Microsoft Exchange 2013 Cookbook

Over 70 simple but incredibly effective recipes to take you through with the common tasks in Exchange 2013

Michael Van Horenbeeck

Peter De Tender

BIRMINGHAM - MUMBAI

Microsoft Exchange 2013 Cookbook

First published: September 2013

Production Reference: 1130913

Published by Packt Publishing Ltd.
Livery Place
35 Livery Street
Birmingham B3 2PB, UK.

ISBN 978-1-78217-062-4

www.packtpub.com

Cover Image by Prashant Timappa Shetty (sparkling.spectrum.123@gmail.com)

Credits

Authors
Michael Van Horenbeeck
Peter De Tender

Reviewers
Paul Cunningham
Anderson Patricio

Acquisition Editor
Kevin Colaco

Lead Technical Editor
Susmita Panda

Technical Editors
Gauri Dasgupta
Dipika Gaonkar
Sonali S. Vernekar

Project Coordinator
Rahul Dixit

Proofreader
Lesley Harrison

Indexer
Priya Subramani

Graphics
Abhinash Sahu
Ronak Dhruv

Production Coordinator
Prachali Bhiwandkar

Cover Work
Prachali Bhiwandkar

About the Author

Michael Van Horenbeeck is a technology consultant, Microsoft Certified Solutions Master (MCSM), and Exchange Server MVP from Belgium, mainly working on projects involving Microsoft Exchange, Office 365, Active Directory, and a bit of Lync.

Michael has been active in the industry for about 12 years and developed a love for Exchange back in 2000. He is a frequent blogger and a member of the Belgian Unified Communications User Group Pro-Exchange, (`www.pro-exchange.be`). Besides writing about technology, Michael is a regular contributor to The UC Architects podcast (`www.theucarchitects.com`) and he speaks regularly at various conferences around the world.

You can follow Michael via twitter (`@mvanhorenbeeck`) or his blog: `michaelvh.wordpress.com`.

Acknowledgments

First and foremost, I would specifically like to thank my wife, Marie, for supporting me in all my crazy and wild undertakings such as this book. I'm very grateful for the unremitting patience and loving support she has given me throughout the writing of this book. I should say sorry for the many hours I have been ignoring her while working on it.

I would also like to thank the two technical reviewers of this book: Paul Cunningham and Anderson Patricio, for willing to take on the humongous task of reviewing all the things I have written. It was a big relief knowing they had my back! Both Paul and Anderson are great people and I would like to thank them again for their continued support to this book and their everlasting efforts in the Exchange community.

- Michael Van Horenbeeck

About the Author

Peter De Tender started his career as an IT professional with over 16 years of experience. Peter has a strong focus on Microsoft Infrastructure technologies, with an expertise in Exchange Server since Version 4.0 back in 1995. He has worked on numerous design and implementation projects in Belgium and with International Customers. He has also worked in SMB environments and on large-scale 50,000 mailbox platforms. Besides doing Exchange consulting, Peter frequently works on general Microsoft Core IO platform integration and consultancy projects as an Infrastructure Architect, mainly working with Windows Server, HyperV, and System Center Operations Manager.

Peter is a also a recognized Microsoft Certified Trainer and out of that expertise he is both country lead for Belgium and European Chairman of IAMCT, the International Association of Microsoft Certified Trainers (`http://www.iamct.org`). He is also a Microsoft Springboard Series member.

For the last few years, Peter has been regularly traveling around the world for speaking at international conferences on Microsoft technologies such as MCT Summits NA and EU, TechFuse Minneapolis and Community Day, or for working as a staff member at Microsoft TechEds NA and EU, MMS, and so on.

Peter started his career as a database admin for an international organization, where he got his first exposure to with Windows Server NT4 back in 1996. He decided to work as an IT engineer on Windows Server, and never looked back. Having worked for some of the largest IT organizations in Belgium, he became the managing partner of a Microsoft technology oriented company in Belgium having 25 high-skilled consultants under his wings. Peter is now working as an independent and has also his own company out of which he is available for hire for giving training, coaching, consulting ,or speaking at your conference.

As a technical writer for TrainSignal (`http://www.trainsignal.com`) and Petri Knowledgebase (`http://www.petri.co.il`), Peter writes many technical how-to articles on a multitude of Microsoft products, always with a twist from his own experience. You can follow Peter via `http://www.twitter.com/pdtit`

Besides this Cookbook, Peter is also the co-author of *Upgrading Skills to Exchange Server 2013*, a courseware training guide published by *MVP-Press* (`http://www.mvp-press.com`).

Acknowledgments

When I got the request from Packt to co-author on an Exchange 2013 Cookbook, I was very thrilled at the thought of doing this, as it would be my first time ever actually writing a real book. And what an adventure it was! I would especially like to thank the Packt Publishing team for their support and patience along the line. I would also like to thank Michael for willing to be the co-author on this book; you did a wonderful job in reviewing my drafts and giving great feedback. Also, thank you to the technical review team, as you gave marvelous feedback and forced me to update the content to even increase the quality of the book. In general, I would like to thank all the people who have ever attended one of my training sessions, workshop sessions, or public speaking gigs in all those different places in the world. It is your feedback and stories that gave me enough inspiration for writing this book, pulling real-life examples out of the discussions and conversations we had.

Last but not least, a more than special thanks goes to my wonderful family for, accepting me being always busy on my PC, hiding in my dark and obscure lab environment, being away for speaking at conferences, or writing on this book. My dear wife Els, thank you so much for supporting me in all that I do. Without your continuous help, this would just have not been possible at all. You are an amazing woman, the best mom our kids can have. Kaylee and Kitana, sweet little girls, you both are so full of energy and joy in life, it puts a smile on my face every time I'm around the two of you, both face to face at home or through the many Skype sessions we have when dad is away from home. I would also like to thank my parents and sister who gave me the opportunity to play and mess around with the computer at home, when you actually needed it for your business. It was there I got bitten by the virus that made me the IT geek I am now. Dad, although you were gone way too soon, you are in my memories for ever. It is with proud and respect to you that I'm making the best of my life as you always taught me.

- Peter De Tender

About the Reviewers

Paul Cunningham is an Exchange Server MVP and messaging specialist from Australia. Paul is working in the IT industry since 1999 in a variety of consulting and support roles. He runs the popular Exchange Server Pro website (`http://exchangeserverpro.com`) and can also be found on Twitter (`http://twitter.com/ExchServPro`).

Anderson Patricio is a Canadian Exchange Server MVP and he is a Messaging consultant based in Toronto, designing and deploying messaging solutions for several clients located in the Americas. He has been working with Exchange since Version 5 and besides his passion with Exchange Server, he works with Active Directory and System Center products.

Anderson is an active member of the Exchange Community and he contributes in forums, blogs, tutorials, articles, and videos. In English, he blogs regularly at `www.AndersonPatricio.ca` and `MSExchange.org` (blog and articles). In Portuguese, his website (`www.AndersonPatricio.org`) contains hundreds of Microsoft articles to help the local community, besides of his speaking engagements such as TechEd speaker in South America and MVA (Microsoft Virtual Academy) training courses.

You can also follow him on Twitter at `http://twitter.com/apatricio`.

He is the reviewer of several books such as *Windows Powershell in Action* by *Bruce Payette*, *PowerShell in Practice* by *Richard Siddaway*, and *Microsoft Exchange 2010 PowerShell Cookbook* by *Mike Pfeiffer*.

www.PacktPub.com

Support files, eBooks, discount offers, and more

You might want to visit www.PacktPub.com for support files and downloads related to your book.

Did you know that Packt offers eBook versions of every book published, with PDF and ePub files available? You can upgrade to the eBook version at www.PacktPub.com and as a print book customer, you are entitled to a discount on the eBook copy. Get in touch with us at service@packtpub.com for more details.

At www.PacktPub.com, you can also read a collection of free technical articles, sign up for a range of free newsletters, and receive exclusive discounts and offers on Packt books and eBooks.

http://PacktLib.PacktPub.com

Do you need instant solutions to your IT questions? PacktLib is Packt's online digital book library. Here, you can access, read and search across Packt's entire library of books.

Why Subscribe?

- Fully searchable across every book published by Packt
- Copy and paste, print and bookmark content
- On demand and accessible via web browser

Free Access for Packt account holders

If you have an account with Packt at www.PacktPub.com, you can use this to access PacktLib today and view nine entirely free books. Simply use your login credentials for immediate access.

Instant Updates on New Packt Books

Get notified! Find out when new books are published by following @PacktEnterprise on Twitter, or the *Packt Enterprise* Facebook page.

Table of Contents

Preface

Microsoft Exchange Server has come a long way since it was first introduced. Back in the days, Exchange was nothing more than a simple mail server. Today, Exchange is much more than that. It has grown to become the cornerstone for collaboration and related technologies within many companies.

On one hand, managing Exchange has never been so easy with the all-new web-based Exchange Admin Center. On the other hand, however, the multitude of features which come built-in to the product can sometimes make it a real challenge to pick the right feature and implement it accordingly.

This book will guide you through the process of installing and configuring Exchange Server 2013. We will tackle how to install Exchange in a green field deployment, and also have a chapter dedicated to migrating from previous versions of Exchange. We will cover everything there is to know to successfully deploy Exchange 2013 and its most used features.

Our goal is to remain as practical as possible. As such, you will find lots of step-by-step examples, which help you reproducing them in your own lab before executing them in production.

What this book covers

Chapter 1, Planning an Exchange Server 2013 Infrastructure, will help you with the architectural part of an Exchange deployment. This chapter will tell you what server hardware, server software you need, how to size your databases correctly, what about security features, and so on.

Chapter 2, Installing Exchange Server, will walk you through the basic concepts and how-to of an Exchange Server installation. Starting with the Active Directory prerequisites, you will learn how to install your first Exchange 2013 server by using GUI and PowerShell.

Chapter 3, Configuring the Client Access Server Role, will dive deeper into the Exchange CAS server role. You will learn what it does, what has changed compared to previous Exchange versions, how to configure SSL certificates, and more.

Chapter 4, Configuring and Managing the Mailbox Server Role, explains all there is to know about configuring and managing your mailbox and public folder databases.

Chapter 5, Configuring External Access, will guide you through configuring mobile access to your mailbox from any device. It will explain the best practices, as well as how to secure these external connections, and more.

Chapter 6, Implementing and Managing High Availability, covers features like Database Availability Groups and Load Balancing, helping you with real-life scenarios on how to deploy an almost 100 percent redundant Exchange environment.

Chapter 7, Transitioning to Exchange Server 2013, is specifically written towards the Exchange admins or consultants who are responsible for doing Exchange server migrations; mainly transitioning from Exchange 2010 to Exchange 2013.

Chapter 8, Configuring Security and Compliance Features, covers the updated security concepts of Exchange 2013, how to secure your mail flow and secure your mail data content.

Chapter 9, Performing Backup, Restore, and Disaster Recovery, is the chapter which talks about specifics there are to know about how to manage Exchange Server backups, which are reliable for doing restores, when needed. We also walk you through some steps that will help you in restoring or rebuilding your Exchange Server in case of a disaster.

Chapter 10, Implementing Security, introduces you to the updates of Role Based Access Control (RBAC), how to configure mailbox access rights and permissions, ending with some technical details on SSL certificate requirements in an Exchange Server environment.

Appendix, Getting to know Exchange Server 2013, is a theoretical guide in learning what has changed with the 2013 version of Exchange server. It describes the newest features, which features are removed, and what has changed from an architecture perspective. Although it's now an appendix, if you are totally new to Exchange 2013, we actually recommend starting here to get you up to speed.

What you need for this book

To complete the recipes in this book, you'll need the following:

- A fully operational lab environment with an Active Directory 2003 or higher forest and domain.
- In order to complete the recipes included in *Chapter 7, Transitioning to Exchange 2013*, you will also need to have Exchange 2007 or Exchange 2010 deployed in your lab.
- Ideally, you have two to four virtual machines running Windows Server 2012 ready, which can be used to install Exchange 2013 on.

- A user account with appropriate permissions to set up, install, and configure Exchange. Depending on your existing lab setup, this could for example, be a member of the Organization Management role group.
- All examples from this book should be run in a lab environment before deploying into production. If you don't have Exchange Server software available for building your lab, you can download the Exchange 2013 180 days trial install bit software from `http://office.microsoft.com/en-us/exchange/`.

Who this book is for

The book is targeted to the so-called accidental admin who needs to master Exchange 2013, yet at the same time has his hands full implementing and managing plenty of other things! However, this doesn't mean that the seasoned Exchange admin or Exchange enthusiast won't find any value in it, as it contains plenty of facts on Exchange 2013 to keep you going!

Conventions

In this book, you will find a number of styles of text that distinguish between different kinds of information. Here are some examples of these styles, and an explanation of their meaning.

Code words in text, database table names, folder names, filenames, file extensions, pathnames, dummy URLs, user input, and Twitter handles are shown as follows: "To create a new mailbox database called `MDB01` on server `EX01`, execute the following command."

Any command-line input or output is written as follows:

```
New-MailboxDatabase -Name "MDB01" -Server "EX01.exblog.be" -LogFolderPath
"E:\MDB01\Logs" -EdbFilePath "E:\MDB01\MDB01.edb"
```

New terms and **important words** are shown in bold. Words that you see on the screen, in menus or dialog boxes for example, appear in the text like this: "clicking on the **Next** button moves you to the next screen".

Warnings or important notes appear in a box like this.

Tips and tricks appear like this.

Reader feedback

Feedback from our readers is always welcome. Let us know what you think about this book—what you liked or may have disliked. Reader feedback is important for us to develop titles that you really get the most out of.

To send us general feedback, simply send an e-mail to `feedback@packtpub.com`, and mention the book title via the subject of your message.

If there is a topic that you have expertise in and you are interested in either writing or contributing to a book, see our author guide on `www.packtpub.com/authors`.

Customer support

Now that you are the proud owner of a Packt book, we have a number of things to help you to get the most from your purchase.

Errata

Although we have taken every care to ensure the accuracy of our content, mistakes do happen. If you find a mistake in one of our books—maybe a mistake in the text or the code—we would be grateful if you would report this to us. By doing so, you can save other readers from frustration and help us improve subsequent versions of this book. If you find any errata, please report them by visiting `http://www.packtpub.com/submit-errata`, selecting your book, clicking on the **errata submission form** link, and entering the details of your errata. Once your errata are verified, your submission will be accepted and the errata will be uploaded on our website, or added to any list of existing errata, under the Errata section of that title. Any existing errata can be viewed by selecting your title from `http://www.packtpub.com/support`.

Piracy

Piracy of copyright material on the Internet is an ongoing problem across all media. At Packt, we take the protection of our copyright and licenses very seriously. If you come across any illegal copies of our works, in any form, on the Internet, please provide us with the location address or website name immediately so that we can pursue a remedy.

Please contact us at `copyright@packtpub.com` with a link to the suspected pirated material.

We appreciate your help in protecting our authors, and our ability to bring you valuable content.

Questions

You can contact us at `questions@packtpub.com` if you are having a problem with any aspect of the book, and we will do our best to address it.

1
Planning an Exchange Server 2013 Infrastructure

Before moving over to the "real stuff", where we walk you through the installation of Exchange Server 2013, we will dedicate this chapter to planning, which might make it the least technical chapter in this book. Considering the fact that Exchange is not only an e-mail system but often the cornerstone for all other unified communication applications in a company, detailed planning is a very important aspect of an Exchange Server 2013 implementation project.

In this chapter, we will cover:

- Gathering the business requirements
- Sizing Exchange 2013
- Preparing for Exchange 2013
- Designing storage for Exchange
- Understanding Active Directory and DNS dependencies
- Planning related platform components

Introduction

When thinking and talking about the design phase elements that come into play in an Exchange 2013 project, people immediately refer to features, such as Outlook Web App, anti-spam, backup, mobile device synchronization. However, other important aspects of the design phase thinking about topics like availability, supportability, and interoperability with third party applications.

Without going into too much detail here, we can safely state that Exchange 2013 has been built with high availability in mind. Although this was probably the case for Exchange 2007 and 2010 too, a lot of the features that safeguard availability have either been updated or completely overhauled to drive this goal. Features and enhancements, such as the new database design, continued usage of the **Database Availability Group** (**DAG**), PowerShell, and the new **Exchange Admin Center** (**EAC**), to name just a few, are living proof of that. Then there's also the addition of Managed Availability which is designed to take action when things go wrong. All these features are designed to keep the Exchange services up and running as much as possible. To quote Microsoft "things break, but the (end user) experience does not".

Although it might seem a bit odd at first, we'd like to include the new management paradigm of Exchange 2013 as part of the planning phase. The new features in PowerShell v3, but mostly the new EAC, drive a change in how Exchange 2013 can be managed. The shift from the traditional console-based administration to a more web-based management will also require rethinking on how your company can or should deal with this. It definitely opens up a whole new world of opportunities!

Once you have an idea about how your future Exchange Server topology should look like, you can start investigating the system requirements from both a hardware and software perspective. Virtualization is also an option here.

If you are already familiar with Exchange Server 2007 or 2010, transitioning your platform to the latest Exchange Server 2013 should not be that complex after all, except for maybe migrating public folders which can be a bit challenging.

As is the case with every Exchange Server version before, Exchange 2013 also requires an Active Directory Schema upgrade. Although this action is far less scary than what it used to be, a lot of companies still require some time to plan and implement these changes.

Besides the Exchange Server installation itself, other components you should integrate in your planning phase are your networking devices including the firewall, reverse proxy, SMTP gateways, and maybe load balancers. Also now is a good time to take a look at your backup infrastructure and anti-malware solutions.

Lastly, another important aspect of your planning phase will be to decide between an on-premises Exchange 2013 infrastructure, Exchange Online in Office 365, or maybe even a hybrid scenario.

Gathering the business requirements

As described in the introduction, there are different things that come into play when designing an Exchange 2013 Infrastructure. This topic will guide you through the process of gathering different business requirements that should help you design and plan for Exchange 2013.

Getting ready

To complete the following steps, you need to identify the different stake holders in your organization. They will be able to help you get the right information you need to get going with your design.

How to do it...

Before diving into the technicalities, let's stop for a moment and have a look at how you can help your company define the business requirements. Part of this process, but focused mainly on how to design for (high) availability, is also described in *Chapter 6, Implementing and Managing High Availability*.

A good point to start is by asking yourself (or the people capable of answering them) the following questions:

- How is the system going to be used? That is, what clients will be connecting to the environment?
- Do I need to provide external access to my clients? That is, are they required to connect over the internet or should clients only be able to connect from within the corporate network?
- Are there any regulatory requirements towards security or data retention?
- What does my support organization look like? Is there a team dedicated to Exchange? Is there a helpdesk? Who is responsible for what?

Next, ask yourself if and what issues you are trying to solve. Maybe your company is looking to move to Exchange Server 2013 to solve a specific business problem? If so, start by outlining how you could solve that problem without going into too much detail. The idea is that you should end up with a list of Exchange features that you need to incorporate into your final design.

Lastly, in order to be able to size the environment properly, you should ask the following questions:

- What is the mailbox size limit?
- Are other limits defined? For instance, ask for the maximum message size.
- You should also gather statistics on the usage of your current system, including the following:
- The amount of messages sent per day, per user
- The average message size
- The total amount of users, including plans for future growth (if any)

> In some cases you'll find that companies don't really enforce a mailbox size or other size limits. In such cases, it's a good idea to propose a size limit yourself. Trying to design for unlimited mailbox sizes is not only very hard, but it's also a recipe for disaster unless your company is operationally mature enough to deal with it.

There's more...

For more information on how to gather usage statistics yourself, have a look at the following section, *Sizing Exchange 2013*.

Sizing Exchange 2013

Proper sizing information for Exchange 2013 was released only a few months after the release of the product. The lengthy blog post and many formulae that the guidance incorporates clearly shows that sizing Exchange 2013 isn't something to take lightly.

Getting ready

In order to properly size your Exchange 2013 environment, you'll need to know the key usage statistics described in the previous topic. They will serve as the basis for your sizing exercise.

How to do it...

To us, it's trivial to have the key figures representing the current system's usage. Without these figures, sizing for Exchange 2013 will become very hard. In fact, all that you would be doing is guessing what your future design should look like. The result will be that you will either underestimate the requirements or overshoot them. Maybe if you're lucky, you'll be spot on. But to be honest, we haven't seen that happen very often.

Step 1—Gathering the data

In short, it all starts with determining your Mailbox profiles. A mailbox profile is a logical unit to identify a certain load for a specific mailbox. This load is based on the overall size of the mailbox, the number of messages being sent and received on a daily basis, as well as the average size of the mail item itself.

In the many Exchange design exercises we've done since Exchange 5.5—we like to classify them in different categories, named Bronze, Silver, Gold, and Platinum—the Exchange 2013 Server **Role Requirements Calculator** talks about different "Tiers".

A great tool to help you identify the different mailbox profiles in your existing Exchange (2003, 2007) environment is the Exchange Profile Analyzer, available for download from the following website:

`http://www.microsoft.com/en-us/download/details.aspx?id=10559&`

Alternatively, Exchange's message tracking logs could help you out as well. You could work some magic with a little help from PowerShell or have a look at the following article by Exchange MVP Paul Cunningham. In this article, he explains how you can get daily message statistics from the Message Tracking Logs using Logs Parser. The article is available at the following website:

`http://exchangeserverpro.com/daily-email-traffic-message-tracking-log-parser/`

Generating these statistics from the message tracking logs is fairly easy, however in order to get an accurate number, you need access to historical info as well. The more data you have, the better!

Step 2—Calculating the requirements

Once you have determined the different mailbox profiles, it is time to start making some calculations. Although Microsoft has done an excellent job in explaining how to size Exchange 2013 through the article in the following website, you would probably want to use the Exchange 2013 Server Role Requirements Calculator tool. This tool is an excel-based spreadsheet that will do the calculations for you using the information you put into it.

Nonetheless, we strongly recommend reading Microsoft's article as it will provide you with a better understanding of where some of the numbers come from. Many will try comparing the results from the tool with Exchange 2010 but, honestly, you shouldn't. The architecture between both versions is so different that comparing them would be like comparing apples and oranges.

You can find Microsoft's article describing the entire process in more detail on the following webpage:

`http://blogs.technet.com/b/exchange/archive/2013/05/06/ask-the-perf-guy-sizing-exchange-2013-deployments.aspx`

Given the great detail of the information from the article, us explaining how to perform them would be waste of paper. However, we did want to give some basic information to get you going with the calculator.

The first sheet, the Input tab, is where you should enter your requirements for your Exchange server deployment. This is the information the tool will use to calculate the sizing requirements. Amongst others things, this information contains the mailbox profile information and architectural information, such as whether you are deploying Exchange in a virtualized environment and/or you are installing multi-role servers. The following screenshot shows the general information the Role Requirements Calculator will ask you for:

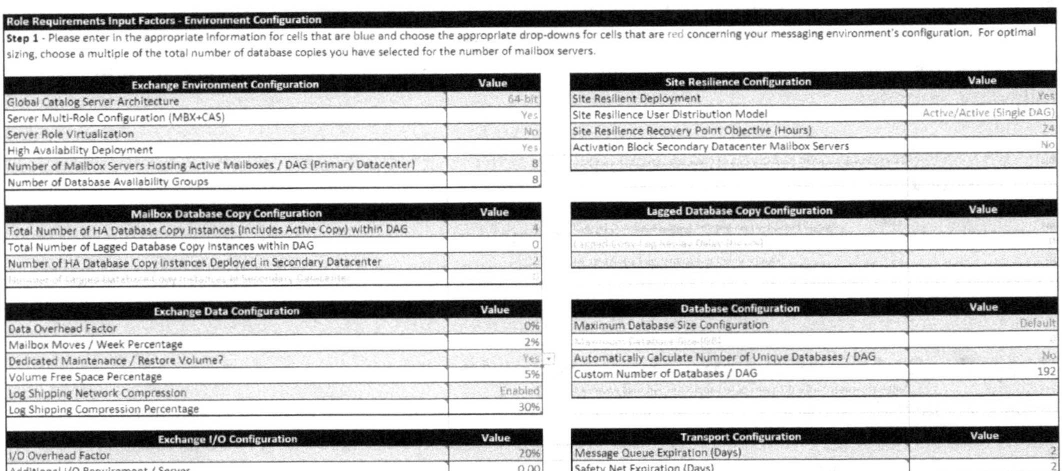

Role Requirements Input Factors - Environment Configuration

Step 1 - Please enter in the appropriate information for cells that are blue and choose the appropriate drop-downs for cells that are red concerning your messaging environment's configuration. For optimal sizing, choose a multiple of the total number of database copies you have selected for the number of mailbox servers.

Exchange Environment Configuration	Value
Global Catalog Server Architecture	64-bit
Server Multi-Role Configuration (MBX+CAS)	Yes
Server Role Virtualization	No
High Availability Deployment	Yes
Number of Mailbox Servers Hosting Active Mailboxes / DAG (Primary Datacenter)	8
Number of Database Availability Groups	8

Site Resilience Configuration	Value
Site Resilient Deployment	Yes
Site Resilience User Distribution Model	Active/Active (Single DAG)
Site Resilience Recovery Point Objective (Hours)	24
Activation Block Secondary Datacenter Mailbox Servers	No
[illegible]	[illegible]

Mailbox Database Copy Configuration	Value
Total Number of HA Database Copy Instances (Includes Active Copy) within DAG	4
Total Number of Lagged Database Copy Instances within DAG	0
Number of HA Database Copy Instances Deployed in Secondary Datacenter	2
[illegible]	[illegible]

Lagged Database Copy Configuration	Value
[illegible]	[illegible]
[illegible]	[illegible]
[illegible]	

Exchange Data Configuration	Value
Data Overhead Factor	0%
Mailbox Moves / Week Percentage	2%
Dedicated Maintenance / Restore Volume?	Yes
Volume Free Space Percentage	5%
Log Shipping Network Compression	Enabled
Log Shipping Compression Percentage	30%

Database Configuration	Value
Maximum Database Size Configuration	Default
[illegible]	[illegible]
Automatically Calculate Number of Unique Databases / DAG	No
Custom Number of Databases / DAG	192
[illegible]	

Exchange I/O Configuration	Value
I/O Overhead Factor	20%
Additional I/O Requirement / Server	0,00

Transport Configuration	Value
Message Queue Expiration (Days)	2
Safety Net Expiration (Days)	2

By clicking on the red triangle on each field, you will be given more information about what the tool is expecting or referring to. Usually the field's names are descriptive enough and self-explanatory. However, the part with regards to the high availability requirements can sometimes seem a little confusing.

Consider the following scenario:

A company has a total of 10.000 mailboxes, all located in a single site. After a first (manual) draft of our sizing, we've calculated that we will need at least 4 servers to store mailboxes and have room for high availability. Not only should the environment be able to withstand a single database failure, but also an entire datacenter failure. Also, the database copies in the second datacenter should not be used automatically. However, if the business decided to switch over to the second datacenter, it should also be able to withstand a single database failure.

This information teaches us that each datacenter should have *at least* two database copies, allowing for a single database failure per datacenter. Because the secondary datacenter should not be activated automatically, the databases in that location should be blocked from activation.

Given that all users are located in a single site, we're actually deploying an Active/Passive scenario. In the real world, this could be the case if you have a primary datacenter and also a secondary one that is solely used for disaster recovery purposes. The latter is sometimes also referred to as a DR-site.

Assuming we would deploy physical multi-role servers, the input for the calculator would look something like this screenshot:

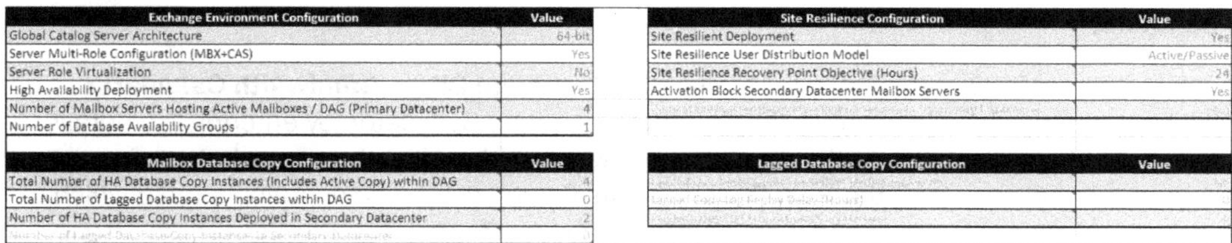

Exchange Environment Configuration	Value
Global Catalog Server Architecture	64-bit
Server Multi-Role Configuration (MBX+CAS)	Yes
Server Role Virtualization	No
High Availability Deployment	Yes
Number of Mailbox Servers Hosting Active Mailboxes / DAG (Primary Datacenter)	4
Number of Database Availability Groups	1

Site Resilience Configuration	Value
Site Resilient Deployment	Yes
Site Resilience User Distribution Model	Active/Passive
Site Resilience Recovery Point Objective (Hours)	24
Activation Block Secondary Datacenter Mailbox Servers	Yes
[illegible]	

Mailbox Database Copy Configuration	Value
Total Number of HA Database Copy Instances (Includes Active Copy) within DAG	4
Total Number of Lagged Database Copy Instances within DAG	0
Number of HA Database Copy Instances Deployed in Secondary Datacenter	2
[illegible]	

Lagged Database Copy Configuration	Value
[illegible]	
[illegible]	
[illegible]	

Next, you need to provide the tool with information on mailbox profiles including the maximum required mailbox size, amount of messages received per mailbox per day, and the retention requirements. This is shown in the following screenshot:

Tier-1 User Mailbox Configuration	Value
Total Number of Tier-1 User Mailboxes / Environment	10000
Projected Mailbox Number Growth Percentage	0%
Total Send/Receive Capability / Mailbox / Day	200 messages
Average Message Size (KB)	75
Mailbox Size Limit (MB)	5120
Personal Archive Mailbox Size Limit (MB)	0
Deleted Item Retention Window (Days)	14
Single Item Recovery	Enabled
Calendar Version Storage	Enabled
Multiplication Factor User Percentage	100%
IOPS Multiplication Factor	1,00
Megacycles Multiplication Factor	1,00
Desktop Search Engines Enabled (for Online Mode Clients)	No
Predict IOPS Value?	Yes
[illegible]	[illegible]
[illegible]	[illegible]

As described earlier, you could define different tiers of users which allow you to define different requirements for different types of users.

The rest of the information on the page is pretty self-descriptive and it shouldn't be too hard to enter or select the correct information except maybe for the part about the **Log Replication Configuration**. This is shown in the following screenshot:

Log Replication Configuration		
Hours in the Day		erated / Hour P
	1	0,00%
	2	0,00%
	3	0,00%
	4	0,00%
	5	0,00%
	6	0,00%
	7	0,00%
	8	0,00%

Network Configuration	Value
Network Link Type	Gigabit Ethernet
Network Link Latency (ms)	50,00

The input from here is used to calculate the bandwidth requirements. In order to do this, the calculator needs to know the amount of logs generated each hour. Without having a live deployment that you could reference to, it's pretty hard to estimate what numbers to enter here.

Luckily, Microsoft has released a tool called the **Exchange Client Bandwidth Calculator** which operates in a similar way to the Role Requirements Calculator, by entering the details of your clients it will calculate the required bandwidth and predict the usage pattern in 24 hours. To help you with the Role Requirements Calculator, it also contains a table which displays the information you can use to enter in the **Log Replication Configuration**. This is shown in the following screenshot:

Hour of Day	%
1	0,00%
2	0,00%
3	0,00%
4	0,00%
5	0,00%
6	0,00%
7	0,02%
8	0,22%
9	1,26%
10	4,43%
11	9,61%

Once you're done entering the information in the Input Sheet, the calculator will automatically generate the results in the other sheets.

The Role Requirements sheet provides you with information on each of the servers, such as the amount of RAM and disk space needed, as well as a calculation of the CPU utilization. If your CPU utilization is too high, you can go back to the Input Sheet and change the CPU information. In such case, you basically have two options, either you buy a CPU that is more powerful or you add more servers to the environment.

This sort of described another widely used approach to sizing Exchange, which is, trial & error. You start by entering information in the Input Sheet, based on what you think the design should look like. Then you go through the other sheets to see if the requirements are feasible. If not, you go back to the input field and change the parameters, such as the amount of servers, disk sizes, or CPU configurations. You keep on doing that until the calculated requirements satisfy your expectations. While this approach might also be effective, we find it to be little efficient. A better approach would be to make the calculations by hand and using the tool to validate and refine them if needed.

The Distribution Sheet contains information on how to layout your database copies throughout your environment. When taking a look at the sheet using the input from earlier, you will see the following screenshot:

Database Name	Active Server	1-Franklin	2-Washington	3-Jackson	4-Jefferson	5-Lincoln	6-Hamilton	7-Perry	8-Scott
DAG1-1	1-Franklin	1	2			3	4		
DAG1-2	2-Washington		1	2			3	4	
DAG1-3	3-Jackson			1	2			3	4
DAG1-4	4-Jefferson	2			1	4			3
DAG1-5	1-Franklin	1		2		3		4	
DAG1-6	2-Washington		1		2		3		4
DAG1-7	3-Jackson	2		1		4		3	
DAG1-8	4-Jefferson		2		1		4		3

Because of the requirement that the second datacenter needs to be able to take on the entire load of primary datacenter and because it should be able to withstand the failure of a single database copy, we actually need to mirror the architecture from the primary datacenter.

There's more...

Have a look at *Chapter 6, Implementing and Managing High Availability* for more information how high availability affects the Exchange 2013 design and ultimately also what you need to input into the Role Requirements Calculator.

Preparing for Exchange 2013

Once you have decided on the topology and know how many servers you are going to deploy, it's time to prepare the introduction of Exchange 2013.

Getting ready

As part of this task, you will need the required permissions in Active Directory (Enterprise Admin) and for the servers on which you plan to install Exchange (local Admin).

How to do it...

Before installing an Exchange Server 2013 in your network, it would be a good practice to go through some of the key requirements and limitations, avoiding unforeseen surprises during the actual implementation.

Supported coexistence scenarios

Exchange 2013 can only coexist when it's running at least Cumulative Update 1 and only in the following situations.

- Coexistence with Exchange 2007 is supported when all the Exchange 2007 servers in the Exchange organization are running Service Pack 3 Update Rollup 10.
- Coexistence with Exchange 2010 is supported when all Exchange 2010 servers in the organization are running at least Service Pack 3. Given the availability of Rollup Update 1, going for that is recommended.

Although you could argue that it's technically possible to coexist, Exchange setup will check that all Exchange 2010 servers in the organization are running at least Service Pack 3. If not, setup will stop and throw a warning. Unfortunately, it does not check the presence of Update Rollup 10 for Exchange 2007. So make absolutely sure that you have deployed it correctly to all your Exchange 2007 servers.

Transitioning from older versions of Exchange Server (2003, 2000, 5.5) is not supported, at least not within the same Exchange organization. If you are still running one of these legacy versions of Exchange, you have to perform a double-hop migration. This means that you have to upgrade your Exchange organization to Exchange 2007 or 2010 first, before you're able to move to Exchange 2013.

Another possibility is to start an Exchange Server 2013 platform from scratch in a new Active Directory forest and use an export/import or cross-forest migration approach to migrate user's mailbox data. Actually, there are only very limited use cases for this approach. Usually this technique is used in situations where multiple AD forests are consolidated into a new one or when a company has decided to create a dedicated resource forest in which Exchange will be installed.

Hardware requirements

The following table lists the minimum hardware requirements for your Exchange Server 2013 infrastructure. However, keep in mind that you should have defined more specific requirements during the sizing exercise!

Component	Minimum sizing
Processor	Any recent Intel x64 or AMD64 based processor.
Memory	▸ 8 GB for Mailbox Server Role. ▸ 4 GB for **Client Access Server** (**CAS**) Role (if the CAS role is installed as a separate server role, we suggest also sizing 8 GB for this role.).

Component	Minimum sizing
System Disk	▸ 50 GB is the recommended disk size for Windows Server 2012, where 30 GB is the Microsoft recommended minimum available space for an Exchange Server 2013. ▸ Recommended RAID system, RAID1, or RAID10.
Storage	▸ DAS, SAN–iSCSI or Fiber Channel. ▸ Any RAID level is supported or **JBOD** (**Just a Bunch of Disks**); disk volumes without RAID. JBOD is only recommended when using 3 or more database copies to guarantee high availability. ▸ SAS, SATA, SSD, Fiber Channel disks. ▸ Recommended best practice is using different volumes for mailbox databases and log files. ▸ Both Windows Basic and Dynamic disks types are supported for Exchange Server 2013. ▸ 64k formatted cluster size for all volumes that contain Exchange data.

For additional information regarding storage in Exchange 2013, have a look at the following Microsoft TechNet website:

`http://technet.microsoft.com/en-us/library/ee832792(v=exchg.150).aspx`

Operating system requirements

In this topic, we will discuss both Windows Server edition requirements as well as Exchange Server 2013 editions.

The following table lists the supported Windows Server operating system versions for Exchange Server 2013:

Operating System Version	Remarks
Windows Server 2008 R2 with SP1	Can be any edition of the operating system: Standard, Enterprise, or Datacenter. Note that the Standard edition doesn't support the failover clustering components which are required for running in a DAG.
Windows Server 2012	Server 2012 exists in both Standard and Datacenter edition. Both these versions support the failover clustering components and can be used for Mailbox Servers running in a DAG.

The following table lists the existing Exchange Server 2013 server editions:

Exchange Server 2013 edition	Remarks
Standard Edition	▸ Supports a maximum of 5 (active or passive) databases
Enterprise Edition	▸ Supports a maximum of 50 databases in case of Exchange 2013 CU1 ▸ Supports a maximum of 100 active and passive databases in case of Exchange 2013 CU2

Although there is technically no difference between the two versions, some features are only supported in the Enterprise edition. To find out more about what features are supported in each edition, have a look at the following website:

`http://office.microsoft.com/en-us/exchange/microsoft-exchange-server-licensing-licensing-overview-FX103746915.aspx`

Exchange Server Editions are defined by the product key; there is no technical difference between the Standard or Enterprise edition. Upgrading from trial to Standard or Enterprise is supported. Upgrading from Standard to Enterprise is also supported and it only requires entering a new Exchange Server license key. However, downgrading from Enterprise Edition to Standard Edition is not possible. If you need to do this, you would have to install a new Exchange Server in the same organization enter a Standard Edition license key. Then you will have to move all mailboxes and content, after which you can decommission the Enterprise Edition server.

How it works...

Planning your Exchange infrastructure is a very important step in the overall process of implementing or migrating. Planning starts by knowing the differences between the Exchange Server 2013 editions. You should also know what edition of Windows you should use to deploy Exchange on. Even though there are shortcuts that can change one Windows edition into another (for example, from Standard to Enterprise), it's not recommended and probably not supported either. So it's important that you get it right from the start.

Designing storage for Exchange

We already talked about storage environments and how they relate to the new Exchange Server 2013 architecture possibilities.

Due to the optimized and redesigned mailbox store architecture, the **Input/Output Operations per Second** (**IOPS**) required for running your Exchange environment decreased dramatically, which lead to possible redesign of your storage infrastructure, or at least consideration of it.

Getting ready

To complete the following steps outlined, make sure to review and understand storage-related terminology. Also, now would be a good time to check whether virtualization is a requirement or an option. Many companies already have some sort of storage solution they want to re-use, but that doesn't necessarily mean it's the best fit for your Exchange environment.

How to do it...

As it is impossible to give you a complete overview of all supported Exchange Server storage vendors, we decided to give you a bullet list of storage considerations in the Exchange Server 2013 context. These guidelines can help you evaluating the right storage solution.

- Exchange Server 2013 supports about any type of storage architecture, including **Direct Attached Storage** (**DAS**) or **Storage Area Network** (**SAN**)—iSCSI or Fiber Channel based.
- Only block-level storage is supported. This means that you can use NAS/SAN storage as long as it's either a direct drive mapping or an iSCSI LUN. NFS nor virtual disks stored on an NFS volume, that present block-level storage to Exchange are supported.
- All currently existing physical disk types are supported for Exchange Server 2013, ranging from SATA, SAS, and Fiber Channel to SSD disks. Key things to watch out for are disk rotation speed and size. Disks with 5400 RPM are considered too slow in performance, so we don't suggest using these in production environments. Any 7200 RPM or 10,000 RPM disk should score well in both sizing and performance.
- Of course, 15,000 RPM disks are also an option. However when it comes to comparing cost versus benefits, they might not be the best fit.

- Exchange 2013 supports multiple RAID levels, depending on the usage. They are as follows:
    - RAID 1/10 are recommended for system partition and log files.
    - RAID 1/5/10 are recommended for database files volumes.
    - RAID 1/5/10 are recommended for database log files volumes, although RAID 0 gives better performance, but no redundancy on storage level.
    - JBOD (disk set without RAID) which is also supported for both database and log files volumes. It should only be considered in a high availability architecture, having three or more database copies!
- Exchange 2013 supports databases up to 2 TB. There is no one-size-fits-all approach. Generally though, it's recommended to keep database sizes to a size which your environment can handle. This is mainly a best practice out of backup/restore and RTO perspective. Imagine needing to perform a restore of a 2 TB Exchange database, when you only have it stored on tape....

How it works...

It is impossible to give you a single answer on how to size and design your Exchange 2013 storage environment. Besides the guidelines we just read, the key on which to base your sizing are IOPS calculations. IOPS is commonly used to reference the performance storage devices, such as hard drives, solid state drives, and SANs.

Microsoft has made tremendous updates to the Exchange database design, resulting in a serious decrease of the required amount of disk IOPS. This is a good thing because disks are growing larger in disk size, but the IOPS they can handle have remained pretty steady over time. So the ideal goal is knowing your Exchange user profile, corresponding IOPS needed, and verifying what IOPS can be delivered by your storage platform.

For each Exchange Server edition since 2003, the Exchange product team provided a Mailbox Server Role Requirements Calculator, which could help with determining the storage requirements so you could match the correct solutions to it. Since the beginning of May 2013 (about 8 months after Exchange 2013 release date though), the calculator for Exchange Server 2013 is (finally) available.

The Exchange 2013 calculator can be downloaded from Microsoft through the following website:

`http://blogs.technet.com/b/exchange/archive/2013/05/14/released-exchange-2013-server-role-requirements-calculator.aspx`

Besides the Microsoft calculator, a lot of storage vendors also provide tools and whitepapers which describe to you best practices, calculated scenarios, and recommended sizing based on their own storage solutions.

To streamline the process of calculating, Microsoft created the **Exchange 2010 Solution**

Reviewed Program (**ESRP**)–**Storage 3.0**, which is a toolset of testing parameters (**JetStress** tests) and documentation guidelines that storage vendors can use for getting their storage solution certified for Exchange Server. This program has recently been upgraded to reflect Exchange 2013 sizing as well.

All information on the ESRP and the different vendor's results can be found at the following website:

`http://technet.microsoft.com/en-us/exchange/ff182054.aspx`

There's more...

The last thing you would want to do is put a storage system into production that doesn't meet the bar when it comes to the amount of IOPS. Storage vendors sometimes try to hide weaknesses or make their solution look better by tweaking some of the numbers or even the results from different tests. Therefore, you should always validate that the solution you chose meets the required amount of IOPS.

A good way to do this is to use the JetStress utility that Microsoft provides. As a matter of fact, running JetStress is also a requirement if you want your storage solution to be fully supported by Microsoft. This doesn't mean they will help you set up the solution, but in case of problems, support might ask for proof that it meets the requirements of your environment.

Because typical JetStress tests can take a while, people often skip them. You shouldn't.

Neil Johnson, a MCS Consultant based in the UK, has created the JetStress field guide for Exchange 2013 which has been released only recently. It is the starting point to understand what JetStress does and how to use it to validate your storage for Exchange 2013.

You can download the guide from the following webpage:

`http://blogs.technet.com/b/exchange/archive/2013/07/10/announcing-the-jetstress-2013-field-guide.aspx`

The way JetStress works is that it will simulate the typical load generated by an Exchange server, based on what parameters you provide to it. It will then monitor the transactions and based on that, return a Pass or Fail for configuring along with additional information that can help you understand why it passed or failed.

While running the JetStress tests, it's also a good idea to simulate a failure in your storage system. If you are using a RAID array, you might want to see what the impact of a rebuild would be on the result of JetStress. If you're running JetStress in a virtualized environment, don't wait until off-business hours to run the test, do it during the day to have more reliable results. After all, you will be running Exchange during business hours, won't you?

Understanding Active Directory and DNS dependencies

As mentioned during the introduction, Exchange 2013—like its predecessors—depends heavily on **Active Directory** (**AD**) and **Domain Name System** (**DNS**). If AD or DNS is not functioning correctly, your Exchange 2013 platform on top of that won't either.

Getting ready

For the following steps and information outlined, we assume you already have an Exchange Server infrastructure in place, meaning you are already using Active Directory (and DNS). Nevertheless, we want to draw your attention to some AD and DNS requirements and changes that are happening as part of your Exchange 2013 platform implementation.

Even if you are not using Exchange in your environment yet, the following items will be of interest to you.

How to do it...

Active Directory system requirements

We are not going to explain you how to set up your Active Directory domain controllers from scratch; we assume you already have that running. What's more important is knowing what the different system requirements for your Active Directory infrastructure are; just to be sure it is according to the Exchange 2013 requirements.

Let us start by giving an overview of the supported Operating System versions for each of the necessary AD components. The following information can also be found on TechNet. The following is the website for TechNet:

`http://technet.microsoft.com/en-us/library/aa996719(v=exchg.150).aspx`

<table>
<tr><th>AD Server Role</th><th>Required Operating System Version</th></tr>
<tr><td>Schema Master</td><td>The Schema Master must be running any of the following OS versions:<ul><li>Windows Server 2012 Standard or Datacenter edition</li><li>Windows Server 2008 R2 Standard or Enterprise edition with Service Pack 1 or later</li><li>Windows Server 2008 R2 Datacenter RTM or later edition</li><li>Windows Server 2008 Standard or Enterprise edition with Service Pack 1 or later (32-bit or 64-bit)</li><li>Windows Server 2008 Datacenter RTM or later edition</li><li>Windows Server 2003 Standard Edition with Service Pack 2 or later (32-bit or 64-bit)</li><li>Windows Server 2003 Enterprise Edition with Service Pack 2 or later (32-bit or 64-bit)</li></ul></td></tr>
<tr><td>Global Catalog Server</td><td>In each Active Directory site where you plan to install an Exchange Server 2013, at least one global catalog server should be running, having one of the following OS versions:<ul><li>Windows Server 2012 Standard or Datacenter edition</li><li>Windows Server 2008 R2 Standard or Enterprise edition</li><li>Windows Server 2008 R2 Datacenter RTM or later edition</li><li>Windows Server 2008 Standard or Enterprise edition (32-bit or 64-bit)</li><li>Windows Server 2008 Datacenter RTM or later edition</li><li>Windows Server 2003 Standard Edition with Service Pack 2 (SP2) or later (32-bit or 64-bit)</li><li>Windows Server 2003 Enterprise Edition with Service Pack P2 or later (32-bit or 64-bit)</li></ul></td></tr>
</table>

AD Server Role	Required Operating System Version
Domain Controller	In each Active Directory site where you plan to install an Exchange Server 2013, at least one writeable Domain Controller server—**Read-Only Domain Controller** (**RODC**) is not supported— should be running, having one of the following OS versions: ▶ Windows Server 2012 Standard or Datacenter edition ▶ Windows Server 2008 R2 Standard or Enterprise edition ▶ Windows Server 2008 R2 Datacenter RTM or later edition ▶ Windows Server 2008 Standard or Enterprise edition (32-bit or 64-bit) ▶ Windows Server 2008 Datacenter RTM or later edition ▶ Windows Server 2003 Standard Edition with Service Pack 2 (SP2) or later (32-bit or 64-bit) ▶ Windows Server 2003 Enterprise Edition with Service Pack 2 or later (32-bit or 64-bit)

DNS infrastructure requirements

Just as with the Active Directory bits of your environment, having a healthy DNS infrastructure is a vital part in your Exchange Server 2013 platform preparation work. While we could again assume this is already all in place and available, we would like to draw your attention to some DNS specifics and best practices.

One of the most recurring questions when designing Exchange (and Active Directory as well, if you will) infrastructure is, How should I decide on defining my DNS namepace? A short answer to this is, "There is no single best solution for this".

It depends on different parameters. The first question is whether you are using a split-DNS configuration or not? Now what does this mean? In most organizations, the internal Active Directory domain name will differ from the public internet domain name (for example, `company.local` and `company.com`). A split-DNS configuration means you will be using the same DNS namespace for your internal network as for your external. Back in the early days, when Active Directory had just come to life, Microsoft used to recommend using a different namespace internally and externally in the Active Directory design guides. Nowadays, it's just the opposite! There are various reasons for this, mainly to simplify the integration between different internal and external resources.

As a side note, we'd like to mention that maintaining a split-DNS setup, requires some additional overhead in the area of managing DNS entries in your DNS namespace. Let's take Outlook Web App as an example. Both URLs (internal and external) could potentially have the same name. Let's say it is set to `https://owa.company.com/owa`.

In your internal DNS namespace `company.com`, you will create a hostname entry which refers to the **internal** IP address(es) of your Client Access Server.

In the external DNS namespace, also `company.com`, you will create a hostname entry which refers to the **public** IP address of your firewall.

It has already been mentioned before that Exchange is highly dependent on DNS. Although no changes are required to your DNS infrastructure as such, it might be a good practice to verify that everything runs well before performing the Exchange 2013 installation.

Troubleshooting DNS

Logging events and debugging

As with a lot of applications and Windows components, your primary source for troubleshooting is the Event Viewer. Although this is also true for DNS, when using Server 2012 the DNS event entries are integrated into the DNS management console itself. In case of major issues with your DNS infrastructure, one might want to activate Debugging logging, which can be achieved as follows:

1. Open the DNS console on one of your DNS Servers
2. In the console, select your DNS server
3. Right-click on **Properties** and select **Debug Logging**
4. Check **Log packets for debugging**

As this is only to be used for detailed troubleshooting, do not forget to turn the checkbox off again when the issue has been resolved.

Basic DNS commands

Without unwrapping all details of how DNS is operating, the following table will help you in verifying and troubleshooting your DNS name resolution mechanism:

Tool/Command Line	Comment
Ipconfig	Gives detailed information about a server or client's network settings, such as IP-address, default gateway.
Nslookup	This command runs a query for a DNS object, such as a hostname record or MX record.
DNScmd	This is the command line version of the DNS Admin Console, allowing for creating and modifying zones, adding or updating records to your DNS infrastructure, and so on.
Ping or Tracert	Verifies a network connection between two machines like a Domain Controller and your Exchange Server, or your Exchange Server and an Outlook 2013 client. While this is only operating on network level, it won't tell you anything about running services such as the Outlook Web App (for example this requires https connection).

How it works...

When the Active Directory Server roles and OS versions we just saw have been verified, check your Active Directory replication and DNS replication to make sure it is working correctly as well. Again, Active Directory and DNS are the foundation for your Exchange 2013 installation!

Active Directory replication can be checked using the tool `repadmin.exe`, which is automatically installed on Server 2008 R2 and 2012 as part of the Remote Server Administration Tools for AD (RSAT-ADDS):

- Open a command prompt with elevated rights. To do this, right-click on the command prompt icon and select **Run as Administrator**. If prompted by **User Account Control** (**UAC**), click on **Yes**.
- Enter the following command:

  ```
  repadmin /replsummary
  ```

- This will give you a summary of the replication status. If no fails/errors are shown, your Active Directory domain controllers are all in sync and replication is working fine, for example:

  ```
  C:\Users\Administrator > repadmin /replsummary
  Replication Summary Start Time : 2013-07-06 18:09:26
  Beginning Data Collection for replication summary, this may take a
  while:
  ...
  Source DSA    largest delta  fails/total%%    error
  Destination DSA  largest delta   fails/total%%    error
  C:\Users\Administrator
  ```

Planning related platform components

In many organizations, Exchange Server 2013 is not the only product that is deployed as part of a greater unified communications and collaborations strategy. Although Microsoft offers a wide range of technologies and products that, together, can fill this need, companies often use other applications.

Describing and understanding these components is another important aspect of your architecture preparation.

How to do it...

First, it's a good idea to start an inventory of what other products and components are tying into your messaging infrastructure. As described earlier, this could go as far as looking at the different networking devices to multi-functional devices e-mailing unauthenticated over SMTP.

Once you have described the different components that are at stake, you should go over each of them and identify the specifics. This means that you will need to review the current configuration and compare that to what's required and what's supported. If there is a gap between what you have today and where you need to be in the future (when deploying Exchange 2013); you need to plan for these changes as well.

In the sections that follow, you'll find some general guidelines around the most common areas of interest which you can use as a reference when looking at each of these components in your deployment.

Firewall and/or reverse proxy

Even though you have a firewall between your Exchange servers internally, they're still required to shield your on-premises environment from the rest of the world. Any firewall these days should be capable of handling Exchange Server traffic. Firewalls, or other networking devices for that matter, can sometimes be challenging. Not because they can become very complex, but because the management of these devices is usually out of the hands of the Exchange admin. Also, unfortunately, the security that manages these devices often has no clue about the Exchange Server design principles or how it interacts with and uses these devices.

In short, all Exchange Server roles should be installed on domain member servers in the LAN, except for the Edge Server role, which needs to be installed in your perimeter network (sometimes also referred to as DMZ).

For securing communications from the outside like Outlook Web App authentication and access, an organization might require the use of a reverse proxy. Have a look at *Chapter 5, Configuring External Access* for more information on the sense or non-sense of using a reverse proxy.

SMTP gateway/Anti-Spam/Malware/Virus appliance

An SMTP gateway is a usually a separate server or appliance placed LAN or perimeter network (DMZ) and is responsible for transporting e-mail inside and outside of the Exchange Server environment. These last few years, several cloud-based solutions—essentially providing the same functionality—have become more and more popular. So, don't be surprised to find out that this gateway is really a service on the Internet. Even though some gateways can perform additional actions, such as address rewriting or journaling, they are mostly used for their security features, such as anti-spam, anti-malware, and anti-virus.

Ever since Exchange 2007, traffic within the Exchange organization is sent after being encrypted by **Transport Layer Security** (**TLS**). By default, if your Exchange Server sends e-mail directly onto the internet, it will always try to use TLS. However, if there's an appliance between your internal and external organization, TLS could break. If you want to make sure TLS encryption is used end-to-end, you need to verify that your gateway supports using it. Alternatively, you could replace the gateway with an Exchange Edge Transport server.

Telephony system or Microsoft Lync Server for voice or unified messaging integration

Since Exchange Server 2007, Microsoft developed the Unified Messaging Server Role in Exchange, which allows for routing and storage of voice messages in your mailbox. Although the separate Unified Messaging Server role as such doesn't exist anymore in Exchange Server 2013, its functionality is largely similar to the unified messaging features from Exchange Server 2010.

Nowadays, IT and telephony systems management is often handled by different teams, which makes communication integration a very difficult thing to achieve sometimes. By integrating voice into your Exchange mailbox, an end user can listen to missed call voice messages, replay voice messages from his mailbox, have voice messages translated to e-mail text in their local language, and so on.

The unified messaging service in Exchange Server 2013 allows for the following:

- Voice mail configuration and integration with existing PBX or Microsoft Lync Server
- Outlook Voice Access (Go through your mailbox by sending voice commands)
- Call answering and call answering rules
- Integration with Microsoft Lync, based on Exchange Autodiscover protocol mechanism
- Play voice messages to another fixed or mobile phone

SharePoint

There was a time when Microsoft actively positioned SharePoint as a replacement of Public Folders. Now, with the new Public Folder architecture, we're not sure if that is still true. However, many companies have adopted SharePoint over the past years and Microsoft continues to improve the functionalities offered by SharePoint and by the integration with other products.

One example of an improved integration between SharePoint and Exchange is Site Mailboxes. Site Mailboxes allow for true collaboration between SharePoint and Exchange, all from within the same client (Outlook). By dragging and dropping e-mails with attachments into a Site Mailbox, the attachment gets stored in SharePoint while the message stays in Exchange.

But as for many good things in life, there's a drawback. To take advantage of Site Mailboxes, you will not only have to deploy Exchange 2013, you'll also need SharePoint 2013.

Faxing solution

The end of Fax has been announced several times before, however up until this very day companies still use and sometimes even rely on sending and receiving faxes to run their business. Exchange 2013 is capable of supporting faxes, but doesn't do a very good job at it. As a matter of fact, for sending and receiving faxes, you will need to use a third-party solution.

There are some pretty good faxing solutions out there. Some are easier to handle than others. Specifically, in the context of Exchange Server 2013 migrations, it is necessary to validate if your faxing application supports Exchange 2013. Maybe there is a new version available, that you need to deploy first. We have seen cases where the faxing solution that was being used didn't exist anymore; the maker decided to stop developing, or even supporting it. If that happens, there aren't many alternatives.... You could move to another product, keep a legacy Exchange server in place for interoperability, or move to a hosted faxing solution. The latter option has gained popularity over the past years, given its flexibility and ease of implementation. It usually only takes setting up a separate namespace for faxes; all the rest happens over SMTP.

Backup and restore

- After going through some high availability, site resilience, and load balancing concepts of Exchange Server 2013 architecture, one might think that taking regular backups is not required anymore. However, even the most redundant, highly available Exchange platform isn't a 100 percent proof against whatever failure that might occur. Therefore, even in Exchange Server 2013, taking backups is necessary.
- Just as with previous Exchange Server editions, Exchange Server 2013 only supports Exchange-aware, **Volume Shadow Services** (**VSS**) based backups. Both Microsoft Windows Server backup and Data Protection Manager have support for VSS-based backups, amongst many other backup solution vendors in the market.
- More information on Exchange 2013 backup and restore is detailed in *Chapter 9, Performing Backup, Restore, and Disaster Recovery*.

Custom developed and other third-party applications

Over the years, many companies bought or developed their own applications on top of Exchange. Depending on which version you are currently running, some of these applications might still use deprecated features. The one that natively comes to mind is WebDAV. Support for WebDAV has already been dropped in Exchange 2010 and is not coming back.

If you are still running Exchange 2003 or Exchange 2007 and have an application that uses WebDAV, you will need to take into account that this application probably needs to be replaced or rewritten. Ideally, you change the application to use one of the two alternatives: Exchange Web Services or the new Outlook Apps model.

Software-based anti-virus

In previous versions of Exchange, anti-virus vendors could be integrated directly with the store process and Exchange databases through the **Virus Scanning Application Interface** (**VSAPI**). This allowed anti-virus programs to perform on-access scans or perform periodical scans of an entire database. Unfortunately, a lot of support calls Microsoft received were due to failing or poorly written code, which could lead to a crashing store process or a corrupted database; ultimately leading to possible data loss.

As a result—and probably for a bunch of other reasons as well—Microsoft decided to pull the plug from the VS API. This means that any anti-virus product still using the API will not work in Exchange 2013. These products will have to be rewritten to either use Exchange Web Services, or shift to scanning for threats as part of the transport pipeline which is still fully supported.

There's more...

To fully understand what the impact of the changes in Exchange 2013 on your environment could be, have a look at the following list of items and features that have been discontinued or aren't available just yet in Exchange 2013. The list is available at the following website:

`http://technet.microsoft.com/en-us/library/jj619283(v=exchg.150).aspx`

2

Installing Exchange Server 2013

In this chapter, we will cover:

- Preparing Active Directory
- Installing Exchange 2013 prerequisites
- Installing Exchange using the Setup wizard
- Installing Exchange from the command line
- Verifying an Exchange 2013 installation
- Introducing the Exchange Admin Center
- Uninstalling an Exchange 2013 Server or Server role

Introduction

This chapter is dedicated to describing and walking you through the installation process of Exchange 2013. Like any other program, ensuring the health and successful operation starts with a solid foundation. As explained in *Chapter 1, Planning an Exchange Server 2013 Infrastructure*, planning your deployment is crucial. Correctly executing the installation steps is at least equally important. Failure to fulfill the prerequisites or correctly install Exchange 2013 might lead to a lot of problems further down the road.

The recipes that are described in this chapter will lead you through the different steps required to introduce Exchange 2013 in your environment. This can be an upgrade from an existing Exchange organization or an installation in an entirely new environment where no Exchange has been installed before. We'll start by preparing your Active Directory inventory and end with showing how you could modify or remove an Exchange server from your environment.

Preparing the Active Directory

As described in *Chapter 1, Planning an Exchange Server 2013 Infrastructure*, important updates to your Active Directory environment are required in order to be able to install Exchange 2013.

In short, the following two steps need to be completed:

1. Extend the Active Directory Schema.
2. Configure Exchange-specific groups and permissions.

We start by showing you how to perform these steps, followed by giving you some additional explanations on how to verify the Schema update ran fine for example.

Getting ready

Before continuing with the following steps outlined, you should understand what the impact extending your schema has on your organization.

To execute the following steps, you need to have the appropriate permissions. Depending on which command you run, this includes membership of:

- Schema Admins
- Enterprise Admins
- Additionally, you should make sure that your Active Directory is healthy and replication is working flawlessly.

How to do it...

Active Directory schema extension

Make sure to execute the following commands from a domain-joined, 64-bit computer in the same Active Directory site as the schema master. To find out what Domain Controller is currently your **Schema master**, run the following command from a command prompt or PowerShell window:

```
netdom query fsmo
```

The following screenshot explains what we just read:

```
[PS] C:\>netdom query fsmo
Schema master               DC01.EXBLOG.BE
Domain naming master        DC01.EXBLOG.BE
PDC                         DC01.EXBLOG.BE
RID pool manager            DC01.EXBLOG.BE
Infrastructure master       DC01.EXBLOG.BE
The command completed successfully.
```

Next, open a command prompt, browse to your Exchange Server 2013 installation directory, and run the following command:

`Setup.exe /prepareSchema /IAcceptExchangeServerLicenseTerms`

Alternatively, you can also abbreviate some parameters:

`Setup.exe /ps /IAcceptExchangeServerLicenseTerms`

The `/IAcceptExchangeServerLicenseTerms` is a required parameter as of Exchange 2013; without this parameter, the setup command will not run. We somehow suspect the Exchange product team was required to add this parameter after some feedback from the corporate lawyers....

The following screenshot explains what we just read:

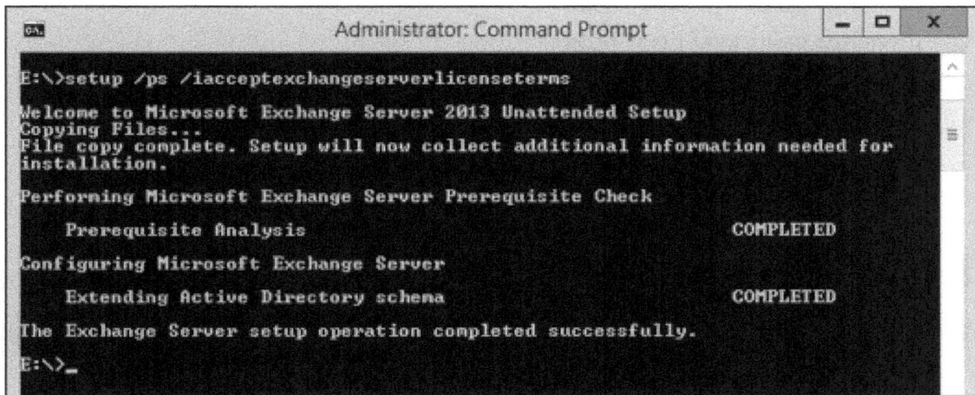

Although the setup process itself will tell you during setup if the Schema Updates were applied successfully, you should verify that the schema was indeed applied successfully.

Instead of going through the manual steps using ADSIEdit, you might want to use a quick PowerShell script, created by Exchange MVP *Michael B. Smith*. The following code shows the quick PowerShell script:

```
$root  = [ADSI]"LDAP://RootDSE"
$name  = "CN=ms-Exch-Schema-Version-Pt," + $root.schemaNamingContext
$value = [ADSI]( "LDAP://" + $name )
"Exchange Schema Version = $( $value.rangeUpper )"
```

The same code is also available as a handy one-liner. The following screenshot shows the one-liner code:

```
[PS] C:\>"Exchange Schema Version = " + ([ADSI]("LDAP://CN=ms-Exch-Schema-Version-Pt," + ([ADSI]"LDAP://RootDSE").schema
NamingContext)).rangeUpper
Exchange Schema Version = 15254
[PS] C:\>_
```

For more information, have a look at his blog available at `http://theessentialexchange.com/blogs/michael/archive/2013/03/14/powershell-quick-script-finding-the-exchange-schema-version.aspx`.

Depending on which version of Exchange you are currently deploying, the value that is returned should be:

- Exchange 2013 RTM: 15137
- Exchange 2013 RTM CU1: 15254
- Exchange 2013 RTM CU2: 15281
- It's likely that future Cumulative Updates will also include schema updates. If so, Microsoft will update the following page to include the new version numbers:
- `http://technet.microsoft.com/en-us/library/bb125224(v=exchg.150).aspx`

After you have executed the `/prepareSchema` command, make sure to wait for Active Directory replication to complete throughout your entire organization.

Preparing Active Directory, groups and permissions

Next, the Active Directory should be prepared, which is done through the following command:

```
Setup.exe /prepareAD :OrganizationName: Organization Name /
IAcceptExchangeServerLicenseTerms
```

Like before, you could abbreviate the parameters as follows:

```
Setup.exe /p /on:OrganizationName /IAcceptExchangeServerLicenseTerms
```

If you are upgrading an existing Exchange organization, for example if you are upgrading from Exchange 2010, you are not required to add the `/OrganizationName` parameter.

The following screenshot shows the Active Directory preparation:

```
Administrator: Command Prompt
Microsoft Windows [Version 6.2.9200]
(c) 2012 Microsoft Corporation. All rights reserved.

C:\Users\administrator.ZOMBIEDUCK>e:

E:\>setup /p /on:"Zombieduck Exchange Organization" /Iacceptexchangeserverlicens
eterms

Welcome to Microsoft Exchange Server 2013 Unattended Setup
Copying Files...
File copy complete. Setup will now collect additional information needed for
installation.

Performing Microsoft Exchange Server Prerequisite Check

    Prerequisite Analysis                                        COMPLETED
 Setup will prepare the organization for Exchange 2013 by using 'Setup /PrepareA
D'. No Exchange 2010 server roles have been detected in this topology. After thi
s operation, you will not be able to install any Exchange 2010 servers.
 For more information, visit: http://technet.microsoft.com/library(EXCHG.150)/ms
.exch.setupreadiness.NoE14ServerWarning.aspx

Configuring Microsoft Exchange Server

    Organization Preparation                                     COMPLETED

The Exchange Server setup operation completed successfully.

E:\>_
```

The last step is to prepare the domain(s) in your Active Directory forest in which you will be installing Exchange or that will contain Exchange recipients. If you have previously executed the `setup.exe /prepareAD` command in the same domain, there's no need to run this command for this domain.

The following command is used to prepare the domain from where the command is run:

```
Setup /preparedomain /IAcceptExchangeServerLicenseTerms
```

Alternatively, you can prepare all domains in your forest at the same time. Please note that you need appropriate permissions in all domains when executing it.

The following command is used to prepare all domains in the Active Directory at the same time:

```
Setup /preparealldomains /IAcceptExchangeServerLicenseTerms
```

The following screenshot shows the results from running the above commands:

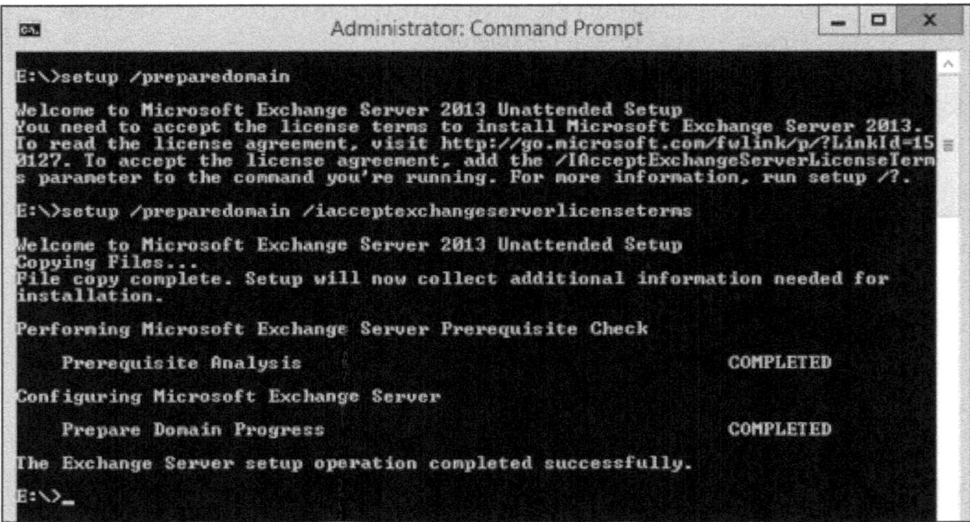

How it works...

By using the `setup.exe /prepareschema` command, the **Lightweight Directory Access Protocol** (**LDAP**) **LDAP Data Interchange Format** (**LDIF**) files that are responsible for the actual update of the schema are being imported into Active Directory. The LDIF files contain updates to classes and attributes. There are about 250 updates to the schema as such. Without these schema updates, it is not possible to install an Exchange 2013 server in your environment.

Executing the `setup.exe /prepareAD` and `/prepareDomain` commands will prepare Active Directory for Exchange 2013 by creating the appropriate objects in the configuration partition as well as creating the required groups in the Microsoft Exchange Security Groups organizational unit and assigning them the required permissions.

There's more...

For a complete overview of the actions executed by these commands, have a look at the following TechNet page:

`http://technet.microsoft.com/en-us/library/bb125224(v=exchg.150)`

Installing Exchange 2013 prerequisites

Getting ready

The following steps assume you have already installed and configured the operating system and drivers. If you have additional software that you need to install, for example, company-specific management tools, this would be a good moment to make sure they have been installed as well.

How to do it...

Windows Server 2008 R2 Service Pack 1 (or higher)

You have to make sure all required Windows Server roles and features are correctly installed. Although it is still possible doing this from the GUI, doing it through PowerShell might save you some time. These are the steps you need to follow to do it through PowerShell:

- Open an elevated Windows PowerShell instance. Open the Start Menu, right click on PowerShell and select **Run as Administrator**
- Load the Server Manager PowerShell Module by running the following command:

```
Import-Module ServerManager
```

Depending on whether you are installing a Mailbox Server, a client Access Server, or a multi-role server, you should execute one of the following commands:

In case of a Mailbox Server or a multi-role server:

```
Add-WindowsFeature RSAT-ADDS,Desktop-Experience, NET-Framework, NET-HTTP-Activation, RPC-over-HTTP-proxy, RSAT-Clustering, RSAT-Web-Server, WAS-Process-Model, Web-Asp-Net, Web-Basic-Auth, Web-Client-Auth, Web-Digest-Auth, Web-Dir-Browsing, Web-Dyn-Compression, Web-Http-Errors, Web-Http-Logging, Web-Http-Redirect, Web-Http-Tracing, Web-ISAPI-Ext, Web-ISAPI-Filter, Web-Lgcy-Mgmt-Console, Web-Metabase, Web-Mgmt-Console, Web-Mgmt-Service, Web-Net-Ext, Web-Request-Monitor, Web-Server, Web-Stat-Compression, Web-Static-Content, Web-Windows-Auth, Web-WMI
```

If you are installing just the Client Access server, use the following command:

```
Add-WindowsFeature RSAT-ADDS,Desktop-Experience, NET-Framework, NET-HTTP-Activation, RPC-over-HTTP-proxy, RSAT-Clustering, RSAT-Web-Server, WAS-Process-Model, Web-Asp-Net, Web-Basic-Auth, Web-Client-Auth, Web-Digest-Auth, Web-Dir-Browsing, Web-Dyn-Compression, Web-Http-Errors, Web-Http-Logging, Web-Http-Redirect, Web-Http-Tracing, Web-ISAPI-Ext, Web-ISAPI-Filter, Web-Lgcy-Mgmt-Console, Web-Metabase, Web-Mgmt-Console, Web-Mgmt-Service, Web-Net-Ext, Web-Request-Monitor, Web-Server, Web-Stat-Compression, Web-Static-Content, Web-Windows-Auth, Web-WMI
```

After the components we just mentioned are installed, install the following additional Microsoft software components as well:

- Microsoft .NET Framework 4.5
- Windows Management Framework 3.0
- Microsoft Unified Communications Managed API 4.0, Core Runtime 64-bit
- Microsoft Office 2010 Filter Pack 64 bit (* only required on Mailbox Server)
- Microsoft Office 2010 Filter Pack SP1 64 bit (* only required on Mailbox Server)
- Microsoft Knowledge Base article KB974405
- Knowledge Base article KB2619234
- Knowledge Base article KB2533623

Windows Server 2012

Just like Windows Server 2008 R2 SP1, you need to install additional server components for Windows Server 2012.

- Open an elevated Windows PowerShell instance. Open the Start Menu, right click on PowerShell and select **Run as Administrator**
- Load the Server Manager PowerShell Module by running the following command:

```
Import-Module ServerManager
```

Depending on whether you are installing a Mailbox Server, a Client Access Server, or a multi-role server, you should execute one of the following commands.

In case of a Mailbox Server or a multi-role server:

```
Install-WindowsFeature AS-HTTP-Activation, Desktop-Experience, NET-
Framework-45-Features, RPC-over-HTTP-proxy, RSAT-Clustering, RSAT-
Clustering-CmdInterface, RSAT-Clustering-Mgmt, RSAT-Clustering-
PowerShell, Web-Mgmt-Console, WAS-Process-Model, Web-Asp-Net45, Web-
Basic-Auth, Web-Client-Auth, Web-Digest-Auth, Web-Dir-Browsing, Web-
Dyn-Compression, Web-Http-Errors, Web-Http-Logging, Web-Http-Redirect,
Web-Http-Tracing, Web-ISAPI-Ext, Web-ISAPI-Filter, Web-Lgcy-Mgmt-Console,
Web-Metabase, Web-Mgmt-Console, Web-Mgmt-Service, Web-Net-Ext45, Web-
Request-Monitor, Web-Server, Web-Stat-Compression, Web-Static-Content,
Web-Windows-Auth, Web-WMI, Windows-Identity-Foundation
```

If you are installing just the Client Access server, use the following command:

```
Install-WindowsFeature AS-HTTP-Activation, Desktop-Experience, NET-
Framework-45-Features, RPC-over-HTTP-proxy, RSAT-Clustering, RSAT-
Clustering-CmdInterface, RSAT-Clustering-Mgmt, RSAT-Clustering-
PowerShell, Web-Mgmt-Console, WAS-Process-Model, Web-Asp-Net45, Web-
Basic-Auth, Web-Client-Auth, Web-Digest-Auth, Web-Dir-Browsing, Web-
Dyn-Compression, Web-Http-Errors, Web-Http-Logging, Web-Http-Redirect,
Web-Http-Tracing, Web-ISAPI-Ext, Web-ISAPI-Filter, Web-Lgcy-Mgmt-Console,
Web-Metabase, Web-Mgmt-Console, Web-Mgmt-Service, Web-Net-Ext45, Web-
Request-Monitor, Web-Server, Web-Stat-Compression, Web-Static-Content,
Web-Windows-Auth, Web-WMI, Windows-Identity-Foundation
```

After the components we just mentioned are installed, install the following additional Microsoft software components as well:

- Microsoft Unified Communications Managed API 4.0, Core Runtime 64-bit
- Microsoft Office 2010 Filter Pack 64 bit (* only required on Mailbox Server)
- Microsoft Office 2010 Filter Pack SP1 64 bit (* only required on Mailbox Server)

The following screenshot shows how this looks like from a PowerShell window:

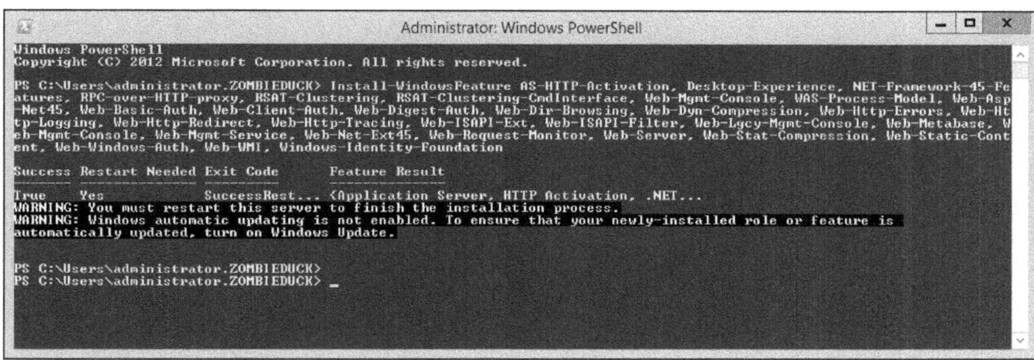

These updates and components represent the minimum required to install Exchange 2013. Next to that, it's always a good idea to make sure the operating system is fully up to date by running Windows Update prior to installing Exchange. Additionally, Microsoft published an article on `http://blogs.technet.com/b/scottschnoll/archive/2013/06/17/recommended-hotfixes-for-windows-server-2012-failover-clusters.aspx` which describe a bunch of additional updates you'd better deploy. Over time, the list of hotfixes to deploy prior is likely to grow. So make sure to verify the latest documentation available before you move on.

How it works...

As Exchange Server depends on a lot of Windows Server roles and features, those need to be installed first. After that, the listed additional Microsoft software components are required as well. Without these, your Exchange Server installation itself will fail.

Once the steps explained are completed, your Windows Server 2008 R2 SP1 or Server 2012 machine is ready for Exchange 2013 installation, which is described in detail in the following recipe.

Installing Exchange 2013 using the Setup Wizard

In this topic, we will walk you through the necessary steps that are required to install your first Exchange Server 2013, by using the Setup Wizard.

How to do it...

The following are the steps necessary for installation:

1. Logon to the Exchange Server machine with an account that has the necessary permissions to install Exchange (see *Chapter 1, Planning an Exchange Server 2013 Infrastructure* planning and designing for the required administrative permissions).
2. From the installation media, launch `setup.exe`.
3. On the first window appearing, make your choice about whether you want to connect to the internet and download the latest available files for doing the setup, or use the version from the installation medium. Depending on your specific situation, you might choose one or the other. Our recommendation is to install the version from the installation media first, making sure all Exchange Servers are running from the same installation media.
4. Click on **next** to continue.

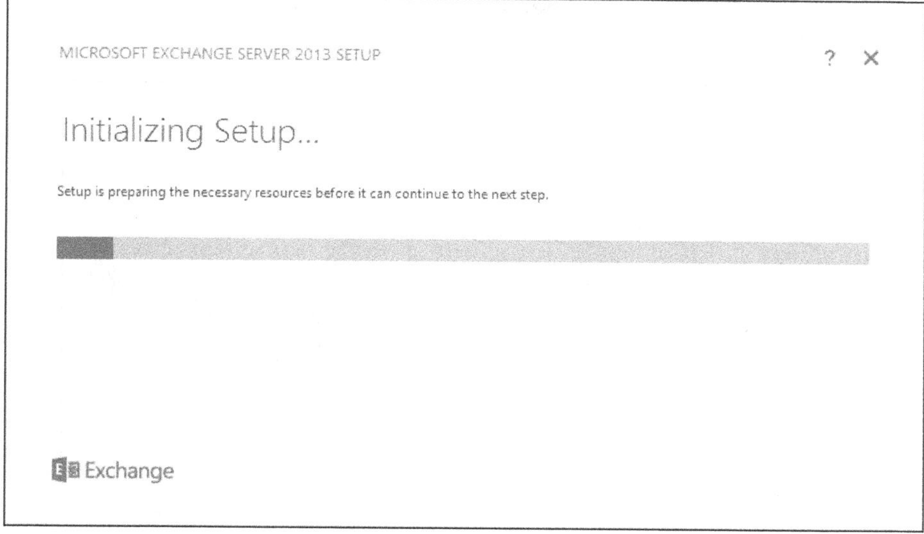

5. Click on **next** on the **Introduction** page.

6. Read through the **License Agreement** and select **I accept...** to continue the installation.

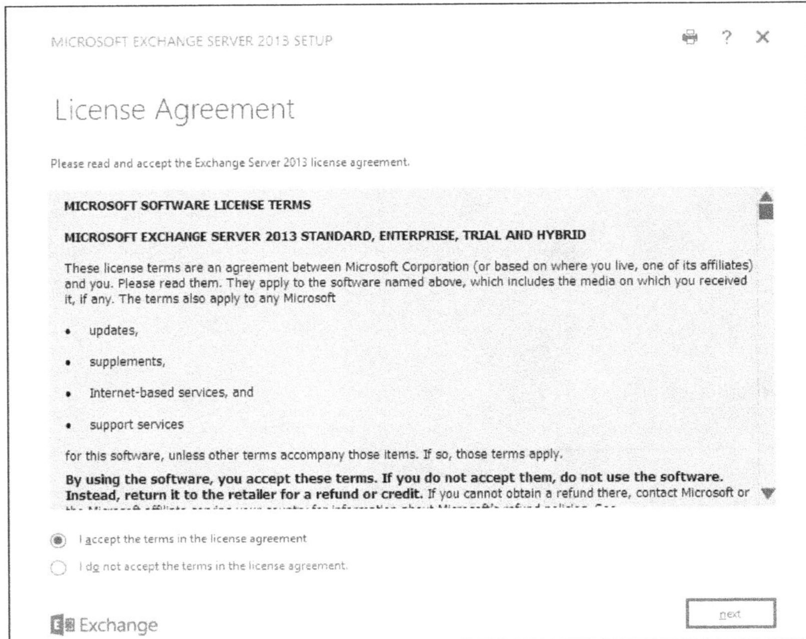
MICROSOFT EXCHANGE SERVER 2013 SETUP

License Agreement

Please read and accept the Exchange Server 2013 license agreement.

MICROSOFT SOFTWARE LICENSE TERMS

MICROSOFT EXCHANGE SERVER 2013 STANDARD, ENTERPRISE, TRIAL AND HYBRID

These license terms are an agreement between Microsoft Corporation (or based on where you live, one of its affiliates) and you. Please read them. They apply to the software named above, which includes the media on which you received it, if any. The terms also apply to any Microsoft

- updates,
- supplements,
- Internet-based services, and
- support services

for this software, unless other terms accompany those items. If so, those terms apply.

By using the software, you accept these terms. If you do not accept them, do not use the software. Instead, return it to the retailer for a refund or credit. If you cannot obtain a refund there, contact Microsoft or

I accept the terms in the license agreement

I do not accept the terms in the license agreement.

7. Select **Don't use recommended settings...** on the **Recommended Settings** page.

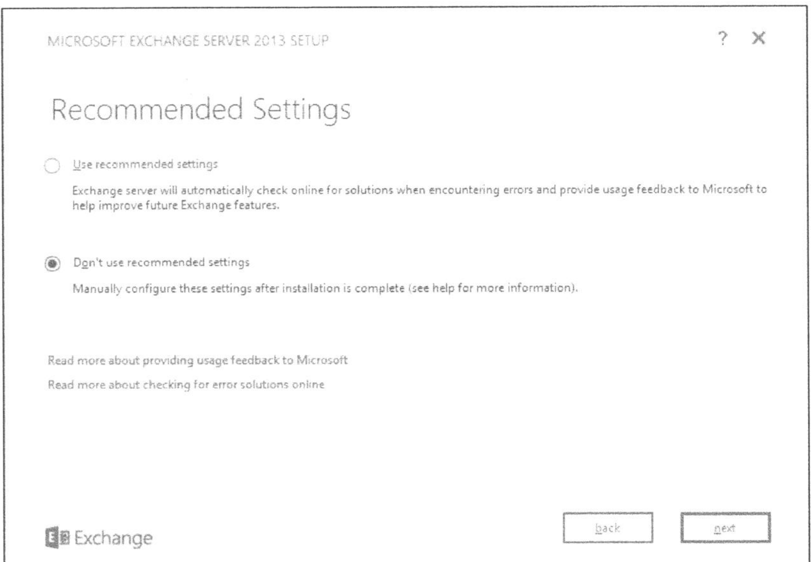

8. Select the **Server Roles** you want to install on the machine. (In our example, we install both **Server Roles** on the same machine) and click on **next** to continue. Notice the **Management Tools** are automatically selected whenever a **Server Role** is selected.

Although it is not required (given we manually installed the components earlier), we suggest that you tick the box to automatically install the required Windows features as this will make sure all required components are verified for installation, and if any are missing, they will automatically be installed.

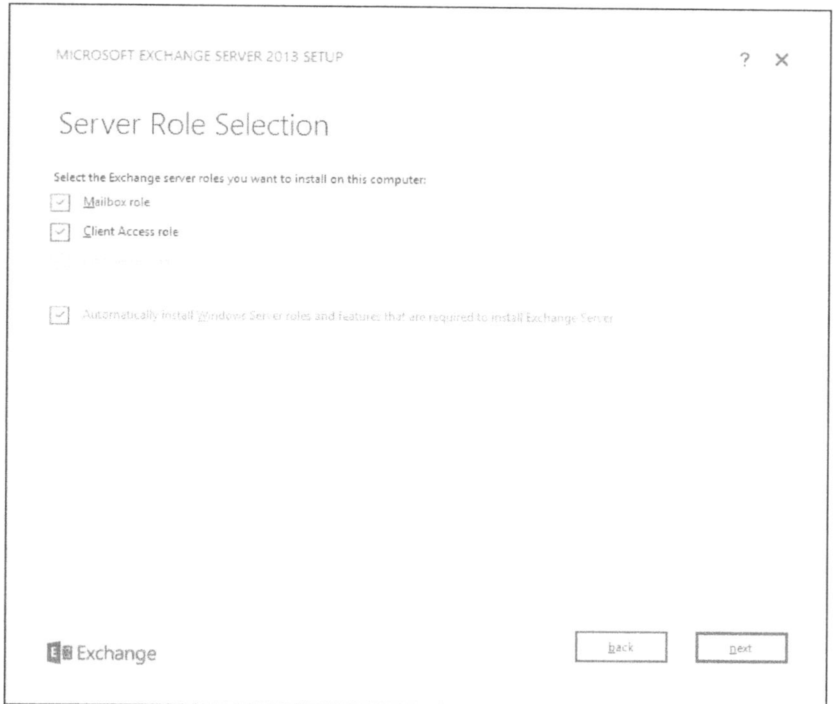

9. Specify the path you want to use for the Exchange 2013 Program Files (default path is `C:\Program Files\Microsoft\Exchange Server\V15`) and click on **next**.

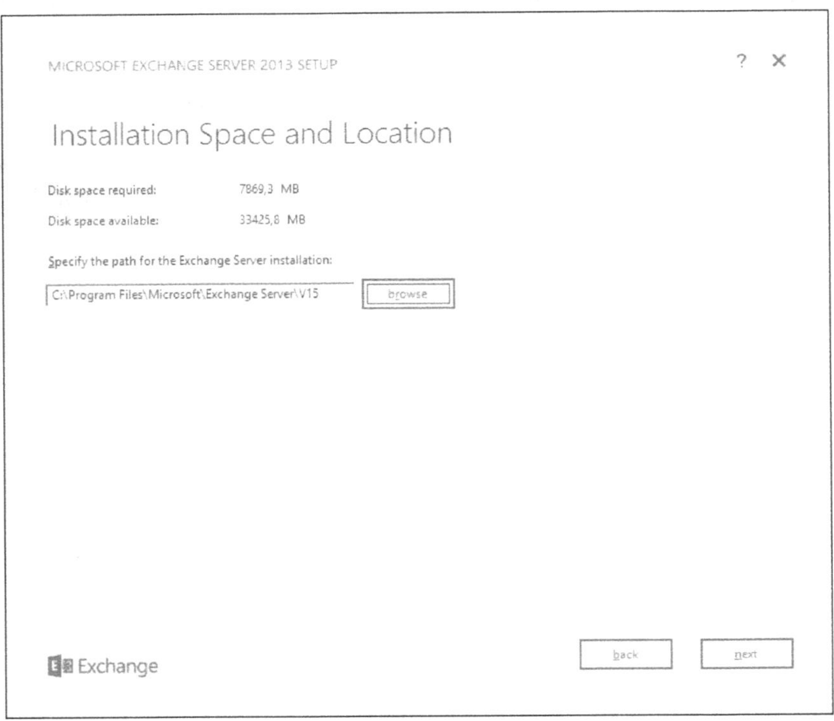

10. Make your choice for enabling or disabling the built-in **Malware Protection Settings** and click on **next** to continue. By default, Microsoft chooses to not disable malware scanning. However, if you have no idea what this feature does (We explain this feature in *Chapter 6, Implementing and Managing High Availability*), it is a good practice to turn this off here during installation, and activate it again later. The reason why Microsoft activates this feature is to make sure that the anti-spam feature is fully operational immediately after the basic installation of the Exchange Server 2013 server.

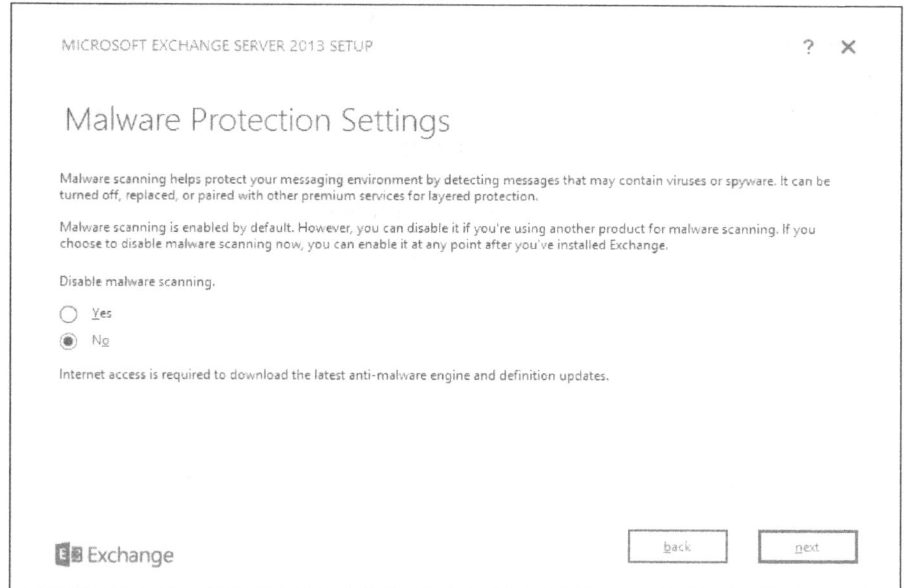

11. The Exchange Server Setup Wizard now starts with the **Readiness Checks**, to verify the machine is compliant with all Exchange Server 2013 system requirements. If the readiness checks pass, you can then click on **install** to proceed with the actual installation.

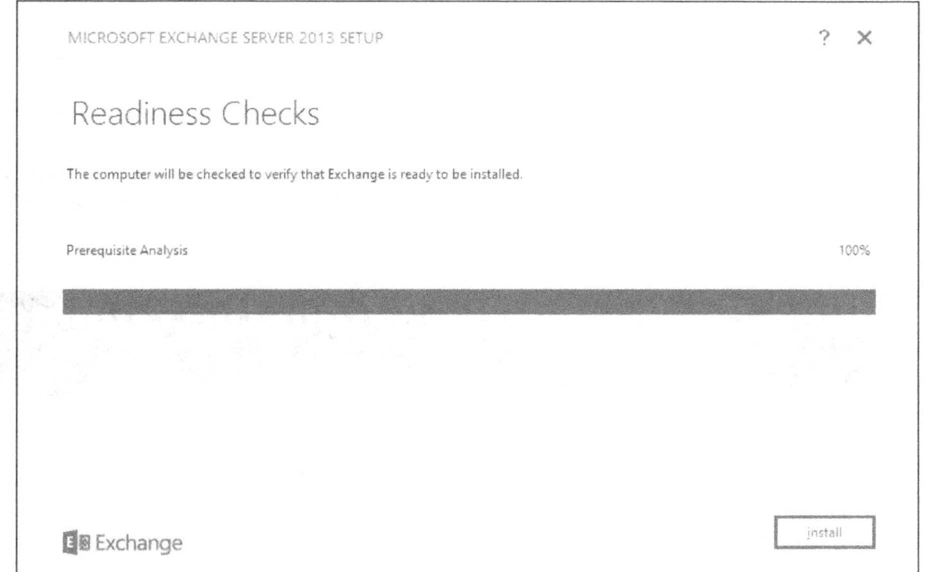

12. During this step, the actual installation of the Exchange Server 2013 application is being executed. In our test setup it took anywhere between 10 to 25 minutes, but this may vary depending of the specs of your servers.
13. When all runs smoothly, you are now at the final stage of the setup installation routine, where setup is completed. Select the option **Launch Exchange Administration Center...** if you want to open up and explore the **Exchange Administration Center** (the new management environment).

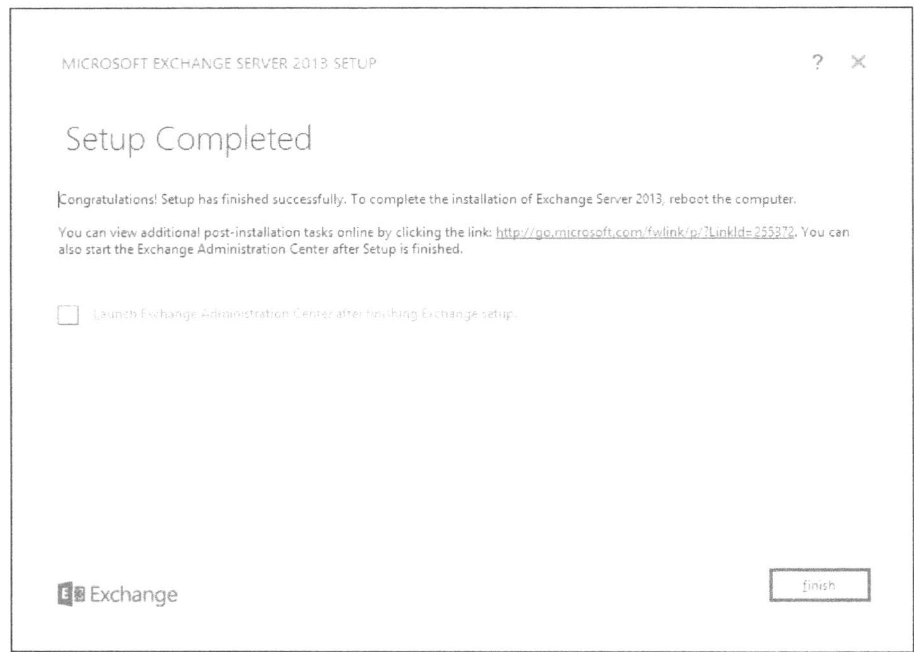

Congratulations, you now have your first Exchange Server 2013 up and running! However, additional configuration steps are required before it is ready for production use. Have a look at our next chapters for this.

Installing Exchange 2013 from the command line

In this recipe we will walk you through the same installation as the Setup Wizard, only this time we are using the command line. Although the Setup Wizard is perfect if you have to do only a few Exchange installations, the command line offers you the ability to quickly set up more servers, even opening up the ability to script the Exchange installation.

A good example of how the command line can be used is the Exchange 2013 Unattended Installation Script by *Michael de Rooij* (`www.eightwone.com`). It's a handy script that we use all the time to quickly build test machines.

To find out more, have a look at the TechNet Gallery available at `http://gallery.technet.microsoft.com/Exchange-2013-Unattended-e97ccda4`.

How to do it...

1. Log on to the Exchange Server machine with an account that has the necessary admin rights for Exchange Server installation. (See *Chapter 1, Planning an Exchange Server 2013 Infrastructure* on what administrative rights are required).
2. Open a command prompt with Administrative Rights, and use the following `setup.exe` command as a minimum:

   /mode

   /IAcceptExchangeServerLicenseTerms

   /Roles

   /OrganizationName (Parameter is only required if this is the first Exchange Server ever introduced in the environment. If you are integrating Excchange Server 2013 in an existing 2007/2010/2013 organization, the OrganizationName is already present).

3. For example:

   ```
   .\Setup.exe /mode:install /Role:MB,CA /
   IacceptExchangeServerLicenseTerms
   ```

Let us give a summarized explanation of each and every important parameter you can include with `setup.exe`. Note that all details for the `setup.exe` parameters can be viewed by typing `setup.exe /help:Install`.

Setup Parameter	Explanation
`/IAcceptExchangeServer LicenseTerms`	This parameter allows you to accept the license terms during the Exchange Installation. This is a required parameter whenever the setup command is used.
`/Mode:` or `/m:`	Defines whether you are: ▸ installing ("install") ▸ uninstalling ("uninstall") ▸ performing a service pack upgrade ("upgrade")

Setup Parameter	Explanation
`/Roles` or `/r:`	Defines which Exchange Server roles you want to install/uninstall: ▸ mailbox or mb ▸ clientacces or ca ▸ management tools or mt or t
`/DisableAMFiltering`	Disables the Anti-Malware built-in filtering during setup
`/DomainController:` or `/dc:`	Specifies which Domain Controller Exchange Server 2013 should use as a reference when performing the installation/uninstallation/upgrade.
`/InstallWindowsComponents`	This parameter is similar to the flag in the Setup Wizard allowing for automatic installation of required Windows Components and/or features if the prerequisites are not ok.
`/OrganizationName:` or `/on:`	Specifies the name of the Exchange Organization (required for first installation). Valid characters for Organization Name is a-z, A-Z, 0-9, hyphen, dash and space.
`/TargetDir:` or `/t:`	Specifies the path where the Exchange Server program files will be installed. (Default install path is `%ProgramFiles*\Microsoft\Exchange Server\V15`.
`/UpdateDir:` or `/u:`	Indicates the source location of Service Pack upgrade files.

To install a new Exchange 2013 multi-role server, run the following command:

```
Setup.exe /Mode:Install /Roles:Mailbox, Client Access, Management Tools /
IAcceptExchangeServerLicenseTerms
```

Or it can be abbreviated in the following way:

```
Setup.exe /m:install /r:mb,ca,mt /IAcceptExchangeServerLicenseTerms
```

After executing the command just explained, you should see the following screenshot during setup:

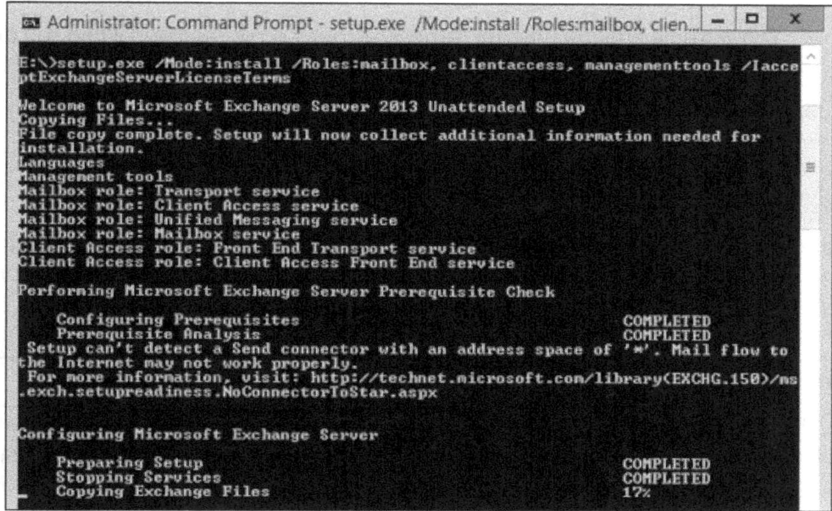

```
E:\>setup.exe /Mode:install /Roles:mailbox, clientaccess, managementtools /IacceptExchangeServerLicenseTerms

Welcome to Microsoft Exchange Server 2013 Unattended Setup
Copying Files...
File copy complete. Setup will now collect additional information needed for
installation.
Languages
Management tools
Mailbox role: Transport service
Mailbox role: Client Access service
Mailbox role: Unified Messaging service
Mailbox role: Mailbox service
Client Access role: Front End Transport service
Client Access role: Client Access Front End service

Performing Microsoft Exchange Server Prerequisite Check

    Configuring Prerequisites                                  COMPLETED
    Prerequisite Analysis                                      COMPLETED
 Setup can't detect a Send connector with an address space of '*'. Mail flow to
the Internet may not work properly.
 For more information, visit: http://technet.microsoft.com/library(EXCHG.150)/ms
.exch.setupreadiness.NoConnectorToStar.aspx

Configuring Microsoft Exchange Server

    Preparing Setup                                            COMPLETED
    Stopping Services                                          COMPLETED
    Copying Exchange Files                                     17%
```

Once the setup process has been completed, you'll see the following:

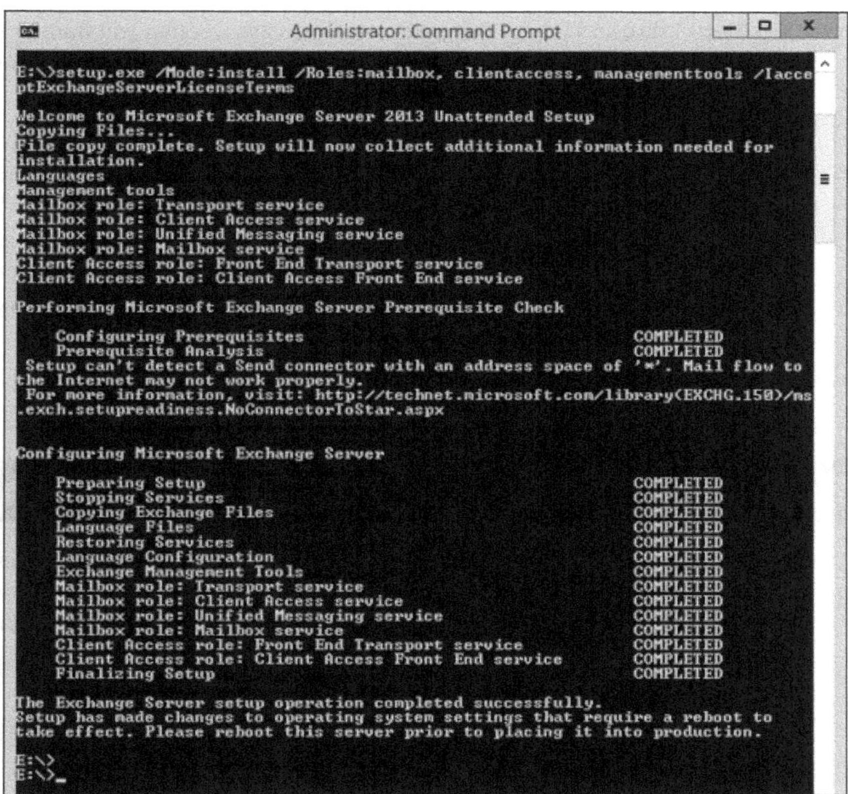

```
E:\>setup.exe /Mode:install /Roles:mailbox, clientaccess, managementtools /IacceptExchangeServerLicenseTerms

Welcome to Microsoft Exchange Server 2013 Unattended Setup
Copying Files...
File copy complete. Setup will now collect additional information needed for
installation.
Languages
Management tools
Mailbox role: Transport service
Mailbox role: Client Access service
Mailbox role: Unified Messaging service
Mailbox role: Mailbox service
Client Access role: Front End Transport service
Client Access role: Client Access Front End service

Performing Microsoft Exchange Server Prerequisite Check

    Configuring Prerequisites                                  COMPLETED
    Prerequisite Analysis                                      COMPLETED
 Setup can't detect a Send connector with an address space of '*'. Mail flow to
the Internet may not work properly.
 For more information, visit: http://technet.microsoft.com/library(EXCHG.150)/ms
.exch.setupreadiness.NoConnectorToStar.aspx

Configuring Microsoft Exchange Server

    Preparing Setup                                            COMPLETED
    Stopping Services                                          COMPLETED
    Copying Exchange Files                                     COMPLETED
    Language Files                                             COMPLETED
    Restoring Services                                         COMPLETED
    Language Configuration                                     COMPLETED
    Exchange Management Tools                                  COMPLETED
    Mailbox role: Transport service                            COMPLETED
    Mailbox role: Client Access service                        COMPLETED
    Mailbox role: Unified Messaging service                    COMPLETED
    Mailbox role: Mailbox service                              COMPLETED
    Client Access role: Front End Transport service            COMPLETED
    Client Access role: Client Access Front End service        COMPLETED
    Finalizing Setup                                           COMPLETED

The Exchange Server setup operation completed successfully.
Setup has made changes to operating system settings that require a reboot to
take effect. Please reboot this server prior to placing it into production.

E:\>
E:\>
```

The warning about a missing `Send Connector` is expected when you are installing an additional server into an existing Exchange environment that you have not finished configuring. It can be safely ignored.

There's more...

Besides the aforementioned more commonly used command line parameters, setup contains another list of parameters, which might be used in specific situations or more advanced environments:

Setup Parameter	Description
`/ActiveDirectorySplit Permissions:`	This parameter allows for Active Directory Split Permissions model when preparing the Exchange Organization. The parameter can be set to True or False.
`/AnswerFile:`	Contains the path to an Answer File with set up parameters.
`/CustomerFeedbackEnabled:`	This parameter specifies whether you want to send customer feedback out of the Customer Experience Improvement Program or not. The parameter can be set to True or False.
`/DBFilePath:`	Specifies the location for the Mailbox Database which gets created when installing the mailbox server role.
`/MdbName:`	Specifies the name of the initially created mailbox database during mailbox server role installation.
`/LogFolderPathUse:`	Specifies the location of the transaction log files.
`/EnableErrorReporting`	Allows for sending critical error and warning information directly to Microsoft for troubleshooting.

Verifying the Exchange 2013 installation

Although the Exchange Server 2013 setup shouldn't be that difficult when all prerequisites are fulfilled, somewhere along the track, something might go wrong or cause an error. Therefore, it is good to know where to look for help, or at least verify whether the installation ran fine or not.

How to do it...

After the installation is completed, you should have two Exchange Server 2013 icons in your Windows Server 2008 R2 Start Menu (or two Exchange Server 2013 tiles in your Windows Server 2012 Start Screen):

Having the icons/tiles available is not a 100 percent bullet-proof test of the installation cycle. Therefore, we use the following additional checks:

Get-ExchangeServer

By using the `Get-ExchangeServer` PowerShell `cmdlet`, you will get an overview of all your Exchange Server 2013 machines in the organization. By default, this is a summarized view, which can be turned into a detailed view by piping the command to a format list.

The summarized or default view is as follows:

```
Get-ExchangeServer
```

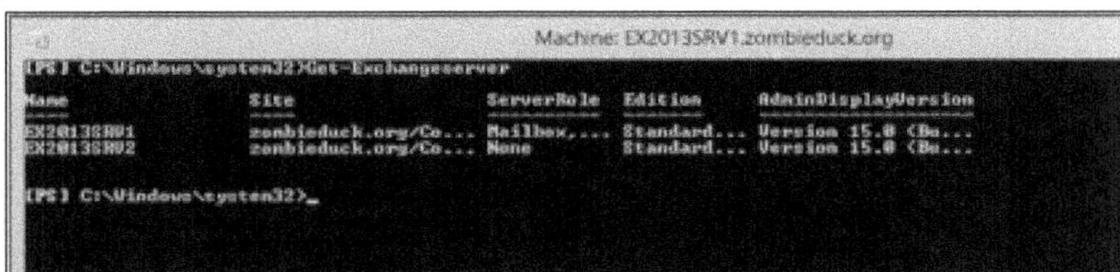

Or the following is the detailed view:

```
Get-ExchangeServer | format-list
```

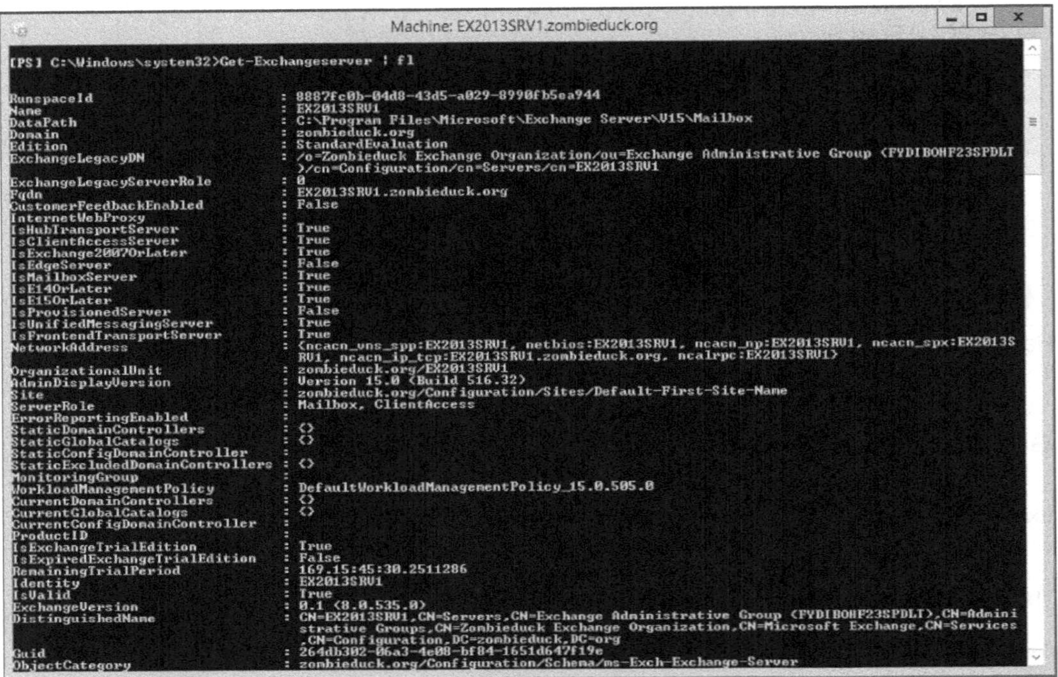

Setup Log file and Event Viewer

Lastly, the best location for validating all went well during the installation process, is the extensively detailed log file that is getting created during installation.

By checking the Setup Log file and/or the Event viewer, a lot of information can be retrieved from the Exchange Server 2013 installation phase.

> By default, the setup log file is created and stored at the following location:
> `system drive\ExchangeSetupLogs\ExchangeSetup.log`

The Setup Log file keeps track of each and every step during the installation, from prerequisites checks, system readiness checks, application installation steps, and all configuration parameters used during the installation process.

A sample **ExchangeSetup.log** looks like the following screenshot:

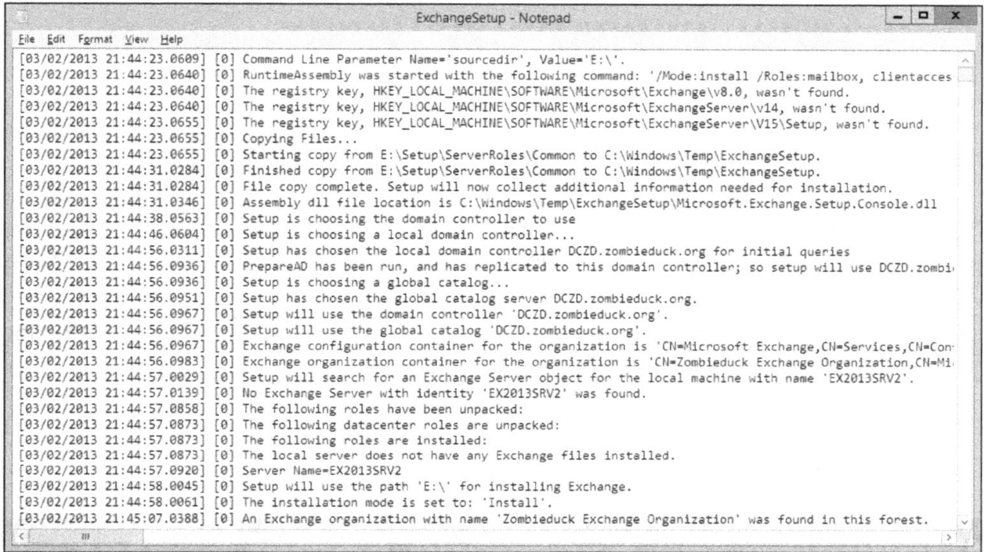

How it works...

As the Exchange installation procedure is mainly based on PowerShell scripts that are running, a lot of detailed logging information is being written into log files and into the Windows Server event viewer.

There's more...

In short, the following setup sequence can be followed throughout the Exchange Setup Log file:

- Detection of the operating system version.
- Verification if any previous Exchange Server registry entries already exist.
- Connect to Domain Controller for AD information gathering, required for setup.

  Based on the command line parameters (for example, `prepareschema`), the required task-sequence for that command will be executed; this will be reported in the log file with multiple sequences, similar to `install-ExchangeSchema -LdapFileName ($roleinstallpath + "setup\Data\"+Roleschemaprefix + "schema19.ldf)`, which are the effective Active Directory Schema extension files that are being applied.

- Next, the actual installation will happen, which will be marked in the log file as the following:

```
**********************************************
* Starting Microsoft Exchange Server 2013 Setup
**********************************************
```

- Investigating when something goes wrong is possible by searching for the keywords **[warning]** or **[error]** or **[failed]**. Note that finding any of these keywords not necessarily means something's wrong. For example, when starting the setup of your first Exchange Server in a fresh configured Active Directory, a warning is raised that no organization name can be found for Exchange, which is of course very normal at that time.
- When the setup routine has completed, it will be marked in the ExchangeSetup log file as follows:

```
"***********************************
* End of Setup
************************************
```

Introducing the Exchange Admin Center

While we will dive into all aspects of the EAC during the next chapters of this cookbook, this recipe is to get you connected to it so you can start learning how to navigate the EAC and find your way around.

As already mentioned in the introduction of Exchange 2013, this new management tool is totally different from the management console in previous versions.

Getting ready

In order to login to the EAC, you will need an account with administrative permissions. For example, an account that is member of the Organization Management role group. If this is the first server you are installing and Exchange wasn't installed in your organization previously, the account you used to install Exchange will automatically have been granted the Organization Management permissions.

How to do it...

Starting the Exchange Admin Center is done by connecting to the following URLs from within your browser:

```
https://internalexchangeserverFQDN/ecp
```

In addition, the following URL can be used when trying to connect to the EAC from external:

https://externalexchangeserverFQDN/ecp

> If you have a mixed Exchange Server 2010-2013 environment and your administrative user's mailbox is still located on the Exchange Server 2010, you will by default be redirected to the Exchange Control Panel of the Exchange Server 2010 environment. If you want to forcefully connect to Exchange 2013, its EAC, you need to use the following URLs:
>
> `https://internal_or_external_exchangeserverFQDN/ECP?ExchClientVer=15`
>
> (for Exchange Server 2013-EAC)
>
> Or
>
> `https://internal_or_external_exchangeserverFQDN/ECP?ExchClientVer=14`
>
> (for Exchange Server 2010-ECP)

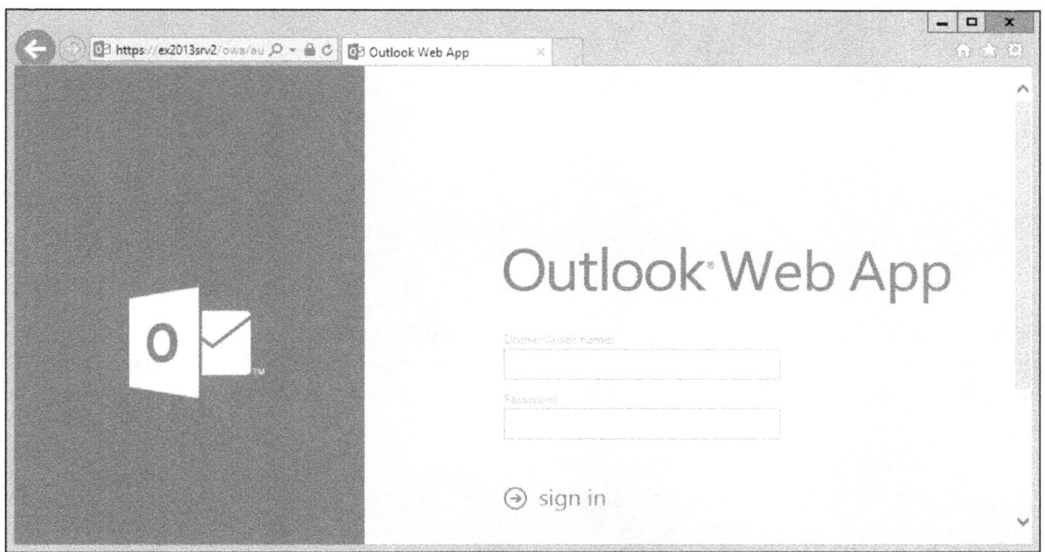

Browsing to the URLs we just saw will bring you to the authentication form. Although configurable afterwards, you should enter your administrative credentials in the domain\username form (or use the UPN).

It's also likely that you will receive a certificate warning when connecting at this point. Given that we haven't configured any certificates yet, this is expected and can be ignored for now. We'll walk through the certificate configuration in *Chapter 3, Configuring the Client Access Server Role*.

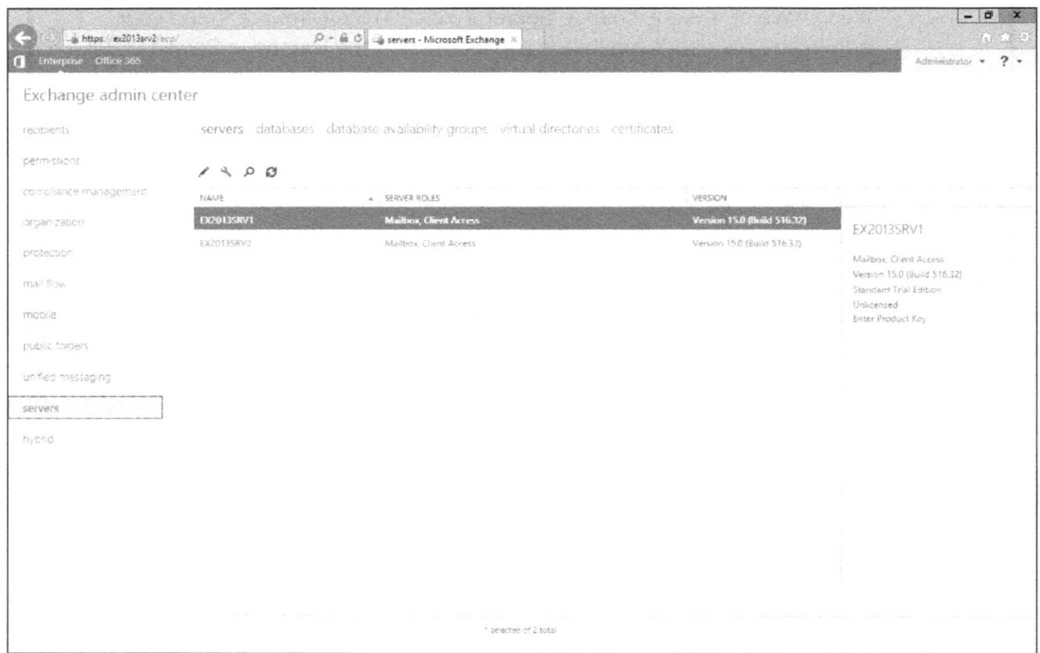

There's more...

Without explaining all ins and outs of the new Exchange Admin Center (EAC) here, we want you to get familiar with(in) the interface as quick and good as possible. The following table summarizes the different components from the EAC and gives a brief description for each of them:

EAC Component	Description
Enterprise/Office365	At the top blue ribbon, you can distinct the EAC from your on-premise Exchange administration or managing your federated Office 365 environment.
Recipients	This is where you manage mailboxes, groups, resource mailboxes, external contacts, and shared mailboxes. This topic also allows you to monitor mailbox move migration batches and their up to date status.

EAC Component	Description
Permissions	This topic is where you control and define admin roles, as well as user role policies and Outlook Web App policies.
Compliance Management	Allows you to configure policies and enterprise-wide mailbox search, auditing, **Data Loss Prevention** (**DLP**), setting retention policies and journaling rules.
Organization	The Organization component is the location where you configure federation trust, as well as the new "Apps" functionality in Exchange Server 2013. Address List management is also done from this topic.
Protection	Allows you to configure Anti-Malware settings and policies.
Mail Flow	This is one of the more important topics, as it contains the necessary components to configure email flow inside and outside of your organization. In here, you also configure the accepted domains, send and receive connectors.
Mobile	Allows management and configuration of mobile devices and mobile device policies.
Public Folders	What was a separate toolbox option in Exchange 2007 and 2010 has now been incorporated in the default admin console again. This topic allows for management of public folders and public folder mailboxes.
Unified Messaging	This topic contains the management interface for Unified Messaging dial plans and gateways.
Servers	Besides the Mail Flow topic, this is another very important part of the EAC. In here, you can configure and manage your servers, databases, DAGs, verify, and set your Exchange Server virtual directories and manage SSL certificates which are used within the Exchange organization.
Hybrid	The last topic contains the configuration wizard (or parameters if already defined) around Office 365 hybrid model.

Although at first sight the EAC looks totally different from any Exchange Admin Console in previous editions, a lot of topics will still look familiar to an experienced Exchange 2007/2010 administrator.

Uninstalling an Exchange 2013 Server or Server role

Although this chapter focusses on installing Exchange Server 2013, we thought it would be of interest explaining how to uninstall a Server or Server Role.

Getting ready

In order to remove Exchange from a server, you need to be a member of the Organization Management role group and either have been delegated permissions on the server or have local Administrator rights.

How to do it...

Somewhere along your Exchange administration timeline, you will probably need to uninstall a server role from an existing multi-role machine. One might think this isn't a difficult task—and to be honest it shouldn't be—but uninstalling a server role from an Exchange Server 2013 is actually not possible. The only option is to completely uninstall Exchange and then only to reinstall the role you want to keep.

Similar to the installation process, uninstalling is possible through the setup wizard or by using the command line. Both examples are explained in this section:

By using the Setup Wizard

Instead of starting from the `setup.exe` from the Exchange Server 2013 setup media location, removing the server is started from **Programs & Features** in the **Control Panel**. The following are the steps for uninstalling the server:

1. Navigate to the **Control Panel** and open **Programs and Features**.

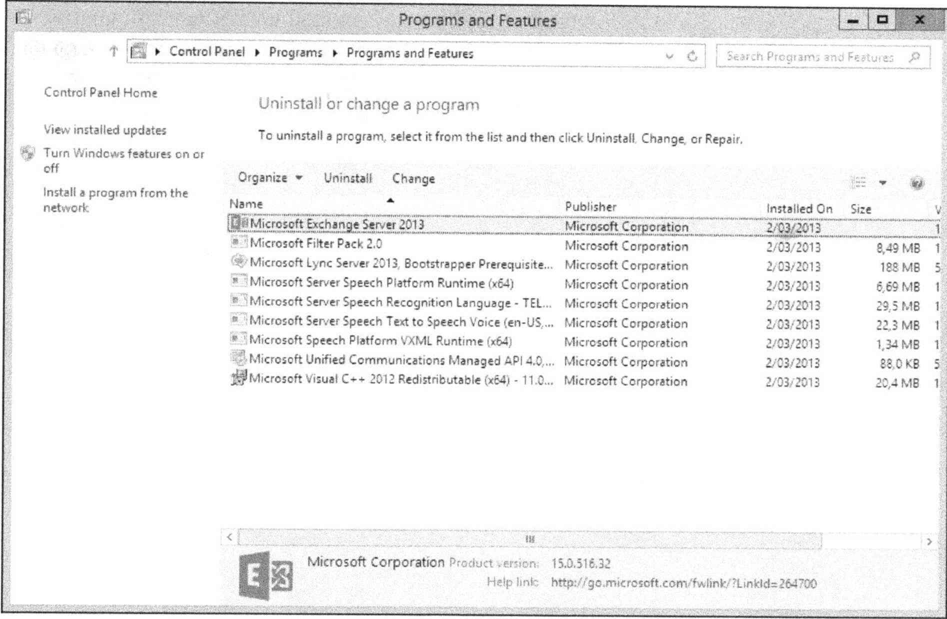

2. Select **Microsoft Exchange Server 2013** and click on **uninstall**.
3. This will start the removal process; click on **next** on the first page appearing.

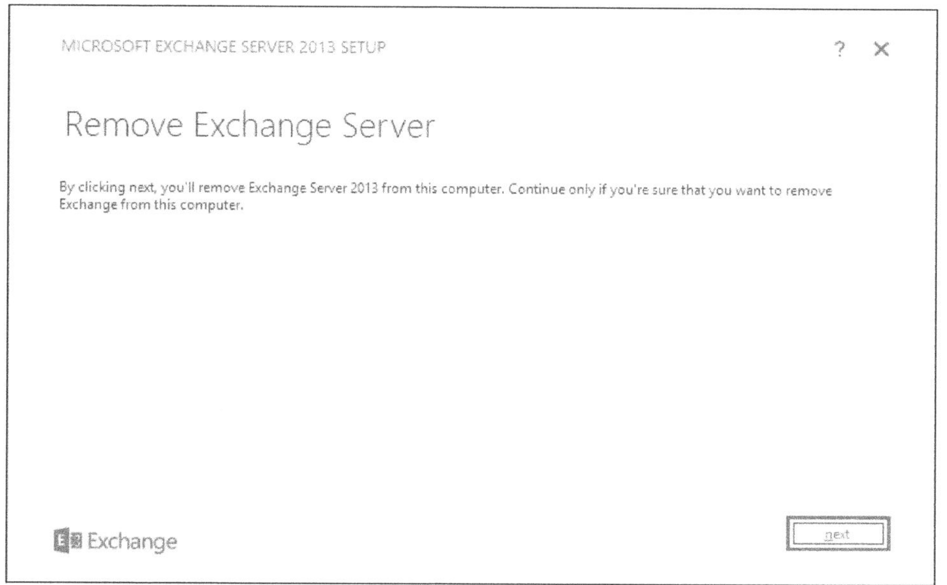

4. Click on **next** to let Exchange Server removal process run some **Readiness Checks** before starting the removal. There might be multiple reasons why uninstalling an Exchange Server 2013 machine is not allowed or possible. For example, when there is still a **Mailbox Database** on the server. Having the `Exchange Server Management Shell` open is another reason for the setup to stop because some files it needs to use are still in use by the PowerShell process.

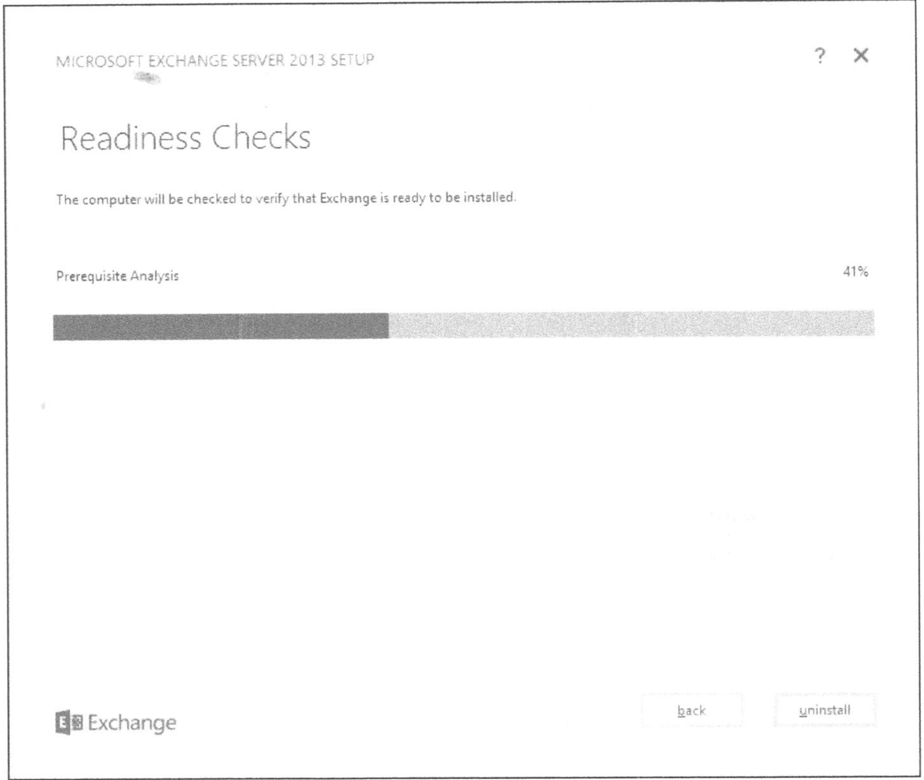

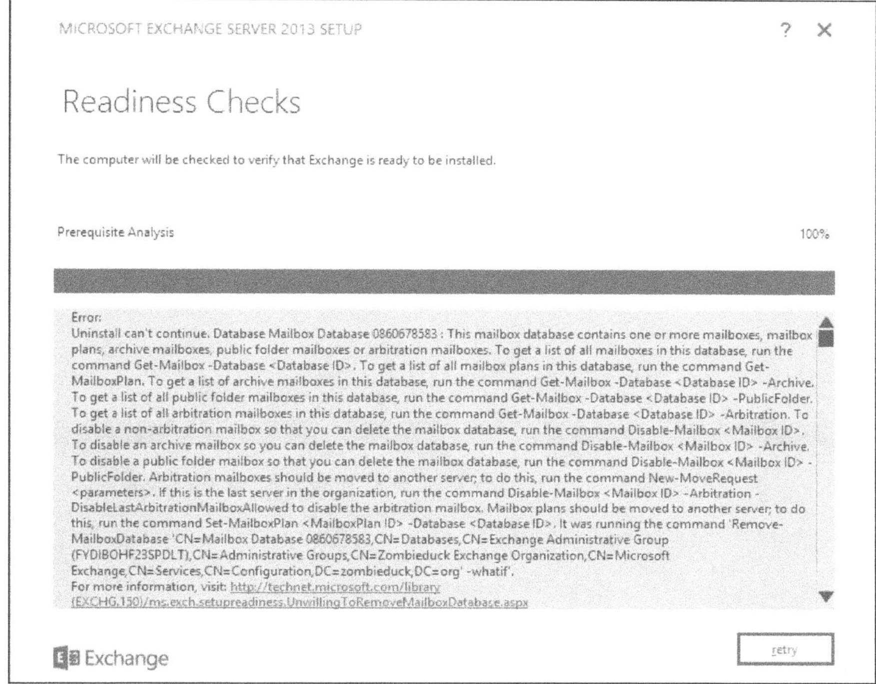

5. When the **Readiness Checks** are completed at 100 percent, click on **uninstall** to continue the removal of Exchange Server 2013 from the server.

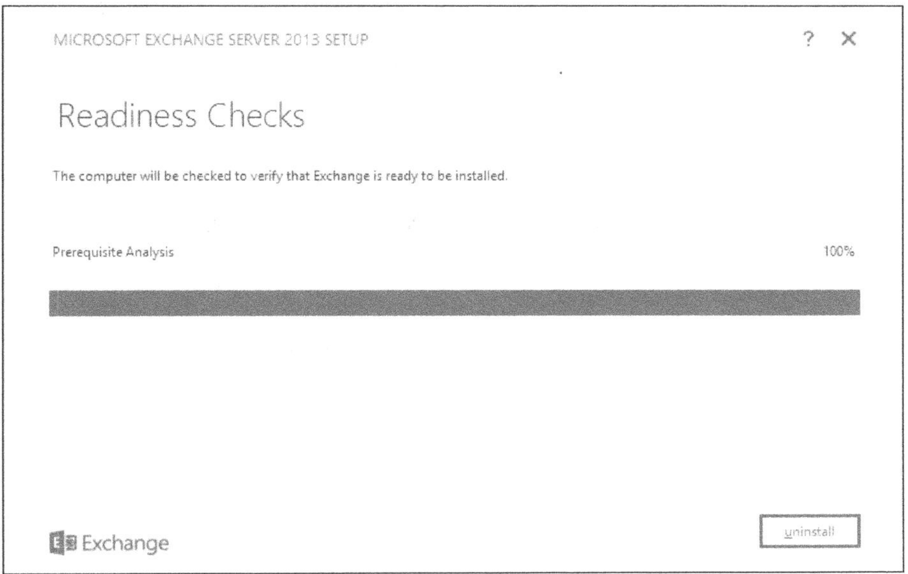

6. At the end of the removal process, Exchange Server 2013 will ask for a **reboot**. This concludes uninstalling the Exchange Server 2013 server machine from your organization.

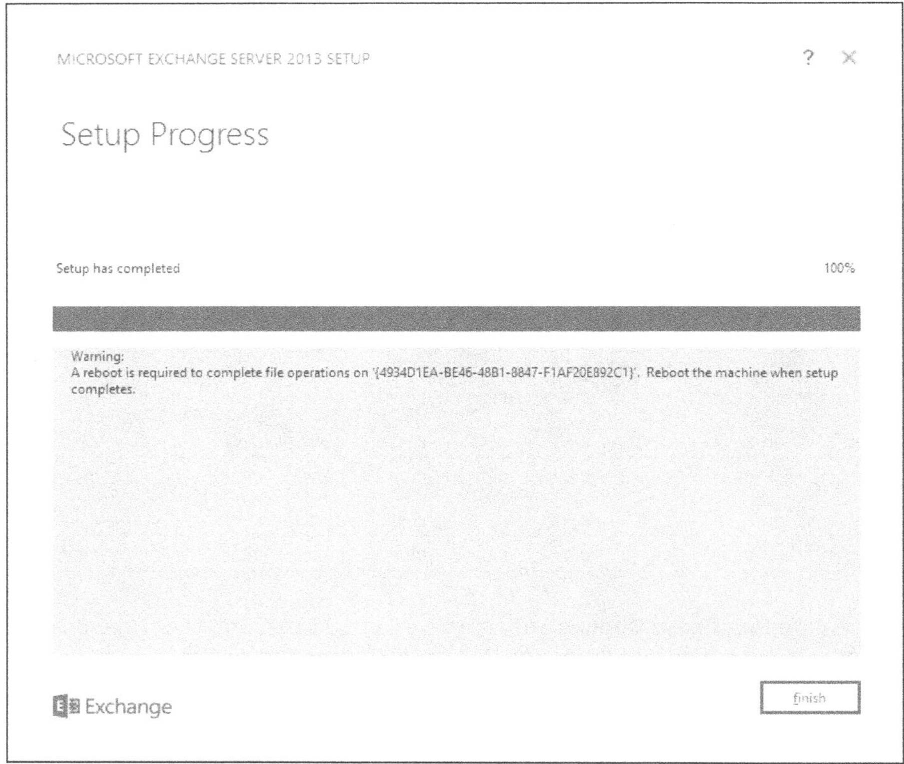

By using the command line

Following are the steps used to uninstall the server by using the command prompt:

1. From the command prompt, browse to your Exchange Server 2013 install media location.
2. Enter the following command:

```
Setup.exe /mode:uninstall /IAcceptExchangeServerLicenseTerms
```

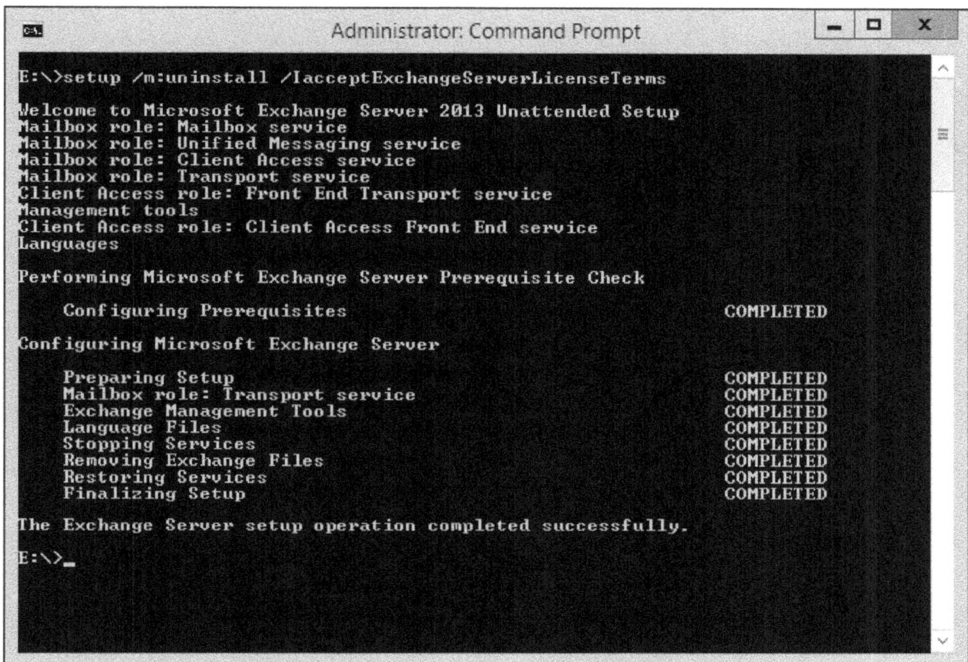

This concludes the removal of Exchange Server 2013 from your server and Active Directory environment.

How it works...

As you could experience from the *How to do it...* section, uninstalling an Exchange Server role or server completely shouldn't be difficult no matter how you do it, whether that is through the Exchange Setup Wizard or by using command line.

After the removal of the server role or server, a reboot is required to complete the process. Doing so, will clean up whatever cached items remain from the removal process and also take the server out of a pending reboot state. This state tells the system that it is waiting for a reboot and might prevent installing or removing other programs.

There's more...

Referring to the installation part as the main content of this chapter, we would like to remind you that at this point, you only have a basic Exchange Server 2013 machine available, and more configuration is required before putting the server into production. How to perform this will be explained in more detail in the following chapters.

3

Configuring the Client Access Server Role

In this chapter, we will cover the tasks related to configuring the Client Access Server Role to successfully accept and forward client requests into the Exchange organization, including:

- Configuring certificates
- Configuring Autodiscover
- Configuring Outlook Anywhere
- Configuring Outlook Web App
- Configuring Exchange Web Services
- Configuring Exchange ActiveSync
- Configuring ActiveSync Device Access
- Configuring SMTP
- Configuring POP and IMAP
- Using non-Microsoft Clients with Exchange Server 2013

Introduction

The Client Access Server role is the main entry point for all client connections into your Exchange organization. Although there are some exceptions where clients may directly make a connection to the Mailbox server, it's in general the first point of ingress into your organization's Exchange environment. This makes it not only a critical but also highly visible part of your Exchange infrastructure. A minor problem with one of these components could potentially knock out all client connections, possibly preventing your users from accessing their mailbox or other Exchange-related services.

This chapter explains how to configure the Client Access Server role, starting with the critical, required, services, such as Outlook Anywhere, Exchange Web Services, and Autodiscover, and ending with some less commonly used protocols, such as POP and IMAP.

Configuring certificates

As briefly touched upon during *Chapter 1, Planning an Exchange Server 2013 Infrastructure*, Exchange 2013 stepped away from familiar RPC-over-TCP connections and now only uses RPC-over-HTTP connections for primary client connectivity. This means that now both internal and external clients connect to Exchange using Outlook anywhere.

By default internal connections are not secured (plain HTTP). Usually though, companies want to secure that traffic using **Secure Sockets Layer** (**SSL**).

SSL has two main functions:

- Authentication
- Encryption

For both of these tasks, SSL relies on certificates. It's not necessary to know all the details of how certificates work. However, it's important to have at least a basic understanding of the implications of working with certificates, especially given the criticality of properly configured certificates in Exchange Server 2013.

Getting ready

Before diving into the configuration of certificates, it's important to understand what **Subject Name** and **Subject Alternative Names** (**SAN**) your certificate should contain. At a bare minimum, an Exchange Server 2013 deployment will always need at least two different namespaces, one for the Autodiscover service and one for the other Exchange workloads, such as Outlook Anywhere, Exchange Web Services, Outlook Web App....

The trick, although it's not really a trick, to having as few as two namespaces for Exchange is to use the same URL for all Exchange workloads, except for Autodisocover. The latter does not share the namespace with the other workloads given that the Autodiscover URLs are hard coded into Outlook and other Autodiscover-capable clients. For more information on how this works, have a look at *Configuring Autodiscover* later in this chapter.

Let's clarify the use of namespaces by using an example. A company named Exblog has an Exchange 2013 deployment. They decided to use `outlook.exblog.be` as namespace for all Exchange workloads. As a result, the certificate should include at least the following Subject (Alternative) Names:

Subject (Alternative) Name	Workload
`Outlook.exblog.be`	Outlook Anywhere, OWA, EWS, EAS, OAB, and so on.
`Autodiscover.exblog.be`	Autodiscover.

Because the certificate only has two namespaces, you're required to use the same namespace both internally and externally. Sometimes, however, a company decides not to use the same namespace. If that's the case, you'll need to list the namespace for each workload and include them on the certificate.

The following table depicts the different entries that you'd have to include on the certificate if you use a different namespace for each workload. This would, for instance, be the case where you decide to use Layer 4 load balancing and still want to have a health check per workload. For more information, check *Chapter 6, Implementing and Managing High Availability*.

Subject (Alternative) Name	Workload
`Webmail.exblog.be`	OWA, EAC
`Outlook.exblog.be`	Outlook Anywhere
`Autodiscover.exblog.be`	Autodiscover
`OAB.exblog.be`	Offline Address Book
`EWS.exblog.be`	Exchange Web Services
`EAS.exblog.be`	Exchange ActiveSync

By now, you should have a picture of what entries should be present on the certificate. However, there are also some special cases to take into account. If you are migrating from Exchange 2007, you need to use a legacy namespace which Exchange 2013 will use to redirect clients to that still have their mailbox on an Exchange 2007 server and try opening it through OWA. Strictly speaking, you don't need to include this namespace on the certificate for Exchange 2013 as you could request a separate certificate for Exchange 2007. However, it's not uncommon to use the same certificate on all Exchange Servers in an organization. If that's the case, make sure to include the legacy namespace on the certificate. For more information on how that works, make sure to have a look at *Chapter 7, Transitioning to Exchange 2013*.

If you haven't previously bought or created a certificate that you'd like to re-use, the steps involved for configuring certificates in Exchange typically include:

1. Create a certificate request.
2. Complete the certificate request.

3. Enable the certificate.

> Because of the way the EAC works, it is also advised to set up a shared folder on the network where you will store the certificates and certificate requests.

How to do it...

When you are using the EAC to create new certificates, you will need a shared folder on the network in which Exchange can save the required files like certificate requests or the certificates themselves.

Creating a shared network folder

In order for Exchange to be able to write to this location, the shared folder should be set up with the correct permissions. The server from where you share the folder can be another Exchange server in the organization, but it does not necessarily have to be.

Below are the steps to setup a shared folder with the necessary permissions:

1. Create a new folder and name it accordingly. For instance call it **Exchange Share**.
2. Right-click on the folder and select **properties**.
3. Navigate to the **Sharing**-tab and click on **Advanced Sharing**.
4. Click on **Share this folder** and make sure to add the following permissions:

   Everyone ~ Full Control

5. Click on **OK**.
6. Navigate to the **Security**-tab and add the following permissions:

   Exchange Trusted Subsystem ~ Modify

7. Click on **OK** twice.

Creating a certificate request

The following steps outline the process to create a new certificate request:

1. Log in to the **Exchange admin center** and navigate to **Servers** | **Certificates**.
2. Click on the **+** sign to open the **new Exchange certificate** wizard.

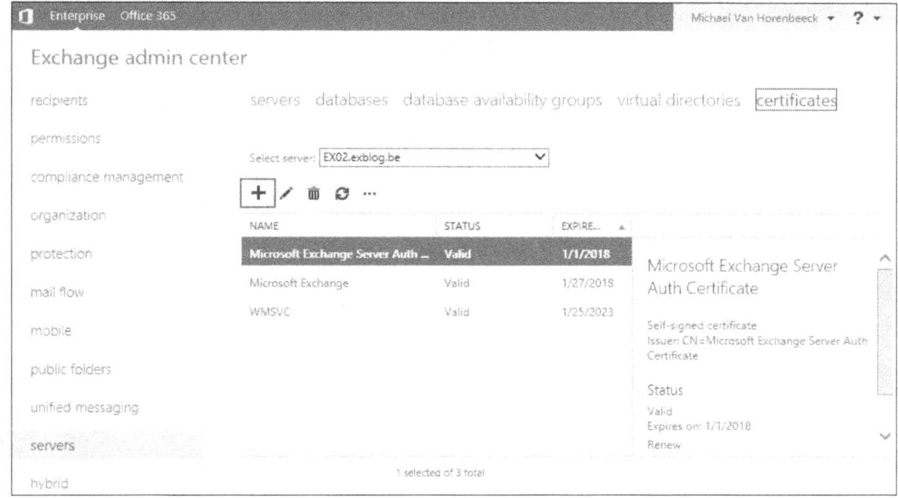

3. Select **Create a request for a certificate from a certification authority** and click on **Next**.
4. Enter a friendly name for the certificate, for instance `Exchange Certificate` and click on **Next**.
5. Leave the checkbox before **Request a wildcard certificate.** unmarked and click on **Next**.
6. Click on **browse...** and select a server on which you want to store the certificate request. Click on **OK** and then click on **Next**.

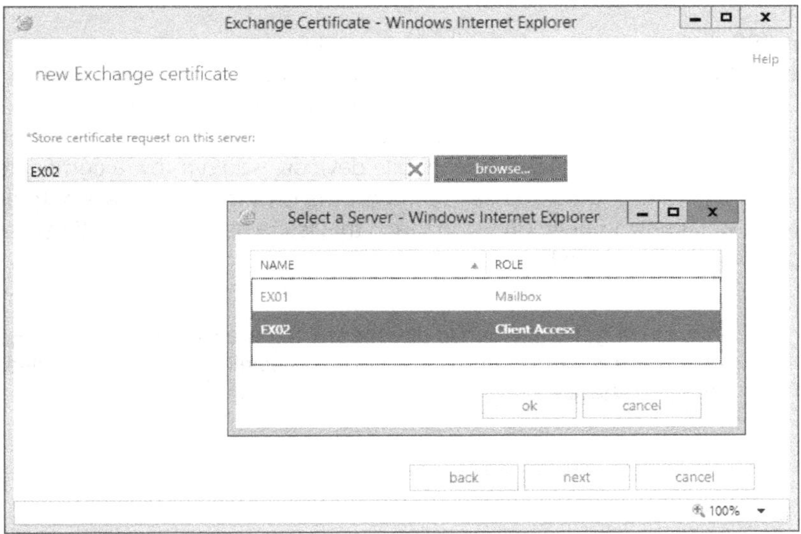

7. Make sure that you update the information in the list to match the host names you chose during planning. When finished, click on **Next**.

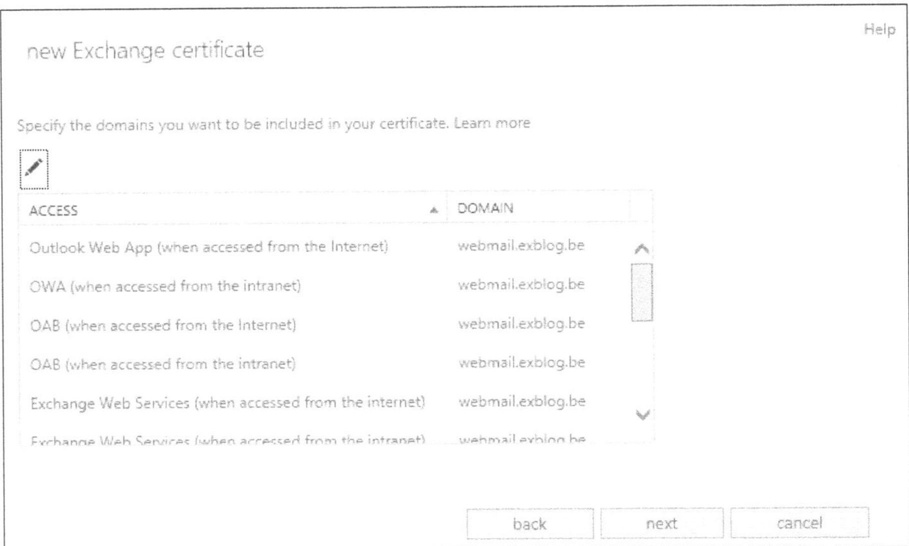

8. Review the list of subject names to be included in the certificate. If you wish to add additional names, now is a good time.
9. Enter your company information and click on **Next**.
10. Finally, enter the UNC path where the certificate request file should be stored and click on **Finish** to create the **Certificate Request File** (**CSR**).

Now, use the CSR that you just created to obtain a certificate from either a public or internal **Certification Authority** (**CA**). Although certificates from either of both will work just fine, using an internal CA is only recommended for lab environments. This is because by default only domain-joined computers trust certificates issued by the internal CA. Without further action, all devices that are not domain-joined, like mobile devices, would throw a certificate warning. To overcome this problem, you would have to import the CA's root certificate onto each device separately. Most well-known public CA's don't face this issue as most operating systems trust a large set of root CA's out of the box.

Unfortunately, not all mobile devices will throw a warning when a certificate's issuers cannot be verified. Especially some Android-based handhelds have a pretty bad track record in this area.

Completing a certificate request

Once you receive the certificate, proceed by completing the certificate request:

1. Log in to **Exchange Admin Center** (**EAC**) and navigate to **Servers** | **Certificates**.

2. From the drop-down list, select the server that you entered in Step 4 when *creating a certificate request*.
3. From the list of certificates, select the certificate with status **Pending Request**.
4. Click on **Complete** under **Pending Request** in the action pane at the right.

5. Enter the UNC path to your SSL-certificate. For instance, `\\servername\share\certificate.crt`.
6. Click on **OK**.
7. Verify the certificate has been imported successfully and that its status is set to **Valid**.

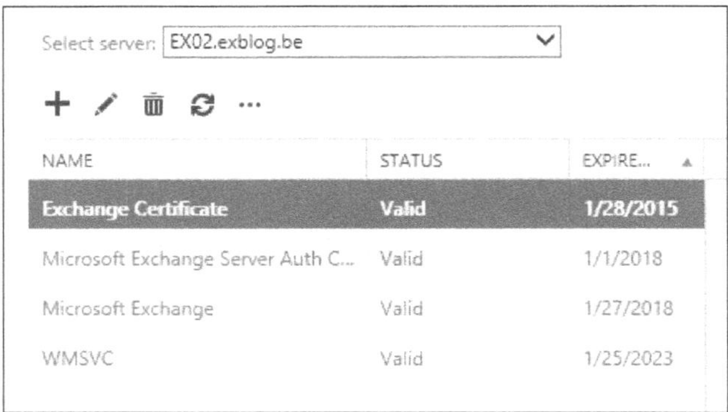

If you have multiple Exchange Client Access Servers in your environment, you will have to import the same certificate to the other servers first.

Exporting a certificate

1. Log in to the **Exchange Admin Center** and navigate to **Servers** | **Certificates**.
2. Select the certificate you wish to export and click on the three dots from the menu and select **Export Exchange certificate**.

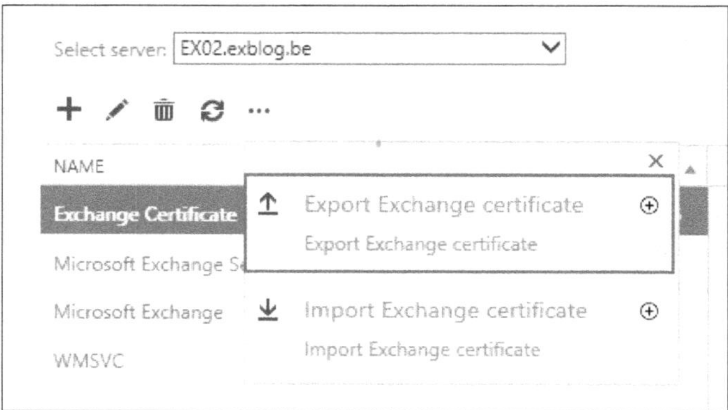

3. In the **Export Exchange certificate**-wizard screen, enter the UNC path where the certificate has to be stored and choose a password to protect the certificate.
4. Click on **OK**.

Importing a certificate

Once you have exported your certificate or you already exported a certificate from another server before, complete the following steps to that certificate to another Exchange Client Access Server.

1. Log in to the **Exchange Admin Center** and navigate to **Servers** | **Certificates**.
2. Click on the three dots from the menu and select **Import Exchange certificate**:

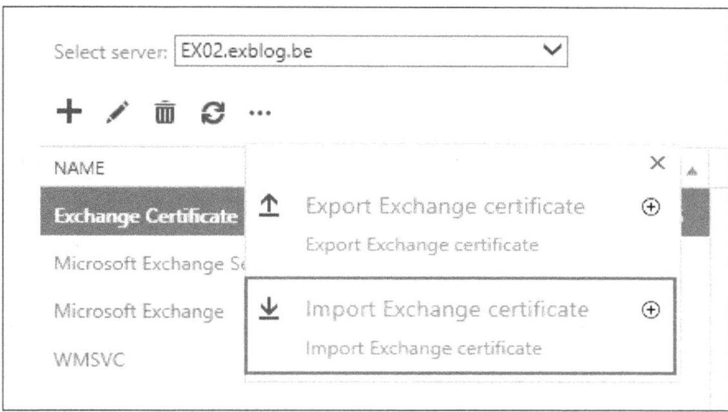

3. Enter the UNC path where you stored the certificate and also the password you used to export the certificate. Then click on **Next**.
4. Click on the plus-sign (**+**) and select the **Exchange server(s)** from the list you wish to import the certificate to. Click on **OK** to confirm.
5. Click on **Finish**.

Enabling a certificate

Before your certificate becomes active, you need to assign specific Exchange services to it, such as IIS, SMTP, or Unified Messaging.

1. Log in to the **Exchange Admin Center** and navigate to **Servers** | **Certificates**.
2. Double-click on the certificate you want to assign services to.
3. Click on **services**.

4. Check the services you want to assign to the certificate. In this example, select **IIS** and click **Save**.

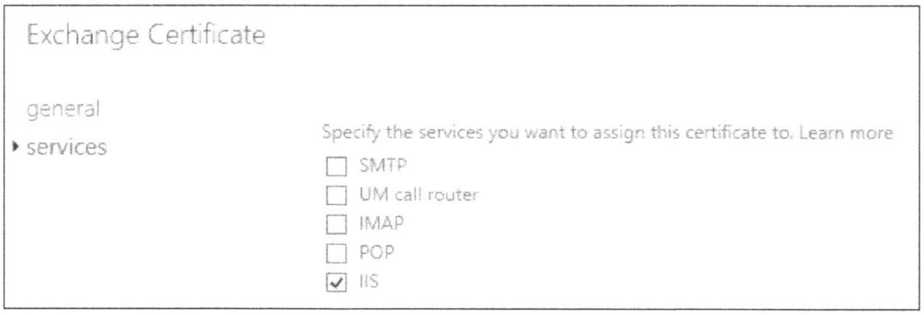

Exchange Certificate

general
services

Specify the services you want to assign this certificate to. Learn more

SMTP
UM call router
IMAP
POP
IIS

You have now successfully configured a certificate for your Client Access Server and are ready to move on to configuring the other services.

How it works...

Whenever a client makes a HTTPS connection to a web server, the server will present its certificate allowing the client to validate the identity of the server. To confirm the validity of the certificate, the following requirements have to be fulfilled:

- The certificate should be within its validity timeframe. Each certificate contains two properties that define this timeframe, Not before <date> and Not after <date>.
- The hostname that is used to connect to the server (for example, `webmail.company.com`) is compared to the entries in the subject name and SAN properties of the certificate and should match.
- The issuer of the certificate must be trusted by the client.
- The certificate hasn't been revoked by the issuer. This means that the issuer has marked the certificate as invalid.

If all of these requirements have been fulfilled, the client will send a request for encryption to the server. The latter will confirm the request by sending back a digitally signed acknowledgement. At this point, the connection is securely established and any data exchange between client and server is encrypted.

When the certificate is deemed invalid because one of the requirements hasn't been met, a warning will be displayed and the connection won't be established.

Proper planning is required to ensure that hostnames on your certificate match the ones you will be using in Exchange. A certificate for Exchange 2013 will always include a bare minimum of two namespaces, one for Autodiscover and one for the namespace your clients will be connecting to. Because of the requirement of having multiple names for your Exchange server, you will need to create SAN certificates, sometimes these certificates are also referred to as UC certificates.

A second point of attention is the CA that will issue the certificate. By default, every Operating System contains a base-list of trusted CAs mostly including the larger, well-known, commercial CAs, such as Digicert, VeriSign, Thawte, and Starfield.

This means that if you purchase a certificate via one of these CA's, almost all clients will be able to trust the certificate from the start.

Wildcard certificates

Sometimes companies like to use wildcard certificates. This type of certificate doesn't have a distinguished hostname (or multiple hostnames) configured. Instead a wildcard certificate will accept any child domain that it's configured for.

For example, a wildcard certificate with a common name of `*.company.com` will accept any hostname that ends with `company.com`. For example, `autodiscover.company.com`, `webmail.company.com`, `mail.company.com`, `owa.company.com` and so on.

Wildcard certificates are well-suited when you have a large number of different hostnames at the cost of trading in some security. Wildcards are actually quite common because of the relative low cost compared to SAN certificates.

See also

- Take a look at *Chapter 2, Installing Exchange Server 2013* for more information on namespace planning.

Configuring Autodiscover

Autodiscover was first introduced with Exchange 2007 and allows any Autodiscover-capable client such as Outlook or most Exchange ActiveSync-enabled mobile devices, to retrieve its profile configuration settings by itself. Before Exchange 2007, it was up to the administrator to configure a user's Outlook profile with the correct server settings. This also meant that if a configuration parameter changed, the profile often had to be updated manually.

How to do it...

Most actions can usually be performed through either the EAC or Management Shell. Sometimes though, we prefer the simplicity of the EAC over PowerShell. In this case however, the EAC is not an option as most of the parameters can only be configured through the Exchange Management Shell.

Configuring the AutodiscoverServiceInternalURI

The value of an `AutodiscoverServiceInternalURI` property corresponds to the URL that will be returned to your Autodiscover-capable clients when they query Active Directory for the related **Service Connection Point** (**SCP**) object. SCPs are objects that are stored in Active Directory which services can use to publish information about their existence within the boundaries of your Active Directory. Clients on their turn query these objects to retrieve specific information about the service. In the case of Autodiscover, clients use the published SCP to retrieve connection information.

To configure the URL a Client Access Server will advertise in the SCP object, run the following command:

```
Set-ClientAccessServer EX02 -AutodiscoverServiceInternalURI
https://autodiscover.exblog.be/Autodiscover/Autodiscover.xml
```

Make sure that you created a name recording within your internal DNS zone that corresponds to the value of this attribute. That way, clients will be able to resolve the name from the DNS and connect to the URL.

Configuring the AutodiscoverSiteScope

This parameter specifies for which AD-site the Autodiscover service is authoritative. It is used for building the in-site and out-of-site list when a client connects to Autodiscover.

The following command will set the Site Scope for the Autodiscover to the AD-Site called `"HQ"`:

```
Set-ClientAccessServer EX02 -AutodiscoverSiteScope "HQ"
```

To test whether Autodiscover has been configured correctly internally, you can use a little script located at: `http://michaelvh.wordpress.com/2012/11/21/retrieving-exchange-autodiscover-scp-information-from-ad-via-powershell/`

The script will query Active Directory for Autodiscover SCPs and output the returned information from it, including the SiteScope, CreationDate and URL.

How it works...

The Autodiscover process is different for internal and external clients. Most part of the process, however, is largely the same.

For internal clients:

1. Outlook queries Active Directory for available SCP objects.
2. The list of objects is sorted into two lists based on the client's location (AD Site). Whether or not a given object is considered to be in-site or out-of-site is controlled by the `AutodiscoverSiteScope` attribute of the Client Access Server.
3. Outlook will first try contacting the servers from the in-site list first. If no servers can be contacted, it will try connecting to servers on the out-of- site list.
4. If no servers (on either lists) can be contacted (or none can be found), Outlook will revert to connecting to the built-in, predefined, URLs:
    1. `https://domain.com/autodiscover/autodiscover.xml`
    2. `https://autodiscover.domain.com/autodiscover/autodiscover.xml`
5. Upon receiving the request from the client, the Autodiscover service will generate an `Autodiscover` response (XML) based on the current location of the user's mailbox.
6. The Autodiscover returns the XML file to the client.
7. The Outlook client uses the information from the XML to configure itself with the correct settings allowing it to connect to the Exchange organization.

For external clients:

The process for external clients is pretty similar to the internal clients. The difference comes from the fact that an external client will not be able to query Active Directory for available SCP objects.

1. Outlook will try to query Active Directory for available SCP objects but fail.
2. Outlook then reverts to using a set of hardcoded URLs:
    1. `https://domain.com/autodiscover/autodiscover.xml`
    2. `https://autodiscover.domain.com/autodiscover/autodiscover.xml`
3. Upon receiving the request from the client, the Autodiscover service will generate an `Autodiscover` response (XML) based on the current location of the user's mailbox.
4. The Autodiscover returns the XML file to the client.
5. The Outlook client uses the information from the XML to configure itself with the correct settings allowing it to connect to the Exchange organization.

Don't forget to add a DNS-record for the Autodiscover service to the external DNS zone of your domain. Otherwise clients won't be able to connect to Autodiscover!

Once you're ready, you can test your Autodiscover setup using the Exchange Remote Connectivity Analyzer. This is a website that Microsoft has set up and allows you if your Exchange services have been setup correctly.

Go to `http://www.testexchangeconnectivity.com` to test the external connectivity to your on-premises organization.

As with many other things in Exchange, Autodiscover basically works out of the box. Without taking into account some of the odd things you might see out there, all you need to do is configure the `AutodiscoverService` properties on the Client Access Server Object.

You might notice that the `AutodiscoverService` property also has a virtual directory that contains an Internal and External URL property (`Get-AutodiscoverVirtualDirectory`). Unlike with other services, these URLs aren't used at all. In fact, configuring these properties will have no impact whatsoever. They can safely be ignored and left with their default setting (null).

See also

- When Autodiscover was first introduced, Microsoft published a whitepaper explaining the details of the Autodiscover service works. If you are looking for more in-depth information, make sure to check the following URL: `http://technet.microsoft.com/en-us/library/bb332063(v=exchg.80).aspx`

Configuring Outlook Anywhere

In Exchange 2010, internal Outlook clients do not use Outlook Anywhere. They connect to the RPC Client Access service which is hosted by the Client Access Server. By default, the Client Access Server's own hostname would be used as the endpoint where clients connect to.

Unless you were configuring a CAS Array, there was nothing specific you had to do to make it work.

In Exchange 2013 the way clients connect to Exchange has changed. Both internal and external clients now connect using Outlook Anywhere (RPC-over-HTTP). To reflect this change in behavior, Outlook Anywhere can now be configured with an internal and an external hostname. Before, only an external hostname could be configured through `Set-OutlookAnywhere` or `Enable-OutlookAnywhere`.

To ensure that things just work, Outlook Anywhere is enabled by default and the Internal Hostname property for each Client Access Server is configured with its own FQDN, without requiring SSL encryption (HTTP).

By ensuring clients can connect over HTTP internally, Exchange 2013 allows clients to connect right away without making any configuration changes. Nonetheless, you still would want to change the hostnames (especially if you are deploying an array of Client Access Servers). Additionally you might want to secure traffic by configuring certificates and enabling SSL.

How to do it...

The options to configure Outlook Anywhere through the EAC are buried deep down with some other options of the Client Access Server. It's far easier to just use the Exchange Management Shell to execute the same task. The command for it is as follows:

```
Get-OutlookAnywhere -Server EX02 | Set-OutlookAnywhere -InternalHostname outlook.exblog.be
```

If you want to secure internal traffic with SSL, add `InternalClientsRequireSSL $true` to the command in the following way:

```
Get-OutlookAnywhere -Server EX02 | Set-OutlookAnywhere -InternalClientsRequireSSL $true
```

Use the following command to change the authentication method. You can choose between Basic, NTLM, and Negotiate:

```
Get-OutlookAnywhere -Server EX02 | Set-OutlookAnywhere -InternalClientAuthenticationMethods NTLM,Basic
```

In order to use Kerberos authentication (Negotiate), additional steps are required, which we describe in *Chapter 10, Implementing Security*.

How it works...

Outlook will use the information received through the Autodiscover process to connect to the Exchange Server. In Exchange 2013, the Autodiscover response now also includes specific connection information that reflect the changes that were made to Outlook Anywhere.

The following code sample is an extract from a typical Autodiscover response. For clarity we've omitted the information irrelevant to this topic:

```
<Autodiscover xmlns="http://schemas.microsoft.com/exchange/
autodiscover/responseschema/2006">
  <Response
    xmlns="http://schemas.microsoft.com/exchange
      /autodiscover/outlook/responseschema/2006a">
```

```
      <Account>
        ...
        <Protocol>
          <Type>EXHTTP</Type>
          <Server>outlook.exblog.be</Server>
          <SSL>On</SSL>
          <AuthPackage>Ntlm</AuthPackage>
          ....
        </Protocol>
        <Protocol>
          <Type>EXHTTP</Type>
          <Server>outlook.exblog.com</Server>
          <SSL>On</SSL>
          <AuthPackage>Basic</AuthPackage>
          ...
          <CertPrincipalName>msstd:*.xylos.com</CertPrincipalName>
        </Protocol>
        ...
      </Account>
    </Response>
  </Autodiscover>
```

Amongst information for other protocols and URLs, the Autodiscover response will include two nodes for Outlook Anywhere:

- The first node contains connection information for internal clients
- The second node for external clients

Both of these nodes are captured under the `EXHTTP` protocol.

Along with the URL where Outlook should connect to, information on what authentication method to use and whether or not the connection requires SSL are also included. This is shown in the following lines of code:

```
<SSL>On</SSL>
<AuthPackage>Ntlm</AuthPackage>
```

When Outlook connects to the URL provided in the Autodiscover response, the connection will be received by a Client Access Server in your internet-facing site. The initial request will include the mailbox GUID of the user who is trying to establish a connection. The CAS will then use that GUID to lookup what mailbox server it should forward the request to.

Once it's determined what the destination of the packet should be, the CAS will proxy the HTTP request to the appropriate mailbox server.

If, for some reason, the mailbox was be located in a different AD-site than where the request was received, CAS will simply proxy the request to a CAS in the AD-site where the mailbox is located.

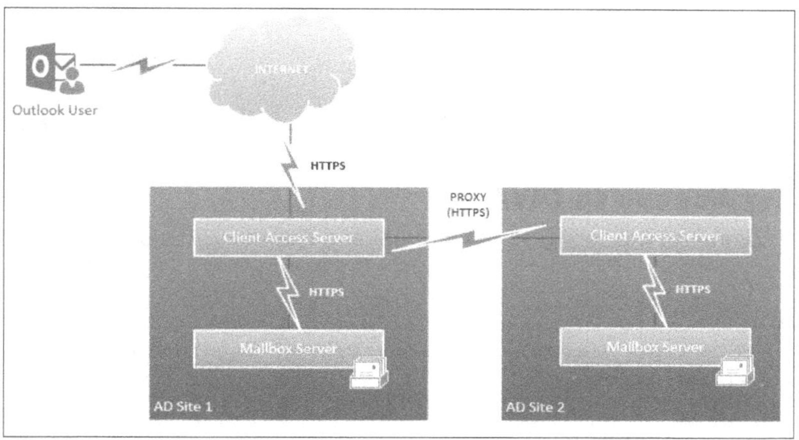

To fully support the changes introduced by Exchange 2013, Outlook 2007 and 2010 require specific patches. Outlook 2010 needs SP1 and the April 2012 Cumulative Update. Outlook 2007 requires at least SP3 and the July 2012 Cumulative Update. Outlook 2013 already contains the necessary logic to connect out of the box.

See also

- *Chapter 5, Configuring External Access* for more information on configuring Outlook Anywhere to support external access.

Configuring Outlook Web App

Outlook Web App (**OWA**) is— next to Outlook—probably one of the most popular ways of connecting to an Exchange server. Over the past Exchange editions, OWA has grown from a simple online mail viewer which could only be used with Internet Explorer to an online mail client offering a feature rich experience to anyone connecting with just about any web browser.

Depending on which browser and device you are using, your user's experience might vary. For a complete overview of the supported browser and the expected client experience, have a look at the following TechNet article:

`http://technet.microsoft.com/en-us/library/jj150522(v=exchg.150).aspx`

Getting ready

In order to make the following configuration changes, you will need to start the Exchange Management Shell.

How to do it...

The following section will explain how you can configure, enable, and control OWA

Configuring Access to OWA

The following command will configure the Internal and External URLs on which OWA will be available:

```
Get-OwaVirtualDirectory -Server EX02 | Set-OWAVirtualDirectory -
InternalURL https://webmail.exblog.be/owa -ExternalUrl https://
webmail.exblog.be/owa
```

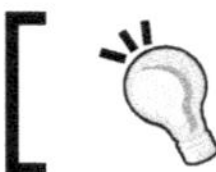

You're not required to use the same URL internally and externally.

By default, OWA will have Forms-Based Authentication enabled:

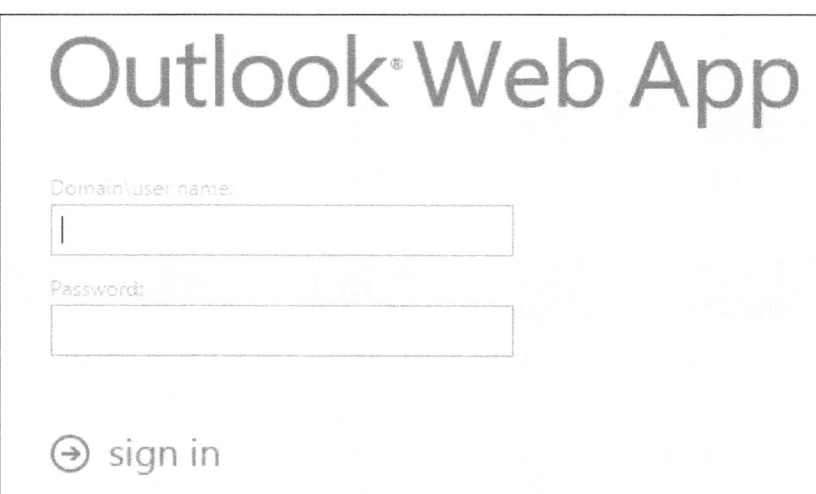

It is possible to define a default logon domain. That way, your users won't have to type in the domain name every time they log on. Execute the following command to configure a default logon domain:

```
Get-OwaVirtualDirectory -Server EX02 | Set-OwaVirtualDirectory -
DefaultDomain "EXBLOG" -LogonFormat UserName
```

When defining a default domain, you are also required to change the logonformat from FullDomain to UserName. Hence why the `-LogonFormat` parameter was included.

Restart IIS after making this change, by using the following line of command:

```
IISReset /noforce
```

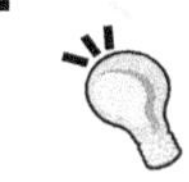

Running IISReset will cause existing connections to be dropped. Make sure to plan accordingly. You wouldn't want to run this command in the middle of a busy day unless you absolutely have to!

Enabling/Disabling OWA

It is possible to turn off OWA completely on a per-user basis. For example, the following command will turn off access through OWA for a user called *Jeff Allen*:

```
Set-CASMailbox -Identity jAllen -OWAEnabled $false
```

To re-enable access through OWA, run the following command:

```
Set-CASMailbox -Identity jAllen -OWAEnabled $true
```

Controlling OWA features globally

OWA is feature rich, but sometimes companies don't want to expose all functionalities to some or all of their users. There are two ways to control what features are available to your users:

- Enable/Disable features globally
- Use OWA Mailbox Policies to control features on a per-user basis

By default all OWA features are enabled. You can control on a per-virtual directory basis what features are available to users connecting through that virtual directory. If you want to enable or disable a certain feature globally, you will either have to use an OWA Mailbox Policy or make a change to each OWA virtual directory in your organization.

To enable/disable features follow these steps:

1. Log in to the **Exchange Admin Center** and navigate to **Servers** | **Virtual Directories**.

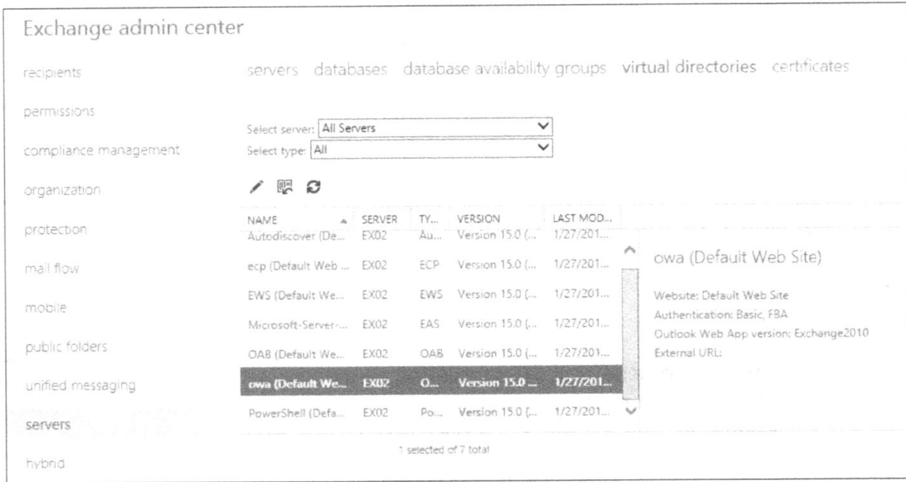

2. Select the server from the drop-down list.
3. In the list of virtual directories, double-click on **owa (Default Web Site)**
4. Select **features**.
5. Uncheck the features you would like to disable.

6. To see and enable/disable advanced features, click **More options**.
7. Click **Save**.

OWA Mailbox Policies

Sometimes enabling or disabling a feature per server or per virtual directory doesn't have the desired effect. What if you would want to make a certain feature available to some of your users and not to others?

By using OWA Mailbox Policies you can control settings on a per-user basis. When an OWA Mailbox Policy is applied to a mailbox, it will override settings configured on the virtual directory. You might also choose not to apply a policy at all. In that case, the user automatically inherits the settings from the virtual directory.

Unsurprisingly, the default policy is called **Default**, as shown in the following screenshot:

To create a new policy, follow these steps:

1. Login into the **Exchange Admin Center** and navigate to **Permissions** | **Outlook Web App policies**.
2. Click on the plus-sign (**+**) to open the **new Outlook Web App Mailbox** policy-wizard.
3. Enter a name (for example, `TEST_OWA Mailbox Policy`)

4. Check/uncheck the features you want to enable/disable

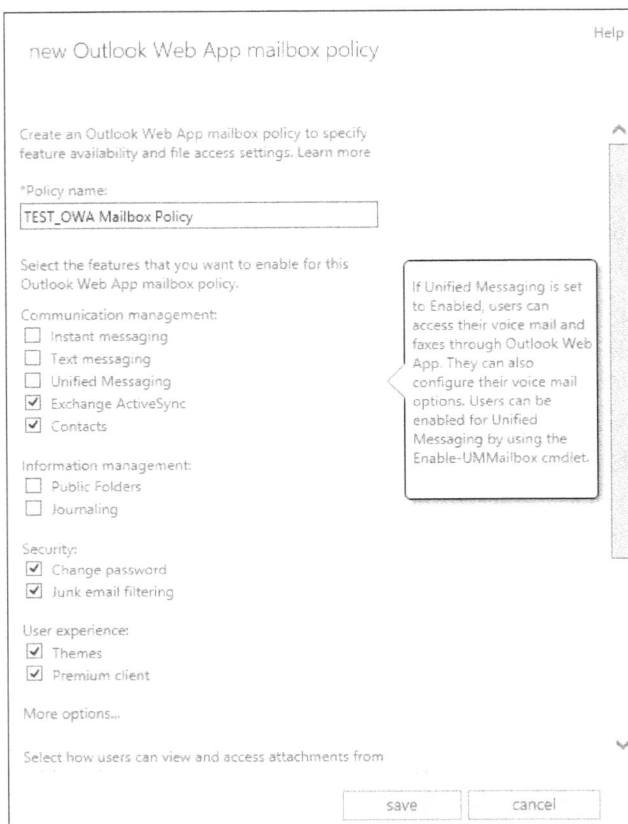

5. Click on **Save**.

Next, you will have to assign the policy to a user.

1. Log in to the **Exchange Admin Center** and navigate to **Recipients** | **Mailboxes**.
2. Double-click on the name of the user you want to assign a new mailbox policy to.
3. Navigate to **mailbox features**.
4. Click on **View details** under **Email Connectivity** and **Outlook Web App**.

5. Click on **browse...** and select the OWA Mailbox Policy you created earlier.
6. Click on **OK**.
7. Click on **Save**, twice.

Applying an OWA Mailbox policy overrides any setting configured on the virtual directory, even if the settings on the virtual directory are more restrictive.

Alternatively, you can use the Exchange Management Shell which we find an easier way to configure an OWA Mailbox Policy:

```
Set-CasMailbox -Identity -OwaMailboxPolicy "TEST_OWA Mailbox Policy"
```

Especially when applying a policy to multiple users, PowerShell can be quite useful:

```
Get-Recipient | Where{$_.Department -like "*IT*"} | Set-CASMailbox -
OwaMailboxPolicy TEST_Owa Mailbox Policy
```

You don't necessarily have to use the same syntax from the example above. Exchange Server 2013 uses PowerShell v3 which allows you to greatly simplify the syntax as follows:

```
Get-Recipient | where Department -eq IT | Set-
CasMailbox -OwaMailboxPolicy "TEST_Owa Mailbox Policy"
```

Configuring Exchange Web Services

Microsoft introduced the **Exchange Web Services** (**EWS**) to expand the ways in which client applications could communicate with the Exchange server. EWS provide access to almost the same Exchange information that is made available through, for example, Outlook. This allows third-party vendors to easily integrate that information within their own applications.

EWS clients (which can be anything from a third-party application to a PowerShell script) can communicate with the server-side EWS by exchanging SOAP calls that are being sent over HTTP.

To control on what endpoints (URLs) the Exchange Web Services are available on a Client Access Server, you configure the InternalUrl and ExternalUrl properties on the Web Services Virtual Directory. The values you configure here will be passed on to your clients through the Autodiscover process, overcoming the need to manually configure these endpoints on your clients. Typically, you wouldn't want to change the value of these properties to reflect the design of your messaging environment and correspond with the namespaces on your certificate(s).

How to do it...

The following command will modify the InternalURL property:

```
Get-WebServicesVirtualDirectory -Server EX02 | Set-
WebServicesVirtualDirectory -InternalUrl https://webmail.exblog.be/EWS/
Exchange.asmx
```

This command changes the ExternalURL property:

```
Get-WebServicesVirtualDirectory -Server EX02 | Set-
WebServicesVirtualDirectory -ExternalUrl https://webmail.exblog.be/EWS/
Exchange.asmx
```

Once you've correctly configured your URLs, run the following command to test your web services configuration:

```
Test-WebServicesConnectivity -ClientAccessServer https://webmail.exblog.be
```

The result should show something similar to the following screenshot:

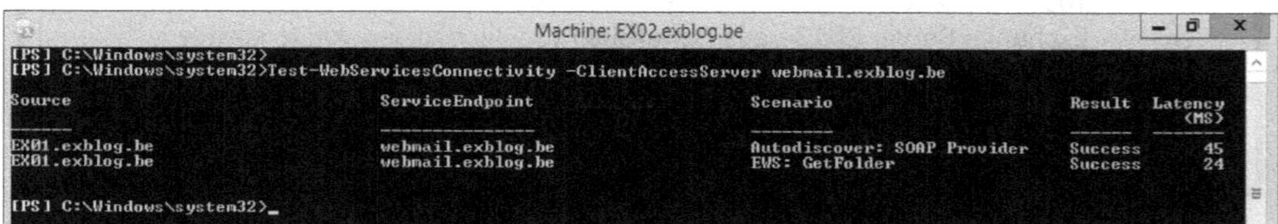

Alternatively, you can also use the Exchange Remote Connectivity Analyzer (`http://www.testexchangeconnectivity.com`) to verify if your Web Services work as expected from the internet as well.

Configuring Exchange ActiveSync

Another popular way of accessing a mailbox is Exchange ActiveSync (EAS). EAS enables devices to synchronize data from your Exchange server mailbox over the air. Typically devices include smart phones and tablets, but regular PC applications have been known to use EAS under the hood as well. A good example of the latter would be the Windows 8 Mail App.

Although Exchange ActiveSync is a stable protocol, its implementation sometimes can be challenging. Every application or mobile OS maker can freely choose what features they will or will not implement. This can lead up to difficult and confusing situations where some devices might work as expected and others don't. Although Microsoft created the `ActiveSync` logo program in the past to overcome these issues, these problems are still very alive today.

Wikipedia has a nice comparative table per device OS of what EAS features are supported and which ones are not. This can be particularly handy when facing different behavior between different types and models of devices:

`http://en.wikipedia.org/wiki/Comparison_of_Exchange_ActiveSync_Clients`

How to do it...

`ActiveSync` is enabled by default. In order to complete the configuration, you would only need to configure the URLs that are required for connecting to the `ActiveSync` service; just like with the EWS.

To configure the Internal URL for the ActiveSync Virtual Directory, execute the following command:

```
Get-ActiveSyncVirtualDirectory -Server EX02 | Set-
ActiveSyncVirtualDirectory -InternalURL https://webmail.exblog.be/
Microsoft-Server-ActiveSync
```

Changing the External URL is pretty similar; execute the following command:

```
Get-ActiveSyncVirtualDirectory -Server EX02 | Set-
ActiveSyncVirtualDirectory -ExternalURL https://webmail.exblog.be/
Microsoft-Server-ActiveSync
```

Unlike OWA where you could turn on or off many features on the virtual directory, ActiveSync features can only be controlled using ActiveSync Mailbox Policies. You can, however, control some ActiveSync settings on a per-mailbox basis. These settings include the option to enable or disable ActiveSync or to configure allowed or blocked devices. We'll talk more about allowing or blocking devices later in this chapter.

The following command will disable ActiveSync for a user named Mark Spencer:

```
Set-CASMailbox -Identity mspencer -ActiveSyncEnabled $false
```

To re-enable ActiveSync, execute the following command:

```
Set-CASMailbox -Identity mspencer -ActiveSyncEnabled $true
```

[Don't expect these changes to become effective immediately. Because some of the caching that happens on the Client Access Server, it might take up to 20 minutes before these settings get enforced.]

As described earlier, ActiveSync Mailbox Policies allow you to create a policy that contains a bunch of custom configuration settings, which you can then apply to an individual mailbox or a group of mailboxes.

To configure a new ActiveSync Mailbox Policy, follow these steps:

1. Log in to the Exchange Admin Center (EAC) and navigate to **Mobile | mobile device mailbox policies**. Click on the **+**-sign to open the **new mobile device mailbox policy** wizard
2. Enter a name (for example, `TEST_EAS Policy`)
3. Select the options that you want to enable in the policy.

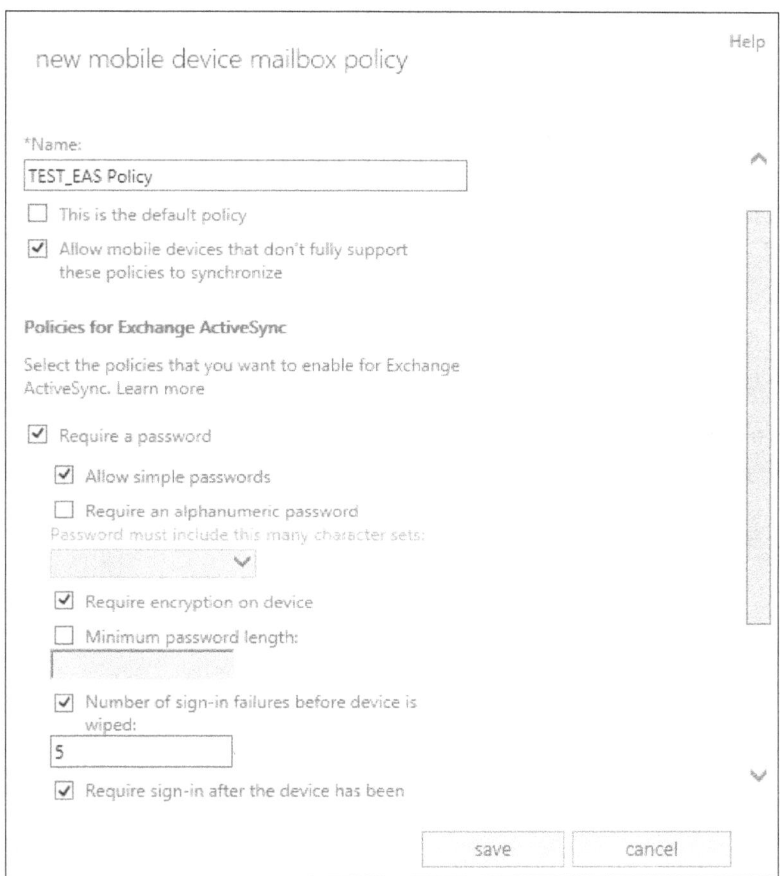

4. Click on **Save**.

Devices that aren't compliant with the settings from your policy will not be able to connect. Unfortunately, there aren't many devices out there that follow the EAS specifications to the letter, not even Windows Phone! If you want these devices to connect anyway, even if that means they'll only implement a subset of the settings from the policy, it's important that you select **Allow mobile devices that don't fully support these policies to synchronize**.

Using the EAC, you can only configure a small subset of the options that are available for configuration through a Mobile Device Mailbox Policy. To configure the following features, you will have to use the Management Shell:

Allow Bluetooth	Allow Browser
Allow Camera	Allow Consumer Email
Allow Desktop Sync	Allow External Device Management
Allow HTML Email	Allow Internet Sharing
Allow IrDA	Allow Mobile Over-the-Air Update
Allow POPIMAPEMail	Allow Remote Desktop
Allow S/MIME encryption	Allow S/MIME software certificates
Allow Storage Card	Allow Text Messaging
Allow Unsigned Applications	Allow Unsigned Installation packages
Allow Wi-Fi	Approved Application List
Attachments Enabled	Device Policy Refresh Interval
IRM Enabled	Max Attachment Size
Max Calendar Age Filter	Max Email Age Filter
Max Email body truncation size	Max email HTML body truncation size
Password recovery enabled	Unapproved InROM application list
Require encrypted S/MIME messages	Require encryption S/MIME algorithm
Require manual synchronization while roaming	Require signed S/MIME algorithm
Require signed S/MIME messages	Require storage card encryption

The following command will configure an existing mobile device mailbox policy to disallow the usage of WiFi or Bluetooth and disable the usage of the storage card:

```
Set-MobileDeviceMailboxPolicy "TEST_EAS Policy" -AllowBluetooth:$false -
AllowWifi:$false -AllowStorageCard:$false
```

Once you have created a policy, you need to assign it to a user's mailbox before the settings are enforced. The following steps will guide you through the process of assigning a policy:

1. Log in to the **Exchange Admin Center** and navigate to **Recipients** | **mailboxes**.
2. Double-click on the user you want to change the policy for.
3. Select **mailbox features**.
4. Click **View Details** under Mobile Devices and Exchange ActiveSync.

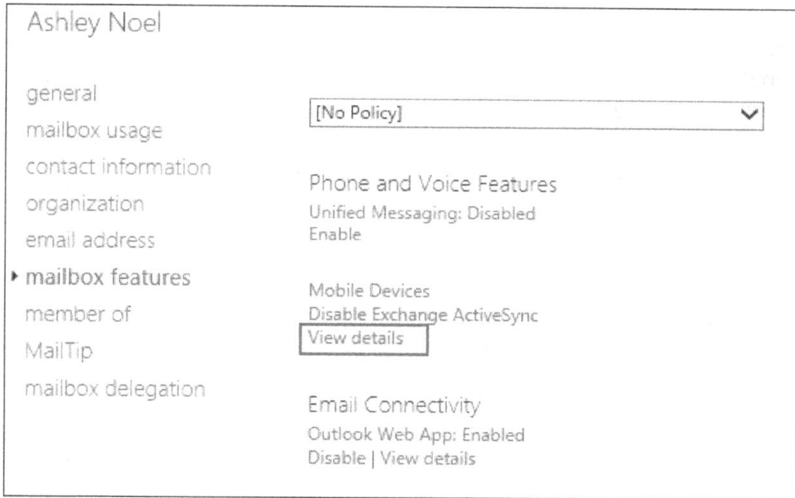

5. Click on **browse...** to display a list of available policies.
6. Select **TEST_EAS Policy** and click on **OK**.
7. Click on **Save**.

Alternatively, you can use the Shell to achieve the same goal in the following way:

```
Set-CAS-Mailbox -Identity mspencer -ActiveSyncMailboxPolicy "TEST_EAS
Policy"
```

See also

- If you're looking for additional information on ActiveSync and how it can help your organization, definitely have a look at the following book from PACKT by *Steve Goodman* available at `http://www.packtpub.com/iphone-with-microsoft-exchange-server-2010/book`.

Configuring ActiveSync Device Access

In the previous module we described how you could configure the ActiveSync service. In this topic, we will have a closer look at how you can control what devices can (or cannot) access your environment.

Although many companies let their employees choose freely what device they want to hook up to Exchange, some companies are subject to specific regulations imposed by the government, for instance because of some of the activities the company is involved with. A good example of this would be ITAR which is a set of US regulations imposed upon companies involved with selling or manufacturing defense-related articles to the US government.

Not so long ago, the landscape of smart phones was dominated by BlackBerry which had and to some point still has a pretty secure platform. The popularity of Apple's iOS and Google's Android, however, didn't really help BlackBerry's cause. Over the past few years many companies switched to alternative platforms, mainly because they had to give in to the pressure caused by everyone wanting an i-device or similar. When the CEO is one of the people yelling, you'd be amazed how fast things can change...

Anyway, switching from one platform to another isn't always as straightforward as one might expect. The BlackBerry Enterprise Server, which went hand-in-hand with the device, provided a pretty good mobile device management platform. Additionally, having a BlackBerry device didn't suffice to make things work. As long as the IT department didn't provision the device through an Enterprise Activation, you had no possibility to configure it to fetch e-mails from the system. Straightforward and simple.

Exchange is by no means a mobile device management platform. But it does offer a set of tools and features that can help the majority of companies out there creating and enforcing a simple mobile device policy. Additionally, the features offered by Exchange can be an interesting addition to third-party mobile device management platforms.

Exchange 2013 offers two features that are particularly interesting in this area. The first feature is the ability to Allow, Block or Quarantine devices based on a number of device characteristics. This feature also existed in Exchange 2010 and didn't really change. Brand new, however, are the ActiveSync Device Auto-Block Thresholds.

This feature is a direct result from the experience Microsoft gained from running a large-scale Exchange deployment like in Office 365. They needed a system which would automatically intervene if devices caused problems on the Exchange servers. Since the OS manufacturer can choose how to implement ActiveSync, there are many things that can potentially go wrong. Not that long ago, a company from Cupertino caused quite some issues on Exchange servers all over the world because they had implemented ActiveSync poorly.

By configuring the ActiveSync Device Auto-Block Thresholds, you allow Exchange to automatically take action against devices that are misbehaving. By misbehaving, we mean devices that are causing ActiveSync to crash, or devices that consume more resources than what you'd expect them to consume within a given timeframe. The difficulty lies in defining what normal behavior looks like...

Getting ready

To complete the following steps, you will need to open the Exchange Management Shell or login into the **Exchange Admin Center**.

How to do it...

Defining the default access level for the entire organization

The organization default will specify what action will be taken on new devices that aren't specifically blocked or allowed. Possible actions are, allow, block, or quarantine.

The following command will ensure that devices that aren't explicitly allowed or blocked through a user or a device access rule, are automatically quarantined:

```
Set-ActiveSyncOrganizationSettings -DefaultAccessLevel Quarantine
```

Blocking specific devices

In the following example, we will use the Exchange Management Shell to create a device access rule which will block all devices with a specific Device OS version. For instance Apple's iOS 6.1:

```
New-ActiveSyncDeviceAccessRule -QueryString "iOS 6.1" -AccessLevel Block
-Name "Block iOS 6.1 Devices" -Characteristic DeviceOS
```

If you are configuring new Device Access Rules, but you do not want to impact already configured device, you will need to make sure that you add existing devices to the list of explicitly allowed devices. To help with this process, MVP *Steve Goodman* has put together a small script which can help you doing this. This script is available at: `http://searchexchange.techtarget.com/tip/An-overview-of-the-Exchange-2010-ActiveSync-Quarantine-feature`.

Explicitly allowing or blocking devices for an individual user

You can also allow or block specific devices for an individual user. This can be handy if you need to make an exception to a Device Access Rule that is already in place as explicitly defined access rights take precedence over the organizational settings and any device access rules.

The following command will configure a specific device for a user called `John Doe`:

```
Set-CasMailbox JohnDoe -ActiveSyncAllowedDeviceIDs ApplF1AB23CDE456
```

If you don't know the ID of a specific device, you can try configuring for a specific user first which will make it show up in the list of devices for that mailbox (even though it might be blocked or quarantined).

To retrieve the list of configured devices for a given user, run the following command:

```
Get-MobileDevice -Mailbox JohnDoe
```

Configuring ActiveSync Auto-Block Thresholds

Currently, there are only a few thresholds which you can configure:

- `UserAgentChanges`
- `Watsons`
- `CommandFrequency`
- `OutOfBudgets`
- `SyncCommands`
- `RecentCommands`
- `EnableNotificationEmail`

Each of these thresholds monitors a certain aspect of an ActiveSync device's behavior. Note that you cannot change what is being monitored. For instance, there is no way to configure specific commands to be included or excluded in the **CommandFrequency** threshold.

What you can configure, on the other hand, are the actual threshold limits using `Set-ActiveSyncDeviceAutoBlockThreshold`:

- `BehaviorTypeIncidenceDuration`
- `BehaviorTypeIncidenceLimit`
- `AdminEmailInsert`
- `DeviceBlockDuration`

Despite the vast experience Microsoft has in this area, they haven't released any information on what good default values would be for each of these thresholds. The problem is that, if you want to start using this feature, you will first have to figure out how normal devices are behaving in your environment.

This is something you could do by looking at the IIS logs with Log Parser Studio, over a longer period of time. The information you get from these logs will help you determine proper values, adjusted to the common usage in your specific environment. After all, every environment is more or less unique, no? It's important that you do not configure thresholds that are too low or you will risk blocking devices too quickly and for no reason.

In the following example we will configure the threshold for repeated commands. Essentially, this means that if a device repeats a given `ActiveSync` command more than 100 times within the configured timeframe, it will automatically get blocked for 10 minutes:

```
Set-ActiveSyncDeviceAutoBlockThreshold -BehaviorTypeIncidenceDuration
00:05:00 -BehaviorTypeIncidenceLimit 100 -DeviceBlockDuration 00:10:00
```

How it works...

Device Access evaluation

Every device that connects to the environment is evaluated against a set or rules to determine whether or not the connection should be allowed. In this process, the following elements are taken into account:

- The organization's default action
- Explicitly configure allow/block actions on an individual mailbox
- Device Access Rules

Explicitly configured allow or block actions take precedence over Device Access Rules or the organization's default action. Similarly, Device Access Rules take precedence over the organization's default action. If no explicit configuration exists, or if there are no device access rules that match the connecting device, the organization's default action is applied. Exchange will implicitly allow all devices for which no explicit configuration is found because the organization's default action is set to Allow out of the box.

ActiveSync Device Auto-Block Thresholds

As described earlier, these thresholds monitor a device's behavior and measure if they exceed the configured limit for a given timeframe. If that happens, devices are automatically blocked for the duration of the `DeviceBlockDuration` timeframe. If you configured the `AdminEmailInsert` property, users that have been blocked will automatically receive an e-mail (which they can read through OWA or Outlook) notifying them they were blocked and the reason why they were blocked.

When the `DeviceBlockDuration` time has run by, devices are automatically unblocked after which they can connect to the environment again. As you can see, when configured properly, this feature can potentially save an admin quite some time.

Configuring SMTP

A part of what once was the Hub Transport Service has been moved to the Exchange 2013 Client Access Server under the name of the Frontend Transport Service.

This service is responsible for proxying inbound traffic to and (if configured) outbound SMTP traffic from your Exchange organization while maintaining the stateless nature of the server role. Despite the fact that SMTP components on the Client Access Server are running at Layer 7, no mail is ever stored or queued locally on the server. As a result, the Client Access Server will not perform actions such as content filtering or attachment scanning. These tasks are set aside for the Mailbox Transport Service which is now part of the Mailbox Server role.

In theory you would expect the service to be able to handle other tasks which do not involve (temporarily) storing messages locally for example, connection filtering. Sadly, that feature somehow didn't make it into the current version of the product. Hopefully we will see it return in later versions...

How to do it...

Like in Exchange 2010, the Frontend Transport Service uses Receive Connectors through which messages are received into the organization. Send Connectors, on the other hand, only exist on the Mailbox Server role.

Creating Receive Connectors

In Exchange 2010 you had to manually (re)configure a receive connector to accept message from the internet, as it wasn't included out of the box. Luckily Exchange 2013 has a connector that is able to receive messages from anonymous connections. This connector is called Default Frontend <servername>.

To view the connector and its settings, run the following command:

```
Get-ReceiveConnector "Default Frontend EX02" | fl *
```

Alternatively, you can also use the EAC to view the connector's properties:

1. Log in to the EAC and navigate to **mail flow** | **receive connectors**.
2. Select server EX02 from the **Select server** drop-down box.
3. Double-click on the **Default Frontend EX02** receive connector.

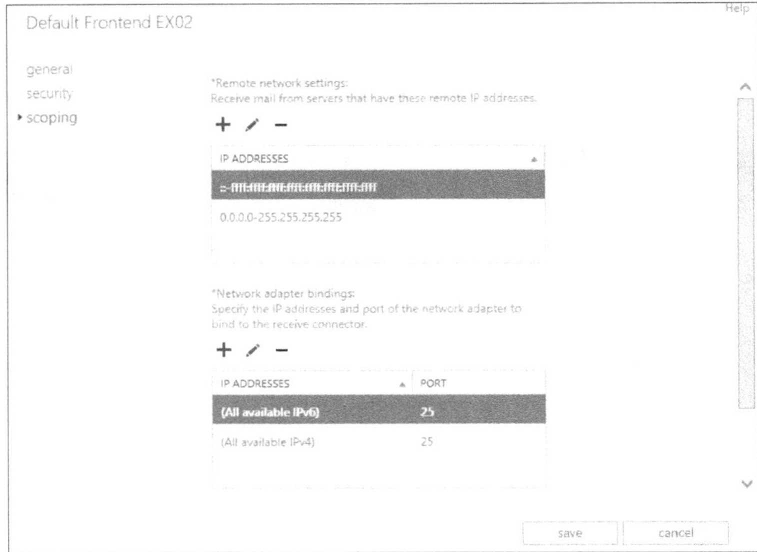

4. Review the settings under **General**, **Scoping**, and **Security**.
5. Click on **Cancel**.

Often companies need a way to route messages to the internet coming from internal devices for example, scanners. Often, these devices do not support authentication, which means that they can only connect anonymously to your mail server. Although the default connector will accept these unauthenticated connections, it will by default not allow these messages to be sent outside the company.

If you want to make this work, you need to create a new Receive Connector explicitly configured to allow external recipients, and scope it to the devices that are allowed to send messages externally.

When configuring a new Receive Connector, the following three key elements need to be taken into account:

- **Authentication Method**: controls what type of authentication mechanisms are offered for incoming connections. This can range from basic authentication to enforcing mutual TLS or IPSEC.
- **Permission Groups**: controls who can connect through this connector from a client-level point of view.
- **Network settings** (**IPs**): controls who can connect through the connector based on the IP address of the sender (remote IP) or the IP address that is connected to (local IP bindings).

Execute the following steps to create a new Receive Connector. Afterwards we will modify this connector to accept unauthenticated connections and allow them to relay.

1. Log in to the EAC and navigate to **mail flow** | **receive connectors**
2. Select server **EX02** from the **Select server** drop-down box
3. Click the plus-sign (**+**) to start the **new receive connector**-wizard
4. Enter a descriptive name for example, **Relay Connector EX02**
5. Under type select Custom and click **Next**.
6. Leave the default binding information and click **Next**.
7. Modify the remote network settings to include the IP address (range) of the devices that are allowed to relay.
8. Click **Finish**.

Now we need to modify some of the settings to accept unauthenticated connections.

1. Log in to the EAC and navigate to **mail flow** | **receive connectors**.
2. Select server **EX02** from the **Select server** drop-down box.
3. Double-click on **Relay Connector EX02**.

4. Click on **security** and select **Anonymous users** under **Permission Groups**.

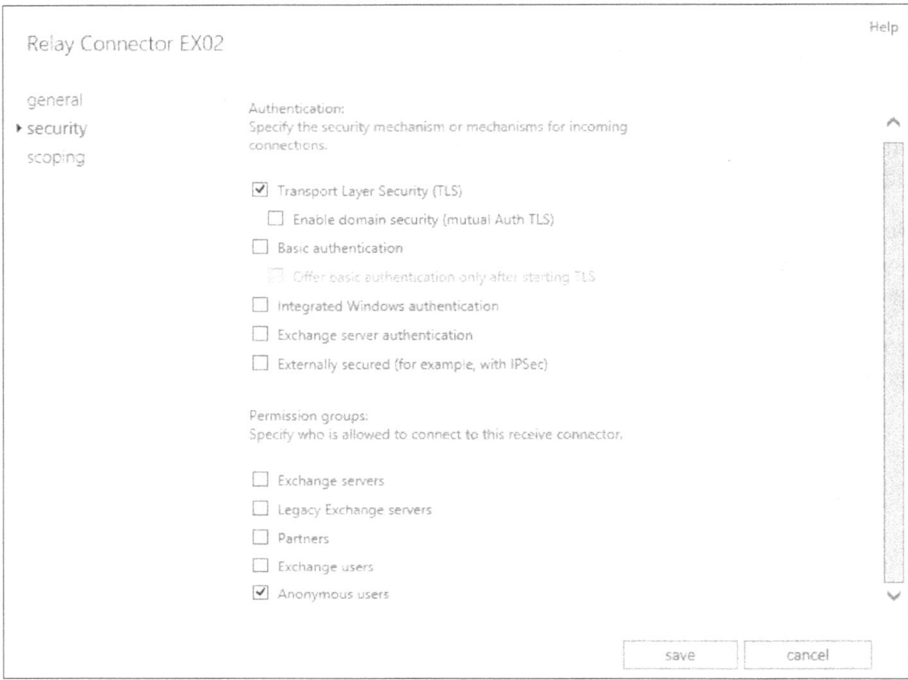

5. Click on **Save**.

Next, we need to modify the connector to allow messages to be sent to external recipients. Execute the following command from the Exchange Management Shell:

```
Get-ReceiveConnector "EX02\Relay Connector EX02" | Add-ADPermission -User
"NT AUTHORITY\Anonymous Logon" -ExtendedRights ms-exch-SMTP-accept-any-
recipient
```

To test if this worked, try sending a mail from one of the devices that you added in the remote IP ranges of the Receive Connector.

Alternatively, you can manually try sending a message over SMTP from a remote server by using the following steps:

1. Open a telnet session on port 25 to EX02.
2. Type the following commands:
    - `EHLO`
    - `MAIL FROM:user@domain.com`
    - `RCPT TO:externaluser@externaldomain.com`

At this point, the remote server should respond with, `250 2.1.0 Recipient OK`, which means that the IP you are sending from is allowed to relay through the connector.

Be careful when configuring a relay connector! Make sure that only trusted devices are allowed to send through that connector. Failing to scope and secure the connector properly might leave the door wide open for malicious individuals to take advantage of this open relay, allowing them to send large amounts of SPAM through it.

Configuring Logging

When troubleshooting incoming connections, verbose logging can sometimes come in handy. By activating the protocol logs for a connector, every SMTP command that is received is written away in a log file.

The following command enables the Protocol Log for the Relay Connector:

```
Set-ReceiveConnector "EX02\Relay Connector EX02" -ProtocolLoggingLevel
Verbose
```

To configure the path where these log files are stored, run the following command:

```
Set-FrontendTransportService -ReceiveProtocolLogPath D:\Logs\SMTPReceive
```

By default, there can be up to a 5 minute delay before entries show up in the protocol log. This is because the Transport Service will only flush these events into the log every 5 minutes. You can control the interval by adding the following two keys to the `FrontEndTransport.config` file in the `%ExchangeInstallPath%\bin` folder:

```
<add key="SmtpSendLogFlushInterval" value="00:00:30" />
<add key="SmtpRecvLogFlushInterval" value="00:00:30" />
```

How it works...

Whenever a message is received by the Front-End Transport Service, it is important that it quickly finds a destination in the organization where to forward the message to. If that process would take too long, the service might seem unavailable to the sender.

To determine what the best destination for an incoming message is, the Front-End Transport Service will look up where the active copy of a user's mailbox is located.

Depending of your topology, the results that are returned can vary and influence how the message will be routed. The destination where a message is routed to is called the delivery group.

As described below, there are different delivery groups:

- When your mailbox is hosted on a Mailbox Server that is not part of a DAG, the message will be forwarded to any of the Exchange 2013 mailbox servers located in the same AD Site as the mailbox server hosting the mailbox. In this case, the delivery group is called the mailbox delivery group.
- When your mailbox is part of a DAG the message will be delivered to an Exchange 2013 Mailbox Server in the DAG which will then become responsible for delivering the message to the correct Mailbox Server within the DAG. Whenever a Mailbox Server is part of the DAG, the delivery group is referred to as the Routable DAG. The Client Access Server will always try to pick the member server closest to its own location. This means that if there's a member server in the same AD site as the Client Access Server, the message will be delivered there, regardless of whether that server has the active copy of the database in which the user's mailbox is stored.
- If none of the recipients have a mailbox (for example, when the message is sent to a distribution list), the Front-End transport service will deliver the message to a random Exchange 2013 Mailbox Server in the local AD Site, if one exists. This delivery group is called the AD Site.

If the message is sent to multiple recipients, only the first 20 recipients are considered for making the routing decision. In the end, only a single message gets sent from the Client Access Server to the Transport Service on a Mailbox Server because the CAS does not perform bifurcation (=creating a copy of the message per recipient).

If the Client Access Server cannot forward the message to Exchange 2013 in the delivery group or a local Exchange 2013 server, it will not try to forward messages to an older version of Exchange. Simply because these versions do not understand the concept of proxying messages. As a result, message delivery will fail with a transient error. This means that the remote server will queue the message and periodically try delivering again.

See also

Chapter 4, Configuring and Managing the Mailbox Server Role.

Configuring POP and IMAP

The last few years **Post Office Protocol** (**POP**) and **Internet Message Access Protocol** (**IMAP**) have become a less attractive way of fetching e-mails from your Exchange server. This is largely because protocols like Exchange ActiveSync have become so popular.

Sometimes legacy applications still rely on either of both protocols. Next to that, we've also seen cases involving an extremely low bandwidth, high latency link (for example, on a boat) where POP3 was the better choice because the connection between the server and the client is closed once messages have been downloaded.

How to do it...

Since Exchange Server 2007, these protocols are not enabled out of the box anymore. This means that you'll have to enable the services manually if you want to start using them.

The following command will configure the POP3 service to start automatically and then start the service:

```
Set-service msExchangePOP3 -startuptype automatic
Start-service msExchangePOP3
```

[Configuring POP3 on the Client Access Servers isn't enough to make it work. You will also have to enable the service on the mailbox server(s), essentially by changing the startup type to automatic on each Mailbox Server as well.]

The process for starting the IMAP service is similar. The following command will configure the IMAP service to start automatically and afterwards start the service:

```
Set-service msExchangeIMAP4 -startuptype automatic
Start-service msExchangeIMAP4
```

[As for POP3, you will also have to enable IMAP on the Mailbox Servers. Take a look at *Chapter 4, Configuring and Managing the Mailbox Server Role* for more information.]

It is possible that you might want to limit the amount of users allowed to connect through these protocols. You can control whether or not to enable them on a per-user basis. By default, however, access through POP and IMAP are enabled.

The following command will disable POP and IMAP access for a user called `Mark Spencer`:

```
Set-CASMailbox mspencer -POPEnabled $false -IMAPEnabled $false
```

To re-enable access through POP3, run this command:

```
Set-CASMailbox mspencer -POPEnable $true -IMAPEnabled $true
```

Because of the limited use of POP and IMAP, we won't dive into more detail. Know, however, there are additional options you can configure with regards to for example, security or logging. The following TechNet article contains more information on how to configure these options:

`http://technet.microsoft.com/en-us/library/jj657728.aspx`

How it works...

Generally, POP clients will connect to the server, download the messages locally and mark the server-side copy for deletion. IMAP, on the other hand, allows for more complex mailbox interaction and messages are generally left on the server until they are explicitly removed.

By default, POP3 connects over port 110. If additional security is required, POP3 traffic can be encrypted using **Transport Layer Security** (**TLS**) or SSL using TCP Port 995.

IMAP is typically configured over TCP port 143. It can also be secured with SSL which typically runs over TCP port 993.

See also

Chapter 4, Configuring and Managing the Mailbox Server Role.

Using non-Microsoft clients with Exchange Server 2013

The chances are that your company is using a multitude of devices, usually not all from the same manufacturer. Even though Microsoft would like the whole world to use their tablets and software, alternative devices like the iPad or mail clients like Outlook for Mac or Entourage have become popular to the point that you cannot ignore them.

Luckily almost all modern mail applications or devices support one or more of the protocols we discussed in this chapter. Unless you are planning to use POP, IMAP, or ActiveSync, not all mail clients are supported with Exchange Server 2013.

- Currently, only the following versions are supported:
- Outlook 2007 SP3 (w/ July 2012 Cumulative Update)
- Outlook 2010 SP1 (w/ April 2012 Cumulative Update)
- Outlook 2013
- Entourage 2008 for Mac (Web Services Edition)
- Outlook for Mac 2011

Mail clients that require DAV are not supported.

4
Configuring and Managing the Mailbox Server Role

In this chapter, you will learn how to perform the tasks necessary to set up, configure, and maintain the Mailbox Server Role, including:

- Creating and removing mailbox databases
- Mounting and dismounting databases
- Moving database files to another location
- Configuring circular logging
- Creating and removing mailboxes
- Managing resource mailboxes
- Configuring mailbox size limits
- Managing personal archives
- Assigning mailbox permissions
- Moving mailboxes to another database
- Managing Public Folders
- Configuring send and receive connectors
- Configuring Accepted domains
- Configuring message size limits

Introduction

Over the years, the Mailbox Server Role has evolved into something more than just a place where mail data is stored. Although its primary role remains storing and managing mail-related data, it inherited large chunks of what used to be the Hub Transport server and Unified Messaging server. This shows that the Mailbox Server role in Exchange 2013 resembles an Exchange 2010 multi-role server in many ways.

Creating and removing mailbox databases

To complete the following steps, you will need to launch the Exchange Management Shell or the Exchange Admin Center. For this example, the Mailbox Server where the new databases are created is configured with an additional disk (E:) that will be used to store the database and its logfiles. Despite earlier examples using multiple disks, we're sticking to a single disk in order to keep things simple. However, if you have stored your logfiles and database files on separate volumes, the same principles apply.

How to do it...

Creating a new mailbox database

To create a new mailbox database called `MDB01` on server `EX01`, execute the following command:

```
New-MailboxDatabase -Name "MDB01" -Server "EX01.exblog.be" -LogFolderPath
"E:\MDB01\Logs" -EdbFilePath "E:\MDB01\MDB01.edb"
```

Unlike the EAC, which offers you to choose whether or not to immediately mount the database, you will need to manually mount the new database after it is created. Have a look later in this chapter for more information on how to mount/dismount databases.

Exchange 2013 no longer dynamically adjusts the amount of memory that is assigned for each database's cache. How much memory is assigned per database depends on the amount of active and passive databases on the servers and is calculated when the Exchange Information Store service starts. That is also why you will see the following message whenever you add or remove a database or database copy to a server:

```
[PS] C:\>New-MailboxDatabase DB05 -Server EX2013-01

Name                     Server          Recovery        ReplicationType
----                     ------          --------        ---------------
DB05                     EX2013-01       False           None
WARNING: Please restart the Microsoft Exchange Information Store service on server EX2013-01 after adding new mailbox
databases.
```

To restart the Exchange Information Store Service, run the following command from an elevated command prompt or PowerShell instance:

```
Restart-Service MSExchangeIS
```

> Restarting the Exchange Information Store service will cause all databases on that server to be dismounted. If that server is not a member of a DAG or it is the sole server that contains a given database copy, that will result in downtime for the user while the service restarts.

Alternatively, the same action can be performed through the Exchange Admin Center:

1. Navigate to **Servers** | **databases**.
2. Click on the plus-sign (**+**) to launch the **new database** wizard. Enter a name for the database.
3. Click on **browse...** and select the Mailbox Server where you want to create the database.
4. Specify the EDB and logfile location.

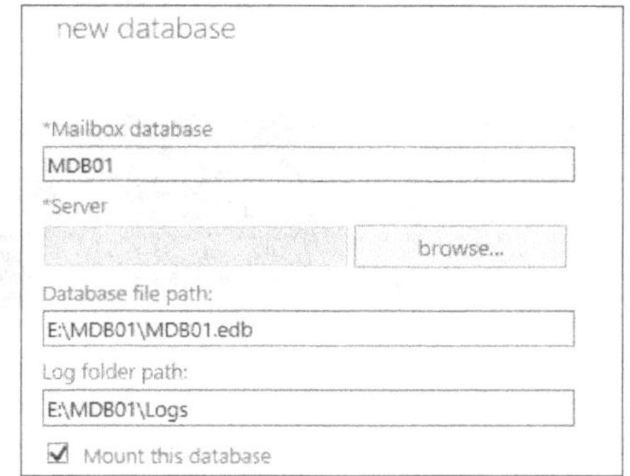

5. Click on **Save**.

Removing a mailbox database

Before you can remove a mailbox database, it must not contain active mailboxes anymore. However, it is possible it still contains disconnected or deleted mailboxes that haven't been purged from the database yet. So before you can remove a database, you need to make sure that all mailboxes have been moved to another database. If you don't, you will get an error as shown in the following screenshot:

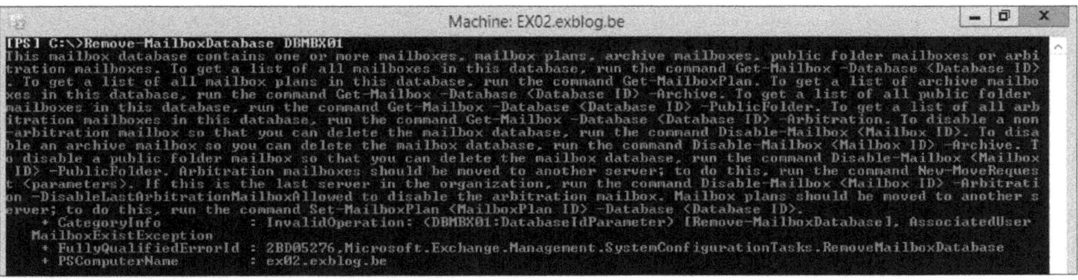

Before you can remove a mailbox database that has multiple database copies in a Database Availability Group, you need to remove the passive copies first. Only when the active database is the only copy that remains and it's empty, you will be able to permanently remove the database.

The following commands will move all mailboxes from database `MDB01` to database `MDB02`, including any system mailboxes that might be hosted in `MDB01`:

```
Get-Mailbox -Database "MDB01" | New-MoveRequest -TargetDatabase "MDB02"

Get-Mailbox -Database "MDB01" -Arbitration | New-MoveRequest -
TargetDatabase "MDB02"
```

Once you made sure that the database is empty, you can go ahead and remove the database using the following command:

```
Get-MailboxDatabase MDB01 | Remove-MailboxDatabase
```

Executing the command will remove the database from Exchange, but it will not remove the database files. You will have to manually delete the remaining files from the disk.

To remove a mailbox database through the EAC, execute the following steps:

1. Navigate to **Servers** | **databases**.
2. Select the database you want to remove and click on the garbage bin icon as shown in the following screenshot:

3. Click on **Yes** to confirm.

How it works...

Creating a mailbox database is in fact a pretty straightforward process. It suffices to provide a name, database - and log file path locations and let Exchange take care of the rest for you. When creating a new database, Exchange will first create an object in Active Directory and then create the EDB file along with the log stream and search catalog files in the locations that you specified earlier.

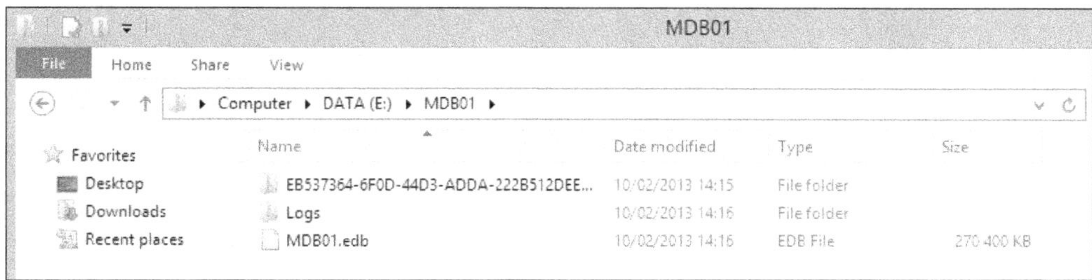

During the installation of Exchange 2013, several so-called arbitration mailboxes are created automatically. These mailboxes are used for system-related actions, such as distribution group moderation, federated delegation and system notification.

The following arbitration mailboxes are created by default and stored in the first (default) mailbox database:

- SystemMailbox{GUID}
- Migration.8f3e7716-2011-43e4-96b1-aba62d229136
- FederatedEmail.4c1f4d8b-8179-4148-93bf-00a95fa1e042

Make absolutely sure that you include these arbitration mailboxes when you are emptying a database before removal. If these mailboxes become unavailable or corrupt, one or more of Exchange's features might stop working. Luckily, Exchange helps you remembering and it won't let you remove a database unless it's considered empty and it's safe to remove it.

There's more...

When trying to physically remove the files immediately after having removed the mailbox database from Exchange, chances are that you will run into the error shown in the following screenshot:

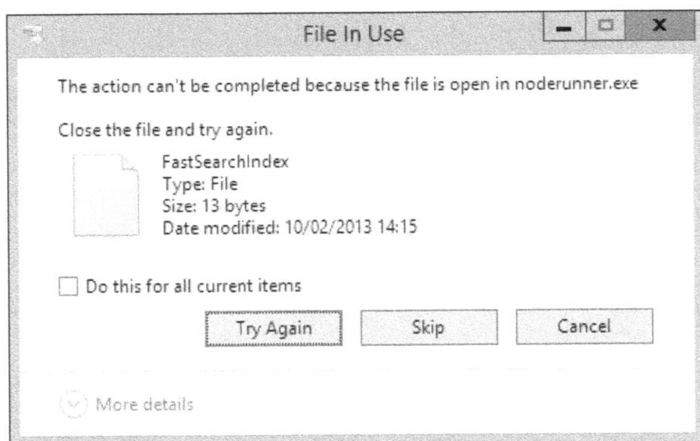

`Noderunner.exe` is a child process of the Microsoft Exchange Search Host Controller service. In order to release the files from the `noderunner.exe` process, you can do any of the following:

1. Restart the Mailbox Server. Unless your server is part of a Database Availability Group and other servers have copies of the databases on this server, you will have to plan for a little downtime while the server is rebooting.
2. Restart `HostControllerService` on the Mailbox Server by executing following command from an elevated PowerShell console:

```
Restart-Service HostControllerService
```

Mounting and dismounting mailbox databases

Although as an Exchange administrator, there shouldn't be many occasions on which you have to manually mount or dismount a database, sometimes you might be required to intervene because of an issue. The most common case is probably when a disk on which a database or logfiles are stored runs out of disk space. To protect the database, Exchange will automatically dismount the database. To recover from this situation, the administrator must free-up some space and manually re-mount the database. Therefore it's not only important to know how to perform these actions, but also to understand what's happening when they are executed.

Getting ready

In order to execute the following steps, you will need to log in to the Exchange Management Shell.

How to do it...

We will learn mounting and dismounting of database in this section.

Mounting a database

The following command will issue a mount-request for database `MDB01`:

```
Mount-Database "MDB01"
```

Dismounting a database:

Executing the following command will dismount the database `MDB01`:

```
Dismount-Database "MDB01"
```

How it works...

Before Exchange 2013, every database ran within the same process (`store.exe`) on the Mailbox Server. The introduction of the new Managed Store in Exchange 2013 changed things quite drastically, but for the better: every database is now running within its own process. This approach has some great advantages, such as whenever a database causes its worker process to hang, only a single database is affected whereas before all databases on the server would have suffered from the hanging process.

When taking a closer look at the new Managed Store, we can distinguish three important services:

- Store Service process
- Store Worker process
- Exchange Replication Service

The Exchange Replication Service could be seen as a sort of traffic control manager that provides a management interface for Exchange databases as it is responsible for issuing mount and dismount requests to the Store Service. Next to that, the Replication Service also keeps an eye on the state of a mailbox database and will, for instance, initiate a database failover when an issue with a database is reported.

For each mount request that is issued, the Exchange Store Service will create a new store worker process for the database being mounted.

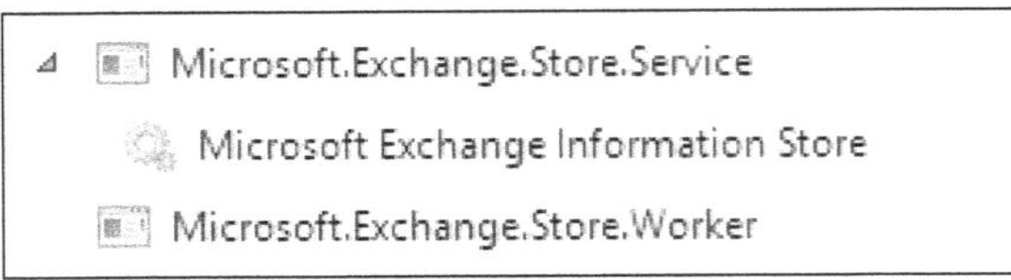

Amongst other tasks, the store worker process itself is responsible for providing effective access to the database. When a database is mounted successfully, Event 3156 will be posted to the Application event log.

Subsequently, the store service will terminate the worker process for a database when a dismount request has been issued. During the dismount process, Exchange will set a flag in the database headers telling that it was cleanly dismounted (also referred to as a "clean shutdown"). If this flag isn't present, the database cannot be re-mounted without being repaired first. When a database is dismounted successfully, an Event 3161 will be posted to the Application event log.

There's more...

To know if and on what server a database is mounted, execute the following steps. Notice the use of the `-Status` parameter in the following command:

```
Get-MailboxDatabase -Status | Ft Name,*mount*
```

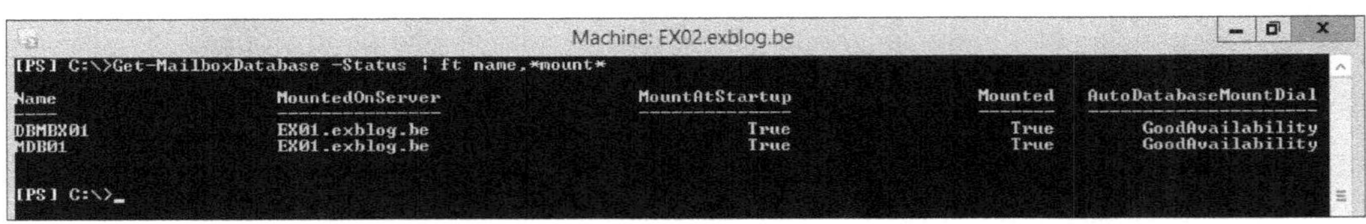

It is also possible to get a quick overview of the databases' status through the EAC. You can do so by navigating to **Servers** | **databases**.

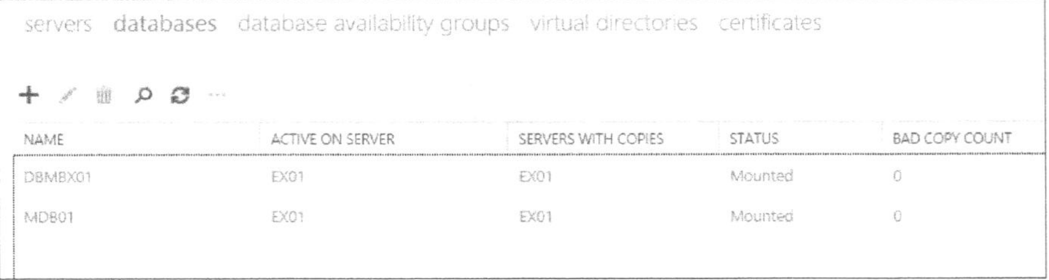

See also

Take a look at *Chapter 6, Implementing and Managing High Availability* and *Chapter 9, Performing Backup, Restore, and Disaster Recovery* which will contain more information on High Availability and Backup and recovery.

Moving database files to another location

If you adequately sized your environment, including taking into account additional disk space for future growth, chances are that you'll never have to physically move a database to another location. However, sometimes lack of disk space, change of underlying storage subsystem or simply a change in the design of your environment might require you to move database file to another physical location.

Getting ready

To execute the following steps, launch the Exchange Management Shell. For more information on how to dismount a database have a look at *Mounting/dismounting mailbox databases* earlier in this chapter.

How to do it...

The following command will move the database files of a database called `MDB01` to another location:

```
Move-DatabasePath -Identity "MDB01" -EdbFilePath "E:\NewPath\MDB01\MDB01.
edb" -LogFolderPath "E:\NewPath\MDB01\Logs"
```

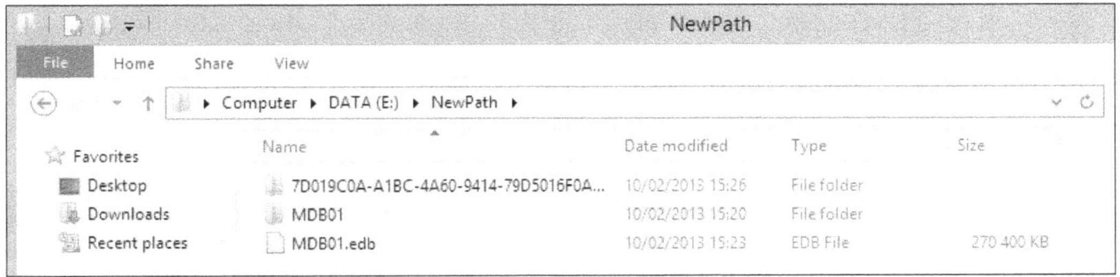

If you run the command while the database is mounted, the Exchange Management Shell will automatically throw a warning and ask for confirmation to dismount the database:

```
[PS] C:\>Move-DatabasePath DB05 -EdbFilePath C:\DB\DB05\DB05.edb -LogFolderPath C:\DB\DB05\Logs

Confirm
Are you sure you want to perform this action?
Moving database path "DB05".
[Y] Yes  [A] Yes to All  [N] No  [L] No to All  [?] Help (default is "Y"): Y

Confirm
To perform the move operation, database "DB05" must be temporarily dismounted, which will make it inaccessible to all
users. Do you want to continue?
[Y] Yes  [A] Yes to All  [N] No  [L] No to All  [?] Help (default is "Y"): Y
```

Dismounting a database will cause a temporary outage until the move has completed.

After the move has completed, Exchange will automatically re-mount the database.

There's more...

In some cases, you might prefer Exchange not to automatically move the physical files to their new location. This could be the case when you are using Mount Points in Windows Server. Mount Points can easily be reassigned to another location, without having to actually copy the data, therefore saving quite some time; especially when you are working with large databases.

Luckily, you can run the same command as before, only this time adding the -`ConfigurationOnly` parameter. The command will only update the database object's properties in Active Directory without physically moving the files' location:

```
Move-DatabasePath -Identity "MDB01" -EdbFilePath "E:\NewPath\MDB01\MDB01.
edb" -LogFolderPath "E:\NewPath\MDB01\Logs" -ConfigurationOnly
```

If you use the `-ConfigurationOnly` parameter, make sure that you manually move/relocate the database files before attempting to mount it again. If you are working with Mount Points, now is the time you would change the mount point location.

Configuring circular logging

Circular logging is the process of truncating logfiles as soon as they have been committed into the database. Normally, logfiles are only truncated after a full back. This allows you to restore a database from an earlier time and replay the transactions up to the latest available one.

Normally there's no need to enable circular logging but it can come in handy to quickly free up some disk space; although we would prefer extending disk space for a full log drive over enabling circular logging. Another point of attention is that using circular logging comes at a cost, if you need to restore a database from an earlier point in time you won't be able to recover to the time when the database failed, inevitably leading to data loss.

That is also one of the reasons why Microsoft recommends only enabling circular logging when you have at least three additional database copies.

Getting ready

In order to execute the following steps, launch the Exchange Management Shell.

How to do it...

To enable circular logging for database `MDB01`, run the following command:

```
Set-MailboxDatabase "MDB01" -CircularLoggingEnabled $true
```

Similarly, the following command will turn off circular logging:

```
Set-MailboxDatabase "MDB01" -CircularLoggingEnabled $false
```

If you enable or disable circular logging for a single database copy, you will have to remount (dismount/mount) the mailbox database for the change to become effective. Databases that are part of a Database Availability Group and have multiple copies don't have to be remounted.

How it works...

Every action that a user performs, generates one (or more) database transactions. These transactions aren't immediately written to the database. Instead, as a safety-measure, these transactions get written into a logfile first. Only when transactions are safely written to a logfile, they are recorded in the database. Each logfile is 1MB in size. When a logfile fills up, a new one is automatically generated.

Transaction logs play an important role at maintaining the consistency of a database. For example, when the store worker process of one of the databases crashes, that database is not dismounted properly and thus it won't have the **clean shutdown** flag set. As a result, you won't be able to mount the database until it is brought back into a clean shutdown state.

Without going into too much detail, the process involved to bring a database back into a consistent state involves replaying logfiles and recording the (partial) transactions from those logfiles into the database. The transactions in the logfiles could be pretty much anything from a new e-mail that was received to a message's read status that has changed. If a logfile that needs to be replayed against the database isn't available, it essentially means that one or more (partial) transactions cannot be recorded and therefore results in data loss.

In large environments, each database can generate hundreds even thousands of logfiles each day and could end up using quite some disk space. Although it's not a recommendation, you can enable circular logging which will flush transaction logs as soon as the transactions have been recorded in the database. If you are running a DAG and your database has multiple copies, transaction logs will be flushed as soon as all database copies have recorded the transactions in the database. In case you have a lagged database copy, the logfile will be flushed from the active and passive database copies as soon as each has recorded the transactions into the database and the logfile has been inspected by the lagged copy.

Circular logging allows you to save on disk space that would otherwise be used to store the transaction logs. However, when a disaster strikes and you need to restore a database from backup, you will not be able to recover the latest transactions therefore losing data up to the latest backup. So, if you enable circular logging, make sure that you have multiple database copies running in a Database Availability Group; preferably at least three. The idea behind this is that the risk of losing three copies at once is relatively small. Just keep in mind that it's not impossible.

See also

- *Chapter 6, Implementing and Managing High Availability*
- The *Recovering mailbox databases* recipe in *Chapter 8, Configuring Security and Compliance Features*

Creating and removing mailboxes

Creating mailboxes might be one of the simplest tasks within an Exchange environment. Even though the EAC wizard is relatively self-explanatory, there are some caveats to look out for. Especially the distinction between removing and disabling mailboxes might be confusing at first.

Getting ready

To execute the following steps, log in to the Exchange Admin Center or launch the Exchange Management Shell.

How to do it...

In this section we will learn how to create and remove mailboxes.

Creating a new user with mailbox

The following command will create a new user named `Mark Sheffield` and create a mailbox for that user:

```
New-Mailbox -UserPrincipalName Mark.Sheffield@exblog.be -Alias MSheffield
-Database "MDB01" -Name "Mark Sheffield" -OrganizationalUnit "Users"
-Password (Converto-Securestring -Asplaintext "P@ssw0rd" -Force) -
Firstname "Mark" -LastName "Sheffield" -DisplayName "Mark Sheffield" -
ResetPasswordOnNextLogon $true
```

In the example we just saw, some parameters are required, others aren't. If you aren't sure, you can have a look at the PowerShell help or you could just run `New-Mailbox`. If you haven't specified all required parameters, PowerShell will automatically query you for them.

```
[PS] C:\>new-mailbox
WARNING: A script or application on the EX2013-01.EXBLOG.BE remote computer is sending a prompt request. When prompted,
 enter sensitive information such as credentials or password only if you trust the remote computer and the application
or script requesting it.

cmdlet New-Mailbox at command pipeline position 1
Supply values for the following parameters:
Name: UserA
Password: **********
UserPrincipalName: userA@exblog.be
```

Creating a new mailbox through the EAC is equally easy, just follow these steps:

1. Navigate to **Recipients** | **Mailboxes**.
2. Click on the plus-sign (**+**) to start the **new mailbox** wizard.
3. Click on **New User** and fill in the other fields, such as **First Name**, **Last Name**, and **Display name**.
4. Click on **more options...** to configure advanced options like:
    - In what database the mailbox should be created
    - Whether or not an archive should be created
    - What address book policy should be used
5. Click on **Save** to create the user.

Enabling a mailbox for an existing user

The following command will create a mailbox for an existing user named `Kirk Jones`:

```
Enable-Mailbox -Identity "Exblog\kjones" -Database "MDB01"
```

To enable a mailbox for an existing user through the EAC refer the following steps:

1. Navigate to **Recipients** | **Mailboxes**.
2. Click on the plus-sign (**+**) to start the **new mailbox** wizard.

3. Click on **Existing user** and click on **browse...** to select the user.
4. Fill in the other fields.
5. Click on **more options...** to configure advanced options such as:
    - In what database the mailbox should be created
    - Whether or not an archive should be created
    - The address book policy
6. Click on **Save** to create the user.

Removing a mailbox

This command will effectively remove the mailbox and the user account of user `kjones`:

```
Remove-Mailbox -Identity kjones
```

To effectively remove the mailbox and the user account through the EAC refer to the following steps:

1. Navigate to **Recipients** | **Mailboxes**.
2. Select the user from the list of users.
3. Click the garbage bin icon and select **delete**.
4. Click **Yes** to confirm.

It's a common error to use Remove-Mailbox to remove a mailbox for a user. Remember that Remove-Mailbox will also remove the user account of that user. If you only want to remove the mailbox (that is, only remove the Exchange-attributes for the user account), run `Disable-Mailbox`.

Disabling a mailbox

The following command will disable the mailbox for user `kjones`, marking the user's mailbox for deletion in the database but without touching the user account itself:

```
Disable-Mailbox -Identity kjones
```

To disable the mailbox for user through the EAC follow these steps:

1. Navigate to **Recipients** | **Mailboxes**.
2. Select the user from the list of users.
3. Click the garbage bin icon and select **disable**.
4. Click **Yes** to confirm.

How it works...

Creating and removing mailboxes is a pretty straightforward action. However, the notion of removing and disabling mailboxes can sometimes be confusing.

When removing a mailbox, you are not only removing the user's mailbox but also the user account in AD. Disabling a user on the other hand will only mark the user's mailbox for deletion in the database, leaving the user account without a mailbox.

Depending on how your databases are configured, the mailbox will remain in the database in a disconnected state until it's past the database's retention time.

For example, to raise the deleted mailbox retention period to 60 days, run the following command:

```
Set-MailboxDatabase MDB01 -MailboxRetention 60.00:00:00
```

There's more...

When a mailbox is disabled, it is removed from the list of mailboxes in the EAC and you won't see it anymore when running the `Get-Mailbox` cmdlet. However, this doesn't necessarily mean the mailbox isn't there anymore.

As long as the mailbox is still within the deleted mailbox retention period of your mailbox database, you can re-enable it for the same user or connect it to another user's account, as long as that user doesn't already have a mailbox associated with it.

Working with disabled mailboxes

Run the following command to see a list of disabled mailboxes for a given database:

```
Get-MailboxStatistics -Database "MDB01" | ? {$_.DisconnectReason -eq
"Disabled"}
```

To reconnect the disabled mailbox of `Ashley Noel` in database `DBMBX01` to the user account of `Ashley Noel`, you can run the following command:

```
Connect-Mailbox "Ashley Noel" -Database "DBMBX01"
```

To connect the disabled mailbox of `Ashley Noel` to another user, `Kirk Jones`, run the following command:

```
Connect-Mailbox "Ashley Noel" -Database "DBMBX01" -User "exblog\kjones"
```

Managing resource mailboxes

Next to regular user mailboxes, Exchange also has a variety of special mailboxes which include the following:

- Arbitration mailboxes used for Exchange internal functions
- Discovery mailboxes, which are in fact regular mailboxes but reserved to be used for Discovery Searches
- Resource mailboxes representing resources, such as Meeting Rooms, Equipment

In this topic we will have a look at some of the more common tasks involved with managing resource mailboxes.

Getting ready

To complete the following steps, you will need to launch the Exchange Management Shell or log in to the Exchange Admin Center.

How to do it...

This section explains us managing resource mailboxes.

Creating a new room mailbox

The following command will create a new room mailbox called `Meeting Room Barcelona` in the specified `Organizational Unit`:

```
New-Mailbox -Room "Meeting Room Barcelona" -OrganizationalUnit "OU=Resources,OU=Accounts,DC=exblog,DC=be"
```

To create a new room mailbox through the EAC refer to the following steps:

1. Navigate to **Recipients** | **Resources**.
2. Click on the plus-sign (**+**) and select room mailbox to start the **new room mailbox** wizard.
3. Enter the details as follows:
    1. **Room name**: `Meeting Room Bremen`
    2. **Email address**: `mrbremen@exblog.be`
    3. **Location**: `Bremen`

    4. **Capacity**: `10`
    5. **Booking requests**: `Accept or decline booking requests automatically`

4. Click on **save** to create the room mailbox.

Configuring booking options

To configure the maximum duration of a booking, execute the following command:

```
Set-CalendarProcessing -Identity "mrbremen" -MaximumDurationInMinutes 480
```

To configure the maximum duration of a booking through the EAC, refer to the following steps:

1. Navigate to **Recipients** | **Resources**.
2. Double-click on the resource you wish to configure.
3. Navigate to **booking options**.
4. Under **Maximum duration (hours)** type: 8.
5. Review the other options and modify if necessary.
6. Click on save.

How it works...

A resource mailbox is a regular mailbox that is connected to a disabled user and can be used to represent rooms or equipment that can be booked through a meeting request in Outlook. There are different types of mailboxes that you can configure:

- Room
- Equipment
- Shared

Each type has its own purpose. Room mailboxes typically represent meeting rooms in your organization whereas Equipment mailboxes can range from anything like a projector to even cars (actually anything that comes into mind).

Shared mailboxes are somewhat different. These mailboxes are used by multiple people in the organization that work together on a project or are perhaps part of the same team. Users that need access to a shared mailbox will need to be given appropriate permissions before they can access the mailbox from Outlook or Outlook Web App.

There's more...

When scheduling a meeting or booking a resource, the scheduling assistant will by default only show the resource type in the resources' description, as shown in the following screenshot:

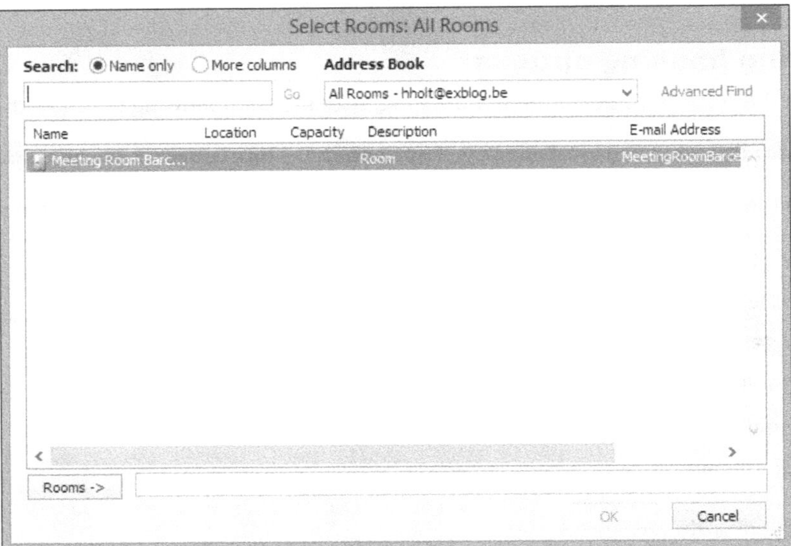

Sometimes companies however, might want to provide additional information in the description like for instance whether the room is equipped with a whiteboard or that it has a projector available. By defining custom resource properties on the resource mailbox, you can add that information to the description field. You cannot, however, add anything you like to that description.

Before you will be able to add additional options, you will have to create them in the Exchange organization by defining additional custom properties. Out of the box, Exchange allows you to configure room mailboxes with the following custom properties, monitor, whiteboard, or projector.

Defining additional custom resource properties

Run the following command to add the following options to the existing option, "air conditioning", "van", "sedan", and "station wagon".

```
$resourceconfig = Get-ResourceConfig
$resourceconfig.ResourcePropertySchema.Add("Room/DigitalWhiteBoard")
$resourceconfig.ResourcePropertySchema.Add("Room/SoundSystem")
Set-ResourceConfig -ResourcePropertySchema $resourceconfig.
ResourcePropertySchema
```

The resource properties you are configuring cannot contain spaces! So instead of using `Room/Digital Whiteboard` you should use `Room/DigitalWhiteboard`.

Adding custom properties to a resource

The following commands will add the options `DigitalWhiteboard` and `SoundSystem` to the equipment mailbox called `Meeting Room Bremen`:

```
$options = @("DigitalWhiteboard","SoundSystem")
Set-Mailbox "mrbremen" -ResourceCustom $options
```

To verify that the resource options have been configured successfully, book a new meeting and click on **add rooms** in the scheduling assistant. You will now see that the description includes the newly configured properties.

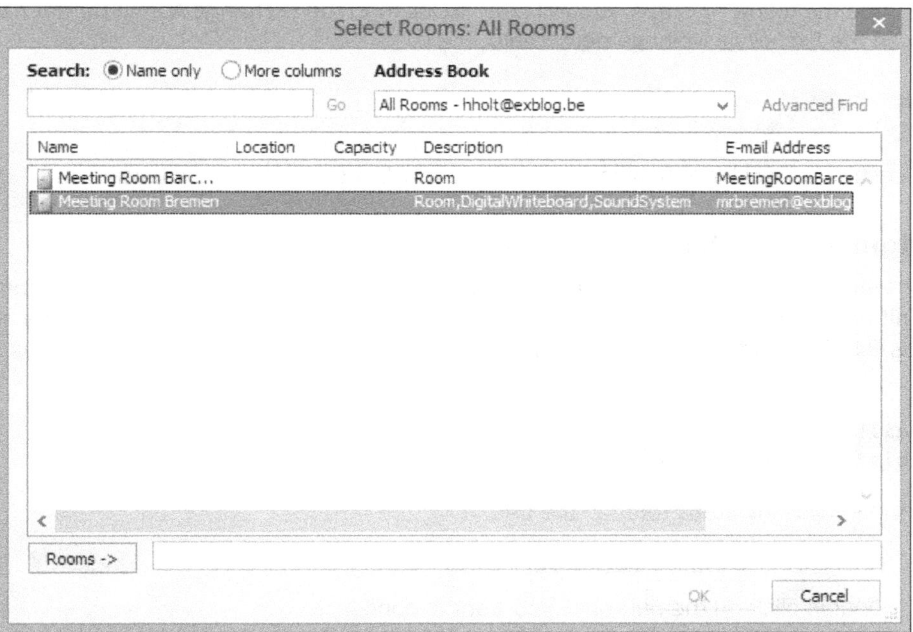

See also

Have a look at the following page for more information on how to configure calendar processing options: `http://technet.microsoft.com/en-us/library/dd335046.aspx`.

Configuring mailbox size limits

In a typical messaging environment, you'll have all sorts of users. Some of them seem to handle e-mail very efficiently and manage to keep their mailbox size very low. It could also be they aren't receiving tons of e-mails. Others do have the tendency to keep everything, therefore possibly using more space than you initially anticipated and sized for.

Even though every design should calculate for additional storage (up to a certain level) without getting into issues, it's important that you keep an eye on the amount of storage that you have left. One way to control how much storage a database can use on disk is to limit the amount of storage mailboxes within that database can use. As such, you can safely predict the maximum database size without getting into storage space related issues.

Getting ready

To complete the following steps, you will need to log in to the Exchange Admin Center as well as launch the Exchange Management Shell.

How to do it...

In this section we will learn how to configure the mailbox sizes at various levels.

Configuring mailbox sizes at database level

The following command will configure mailbox database `MDB01` with a default maximum size limit of 10 GB. At the same time, sending messages will be prohibited when the mailbox reaches 9.5 GB and the user will start receiving warnings once their mailbox reaches 9 GB in size:

```
Set-MailboxDatabase MDB01-ProhibitSendReceiveQuota "10GB" -
ProhibitSendQuota "9.5GB" -IssueWarningQuota "9GB"
```

Perform the following steps through the EAC:

1. Navigate to **servers** | **databases**.
2. Double-click on the database you want to configure.
3. Click on **limits**.
4. Configure the limits as follows:
    - **Issue a warning at (GB)**: `9`
    - **Prohibit send at (GB)**: `9.5`
    - **Prohibit send and receive at (GB)**: `10`
5. Click on **save**.

Configuring mailbox sizes at user level

The following command will limit the size of `Ronald White` mailbox to 5 GB while already preventing messages to be sent when it reached 4.8 GB. The user will be warned once he reaches 4 GB:

```
Set-Mailbox "Ronald White" -ProhibitSendQuota "4.8GB"
-ProhibitSendReceiveQuota "5GB" -IssueWarningQuota "4GB"
-UseDatabaseQuotaDefaults $false
```

Perform the following steps through the EAC:

1. Navigate to **recipients** | **mailboxes**.
2. Double-click on the mailbox you want to configure.
3. Click on **mailbox usage** and then click on **More options...** as shown in the following screenshot:

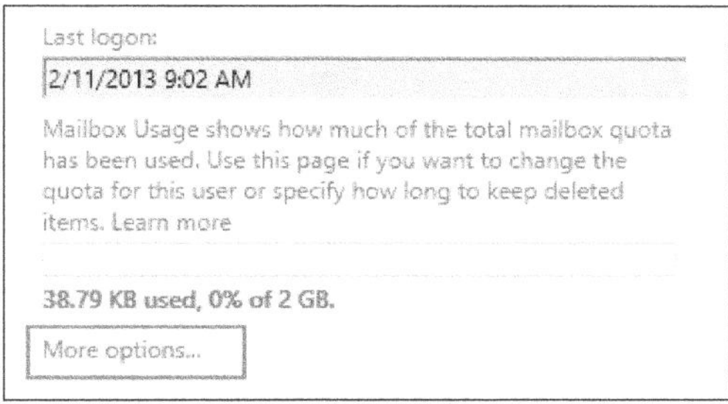

4. Click on **Customize the settings for this mailbox** and configure the following values:
   - **Issue a warning at (GB)**: `4`
   - **Prohibit send at (GB)**: `4.8`
   - **Prohibit send and receive at (GB)**: `5`
5. Click on **save**.

How it works...

Configuring mailbox size limits on the database level, allows you to easily control mailbox sizes without having to configure mailbox-level restrictions: every mailbox stored on the mailbox database will, by default, inherit the settings of that mailbox database.

The size limits on the mailbox level can be used to override the default values inherited from the database. It allows you to define individual limits for a single mailbox or a group of mailboxes. Another option would be to configure multiple databases in your environment, each with a different size limit, and move mailboxes between databases as their size limit should change.

Message size limits configured at the mailbox level will always override settings configured at the database level. To restore the default settings, you will have to set the UseDatabaseQuotaDefaults parameter to `$true` when using the Exchange Management Shell or set it to **Use the default quota settings from the mailbox database** in the EAC.

Managing personal archives

Personal archives were first introduced in Exchange 2010 and can be used to offload data from the primary mailbox. There are many good reasons to implement personal archives. For instance, they can be used to limit the size of the primary mailbox or because of some legal requirements that force you into keeping e-mail for a certain amount of time.

In this topic, we will go through the process of creating and managing archives.

Getting ready

To complete the following steps, you will need to launch the Exchange Management Shell or log in to the Exchange Admin Center.

How to do it...

The steps for enabling a personal archive for an existing mailbox-enabled user are explained in this section.

The following command will create a personal archive for a user called `Holly Holt` which already has a mailbox:

```
Enable-Mailbox "Holly Holt" -Archive
```

You can execute the same task through the EAC as well:

1. Navigate to **recipients** | **mailboxes**.
2. Double-click on the mailbox you want to enable an archive for.
3. Click on **mailbox features** and scroll down to **Archiving** as shown in the following screenshot:

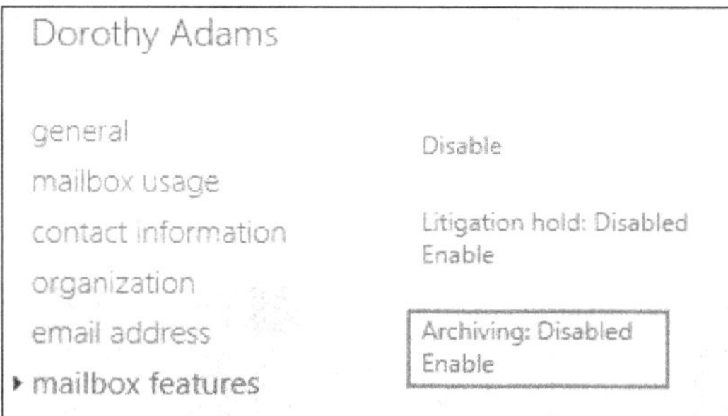

4. Click on **Enable**.
5. Click on **browse...** and select the mailbox database where to store the archive.
6. Click on **ok**.
7. Verify that the status now says: **Archiving: Enabled**.
8. Click on **save**.

The steps for creating a new user with mailbox and archive are explained in the following section.

The following command creates a new user `Mark Sheffield`, creates a mailbox, and enables a personal archive:

```
New-Mailbox -UserPrincipalName Mark.Sheffield@exblog.be -Alias user1 -
Archive -Database "MDB01" -Name "Mark Sheffield" -OrganizationalUnit
"Users" -Password (Converto-Securestring -Asplaintext "P@ssw0rd" -Force)
-Firstname "Mark" -LastName "Sheffield" -DisplayName "Mark Sheffield" -
ResetPasswordOnNextLogon $true
```

Perform the following steps through the EAC:

1. Navigate to **recipients** | **mailboxes**.
2. Click on the plus-sign (**+**) to launch the **new mailbox** wizard.
3. Enter the user's details like the **First name**, **Last Name**, and so on.
4. Click on **more options...**.
5. Click on **Create an on-premises archive mailbox for this user**.
6. Click on **browse** to select the mailbox database where to store the archive.
7. Click on **save**.

This section explains reviewing the personal archive properties.

The following command will output the archive details of `Holly Holt`:

```
Get-Mailbox "Holly Holt" | fl Name,*archive*
```

The screenshot for the preceding command is as follows:

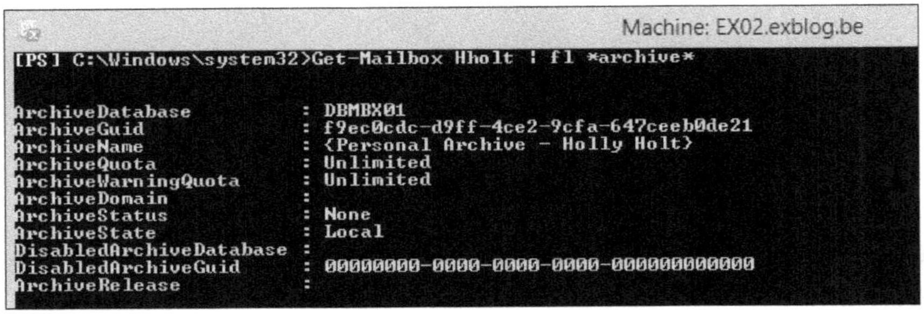

```
Machine: EX02.exblog.be
[PS] C:\Windows\system32>Get-Mailbox Hholt | fl *archive*

ArchiveDatabase         : DBMBX01
ArchiveGuid             : f9ec0cdc-d9ff-4ce2-9cfa-647ceeb0de21
ArchiveName             : {Personal Archive - Holly Holt}
ArchiveQuota            : Unlimited
ArchiveWarningQuota     : Unlimited
ArchiveDomain           :
ArchiveStatus           : None
ArchiveState            : Local
DisabledArchiveDatabase :
DisabledArchiveGuid     : 00000000-0000-0000-0000-000000000000
ArchiveRelease          :
```

Perform the following steps through the EAC:

1. Navigate to **recipients** | **mailboxes**.
2. Double-click on the mailbox you want to view details for.
3. Click on **mailbox features** and scroll down to **Archiving: Enabled**.
4. Click on **View details**.

How it works...

One could argue that personal archives are no more (or less) than a secondary mailbox for a user. Although there is some truth in that statement, an archive mailbox cannot be used to send or receive e-mails, nor is it possible to directly assign permissions to it. On the other hand, if someone has received full Access to a mailbox that has an archive, that person will also have access to the archive.

Given the right client version and license, archives can be viewed from either Outlook or Outlook Web Access. There's one catch though: archives can only be viewed when the client is online and connected to the Exchange server. This means they will not be available when Outlook Web App or Outlook are working in offline mode.

The following screenshot depicts how a personal archive appears in Outlook:

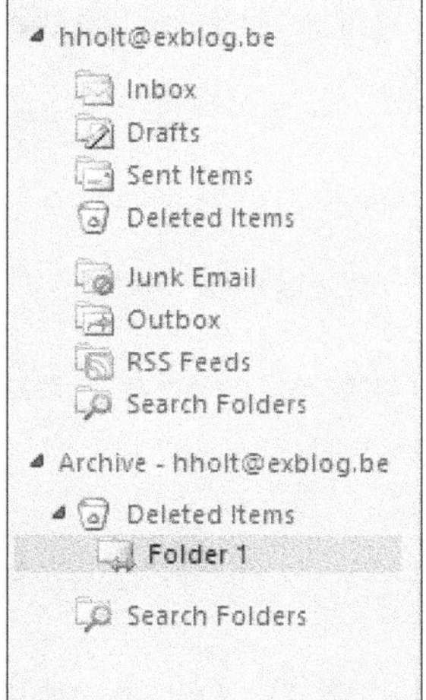

By default, if you don't specify an alternate location, the archive will be created in the same database as the user's primary mailbox. However, this is not a requirement and you are more than welcome to specify an alternate location for it.

Personal Archives are a so-called premium feature and require **Enterprise Client Access Licenses** (**eCALs**). They also require specific version of Outlook to work with. For more information have a look at the following web page: `http://office.microsoft.com/en-us/outlook-help/license-requirements-for-personal-archive-and-retention-policies-HA102576659.aspx`

See also

- *Chapter 8, Configuring Security and Compliance Features*

Assigning mailbox permissions

One of the tasks that you will be faced with is granting access to other user's mailboxes. Although this task could be expedited to your help desk by using RBAC, typically changing permissions isn't something that many companies allow to be done by a lot of people.

Getting ready

To complete the following steps, you will need to launch the Exchange Management Shell or log in to the Exchange Admin Center.

How to do it...

In this section we will learn about assigning mailbox permissions.

Assigning full access permissions to a mailbox

The following command will grant a user `Mark Johnson` full access permissions to the mailbox of `Ronald White`:

```
Add-MailboxPermission -Identity "rwhite" -user "exblog\mjohnson" -
AccessRights "FullAccess"
```

Assigning full access permissions through the EAC can be done as follows:

1. Navigate to **recipients** | **mailboxes**.
2. Double-click on the mailbox you want to grant access to.
3. Click on **mailbox delegation**.
4. Click on the plus-sign (**+**) under **Full Access**.
5. Select the user you want to grant full access and click on **ok**.
6. Click on **save**.

Assigning send-as or send on behalf of permissions

The following command will grant user `Mark Johnson` send-as permissions on the mailbox of `Ronald White`:

```
Add-ADPermission "Ronald White" -User "Exblog\mjohnson" -Extendedrights
"Send As"
```

Perform the following steps through the EAC:

1. Navigate to **recipients** | **mailboxes**.
2. Double-click on the mailbox you want to grant access to.
3. Click on **mailbox delegation**.
4. Click on the plus-sign (**+**) under **Send As**.
5. Select the user you want to grant full access and click on **ok**.
6. Click on **save**.

The following command grants user `Mark Johnson` "send-on behalf of" permissions on the mailbox of `Ronald White`:

```
Set-Mailbox "Ronald White" -GrantSendOnBehalfTo "Exblog\mjohnson"
```

Perform the following steps through the EAC:

1. Navigate to **recipients** | **mailboxes**.
2. Double-click on the mailbox you want to grant access to.
3. Click on **mailbox delegation**.
4. Click on the plus-sign (**+**) under **Send on Behalf Of**.
5. Select the user you want to grant full access to and click on **ok**.
6. Click on **save**.

Granting receive-as permission

The following command grants user `Mark Johnson` "receive-as" permissions on the mailbox of `Ronald White`:

```
Add-ADPermission -Identity "Ronald White" -User "exblog\mjohnson" -
ExtendedRights "receive-as"
```

It is not possible to assign receive-as permissions through the EAC.

How it works...

Full access permissions should be relatively self-explanatory, they grant a user (or distribution group) full access to the mailbox for which the permission was applied.

Send-as permissions allow someone to send an e-mail from the mailbox the permission is applied to. E-mails sent from that mailbox appear to be coming from the mailbox owner.

The send on behalf of permission is different from the send-as permission; it also allows someone to send e-mails from the mailbox for which the permission was applied, however, the recipient will see that the message was sent by one of the mailbox's delegates.

Send-as and send on behalf of permissions cannot be used at the same time. When configuring these permissions, you'll have to choose either of them.

An example screenshot of send-as on behalf of permission is as follows:

Receive-as permissions are used to grant someone access to a mailbox without granting the ability to send mails. For example, this could be the case when you are performing a legal search for content in the mailbox.

There's more...

In Exchange 2010 SP1 a new feature called Auto-Mapping was introduced. This feature will automatically map any mailbox a user has full access to in Outlook:

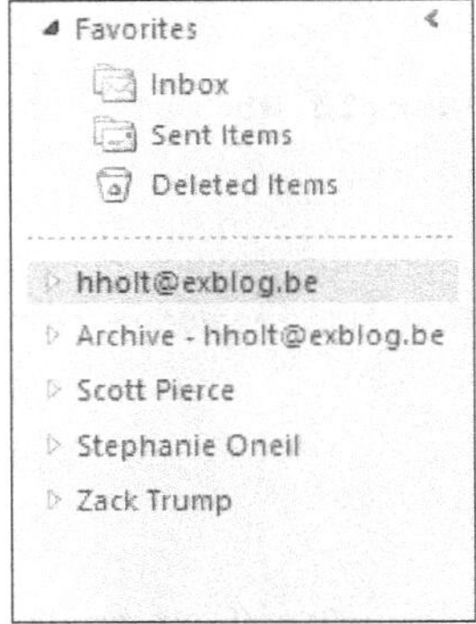

Auto-Mapping is enabled by default when granting someone full access to a mailbox. It can only be disabled when adding the permission and only through the Exchange Management Shell by adding `-Automapping $false` to the command:

```
Add-MailboxPermission -Identity "rwhite" -user "exblog\mjohnson" -
AccessRights "FullAccess" -AutoMapping $false
```

If you want to disable Auto-Mapping feature for previously applied permissions, you will have to remove and re-apply the permission with the feature disabled.

See also

Take a look at the following TechNet article for more information on mailbox permissions: `http://technet.microsoft.com/en-us/library/aa997244.aspx`.

Moving mailboxes to another database

Earlier in this chapter we talked about moving databases to another location. Similarly, you can also move mailboxes from one database to another. This is typically something you'd do when a user moves between regions or sites that have their own Exchange Servers. Another use-case for moving mailboxes is to redistribute the load on your databases as not all mailbox databases will grow at the same pace.

Getting ready

To execute the following steps, log in to the EAC or launch the Exchange Management Shell.

How to do it...

This section explains how to move mailboxes.

Moving mailboxes using migration batches

The following command will move a batch of users, specified in a file called `users.csv`, to database `MDB01`:

```
New-MigrationBatch -Name <name> -CSVData ([System.
IO.File]::ReadAllBytes("C:\temp\users.csv")) -Local -TargetDatabase MDB01
-AutoStart
```

The CSV file that you are using, will have to be in the following format:

Executing the same steps through the EAC:

1. Navigate to **recipients** | **migration**.
2. Click on the plus-sign (**+**) to start the new local mailbox move wizard.
3. Click on the plus-sign (**+**) and select the users you want to move to another database.
4. Click on **next**.
5. Enter a descriptive name for the migration batch.
6. Select **Move archive mailbox along with primary mailbox**.
7. Click on **browse...** under **Target database** and select the database you want to move the user to.
8. Click on **next**.
9. Click on **browse...** and select the recipient that should receive the migration reports by e-mail.
10. Select **Automatically start the batch** and **Automatically complete the migration batch**.
11. Click on **new**.

If you are using a CSV file instead of selecting the users, make sure the file is in the same format as when used with PowerShell.

Moving mailboxes using move requests

The following command will initiate a move request to move the mailbox of `Holly Holt` to database `MDB01`:

```
New-MoveRequest -Identity "Holly Holt" -TargetDatabase "MDB01"
```

Although it is possible to move a single mailbox using the EAC, it will still create a new migration batch for it. Regular mailbox moves cannot be created through the EAC.

Checking the progress of a mailbox move

The following command will output an overview of the existing move requests and their current status and progress:

```
Get-MoveRequest | Get-MoveRequestStatistics
```

Checking the status of a migration batch

The following command show detailed information a given migrationbatch:

```
Get-MigrationBatch "Batch1"| FL *
```

It is also possible to get an overview per individual user in a migration batch. The following command will report the current migration status for a user called `Carrie Wood`:

```
Get-MigrationUserStatistics cwood@exblog.be
```

Removing completed move request

The following command will remove all completed move requests:

```
Get-MoveRequest | Where Status -eq "Completed" | Remove-MoveRequest
```

> You might have noticed the simplified syntax in the preceding example. This is new to PowerShell v3 that was introduced with Windows Server 2012. This new syntax is exactly the same as the following: `Get-MoveRequest | where{$_.Status -eq "Completed"} | Remove-MoveRequest`. Much simpler, isn't it?

How it works...

The most obvious time to move mailboxes is during a migration from one version of Exchange to another, but even during the lifetime of your Exchange environment, there are many reasons to perform a mailbox move, for instance to:

- Fix mailbox corruption
- Re-balance databases
- Move a mailbox to another physical location
- Change a mailbox' properties such as quotas
- Change permissions applied at database level
- Investigate issues

New move requests, whether they were initiated directly using the `New-MoveRequest` cmdlet or via a migration batch, are automatically picked up by the **Mailbox Replication Service** (**MRS**). This service is responsible for handling mailbox moves and runs on each Mailbox Server Role in the organization. The MRS regularly scans the environment for new move requests and will automatically start processing new requests on a first created, first served basis.

As soon as a move request is detected, one of the MRS' in the AD Site of the source mailbox will take ownership of the request and initiate the actual move of the data. This move consists of pulling the data from the source mailbox and copying it to the target mailbox.

Mailbox moves are also referred to as online mailbox moves, essentially pointing out that a user can continue working while a move is being executed. Because of this, chances are that a user makes changes (create or delete new e-mail messages) while data is being copied to the target mailbox. To overcome that mailbox data isn't necessarily static and make sure that these changes are also copied, the MRS will use multiple passes to copy the data from the source mailbox: while copying data it will monitor the source mailbox for changes and copy those changes over in a subsequent pass of the mailbox.

Only during the last pass, the source mailbox will be locked to avoid conflicts and missed data between the source and the target mailbox. This last phase of the move (**CompletionInProgress** status) can last anywhere from a few seconds to a few minutes.

Mailbox move requests are pretty straightforward: they are created, processed, and completed. Once a move request is completed, you will have to clear it before you can create a new move request for that mailbox.

Migration batches also rely on the Mailbox Replication Service to effectively move data to the target location. In fact, when a migration batch is processed it will automatically create new move requests for the mailboxes in that batch.

Migration batches can be seen as a sort of management architecture around regular move requests that provide you some additional capabilities such as e-mail notifications and incremental synchronizations. The latter can prove useful if you have to copy large amounts of data, but do not want to switch over to the target mailbox just yet. This could be the case when you want to move data to another physical location ahead of time, for instance, during the weekend or nights. The incremental synchronizations that will happen after the initial sync will be much smaller in size and therefore have less impact on the bandwidth that is used.

There's more...

Regular move requests are handled asynchronously. This means that the Mailbox Replication Service will treat a mailbox move "when it has time to do so". In large and busy environments, it could take a while before a mailbox gets effectively moved!

Synchronous mailbox moves

In the rare scenarios where you want a mailbox move to be executed immediately, you can revert to using a built-in PowerShell script that will initiate a synchronous mailbox move: it is executed immediately!

The following command will perform a synchronous mailbox move for a user called `Jeff Allen` to `DBMBX01`:

```
Cd $exscripts
.\MoveMailbox.ps1 -Identity jLittle -TargetDatabase MDB01
```

The screenshot for the output of the preceding command is as follows:

Bad item limit

As described earlier, move request can be used to fight corruption in a mailbox. Sometimes you might find that a move request (or migration batch) fails because of a high number of bad items that were found during the move. By default, the bad item limit for a move is zero. This means the move will fail when a single corrupt item is found.

Items can become corrupted for various reasons. It's very likely that an item has been around for a while and has remained untouched for a long period of time, possibly rendering it corrupt. In such a case, there's nothing much you can do and it certainly serves no point in trying to move them along.

By specifying a custom bad item limit for a move request, you tell the MRS to ignore corrupt items it encounters until it reaches the threshold.

The following command will create a new move request for user `Jef Allen` to `DBMBX01` and set the `BadItemLimit` to `15`:

```
New-MoveRequest -Identity "JAllen" -TargetDatabase "MDB01" -BadItemLimit
15
```

See also

Take a look at the following TechNet article for more information on mailbox moves: `http://technet.microsoft.com/en-us/library/jj150543.aspx`.

Managing public folders

Public folders have changed quite dramatically compared to before. Prior to Exchange 2013 public folders were stored in their own databases. As such, they were managed in a completely different way than regular mailboxes. In this topic we will go through some of the common management tasks related to public folder management.

Getting ready

To execute the following steps either log in to the Exchange Admin Center or launch the Exchange Management Shell.

How to do it...

We will learn how to manage folders in this section.

Creating new public folder mailboxes

The following command will create a new public folder mailbox named `Accounting` on mailbox database `MDB01`:

```
New-Mailbox -Name "Accounting" -Database "MDB01" -PublicFolder
```

Execute the following steps to create a new public folder mailbox name `Accounting` using the EAC:

1. Navigate to **public folders** | **public folder mailboxes**.
2. Click on the plus-sign (**+**) to start the new public folder mailbox wizard.
3. Under **Name**, type `Accounting`.
4. Under **Organizational Unit**, click on **browse...** and select an OU to store the PF Mailbox' user account in.
5. Under **Mailbox database**, click on **browse...** to select the database where to store the public folder mailbox.
6. Click on **save**.

When you have no public folder mailboxes, the first time you navigate to the public folder tab, you will get the following error:

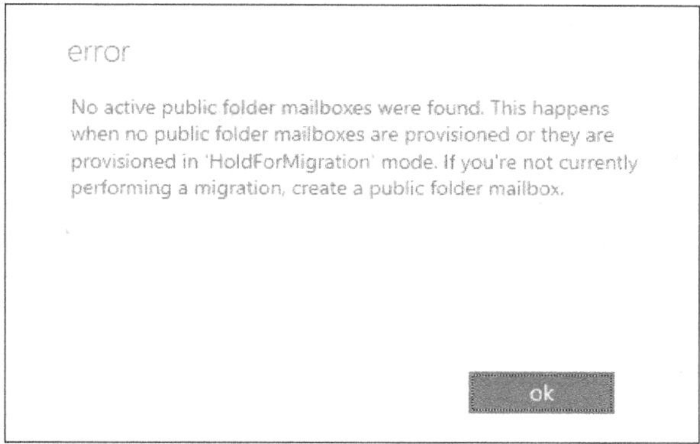

This error can safely be ignored as it just informs you there are no public folder mailboxes found or they are in course of being migrated.

Creating public folders

The following command will create a new public folder called `Sales Results` in the public folder mailbox `Accounting`:

```
New-PublicFolder -Name "Sales Results" -Mailbox "Accounting"
```

Perform the following steps through the EAC:

1. Navigate to **public folders** | **public folders**.
2. Click on the plus-sign (**+**) to start the **new public folder** wizard.
3. Type `Sales Results` in the **Name** field.
4. Click on **save**.

By clicking on a public folder, you navigate one level down the folder hierarchy. If you run the **new public folder** wizard while in another public folder, you can create a hierarchy of folders.

Managing public folder permissions

The following command will grant user `Carol Wood` owner rights on the `Accounting` public folder:

```
Add-PublicFolderClientPermission -Identity "\Accounting" -User "CWood" -
AccessRights "Owner"
```

Perform the following steps through the EAC:

1. Navigate to **public folders** | **public folders**.
2. Highlight the public folder you want to provide access to and click on **manage** under **Folder permissions** in the action-pane at your right-hand side.
3. Click on the plus-sign (**+**) and then click on **browse...** to select the user you want to grant permissions to.
4. Select the appropriate permissions from the **Permission level** dropdown menu. If required, you can also create custom permissions by selecting the appropriate permissions yourself.
5. Click on **save**.
6. In the **Public Folder Permissions** window, click on **save** again.

Removing permissions is as easy as granting them. You need to execute the exact same steps, only instead of adding another user or changing existing permissions, you simply remove a user's permissions by highlighting the user and clicking on the minus sign (-).

How it works...

Once, public folders were the best way for sharing messages and collaborating with a group of people. Even with the raise of SharePoint and new features like Site Mailboxes that bring both Exchange and SharePoint closer together, public folders often remain loved for their integration with Outlook and simplicity. In order to provide some sort of high availability and resiliency, you could store multiple instances of public folders in different locations. A copy of a public folder is also referred to as a replica. Because public folders operated as a multi-master model, it was possible to make changes to a document in a public folder from each location that had a replica.

To keep the different replicas in sync with each other, Exchange relied on a built-in replication mechanism which was, unlike a Database Availability Group, based on SMTP messages. A server hosting a given copy of a public folder would exchange SMTP messages containing updated information and content of that public folder with other servers hosting that had a copy of that public folder. Even though the replication mechanism was robust, it lacked a set of management features; often leaving the administrator to the Exchange server's mercy.

Public folders in Exchange 2013 are no longer stored in a separate database. Instead, public folders are now stored in a new type of mailbox, unsurprisingly called the public folder mailbox. Because these mailboxes are now stored in regular mailbox databases, they can take advantage from the exact same high-availability and resiliency features like the Database Availability Group.

These changes come with a trade-off though: the public folder architecture is no longer based on a multi-master model. This means there can only be a single (active) copy of a public folder mailbox, and therefore of a public folder, at any given time.

In the entire Exchange organization, there is only a single public folder mailbox that is responsible for maintaining a writeable copy of the public folder hierarchy. This mailbox is referred to as the hierarchy mailbox. All other public folder mailboxes have a read-only copy of the hierarchy. By default, a user will be pointed to his or her default public folder mailbox, which is a configurable property on the user's mailbox.

Whenever the user makes a change to the public folder hierarchy like adding or removing a new folder, the public folder mailbox will pass that change on to the master hierarchy mailbox, which will then in turn dispatch the change to all other public folder mailboxes so that they can update their read-only copy of the hierarchy. The diagram depicting the same is as follows:

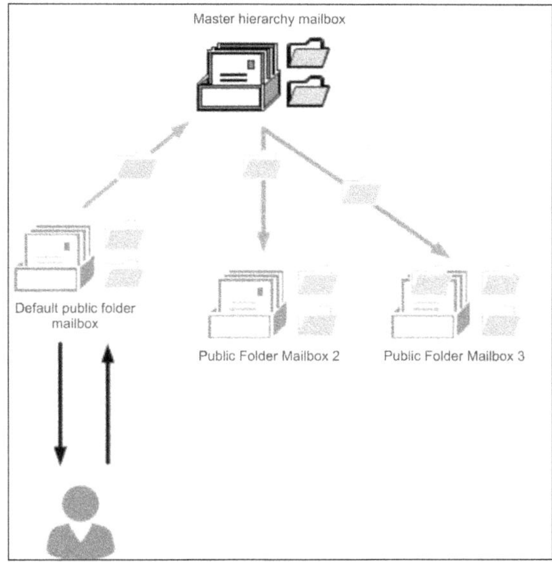

Surely you can have multiple copies stored at different locations, but access to a public folder always happen from the Mailbox Server hosting the active copy of the mailbox database in which the public folder mailbox is stored. This will certainly have its impact in organizations that require access to the same public folders over different locations, but lack the bandwidth to support the direct connections. In such a case, you might want to rethink your public folder placement, if not perhaps move them to a more suitable solution such as SharePoint.

See also

Take a look at the following web page for more information on public folders in Exchange 2013: `http://technet.microsoft.com/en-us/library/jj150538.aspx`.

Configuring outbound mail flow

Mail flow is essentially what a messaging platform is all about. When talking about mail flow, we can make two major distinctions: internal traffic and external traffic.

When talking about external traffic, I'm referring to all mail traffic where the destination of the message is outside the company's internal Exchange organization.

Getting ready

To execute the following steps, either log in to the Exchange Admin Center or launch the Exchange Management Shell.

How to do it...

The steps for creating a send connector to send messages to the internet are explained in this section.

The following command will create a new send connector that will route messages to the internet:

```
New-SendConnector "Default Internet Connector" -AddressSpace "*" -
Internet -Enabled $true
```

Perform the following steps through the EAC:

1. Navigate to **mail flow** | **send connectors**.
2. Click on the plus-sign (**+**) to start the **new send connector** wizard.
3. Type `Default Internet Connector` in the **Name** field.
4. Select **Internet** as the connector type and click on **next**.
5. Select **MX record associated with recipient domain** and click on **next**.
6. Click on the plus-sign (**+**) to add an address space.
7. Type `*` in the **FQDN** field, leave the other default values and click on **save**.
8. Click on **next**.
9. Click on the plus-sign (**+**) to select the source servers associated with this connector.
10. Click on **finish**.

The steps for creating a send connector to route emails through a smart host are explained in the following section.

The following command will create a new send connector that will route all e-mails for the domain `PartnerCompany.com` through a smarthost (`10.20.30.40`):

```
New-Sendconnector "Connector to PartnerCompany.com" -SmartHosts
"10.20.30.40" -AddressSpace "SMTP:partnercompany.com;1" -Enabled $true
```

Or, perform the following steps through the EAC:

1. Navigate to **mail flow** | **send connectors**.
2. Click on the plus-sign (**+**) to start the **new send connector** wizard.
3. Type `Connector to PartnerCompany.com` in the **Name** field.
4. Select **Custom** and click on **next**.
5. Select **Route mail through smart hosts** and click on the plus-sign (**+**) to add one or more smart hosts:

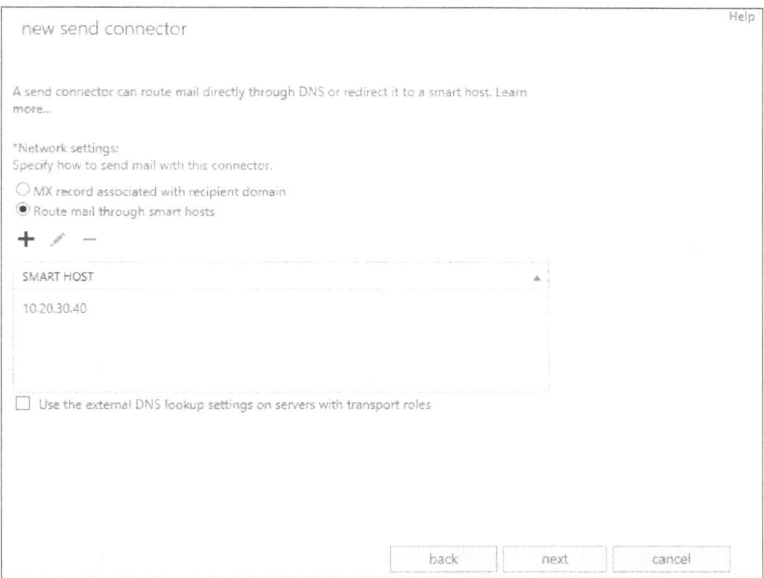

6. Click on **next**.
7. Leave the default authentication value (**None**) and click on **next**.
8. Click on the plus-sign (**+**) to add the following address space: **PartnerDomain.com**; leave both **Type** and **Cost** by their default values and click on **save**.
9. Click on **next**.

10. Click on the plus-sign (**+**) to select the source servers associated with this connector.
11. Click on **finish**.

How it works...

Connectors are an essential part of the mail flow mechanism in your Exchange organization. Unsurprisingly, receive connectors are used to accept messages from other sources into your Exchange organization. These sources can be anything ranging from another Exchange server in your organization to an unknown source on the Internet.

Send connectors (how could you guess?) are used to route e-mails outside of your organization.

During the installation of Exchange, the necessary receive connectors to allow for basic mail flow are already created. In a typical Exchange deployment, you wouldn't even have to configure additional receive connectors.

However, before you are able to send messages to the Internet, you will have to create at least one send connector with the default address space "*" to route messages to the Internet, as described previously.

There's more...

There is more in store and explained in the following section.

Send connector costs

How Exchange 2013 routes e-mails within the organization deserves a chapter at its own right. However, in order to keep things short and to the point we won't discuss the inner workings in detail. Essentially, Exchange looks at various parameters to determine the least-cost route to a destination. Elements that can influence the cost of a route to the destination of a message can be, but are not limited to:

- Active Directory sites, site link costs and Exchange-specific site link costs
- Hub Sites
- Costs associated with send connectors

Assigning a specific cost to a send connector can be an effective way to control by what Exchange Servers that connector will be used. Consider the following situation:

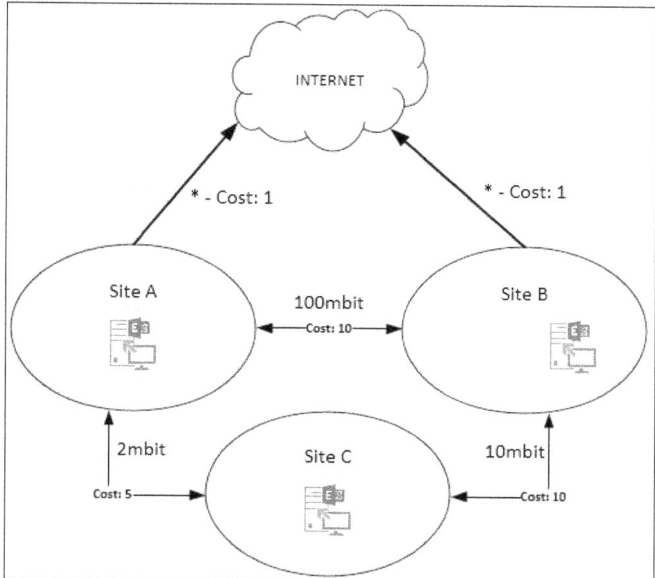

In this example, whenever a mailbox on **Site C** would send a message to a recipient on the Internet, the message would get routed to the connector on **Site A** because it has the lowest total cost: the cost of the site link between **Site A** and **Site C** plus the cost of the connector in **Site A**, 6 is lower than the cost of the site link between **Site C** and **Site B** and the connector in **Site B**, being 11.

To make sure that outgoing messages from **Site C** to the Internet are routed over the connector in **Site B**, you have several options:

- Lower the site link cost between sites B and C
- Increase the site link cost between site A and C
- Assign a higher Exchange-specific cost to the site link between sites A and C
- Increase the cost of the connector in site A

Even though all these options are valid, let's zoom in onto the latter one and change the cost of the connector in **Site A** to, for example, 9, the total cost from **Site C** to the Internet through **Site A** would now be 14 (5 + 9) which is higher than the cost through **Site B** (11). As a result, all message will flow through **Site B**. This change has also the additional benefit of not changing the routing behavior for mailboxes in **Site A**. The cost of sending a message to the Internet might have changed from 1 to 9, but it's still lower than routing messages through **Site B** which has a total cost of 11 (10+1).

Note that when you have multiple send connectors that are valid for the same mail domain, Exchange will always use the send connector with the lowest cost. It will not attempt to use the other send connector, even if the send connector with the lowest cost is temporarily unavailable. Instead, if this happens, it will queue the mails until the connector becomes available again.

To force messages to be re-routed through another connector with the same cost, you must manually disable the connector and resubmit the messages in the queue using the `Retry-Queue` command with the `-Resubmit` parameter.

Configure a send connector to route e-mails through the Client Access Server

By default a new send connector will send messages either directly to the Internet or through a configured smart host. You can configure a send connector to route messages through the front-end transport service on the Client Access Server as well; this gives you the benefit that both inbound and outbound messages go through a single point.

The following command will configure the default Internet connector we created earlier to route messages through the Client Access Server:

```
Set-SendConnector -Identity "Default Internet Connector"
-FrontEndProxyEnabled $true
```

Perform the following steps through the EAC:

1. Navigate to **mail flow | send connectors**.
2. Double click on the **Default Internet Connector**.
3. Select **Proxy through client access server** and click on **save**.

See also

Have a look at the following TechNet article on connectors in Exchange 2013: `http://technet.microsoft.com/en-us/library/jj657461.aspx`.

Configuring accepted domains

Simply put, by creating accepted domains you control for what domains your Exchange environment will accept messages. The following chapter will explain how to create accepted domains and how they're used in Exchange.

Getting ready

To execute the following commands, log in to the Exchange Admin Center or launch the Exchange Management Shell.

How to do it...

The following command will create a new accepted domain for the domain name `exblog.com`:

```
New-AcceptedDomain -Name "exblog.com" -Domainname "exblog.com"
```

Perform the following steps through the EAC:

1. Navigate to **mail flow** | **accepted domains**.
2. Click on the plus-sign (**+**) to start the **new accepted domain** wizard.
3. Type in a descriptive name.
4. Type: `exblog.com` under ***Accepted domain**.
5. Select **Authoritative domain. Email is delivered to a recipient in this Exchange organization**, as shown in the following screenshot:

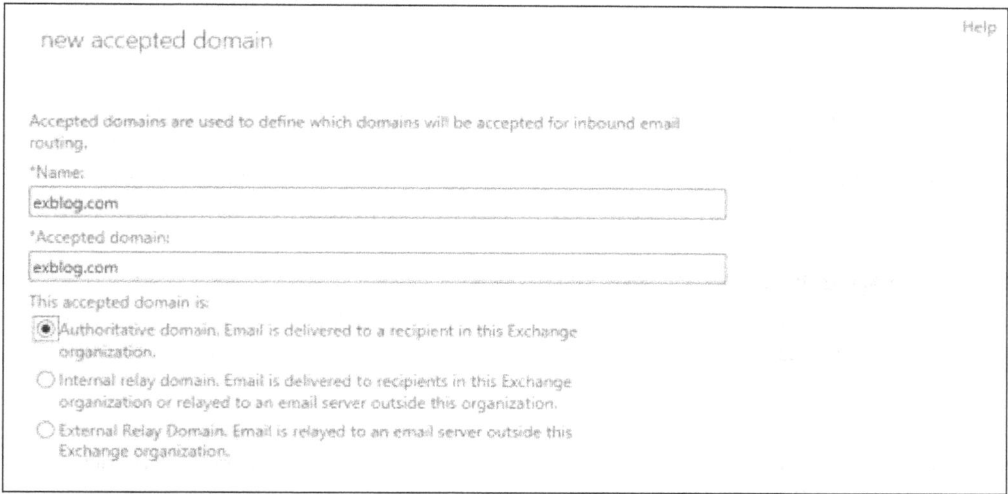

6. Click on **save**.

How it works...

Accepted domains are used to control what e-mail domains your Exchange server is allowed to receive e-mails for. There are three types of accepted domains:

- Authoritative
- Internal relay
- External relay

A domain is considered authoritative if the Exchange organization is the point of delivery and recipients for that domain have mailboxes in the Exchange organization. During the installation of Exchange, the local active directory domain name is configured as default accepted domain.

Internal relay domains are used when some recipients for that domain have mailboxes in the Exchange organization and some don't. This could, for example, be the case where you have a domain name that has to coexist with other messaging platforms within the company.

External relay domains are used when none of the recipients for that domain have a mailbox in the Exchange organization. Messages for that domain are relayed outside the Exchange organization, possibly even outside the company.

There's more...

E-mail address policies are used to provide users an e-mail address. Depending on your organizational structure and the number of accepted domains you have, you might end up with multiple e-mail address policies. This allows you to define a different set of e-mail addresses for different groups of people, for instance, per department or business unit.

Configuring e-mail address policies

The following command will create a new e-mail address policy that will give all recipient types in the `Accounting` department a default e-mail address in the following format: `firstname.lastname@exblog.com`:

```
New-EmailAddressPolicy -name "exblog.com" -ConditionalDepartment
"Accounting" -EnabledPrimarySMTPAddressTemplate "%g.%s@exblog.com" -
IncludedRecipients "All"
```

Perform the following steps through the EAC:

1. Navigate to **mail flow** | **email address policies**.
2. Click on the plus-sign (**+**) to start the **new email address policy** wizard.

3. Type a descriptive name, for example, `exblog.com`.
4. Click on the plus-sign (**+**) to create a new e-mail address format.
    - Select **exblog.com** from the list of accepted domains
    - Select **John.Smith@contoso.com**
    - Click on **save**
5. Select **All recipient types**.
6. Click on **add a rule** and select **Department**.
7. Type `Accounting` and click on **ok**.
8. Click on **save**.

See also

For more information on how domains are used in Exchange 2013, have a look at the following TechNet article: `http://technet.microsoft.com/en-us/library/jj673041.aspx`.

Configuring message size limits

This section explains us configuring message size limits.

Getting ready

To execute the following steps, log in to the Exchange Admin Center or launch the Exchange Management Shell.

How to do it...

The steps are explained in the following sections.

Configuring message size limits at organizational level

The following command will set the default organizational message size limits to 35 MB and will also limit the maximum amount of recipients per message to 250:

```
Set-TransportConfig -MaxReceiveSize "35MB" -MaxSendSize "35MB" -
MaxRecipientEnvelopeLimit "250"
```

Perform the following steps through the EAC:

1. Navigate to **mail flow** | **receive connectors**.
2. Click the three dots (**...**) to show more options and click organization transport settings.
3. Configure the limits as follows:
    - **Maximum number of recipients**: `250`
    - **Maximum receive message size (MB)**: `35`
    - **Maximum send message size (MB)**: `35`
4. Click on **save**.

Configuring message size limits at connector level

The following command will configure the default receive connector on `EX01` to only receive messages up to 35 MB:

```
Set-ReceiveConnector "EX01\Default EX01" -MaxMessagsize "35MB"
```

Perform the following steps through the EAC:

1. Navigate to **mail flow** | **receive connectors**.
2. Double-click on the connector you would like to edit.
3. Scroll down on the **general** tab and configure the following limit:
    - **Maximum receive message size (MB)**: `35`
4. Click on **save**.

Message size limits can be configured on all connector types: receive connectors and send connectors. They can also be applied both at the Client Access Server as the Mailbox Server role.

Configuring message size limits at mailbox level

Executing the following command will configure the mailbox of `Mark Spencer` so that it can receive and send messages up to 20 MB:

```
Set-Mailbox "mspencer" -MaxSendSize "27MB" -MaxReceiveSize "27MB"
```

Because of the conversion of messages in Exchange, you should make sure to configure a value that is approximately 33 percent higher than the size you want to limit. So for a messages size of 20 MB, you would configure 27 MB.

Perform the following steps through the EAC:

1. Navigate to **recipients** | **mailboxes**.
2. Double-click on the user you want to configure limits for.
3. Click on **mailbox features** and scroll down to **Message Size Restrictions**.
4. Click on **View details**.
5. Check **Maximum message size (KB)** and type: `27648` for both **Sent** and **Received** messages.
6. Click on **ok** and then click on **save**.

How it works...

Having to manage message size limits at various levels might be confusing at first, but it allows you to granularly apply different message sizes for different scenarios. There are three levels that size limits can be applied to:

- Organizational level
- Connector level
- Mailbox level

The best practice is to configure the most restrictive message size limit where messages enter your organization. Typically, this is at the connector level. By doing so, you avoid that the transport service will waste precious resources by processing a message that will be rejected by the organizational or user-level size limits anyway.

The organization level setting should always be the least restrictive setting within the organization. Limits configured at mailbox level take precedence over other configured size limits. At least this is the case when the limit at user level is configured as the most restrictive size limit.

If the size limit at mailbox level exceeds the one that is configured at the organizational level, the user-level size limit only takes precedence for messages that are sent within the organization. For all other traffic like from and to the Internet, the most restrictive size limits configured at the organizational level or connector level apply.

See also

For more information on message sizes and other configurable limits, have a look at the following TechNet article: `http://technet.microsoft.com/en-us/library/bb124345.aspx`.

5 Configuring External Access

In this chapter, you will learn how to perform the tasks necessary to successfully make Exchange available outside of your network by taking a closer look at the following tasks:

- Configuring Exchange workloads for external access
- Configuring the Autodiscover service to work externally
- Configuring Outlook Anywhere to support external access
- Publishing Exchange 2013 to the Internet using TMG 2010
- Publishing Exchange 2013 to the Internet using UAG 2010
- Publishing Exchange 2013 to the Internet without using a reverse proxy solution

Introduction

In a world where almost everyone and everything is connected to the Internet, it's a no-brainer to provide employees with access to corporate e-mail from outside the boundaries of the corporate network, like for example from home. There are various ways how to interact with Exchange remotely, including the use of smart phones, tablets or regular desktops and laptops. In the early days, the IT department usually had control over all these devices as well as what devices were allowed to connect. Nowadays, with the hype around **Bring-Your-Own-Device** (**BYOD**), it seems that companies stray away from this ideology and encourage people to use their own devices.

Because the IT department cannot always control the endpoints, it's important that when Exchange is made available externally, it's done securely.

Securely providing remote access to Exchange can be done in different ways and usually involves multiple configuration steps that range from configuring Exchange to support external access to publishing the different workloads onto the Internet; with or without a reverse proxy.

A reverse proxy is a server or appliance that usually resides in the perimeter network and serves as an endpoint for external connections. It acts as a sort of "man-in-the-middle" and will fetch the requested internal resources on the behalf of the connecting user and return them as if the reverse proxy was the originator.

Aside from its primary function, many reverse proxies can also perform additional tasks like, for instance, (pre-) authentication or connection filtering. Strictly seen, these features are not required to allow Exchange to be available from the Internet. However, sometimes company policies dictate additional security be implemented, which might require you to configure these features.

Configuring Exchange workloads for external access

To complete the following steps, you can either use the Exchange Management Shell or the Exchange Admin Center. We assume a single external hostname (`outlook.exblog.be`) is used for all workloads.

How to do it...

In this section we will cover the different tasks involved with configuring different Exchange workloads for external access:

Configuring Outlook Web App

To configure an external URL for the Outlook Web App Virtual Directory, run the following command:

```
Set-OwavirtualDirectory -Identity "owa (Default WebSite)" -
  ExternalUrl https://outlook.exblog.be/owa
```

To make these changes for multiple servers at once, you could pipe the results from the `Get-OwaVirtualDirectory` command to the `Set-OwaVirtualDirectory` as shown in the following command line:

```
Get-OwaVirtualDirectory | Set-OwavirtualDirectory -Identity "owa (Default
WebSite)" -ExternalUrl https://outlook.exblog.be/owa
```

Also, if you want to change the OWA Virtual directory for a specific server, you could do so like this:

```
Get-OwaVirtualDirectory -Server EX2013-01 | Set-OwavirtualDirectory
  -Identity "owa (Default WebSite)" -ExternalUrl
  https://outlook.exblog.be/owa
```

Alternatively, the same actions can be performed through the Exchange Admin Center:

1. Navigate to **Servers** | **virtual directories**.
2. Double-click on **owa (Default Web Site)** on the Internet-facing Client Access Server.
3. On the **general** tab, enter `https://outlook.exblog.be/owa` in the **External URL** field.

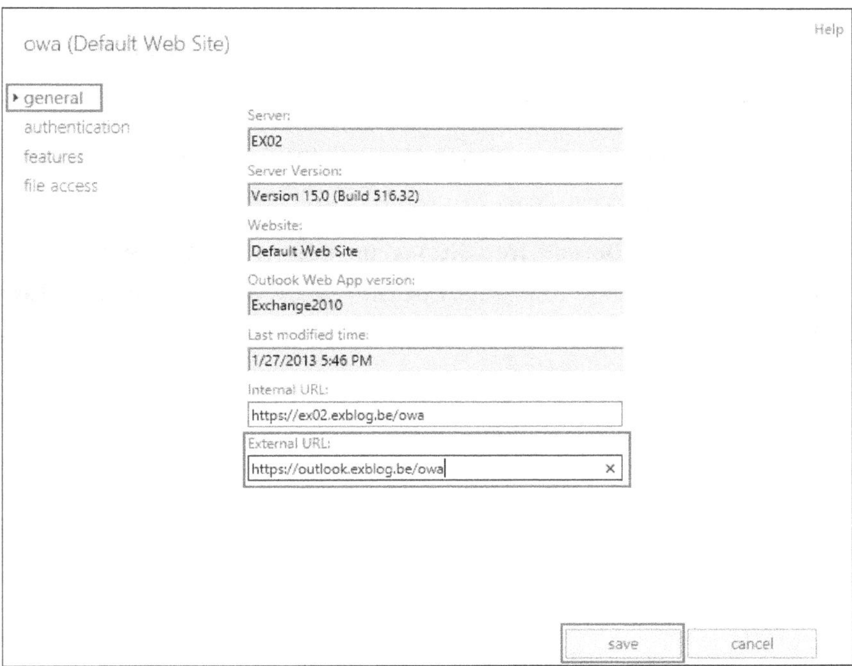

4. Click on **save**.

Remember to execute this step for each Internet-facing Client Access Server.

Configuring the Exchange Admin Center

Run the following command to configure an External URL for the Exchange Admin Center virtual directory (ECP):

```
Set-EcpvirtualDirectory -Identity "ecp (Default WebSite)" -
  ExternalUrl https://outlook.exblog.be/ecp
```

To make these changes for multiple servers at once, you could pipe the results from the `Get-EcpVirtualDirectory` command to the `Set-EcpVirtualDirectory`:

```
Get-EcpVirtualDirectory | Set-EcpvirtualDirectory -Identity "ecp
  (Default WebSite)" -ExternalUrl https://outlook.exblog.be/ecp
```

Also, if you want to change the ECP Virtual directory for a specific server, you could do so like this:

```
Get-EcpVirtualDirectory -Server EX2013-01 | Set-EcpvirtualDirectory
  -Identity "ecp (Default WebSite)" -ExternalUrl
  https://outlook.exblog.be/ecp
```

Alternatively, the same action can be performed through the Exchange Admin Center:

1. Navigate to **Servers** | **virtual directories**.
2. Double-click on **ecp (Default Web Site)** on the Internet-facing Client Access Server.
3. On the **general** tab, enter `https://outlook.exblog.be/ecp` in the **External URL** field.

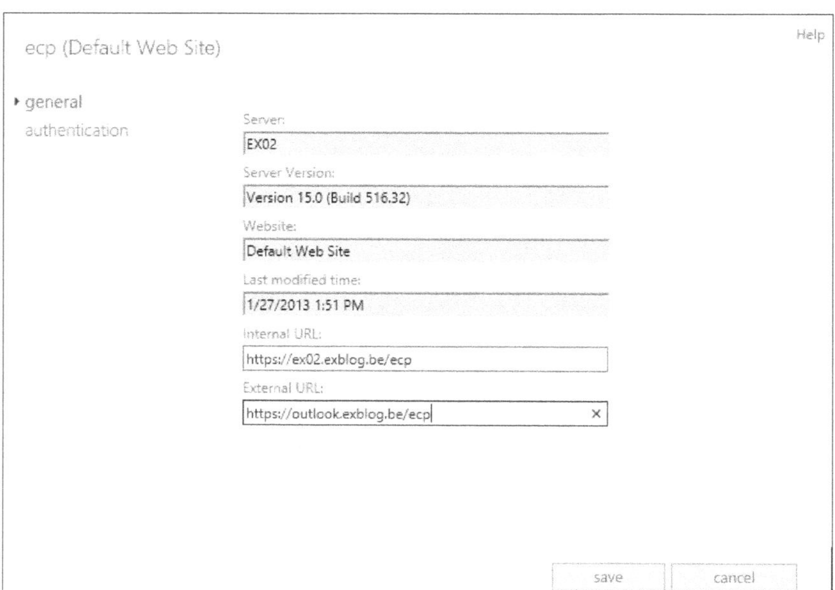

4. Click on **save**.

[ Remember to execute this step for each Internet-facing Client Access Server.]

Configuring Exchange Web Services

Run the following command to configure an External URL for the **Exchange Web Services** (**EWS**) virtual directory:

```
Set-WebServicesvirtualDirectory -Identity "EWS (Default WebSite)"
  -ExternalUrl https://outlook.exblog.be/EWS/Exchange.asmx
```

To make these changes for multiple servers at once, you could pipe the results from the `Get-WebServicesVirtualDirectory` command to the `Set-WebServicesVirtualDirectory`:

```
Get-WebServicesVirtualDirectory | Set-WebServicesvirtualDirectory
  -Identity "EWS (Default WebSite)" -ExternalUrl
  https://outlook.exblog.be/EWS/Exchange.asmx
```

Also, if you want to change the EWS Virtual directory for a specific server, you could do so like this:

```
Get-WebServicesVirtualDirectory -Server EX2013-01 | Set-
  WebServicesvirtualDirectory -Identity "EWS (Default WebSite)"
  -ExternalUrl https://outlook.exblog.be/EWS/Exchange.asmx
```

Alternatively, the same action can be performed through the Exchange Admin Center:

1. Navigate to **Servers** | **virtual directories**.
2. Double-click on **EWS (Default Web Site)** on the Internet-facing Client Access Server.
3. Click on **general**.

4. Enter `https://outlook.exblog.be/EWS/Exchange.asmx` in the **External URL** field.

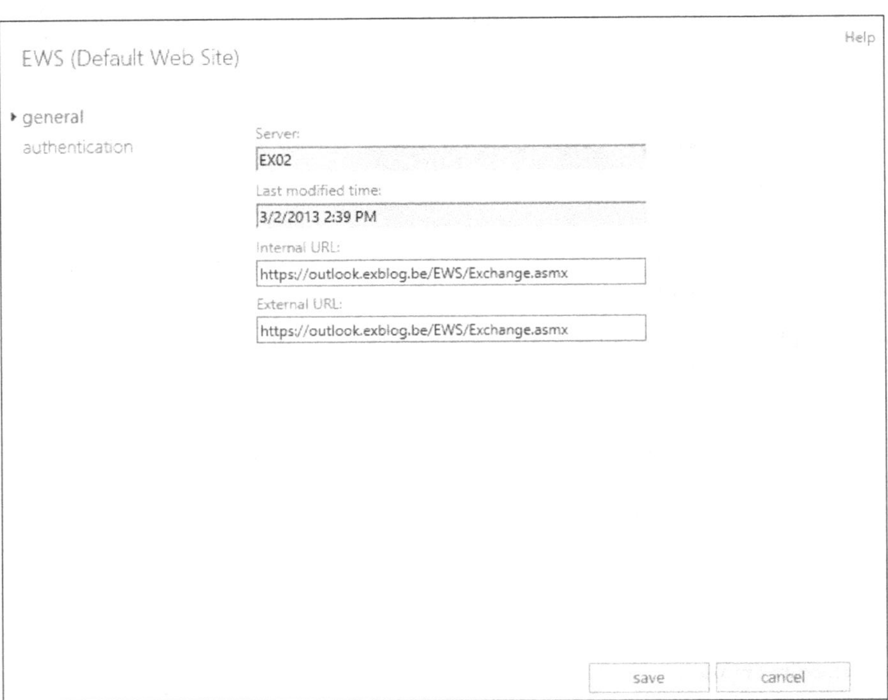

5. Click on **save**.

Remember to execute this step for each Internet-facing Client Access Server.

Configuring the Offline Address Book

Run the following command to configure an External URL for the **Offline Address Book** (**OAB**) virtual directory:

```
Set-OABvirtualDirectory -Identity "OAB (Default WebSite)"
  -ExternalUrl https://outlook.exblog.be/OAB
```

To make these changes for multiple servers at once, you could pipe the results from the `Get-OABVirtualDirectory` command to the `Set-OABVirtualDirectory`:

```
Get-OABVirtualDirectory | Set-OABvirtualDirectory -Identity "OAB
  (Default WebSite)" -ExternalUrl https://outlook.exblog.be/OAB
```

Also, if you want to change the OAB Virtual directory for a specific server, you could do so as follows:

```
Get-OABVirtualDirectory -Server EX2013-01 | Set-OABvirtualDirectory
  -Identity "OAB (Default WebSite)" -ExternalUrl
  https://outlook.exblog.be/OAB
```

Alternatively, the same action can be performed through the Exchange Admin Center:

1. Navigate to **Servers | virtual directories**.
2. Double-click on **OAB (Default Web Site)** on the Internet-facing Client Access Server.
3. Click on **general**.
4. Enter `https://outlook.exblog.be/OAB` in the **External URL** field.

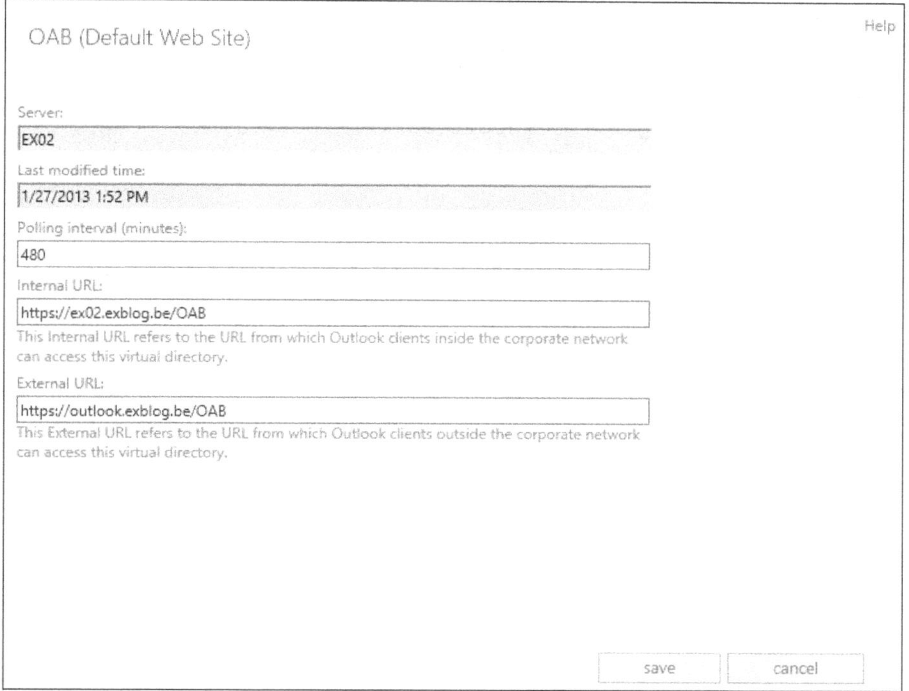

5. Click on **save**.

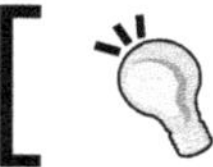

Remember to execute this step for each Internet-facing Client Access Server.

Configuring ActiveSync

Run the following command to configure an External URL for Exchange ActiveSync:

```
Set-ActiveSyncvirtualDirectory -Identity "Microsoft-Server-ActiveSync
  (Default WebSite)" -ExternalUrl
  https://outlook.exblog.be/Microsoft-Server-ActiveSync
```

To make these changes for multiple servers at once, you could pipe the results from the `Get-ActiveSyncVirtualDirectory` command to the `Set-ActiveSyncVirtualDirectory`:

```
Get-ActiveSyncVirtalDirectory | Set-ActiveSyncvirtualDirectory -Identity
"Microsoft-Server-ActiveSync (Default WebSite)" -ExternalUrl https://
outlook.exblog.be/Microsoft-Server-ActiveSync
```

Also, if you want to change the ActiveSync Virtual directory for a specific server, you could do so like this:

```
Get-ActiveSyncVirtalDirectory -Server EX2013-01 | Set-
  ActiveSyncvirtualDirectory -Identity "Microsoft-Server-ActiveSync
  (Default WebSite)" -ExternalUrl
  https://outlook.exblog.be/Microsoft-Server-ActiveSync
```

Alternatively, the same action can be performed through the Exchange Admin Center:

1. Navigate to **Servers** | **virtual directories**.
2. Double-click on **Microsoft-Server-ActiveSync (Default Web Site)** on the Internet-facing Client Access Server.
3. Click on **general**.
4. Enter `https://outlook.exblog.be/Microsoft-Server-ActiveSync` in the **External URL** field.

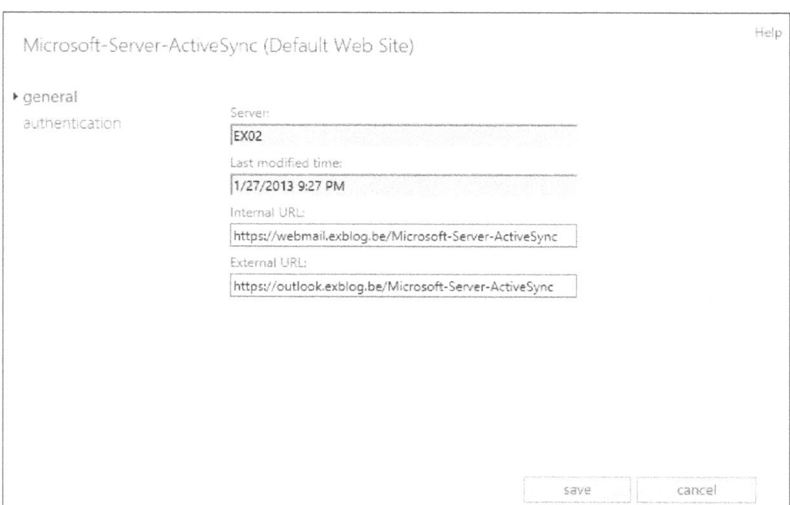

5. Click on **save**.

Remember to execute this step for each Internet-facing Client Access Server.

How it works...

By defining an External URL for each Exchange workload, you ensure that the connection information for these workloads is discoverable through the Autodiscover process.

Without the configuration of these URLs, the values wouldn't be exposed to the client and therefore the client would not know where to connect to. Except for configuring the different URL values, possibly changing the authentication methods and making sure that certificates are configured correctly, there isn't much configuration work required on the Exchange-side of things to make these workloads available externally.

However, only configuring the External URL values, by itself, won't provide external access. You will also have to make sure that, for each External URL value that you configured, a matching host record is available in your domain's external DNS zone and that the Exchange workloads are published correctly onto the Internet.

Make sure to read the *Configuring Certificates* section in *Chapter 3, Configuring the Client Access Server role* for more information on correctly configuring Certificates.

There's more...

Some companies rather don't expose their management tools directly onto the Internet. Because a great part of the management tasks related to Exchange can be performed using the EAC, it might fall under umbrella of tools that have to be disabled.

The article on `http://technet.microsoft.com/en-us/library/jj218639.aspx` describes how to turn off EAC for users coming from the Internet. However, Exchange has no way of knowing the difference between internal and external traffic. Following the steps outlined in the article won't really help you as it would turn off the EAC for everyone.

The only way to work around this problem, is to create a dedicated CAS or array of Client Access Servers that will be used for inbound access to the EAC from the Internet. Then you disable the EAC on those servers. Basically, you make sure that internal traffic and external traffic are using different Client Access Servers for EAC.

Turning off the Exchange Admin Center

When you're ready to disable the EAC, run the following command from the Exchange Management Shell:

```
Set-ECPVirtualDirectory -Identity "EX2013-2\ecp (default web site)"
  -AdminEnabled $false
```

See also

Have a look at *Chapter 2, Installing Exchange Server 2013* for more information on namespace planning and design.

Configuring Autodiscover

Making Autodiscover available externally is relatively easy. Normally, there is little to no additional configuration required within Exchange itself. Just like other Exchange workloads, the Autodiscover service uses a Virtual Directory that has an internal and External URL value. In contrast to the other workloads these values aren't used at all. In fact, the Exchange 2013 Management Shell won't allow you to configure these values anymore.

In order for the Autodiscover service to work externally, you'll need to have the following:

- An entry for the Autodiscover hostname on your Exchange Certificate. This can either be the certificate's Subject Name or one of the Subject Alternative Names (SAN). For example: Autodiscover.exblog.be
- A host entry in the external DNS zone for your domain that points to your on-premise Exchange environment. For example:

Type	Name	TTL	IP
A	`Autodiscover.exblog.be`	3600 s.	10.20.30.40

As long as you have a single primary e-mail domain, this configuration ought to be enough. However, when you are using multiple (primary) e-mail domains, configuring Autodiscover can sometimes become challenging because of the additional certificate requirements.

Of course, creating the DNS records isn't enough. You will also have to expose the Autodiscover virtual directory to external clients by publishing it onto the Internet.

Getting ready

To execute the following steps, you will need access to the IIS Manager on the Client Access Server(s). The server(s) that you will be configuring require an additional IP address that isn't bound to the Default Web Site.

Publishing SRV records will require you to logon to the administration tool of your external DNS zone. The tool or web application that is used to make these changes usually depend on the DNS provider you are working with.

Both examples below also assume that the "primary" Autodiscover URL (the one that is on the Exchange certificate) is "Autodiscover.exblog.be".

How to do it...

Redirecting Autodiscover is one of the solutions you can implement when you have additional, potentially a large amount, of primary e-mail domains in your Exchange organization.

Configuring Autodiscover redirection when using multiple primary e-mail domains through IIS

First, we will create a new website that is bound to an IP address:

1. Open the IIS Manager on your Internet-facing Client Access Server(s).
2. Right-click on your server node and select **Add Website...**.
3. Enter `RedirectAutodiscover` in the **Site Name** field and select a path where to store the new website. For example: `C:\inetpub\ RedirectAutodiscover`.
4. Under **Binding**, enter the IP address that isn't configured on the default website yet.

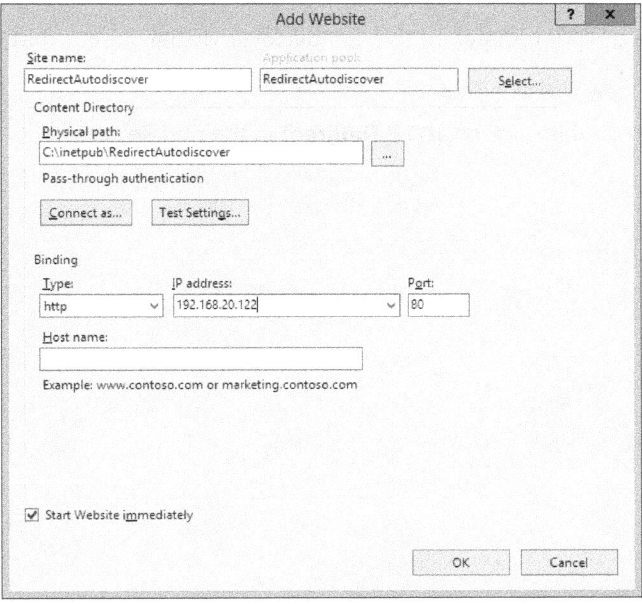

5. Click on **OK**.

Next, we will configure a new Autodiscover virtual directory in the website we just created:

1. Right-click on the newly created website and click on **Add Virtual Directory...**.
2. Under **Alias**, enter `Autodiscover`.
3. Select `C:\inetPub\RedirectoAutodiscover\Autodiscover` as the Physical Path.

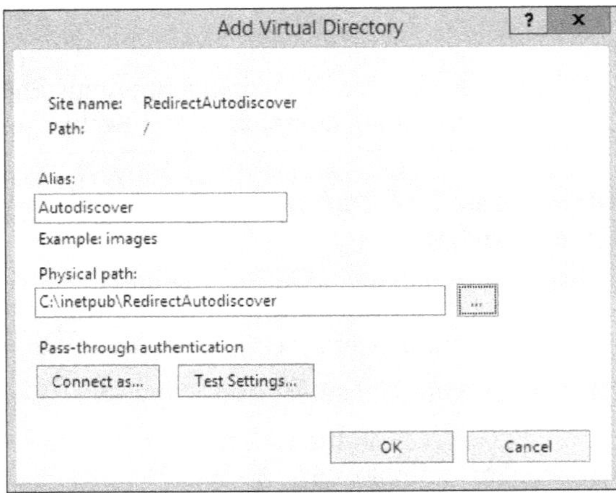

4. Click on **OK**.

Next, we will create a HTTP redirect on the Autodiscover virtual directly that was just created:

1. Select the new virtual directory.
2. Locate and double-click on **HTTP Redirect** in the middle pane.

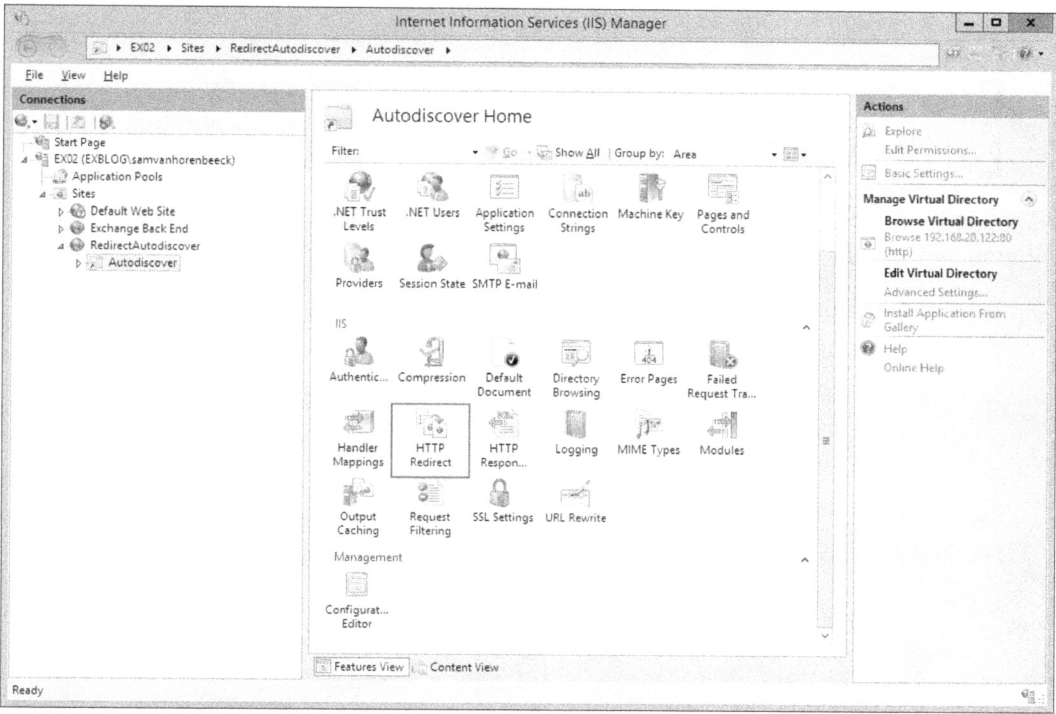

3. Select **Redirect requests to this destination:** and enter the following hostname: `https://Autodiscover.exblog.be/Autodiscover`.
4. Select **Redirect all requests to exact destination...** and **Only redirect requests to content in this directory....**
5. Make sure to select **Found (302)** from the drop-down list.

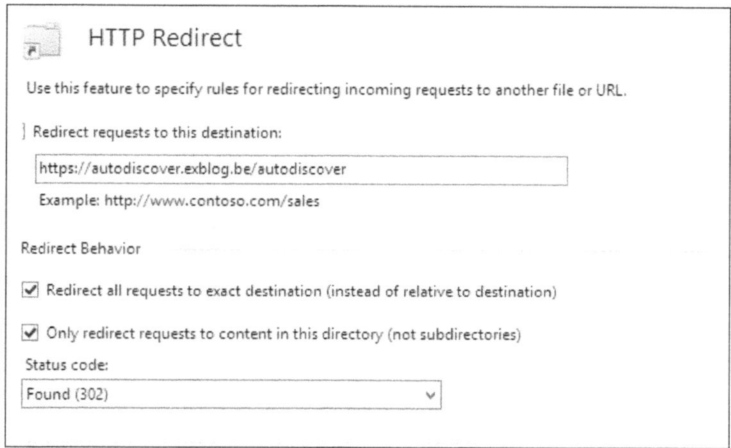

6. Click on **Apply** in the action pane.

There is no hard requirement to use IIS to configure the redirection. Other ways, including the usage of TMG, UAG, or a load balancer to issue the redirect are also supported.

Optionally, you can configure the website to only respond to requests coming from your different Autodiscover hostnames:

1. Right-click on the **RedirectAutodiscover** website and select **Edit Bindings...**.
2. Click on **Add...**.
3. Select the IP Address that is bound to this website. Make sure port **80** is selected.
4. Enter the Autodiscover hostname for one of your domains. For example: `Autodiscover.domain2.com`.
5. Repeat steps 2 to 4 for each primary e-mail domain.

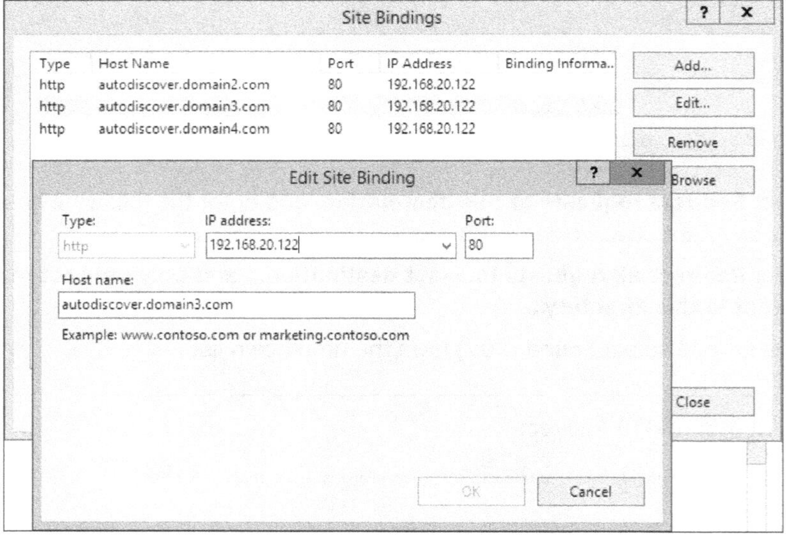

The last step is to publish a CNAME record for each of the e-mail domains that require to be redirected. The following table provides an example of the records you might need to create:

Type	Host	TTL	Target
CNAME	Domain2.com	300	`Autodiscover.exblog.be`
CNAME	Domain3.com	300	`Autodiscover.exblog.be`

Using SRV records record

We cannot show you how to configure SRV records for your domain as that will depend on the DNS provider you are working with.

However, the following table will provide you with an overview of the values you need to configure for the SRV records in each domain:

Type	Service	Protocol	Priority	Weight	Port	Host
SRV	_Autodiscover	_tcp	1	100	443	Autodiscover.exblog.be

How it works...

Clients that support Autodiscover will automatically construct the URL they need to connect to from the user's primary e-mail address. For that, they'll use the e-mail domain of the primary e-mail address.

For example, the e-mail address `mark@exblog.be` will automatically yield the following URLs:

- `Exblog.be/Autodiscover`
- `Autodiscover.exblog.be`

In an ideal world, you would create an entry on your Exchange certificate for each e-mail domain that is used in primary e-mail addresses. Basically, you have to create an additional subject name for each e-mail domain and add it to the **Subject Alternative Names** (**SAN**) of the certificate. Given that most Certificate Authorities charge a few dollars extra per SAN, companies that have a large number of e-mail domains might end up having to pay quite a lot for their certificate.

In that case, you have two options to work around this problem:

- Redirect Autodiscover traffic for other e-mail domains to the one e-mail domain hat is configured on the certificate

  OR

- Create a SRV record in the external DNS zone for each (primary) e-mail domain

Each option has its upsides and downsides: redirecting Autodiscover usually works very well (on all types of devices), but it requires additional configuration which can be a bit tricky. Configuring a SRV record is far less complicated than configuring redirection but it might not work for all devices. Especially mobile devices such as tablets and smart phones in particular have a bad track record with the latter method.

The following steps outline the process of how redirection works when an Outlook client tries to connect:

1. The external client tries connecting to the Autodiscover URL that was constructed from the user's primary e-mail domain. This could for example be `Autodiscover.domain2.com`.
2. After being unable to connect over HTTPS, the client will automatically try connecting using HTTP. This connection is now allowed and will issue an HTTP-redirect (302) to the primary Autodiscover URL, which is the URL for which we do have an entry on the Exchange certificate.
3. The user is prompted with a warning, asking them to confirm the redirection.
4. After confirming, the client connects to "primary" Autodiscover URL and can now successfully request Autodiscover information.

When choosing to use a SRV record in the external DNS zone, no additional configuration in Exchange is required. Whenever a client cannot connect to `domain.com/Autodiscover` and it does not find a host record for Autodiscover, it will try locating the Autodiscover service by querying DNS for a SRV record.

This SRV records will, just like the host name, point to the primary Autodiscover namespace, which results in the exact same behavior (including the warning) as when a client is redirected.

Please note that the SRV method only works with Outlook 2007 clients and newer. Given Outlook 2007 and higher are the only versions of Outlook supported with Exchange 2013, that shouldn't be much of a problem.

Not all clients that connect to Exchange support the use of SRV records. Usually mobile devices have a bad track record when it comes to supporting this feature.

Another problem with using SRV records is that not all DNS providers support creating them, possibly leaving you with no other alternative than to use redirection.

The table below summarizes the different options you have for making Autodiscover available externally:

	Pros	**Cons**
"Regular" configuration	Works as expected. Fully transparent to the user.	Requires an Autodiscover-entry on the Exchange certificate for every primary e-mail domain.

	Pros	Cons
Redirection	No additional namespaces required on the Exchange certificate	Harder to setup, requires additional configuration. Not transparent to users. They get a warning (which they can choose to ignore). Requires additional IP address on Exchange server.
SRV record	No additional namespaces required on the Exchange certificate	Not transparent to users. They get a warning (which they can choose to ignore). Not supported on all devices. Some DNS providers do not allow creation on SRV records.

See also

The feature that allows accessing Autodiscover externally by publishing SRV records to the external DNS zone, is also described in the article at `http://support.microsoft.com/kb/940881`.

Check "Publishing Exchange onto the Internet through TMG 2010" for more information on how to configure redirection using TMG 2010.

Configuring Outlook Anywhere to support external access

In order to execute the following steps, you either need to login to the Exchange Admin Center or run the Exchange Management Shell.

How to do it...

The following command will configure an external hostname and set the authentication mechanism to basic:

```
Set-OutlookAnywhere "EX02\Rpc (Default Web Site)" -ExternalHostName
  outlook.exblog.be -ExternalClientAuthenticationMethod Basic
```

Alternatively, you can achieve the same goal using the Exchange Admin Center:

1. Navigate to **servers** | **servers**.
2. Double-click on the Client Access Server EX02.
3. Go to Outlook Anywhere.
4. Enter the external hostname as `outlook.exblog.be`.
5. Change the external authentication method to **Basic** and click on **Save**.

Please note that it might take up to 15 minutes before these changes become effective. When the Outlook Anywhere settings are updated, you'll see an Informational event (Event ID 3025) from "MSExchange RPC over HTTP Autoconfig" in the Application Event Log.

How it works...

Just like other virtual directories, you are required to specify an external hostname for Outlook Anywhere. This hostname is returned to the client during the Autodiscover process, allowing it to connect to Exchange even when they're not within the boundaries of the corporate network.

Internal and external connections can be configured to use different authentication mechanisms. However, in a split-DNS configuration the internal and external hostname could potentially be the same. In such case, the internal authentication methods is used both internally as externally. Only when the authentication fails, the client would fall back to using the external authentication method.

See also

Be sure to check *Chapter 4, Configuring and Managing the Mailbox Server Role* for more information on how RPC-over-HTTPS (Outlook Anywhere) works under the cheats.

Publishing Exchange onto the Internet through TMG 2010

Although Microsoft stopped distribution and active development of their TMG product in December 2012, it remains supported until 2015. Some customers are already using TMG and at the moment there are vendors that still sell TMG 2010 as an appliance for which they will continue to offer support for a while to come. Therefore, it is useful to have a look at how you can configure the TMG to work with Exchange 2013.

Despite all the modifications to make the TMG work in combination with Exchange 2013, it will present the user with an Exchange 2010-based login form. If you do not want this, for example because your users find it confusing, you will either have to create a custom login form for the TMG or revert to using another reverse-proxy solution.

Getting ready

In order to execute the following steps, you will need to have a server running the latest version of Microsoft's **Threat Management Gateway 2010** (**TMG**). This server needs to be Internet connected and have at least a single free external IP address. You should also have installed the Exchange certificate onto the machine. Although it's not a requirement, we assume that you have created a server farm to which you've added your Exchange Client Access Servers. Like in the previous examples, we will be using a single external hostname for all workloads: `outlook.exblog.be`.

Lastly, in all of our examples, our environment is configured for split DNS. Split DNS means that your internal and external DNS zones have the same name. For example: "exblog.be".

How to do it...

First, we will create a new listener. This listener will be bound to the external IP Address for your Exchange environment and configured with the Exchange certificate. Perform the following steps:

1. Open the TMG Management console and navigate to **Firewall Policy**.
2. In the right-hand side pane, click on **Network Objects**, then right-click on **Web Listeners** and select **New Web Listener...**.
3. Enter a name for the listener, for example `Exchange SSL`.
4. On the next page, select **Require SSL** secured connections with clients and click on **Next**.
5. Select the network through which incoming requests are sent to the TMG server. Depending on your TMG configuration this will likely be the External network. Click on **Next**.
6. Select **Use a single certificate for this Web Listener** and click on **Select Certificate...**. From the Select Certificate screen, select the Exchange certificate that you installed previously and click on **Select**.
7. Click on **Next**.
8. Select **HTML Form Authentication** from the drop-down list, select **Windows (Active Directory)** and click on **Next**.

9. Select **Enable SSO for Web sites...** and enter your domain name in the **SSO Domain name** field. For example `exblog.be`.
10. Click on **Finish**.

Now that we have created a listener, we can continue publishing Exchange onto the Internet. We will be using the built-in Publishing Rule Wizard, therefore having to run it three times. Once for ActiveSync, Once for OWA and one time for Outlook Anywhere.

Creating a publishing rule for ActiveSync

1. Right-click on **Firewall Policy**. Hover over **New** and select **Exchange Web Client Access Publishing Rule....**
2. Enter `Exchange ActiveSync` as name for the rule. Click on **Next**.
3. Select **Exchange Server 2010** as the Exchange version, then select **Exchange ActiveSync** and click on **Next**.
4. Select **Public a server farm of load balanced Web servers** and click on **Next**.
5. Select **Use SSL to connect...** and click on **Next**.
6. Enter `outlook.exblog.be` for the internal site name and click on **Next**.
7. Select the server farm you created earlier and click on **Next**.
8. Select **This domain name (type below)** and enter the external hostname of your Exchange. For example: `outlook.exblog.be`.
9. Select the web listener you created earlier and click on **Next**.
10. Select **Basic Authentication** from the drop-down list and click on **Next**.
11. Make sure that **All Authenticated Users** is in the list of user sets. However, if you want to limit access to a specific group of people, you can define other groups. Click on **Next**.
12. Click on **Finish**.

The TMG server will delegate credentials to the Client Access Servers using basic authentication. For this to work, however, the virtual directories on the Client Access Servers have to be configured for basic authentication. Have a look at the *Configuring basic authentication* section for more information.

You now successfully configured Exchange ActiveSync for external access. There are no additional configuration steps to make it work except for adding a host name (`outlook.exblog.be`) in your external DNS zone that points to the external IP address of the TMG.

Creating a publishing rule for OWA

1. Right-click on **Firewall Policy**. Hover over **New** and select **Exchange Web Client Access Publishing Rule...**.
2. Enter `Exchange OWA` as name for the rule. Click on **Next**.
3. Select **Exchange Server 2010** as the Exchange version, then select **Outlook Web Access** and click on **Next**.
4. Select **Publish a server farm of load balanced Web servers** and click on **Next**.
5. Select **Use SSL to connect...** and click on **Next**.
6. Enter `outlook.exblog.be` for the internal site name and click on **Next**.
7. Select the Server farm you created earlier and click on **Next**.
8. Select **This domain name (type below)** and enter the external hostname of your Exchange. For example: `outlook.exblog.be`.
9. Select the web listener you created earlier and click on **Next**.
10. Select **Basic Authentication** from the drop-down list and click on **Next**.
11. Make sure that **All Authenticated Users** is in the list of user sets. However, if you want to limit access to a specific group of people, you can define other groups. Click on **Next**.
12. Click on **Finish**.

The TMG server will delegate credentials to the Client Access Servers using basic authentication. For this to work, however, the virtual directories on the Client Access Servers have to be configured for basic authentication. Have a look at the *Configuring basic authentication* section for more information.

Before putting it into production, the publishing rule needs to be modified in order to fully work with Exchange 2013. First the logoff URL needs to be modified:

1. Double-click on the **Exchange OWA** publishing rule.
2. Click on the **Application Settings** tab and change the Published server logoff URL to `/owa/logoff.owa`.

3. Next, in order to support the new App model, a new publishing rule needs to be created and modified accordingly. However, before moving on, execute the following steps to record the `ExchangeGUID` of your organization mailbox. We will use this GUID in the next steps.
4. Open the Exchange Management shell and run the following command:

```
Get-Mailbox -Arbitration | where {$_.PersistedCapabilities
  -like "OrganizationCapabilityClientExtensions"} | fl
  exchangeGUID, PrimarySmtpAddress
```

5. From the output, copy the value of the ExchangeGUID between brackets:

6. Add `@domain` after the GUID you just copied. The result should be something similar to `bb558c35-97f1-4cb9-8ff7-d53741dc928c@exchangelab.be`. Write down or copy this value for later use.

The last step involves creating and editing a new Publishing Rule:

1. Create a new publishing rule for OWA using the steps outlined earlier. You could for instance name this new publishing rule **Exchange OWA 2013**.
2. Make sure to assign this new publishing rule a higher priority than the existing one for OWA:

3. Double-click on the new publishing rule and select the **Paths** tab.
4. Remove all pre-filled paths and add a new one, constructed from the value you recorded earlier: `/owa/ bb558c35-97f1-4cb9-8ff7-d53741dc928c@exchangelab.be/*`.

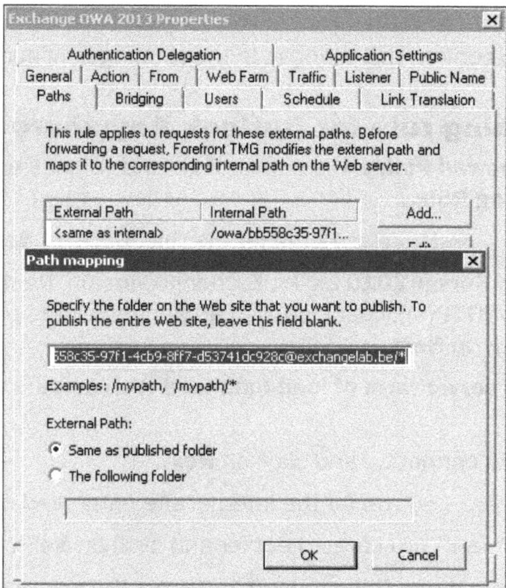

5. Click on the **Users** tab and change **All authenticated users** to **All users**.

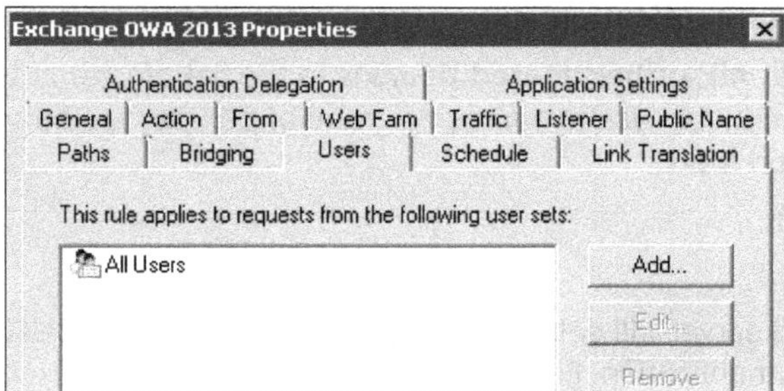

6. Click on the **Authentication Delegation** tab and select **No delegation, but client may authenticate directly** from the drop-down list.

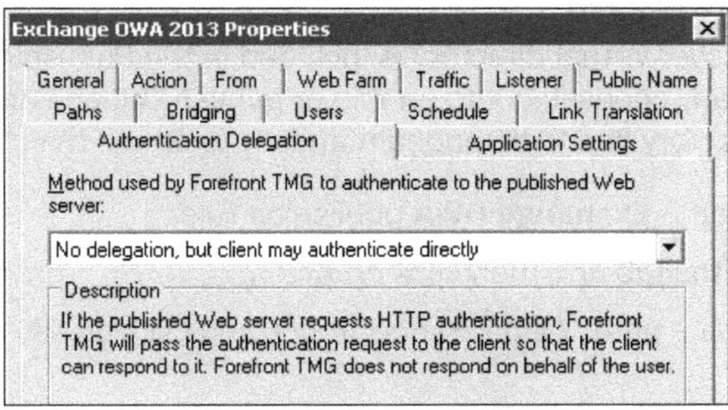

7. Click on **OK**
8. Click on **Apply** to confirm the changes to the running configuration of the TMG.

Creating a publishing rule for Outlook Anywhere

1. Right-click on **Firewall Policy**. Hover over **New** and select **Exchange Web Client Access Publishing Rule...**.
2. Enter `Outlook Anywhere` as name for the rule. Click on **Next**.
3. Select **Exchange Server 2010** as the Exchange version, then select **Outlook Anywhere (RPC/HTTP(s))**, check publish additional folders on the **Exchange Server...** and click on **Next**.
4. Select **Publish a server farm of load balanced Web servers** and click on **Next**.
5. Select **Use SSL to connect...** and click on **Next**.
6. Enter `outlook.exblog.be` for the internal site name and click on **Next**.
7. Select the Server farm you created earlier and click on **Next**.
8. Select **This domain name (type below)** and enter the external hostname of your Exchange. For example: `outlook.exblog.be`.
9. Select the web listener you created earlier and click on **Next**.
10. Select **Basic Authentication** from the drop-down list and click on **Next**.
11. Make sure that **All Authenticated Users** is in the list of user sets. However, if you want to limit access to a specific group of people, you can define other groups. Click on **Next**.
12. Click on **Finish**.

The TMG server will delegate credentials to the Client Access Servers using basic authentication. For this to work, however, the virtual directories on the Client Access Servers have to be configured for basic authentication. Have a look at the *Configuring basic authentication* section for more information.

Publishing Autodiscover

By default, the Autodiscover virtual directory is included in the Publishing Rule for Outlook Anywhere. If your company chooses not to enable or publish Outlook Anywhere, the Autodiscover virtual directory has to be added manually to one of the other publishing rules:

1. Double-click on the **Exchange OWA** publishing rule.
2. Click on the **Paths** tab and then click on **Add...**.
3. Enter the following path: `/Autodiscover/*` and click on **OK**.
4. Click on **Apply**.

Configuring basic authentication

Run the following commands to enable the virtual directories for basic authentication:

```
Set-OABVirtualDirectory "EX02\*"-BasicAuthentication:$true
Set-WebServicesVirtualDirectory "EX02\*" -BasicAuthentication:$true
Set-OwaVirtualDirectory "EX02\*" -BasicAuthentication:$true
Set-EcpVirtualDirectory "EX02\*" -BasicAuthentication:$true
```

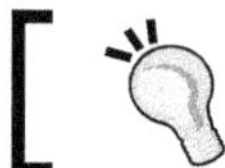

Make sure to run `iisreset` on the Client Access Server(s) after changing the authentication method.

How it works...

Typically, a topology including a TMG would look something like the following diagram:

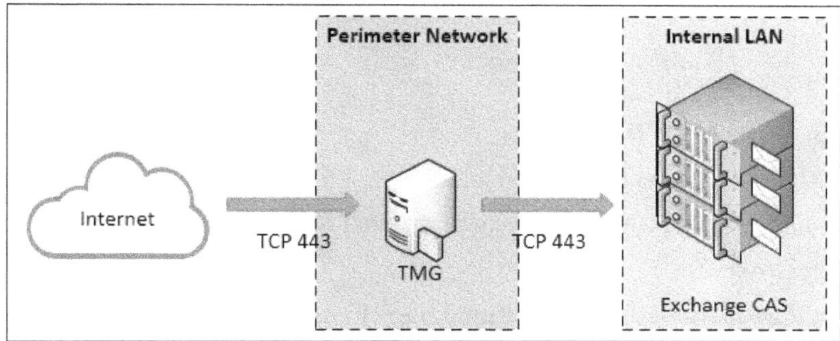

The TMG server acts as a "barrier" between the Internet and your on-premises Exchange organization. External traffic will flow through your TMG server, where it will be authenticated before hitting your internal CAS servers. This process is also referred to as pre-authentication.

Despite the fact that the Client Access Server in Exchange 2013 also does some form of pre-authentication, companies sometimes still require traffic to be authenticated before entering the corporate network. Because a Client Access Server must not be placed in the perimeter network, but the TMG typically is, the latter might be a better choice.

Additionally, a TMG integrates more easily with one-time password (OTP) solutions making it the overall better choice if dual factor authentication is a requirement.

Publishing Exchange onto the Internet through UAG 2010 SP3

Getting ready

In order to execute the following steps, you will need to have a server running UAG 2010 Service Pack 3. The server needs to be Internet connected and have at least two network adapters: one connected to the internal network and to the perimeter network.

Furthermore, we assume that you already installed the Exchange certificate onto the server and that you configured an authentication server using the **Authentication and Authorization Servers...** wizard from the **Admin** menu.

Although Service Pack 3 for UAG 2010 officially added support for Exchange Server 2013, users will be presented with an Exchange 2010 Login-form for OWA. If this isn't something you want, you'll have to use another reverse-proxy solution.

How to do it...

Creating a new HTTPS-trunk

1. Open the UAG Management Console.
2. Right-click on **HTTPS Connections** and select **New Trunk**.
3. Click on **Next**.
4. Select **Portal Trunk** and check **Publish Exchange applications via the portal**.

It might be a bit confusing, but even though you are selecting to publish Exchange applications via the portal, running this wizard will not require users to login to the portal first.

5. Specify a trunk name, for example `ExchangeTrunk` and enter the public host name: `Outlook.exblog.be`.
6. Select the external IP address of the UAG server and click on **Next**.
7. Click on **Add...** to add the authentication server(s) you created previously. Leave the other settings by their defaults and click on **Next**.
8. Make sure to select the Exchange certificate and click on **Next**.
9. Select **Use Forefront UAG access policies**, then click on **Next**.
10. On the **Endpoint Policies** page, leave the defaults and click on **Next**.

11. On the **Select Exchange Services** page, choose **Microsoft Exchange Server 2013** from the version list and only check the box next to **Outlook Web Access**. Then click on **Next**.
12. Enter the following name: `OWA 2013` and click on **Next**.
13. Leave the default endpoint policies and click on **Next**.
14. Select **Configure a farm of application servers** and click on **Next**.
15. Add your Client Access Servers to the list of addresses. In our example, we added only `EX02.exblog.be`. Then click on **Next**.
16. Given that Exchange 2013 does not require any affinity, you can select the option **IP-based affinity** under **Balance requests using** Click on **Next**.
17. On the **Configure Connectivity Verifiers** page, select **Establish a TCP connection** and click on **Next**.
18. Add your previously create Authentication servers to the list and click on **Next**.
19. Leave the default values and click on **Next**.
20. On the **Exchange Application Authorization** page, leave the defaults and click on **Next**.
21. Click on **Finish**.

Before the new trunk is operational, you will need to save and activate the current configuration:

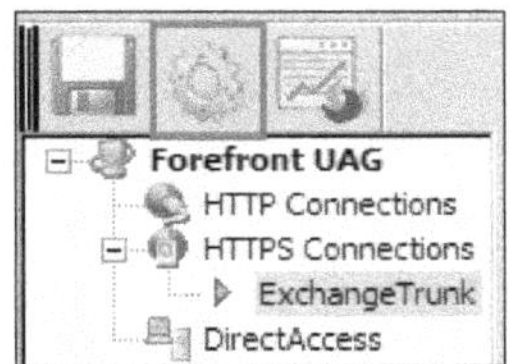

While creating the new trunk, we already published Outlook Web App to the Internet. It's a good practice not to select OWA, Outlook Anywhere and Exchange ActiveSync at the same time. However, there's no problem in configuring Outlook Anywhere and Exchange ActiveSync separately from OWA.

Configuring Outlook Anywhere and Exchange ActiveSync

Perform the following steps to configure Outlook Anywhere and Exchange ActiveSync:

1. Open the UAG Management console and navigate to the trunk you created previously.
2. Under **Applications**, click on **Add...**.
3. Click on **Next** on the **Welcome** page.

4. Click on **Web** and select **Microsoft Exchange Server (all versions)**, then click on **Next**.
5. On the **Select Exchange Services** page, choose **Microsoft Exchange Server 2013** from the version list and check the boxes next to **Outlook Anywhere (RPC over HTTP)** and **Exchange ActiveSync**. Then click on **Next**.
6. Enter an application name, for example `Exchange-OA-EAS`. Click on **Next**.
7. Leave the default endpoint policies and click on **Next**.
8. Select **Configure a farm of application servers** and click on **Next**.
9. Add your local Client Access Server(s) to the list and click on **Next**.
10. On the **Configure Connectivity Verifiers** page, select **Establish a TCP connection** and click on **Next**.
11. Click on **Add...** to add the Authentication servers you created earlier. Then click on **Next**. If you get a warning about rich clients and basic/NTLM authentication, accept it.
12. Select basic authentication for both **Outlook Anywhere Authentication** and **Autodiscover Authentication**. Click on **Next**.

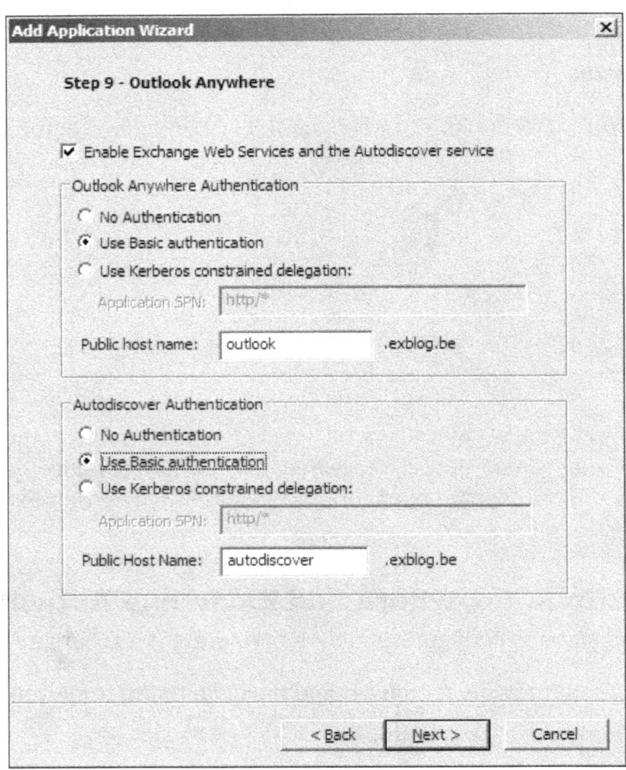

13. Accept the default authorization settings and click on **Next**.
14. Click on **Finish**.
15. Save and activate the configuration changes.

You should now see the following configured applications in the trunk we created earlier:

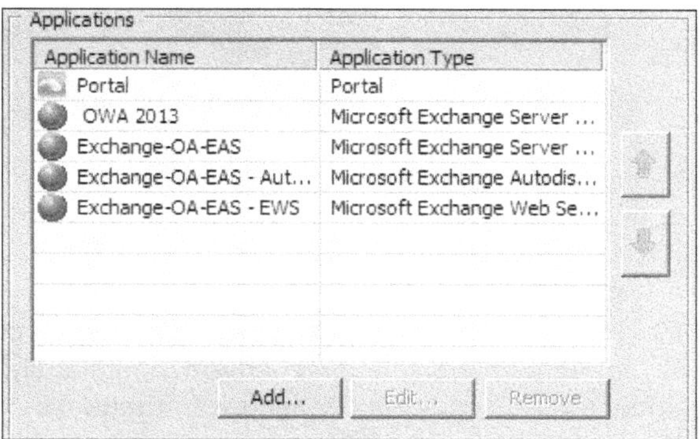

Configuring Exchange for basic authentication

During the wizard for Outlook, Outlook Anywhere and Exchange ActiveSync we configured the UAG to use basic authentication. Because the configuration between UAG and Exchange must match, you will need to configure basic authentication in Exchange as well.

Run the following commands to enable the virtual directories for basic authentication:

```
Set-OABVirtualDirectory "EX02\*"-BasicAuthentication:$true
Set-WebServicesVirtualDirectory "EX02\*" -BasicAuthentication:$true
Set-OwaVirtualDirectory "EX02\*" -BasicAuthentication:$true
Set-EcpVirtualDirectory "EX02\*" -BasicAuthentication:$true
```

Make sure to run `iisreset` on the Client Access Server(s) after changing the authentication method.

How it works...

The way UAG publishes Exchange application onto the Internet is pretty similar to how TMG does it. In fact, a lot of the TMG's components can be found in the UAG. The difference mostly comes from the different way of publishing Exchange.

A typical UAG deployment would therefore look very similar to a TMG deployment:

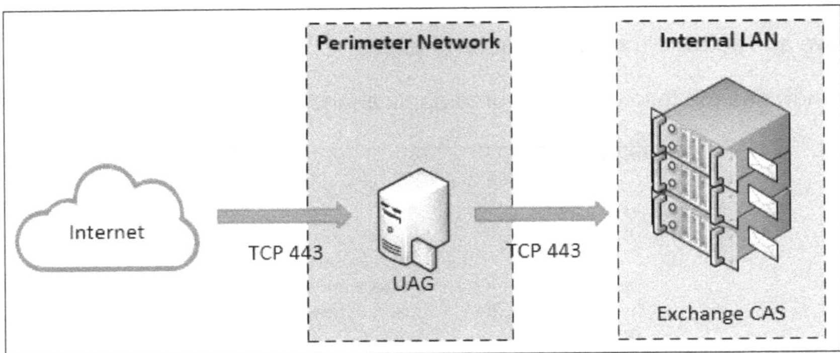

The UAG also acts like a barrier between the Internet and your internal deployment, filtering and authenticating traffic before it enters your environment. Additionally, A UAG also allows you to evaluate the health of a remote system connecting to Exchange. If the system doesn't match the required health state, you could disallow the connection.

Publishing Exchange 2013 to the Internet without using a reverse proxy solution

The previous topics explained how you could publish Exchange using one of Microsoft's reverse proxy solutions. However, a reverse proxy is not a required component to make Exchange available from the Internet.

Typically, a reverse proxy is used to provide additional security by providing features such as, pre-authentication or connection filtering. While both of them can be useful, there is no definite need for them.

When taking a look from a distance, one could argue that the Client Access Server basically performs somewhat the same tasks as a reverse proxy: it authenticates the user and fetches the requested information from the internal servers, in this case being the Exchange Mailbox servers.

I admit the reasoning behind the above statement might seem a bit blunt, but in essence it does represent what's happening. If there is no requirement stating some of the additional security features like pre-authentication are a must, I would personally opt to publish Exchange directly onto the Internet through the firewall.

Getting ready

In order to execute the steps outlined in the following, you need access to the firewall connecting your internal network to the Internet.

How to do it...

Next to port TCP 25 (SMTP), there's only one additional port you need to make available through the Internet in order to make your Exchange server available to clients from outside of your network: TCP 443.

You need to create a firewall rule that "forwards" traffic from the external IP address which corresponds to your external namespace, to the internal IP address of your Client Access Server or Virtual IP Address of the load balancer in front of your array of servers.

Consider the following scenario:

Your company has an external namespace `outlook.exblog.be`, which has `24.25.26.27` as its IP address. The load balancer on your internal network has been configured for Exchange on the IP address `10.10.10.100`.

The configuration in your firewall would therefore look something like the following table:

External IPaddress	Source Port	Target Port	Internal IP Address
24.25.26.27	443	443	10.10.10.100
24.25.26.27	25	25	10.10.10.100

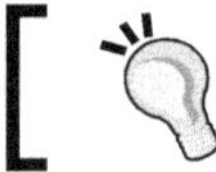

This process is sometimes also referred to as port forwarding.

How it works...

In this scenario, the firewall is providing additional security for your Exchange servers. First, it will only allow connections over either TCP port 443 or TCP port 25. If someone tries to connect to a port other than these two, the connection will be dropped by the firewall.

Secondly, many firewalls offer security features such as, **Intrusion Prevention System** (**IPS**), **Deep Packet Inspection** (**DPI**), **Denial-of-Service** protection (**DOS**), and more than likely a whole bunch of other things whose acronyms I can't remember. Each of these features play their own role in detecting and preventing all sorts of threats your on-premises environment might be subject to.

By inspecting the traffic that is flowing through it, a firewall can catch potentially malicious connections and take appropriate action by dropping or denying them. To do so, it uses a set of rules or algorithms to search for and detect known threats. What your firewall protects you from, and how it does so, varies from vendor to vendor. So make sure to ask your current vendor what features your firewall supports.

Personally, if I was publishing Exchange directly through the firewall, I would make sure my firewall was able to detect and protect me against DOS attacks. A DOS or Distributed DOS attack is when someone repeatedly launches a massive amount of requests towards your Exchange server from one or more places on the Internet. The originators of these requests are usually computer systems that got infected with one or the other malware and can be located anywhere in the world.

The result is that your Exchange environment gets flooded by a large number of requests. The goal of such an attack is to try and overload the system and make it "fall over"; taking the service down. If this happens, not only are your external users are affected, but also your internal users. Not really something you'd want to happen, right?

Many firewalls offer protection from this for these types of attacks, as well as other threats. How they detect or try to step them, depends on the model and brand of your firewall. Usually though, actions include throttling or simply blocking connections. Although modern firewalls have a pretty good accuracy rate, they might (temporarily) block connections from legitimate users as well, because they were mistakenly seen as part of the attack (false positives). While this is far from ideal, at least your internal users won't be affected as the additional load the attacks generates never gets to your Client Access Servers. However, your external users might see some delays or intermittent connectivity.

Essentially, the firewall is taking over part of the tasks that you'd typically find a reverse proxy is doing. Funny enough, people usually deploy a reverse proxy behind a firewall; thus sometimes performing the same task twice.

6
Implementing and Managing High Availability

In this chapter, you will learn how to create an Exchange environment that is more resilient to failure by making different aspects of your deployment highly available. We will cover the following recipes:

- Designing for high availability
- Creating a highly available Client Access Server infrastructure
- Load balancing at layer 4 using DNS round robin
- Load balancing at layer 4 using a single IP address and a load balancer
- Load balancing at layer 4 using multiple IP addresses and a load balancer
- Load balancing at layer 7 using a load balancer
- Creating a highly available mailbox server infrastructure
- Configuring a DAG
- Managing a DAG
- Configuring transport high availability
- Configuring redundant inbound mail delivery
- Performing maintenance in a highly available environment

Introduction

In its early days, e-mail was, next to the already existing and more traditional methods, no more than another way of communicating. At that time, people used the phone, written letters and fax as their main way of communication. Even if you wanted to switch to primarily using e-mail, you would not have been able to. Not everyone that was connected to the Internet—if at all, had an e-mail address or used one.

The popularity of the personal computer at home definitely contributed to the fast-growing adoption of e-mail. Many probably realized that e-mail is easy to use, usually delivered promptly and cheap when compared to other communication channels, especially for a message that is traveling half way around the globe.

Over the years, e-mail has grown from yet another way of communicating with people to probably the most important way of non-direct communication.

In our modern world, one could state that—at least for some, e-mail has become a commodity like electricity or water. Many companies rely on e-mail to run their business. Not being able to send or receive e-mail potentially makes them lose money which in turn feeds the company's need for a resilient, highly available messaging environment.

Designing for high availability

Prior to taking on the design task, it's highly recommended that you go talk to the business to understand where the need for high availability comes from and what exactly their need is. There's nothing easier than to overestimate the actual needs, increasing the overall complexity and thus the costs related to setting up and maintaining the solution.

How to do it...

Before heading off and diving into the technical details, it's important that you know what you are actually designing for. There's more than only Exchange that comes into play in a resilient and highly available messaging solution. Consider the effect a single non-Exchange component might have on your end user's experience. For instance, what good is your Exchange infrastructure, only to find out that none of your messages were delivered in a timely fashion because your Internet connection went down for a few hours?

In order to determine what aspects of your environment you need to take into account, you can start with asking yourself (and the business!) some simple questions. Use the following table as a guideline to determine what parts of your messaging environment are required to be highly available. Do add functional areas that are specific to your organization to the table. For example, if your company is storing voice mails in Exchange, it might be a functional requirement to make access to these voice mails highly available.

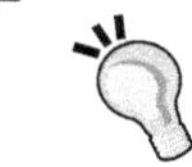

This might also be a good time to explain your superiors that answering "yes" to every question will likely influence their budget rather negatively.

Functional area	Is HA required?
Individual mailbox access (regardless of the location of the client)	yes
External mailbox access (from outside the companies network boundaries)	yes
Internal mail flow (messages sent/received within in the organization)	yes
External mail flow (messages sent/received outside of the organization)	yes
Messaging security (for example, anti-spam, anti-virus, and so on)	yes

Once completed, the preceding table will indirectly tell you a lot about what components you will need to make highly available or otherwise resilient.

Let's take the example of external mailbox access, which represents your internal users connecting to your Exchange environment over the Internet through Outlook, OWA, smartphones, and so on.

First, we need to create a list of all functional domains that might interfere with the availability of the Exchange environment to your external users. Look at these functional domains as the different layers upon which your Exchange environment is built.

This exercise might leave you with a relatively short list, possibly looking something like the following:

- Internet connection
- Network
- Storage
- Power
- Server(s) (for example: blades)
- And so on

You might see the items from this list also be referred to as **failure domains**.

Once you have created this list, you will need to identify what potential risks are involved for each of these failure domains. Then, you need to determine what you can do about each of the identified risks.

> Each risk that you identify must either be mitigated or simply accepted, meaning that you will either try to resolve or work around the risk or that you know about the risk but that you deliberately choose to not do anything about it. What action you decide on will strongly depend on a number of things, including the availability rate you agreed upon with the business and the available budget. Discussing why (or why not) you should do something about a risk would carry us way too far from the purpose of this chapter and will therefore not be discussed. However, in the light of your own deployment, it is important that you take a look at each risk and see how it can potentially impact the agreed service level. When a risk is deemed too high to ignore, there are basically two options: either you do something about it in your design, which usually leads to an increased cost or you go back to the business and re-negotiate the service level.

Let's move on and take a closer look at one of the earlier defined failure domains and take the Internet connection as example. Let's assume you have only a single DSL Internet connection. The fact that you only have a single connection represents a risk of you losing external access to your entire infrastructure (including Exchange) when that connection becomes unavailable. As possible solution for this risk would be to put in an additional Internet connection alternatively, you could try negotiating better service levels with your ISP, if at all possible.

After you go through each of the potential risks and defined what actions you will (or will not) take, go through them again. You will notice that some of the mitigating actions that you wrote down might bring in new risks that require your attention.

For example: you defined that adding a second Internet connection might solve the risk of losing external access. But what if there's only a single operator in the area? What if that operator experiences an outage? What if you choose to use to separate carriers, only to find out that both operators share the same physical cable for the so-called "last mile" to your company infrastructure?

As you can see, solving one problem might raise others. How far you go in your quest for a solution, again, depends on the agreements you have made (if at all) with the business.

> In order to evaluate whether or not you should do something about a risk depends of a few criteria including the impact on the business (or service levels), the probability that the risk would occur and the cost of mitigating the risk.
>
> For example, a risk that has high impact but is unlikely to happen is more easily decided to be accept able than a risk that has a lower impact but a higher chance of happening.

If you decide to mitigate a risk, a part of the strategy might include making the component that is responsible for the risk more resilient and more highly available. That way, the failure of a single device or component doesn't necessarily cause a service outage leading to an infringement of your service levels with the business.

If we go back to our example of the single Internet connection, the mitigation strategy will likely include the addition of a second firewall, router, and switch next to adding in a second Internet connection.

In the end, how to create high availability for a given component depends on the product or device that you are working with. Exchange Server 2013 definitely made some vast improvements in that area, which makes that creating a resilient, highly available messaging solution with Exchange has never been so easy.

Creating a highly available Client Access Server infrastructure

In order to make your CAS infrastructure highly-available, you need to load balance traffic across the different servers in the CAS pool. That pool of Client Access Servers by itself doesn't necessarily create high availability. There are other components and mechanisms that play an equal important part in the process. For example, the load balancing solution should be able to determine whether or not a Client Access Server is still a viable endpoint. If not, you risk ending up sending traffic to a non-functional server, therefore impacting on an end user's experience.

Unlike Exchange 2010, Exchange 2013 offers you the ability to load balance traffic between two or more Client Access Servers over **layer 4** (**L4**). This means that load balancing is now effectively performed at the transport layer (remember the OSI model?!), opening the door for solutions like DNS round robin.

Load balancers operating at layer 4 are content-agnostic because they have no clue of what data or type of traffic is passing through. Basically, it boils down to this: traffic is load balanced based on its destination IP address. No more, no less.

On the other hand, if you are load balancing at layer 7, the load balancer is operating at the application layer and has full access to the protocol stack and/or the data that is passing through it. This allows for more advanced load balancing scenarios where routing decisions can be taken based on the content flowing through the load balancer.

When traffic is unencrypted, most load balancers can operate natively at layer 7. However, because most Exchange traffic is encrypted with SSL by default, the load balancer needs to decrypt the content first in order to get access to it. Some vendors require you to buy additional licenses for this feature, also known as "SSL Decryption". Also, because SSL decryption requires additional resources on the load balancer it can drive up the cost as it might force you into buying a higher-end model.

The reason that Exchange 2013 no longer requires a layer 7 load balancer is because Microsoft removed the need to keep affinity between the source (client) and the destination (server). Before, some workloads like Outlook Web App required that—once the connection was built—subsequent traffic within that particular session was always exchanged between the client and the same backend server. To do this, the load balancer keeps a routing table where mappings between clients and servers are stored. However, in order to identify what session a packet belongs to, the load balancer needed to be able to access the content. Hence the need for layer 7 load balancing.

Even though layer 7 load balancing is no longer a requirement in Exchange 2013, it doesn't mean that you cannot use it anymore. In fact, as you will see later in this chapter, load balancing at layer 7 still offers some benefits over layer 4 load balancing.

There are several solutions that you can use to load balance Exchange 2013 Client Access Servers. Basically, we can make the following distinction:

- DNS round robin
- Load balancing at layer 4
- Load balancing at layer 7
- **Windows Network Load Balancing** (**WNLB**)

Strictly speaking, WNLB is a valid and supported solution for load balancing Exchange 2013. However, its use is not very recommended. Personally, I'm no big fan of WNLB either because of its limitations and the issues that might arise from a networking point-of-view. That, and the fact you cannot use WNLB when you're deploying a multi-role Exchange server are some of the reasons why we won't be discussing here how it works or how to set it up.

Instead, we will focus on the following four scenarios:

- Load balancing at layer 4 using DNS Round Robin
- Load balancing at layer 4 with a single IP address and using a load balancer
- Load balancing at layer 4 with multiple IP addresses and using a load balancer
- Load balancing at layer 7 using a load balancer

Load balancing at layer 4 using DNS round robin

DNS Round Robin is the easiest way of load balancing. Although it's not as powerful as the other solutions, it doesn't require setting up a load balancing device. Instead, it's leveraging features in DNS that have already been there for a while. In this recipe we will guide you through the different steps of setting up DNS round robin using Windows DNS.

Getting ready

In order to execute the following tasks, you need access to the Windows DNS Management console for your domain. In order for load balancing to work properly, you need to ensure that all Client Access Servers are configured with the same certificate.

How to do it...

1. Open the DNS management console on one of your domain controllers.
2. Navigate to your internal DNS zone.
3. Right-click on the internal zone and select **New Host (A or AAAA)...**.

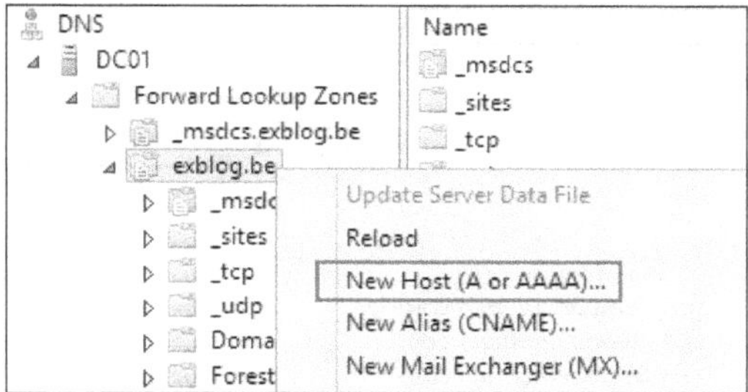

4. Choose a name for the host. For example: `outlook.yourdomain.com`.
5. Enter the IP address of your first Client Access Server and click on **OK**.
6. Repeat step 3 to step 5 for every Client Access Server in the site. This time, do use the same name as in step 4, but change the IP address to match the one of the additional Client Access Server(s).

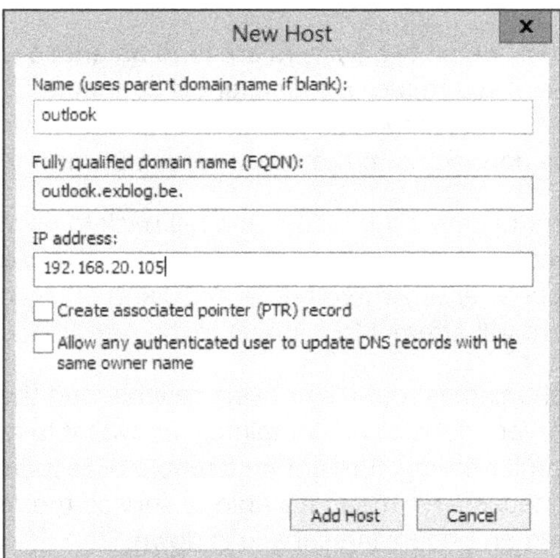

How it works...

DNS Round Robin is easy to setup and it definitely beats having no form of high availability at all. However, there are some major drawbacks to the client's experience in case of an outage. The way DNS round robin works is as follows: in order to connect to the Exchange server, the client will first perform a DNS query to translate the FQDN it got into an IP address. Because the DNS server has multiple records for the same host (FQDN), it will send back an ordered list containing all the IP addresses that were tied to that hostname. The DNS server will reorder the list by shifting the first result to the bottom for every new request:

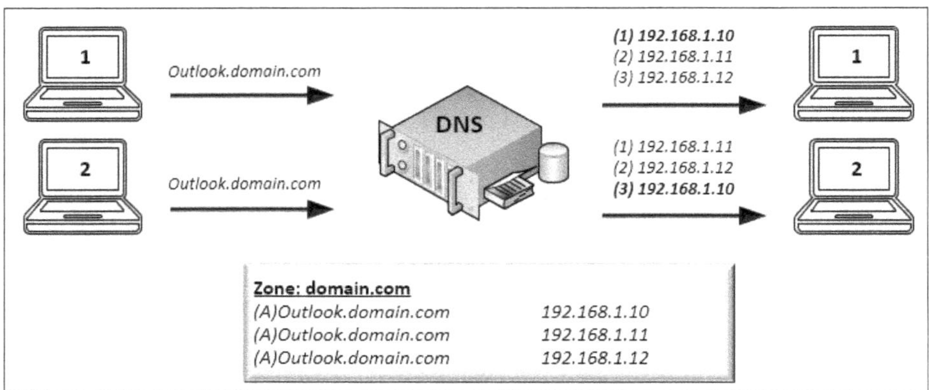

When receiving the results of the query back, the client will try connecting to the server(s) in the order that it received the results from the DNS server. That way a very basic form of load balancing is achieved as only every *nth* client will first try connecting to the same server (where n is the amount of Client Access Servers you are load balancing between). However, this form of load balancing is static and DNS Round Robin does not perform any health checking to determine whether a server should still be addressed or not.

Now, consider the scenario in which two servers are load balanced using DNS Round Robin and one of the servers fails. If you're lucky, your client is connected to the other server and won't notice the outage. In real life, however, you're likely to have more than one client and surely some of them will be connected to the failed server. Bummer!

It's now up to the HTTP client to detect the failure and fall back to using any of the other IP addresses on the list it received earlier. Depending on the configuration of the client, a connection timeout will occur after anywhere between 20 and 45 seconds. It's only after this timeout period that the client will attempt to connect to the next IP address from the list.

The problem with this mechanism is that it's not very reliable and the user's experience isn't all that good either. The server needs to be completely unavailable for the "fall back" to work. If your Exchange Server is still running, it might be capable of responding to connection requests, but that doesn't necessarily mean it's able to service the requests that it receives. This could be the case when an underlying service is down.

In such cases, no timeout will occur and your clients will experience a service outage. Whenever a complete server failure does occur, connected clients will still have to wait for about one minute before they will automatically try connecting to another server.

Lastly, an administrator will have to manually remove the corresponding host record from DNS for the duration of the outage to avoid new clients from still receiving the IP address of the failed server.

All in all, DNS might do the trick but isn't really suited for larger deployments. In fact, I wouldn't recommend using DNS Round Robin but for the smallest deployments or in deployments where there's no room (or budget) for other solutions. It's better to have some high availability than it is to have none, right?!

If you really want to carry on through with this solution, you might want to have a look at alternate methods that might help making DNS Round Robin a more viable solution. For instance, System Center Orchestrator could help you to automatically remove the records from DNS when a certain condition is detected. Alternatively, creating a script in PowerShell might prove useful in order to limit the amount of manual steps that you need to take. One thing I'd do for certain when using Round Robin, is lower the **Time-To-Live** (**TTL**) value for the Exchange-related DNS records to about 5 minutes. This ensures that the client-side cache for these DNS records expires after 5 minutes and as a result changes to DNS, such as removing a bad server entry from your DNS, get carried through to your clients more quickly.

Load balancing at layer 4 using a single IP address and a load balancer

Unlike DNS Round Robin, load balancing at layer 4 usually requires some sort of load balancing device to be configured. Although, technically speaking, Windows Network Load Balancing would also be a valid option and doesn't require a load balancing device.

In the following recipe we will describe the steps that are necessary to set up your load balancing device for layer 4 load balancing. Because there are many vendors and device models out there, we will describe the principles to this setup but we won't be covering product-specific configuration steps.

Getting ready

To complete the following steps, you will need to use a virtual or hardware load balancer. The load balancer does not need to have any SSL offloading capabilities. In order for load balancing to work properly, you need to ensure that all Client Access Servers are configured with the same certificate. To guarantee the user experience, the configuration of the different web services should match as well.

How to do it...

Please note that depending on the model and make of the load balancer you are using, the terminology that is used might be different. Nonetheless, the same principles apply.

Execute the following tasks on your load balancer:

1. Create a new Virtual Service/Server (VS).
2. Configure the VS to perform the following:
    1. Accept requests for a single IP address on port 443 (the one from the example is `192.168.1.100`).
    2. Perform a health check on one of the virtual directories (for example, the "/OWA" virtual directory).
    3. Include all the CAS servers between which you want to load balance traffic.
    4. Use a load balancing mechanism between the different Client Access Servers. This could for instance be "round robin" or "least connections".
3. In the end, your configuration should look similar to the following diagram:

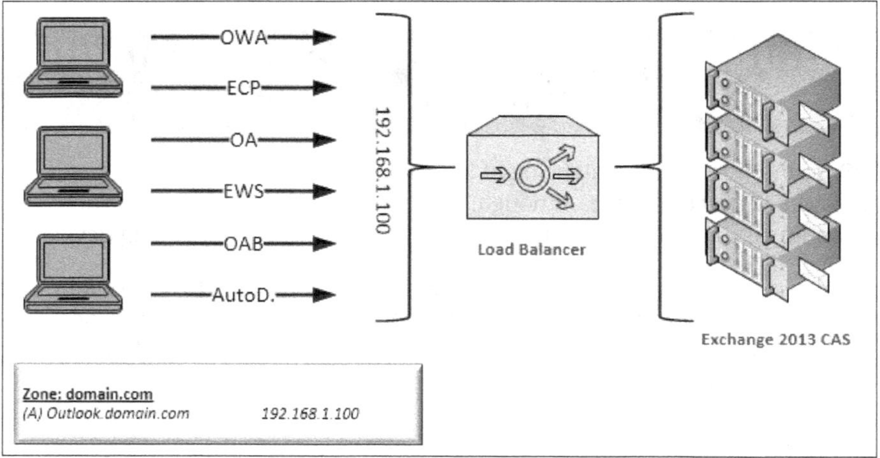

How it works...

As the diagram above already outlined, the load balancer "listens" on a single IP address (192.168.1.100) for incoming connections. Because it is operating at layer 4, it will not analyse the traffic but rather just pass traffic along to one of the servers in the array as it hits the virtual service.

How the load balancer will distribute the load between the servers in the array depends on the load balancing mechanism that you configured. Sometimes this mechanism is also referred to as scheduling mechanism. Typically, load balancers support a multitude of options, including "Round Robin", "Least Connections", "Random", "Weighted Round Robin", and so on. While most vendors mechanism will pretty much work the same, some differences might exist between devices from different vendors.

The following bullet list will provide some basic information on the aforementioned scheduling methods:

- **Round robin**: The load balancer will cycle through the list of servers, one by one. Each new connection will be sent to the next server in the list.
- **Least connections**: The load balancer will evaluate which server currently has the least amount of active connections and forward the new connection to that server.
- **Random**: As it says a random server will be picked.
- **Weighted round robin**: You can assign a weight to the servers in your array. The load balancer will cycle through the list of server, taking into account the weight that was assigned to a server. Servers with a higher weight will automatically be revised more and get more connections.

In most situations "round robin", which will distribute load between servers by cycling through them one at a time, will do the trick. Of course, this is only true when all servers in your array are identical. Sometimes, however, you might have to deal with servers that have different CPUs or even memory. In such cases, you can for example use "weighted round robin", which allows you to assign a different weight to your servers. When load balancing traffic, across your servers, this weight is taken into account. Servers with a higher weight will automatically get more connections.

Aside from more advanced load balancing mechanisms, hardware (or virtual) load balancers also offer the ability to perform health checking against the servers in the array. The purpose of a health check is to verify whether a server in the array is still working as expected. Health checks can be performed in many ways, ranging from a simple ping, to verify if the server is still responding, to more advanced checks that execute scripts on the server. The problem with using ping to verify if a server is healthy or not is that it doesn't take into account if the service is actually behaving properly. An Exchange server might respond properly to a ping, but that doesn't necessarily mean OWA is working as it should.

If a health check fails or returns improper results, the server is deemed offline and will automatically be taken out of the array. That way, the load balancer ensures that no new traffic is sent to the failed server.

Because the load balancer is operating at layer 4, you can only use a single health check to verify the health of your servers. This could cause all sorts of issues. Let's take a closer look by using an example.

You have configured the virtual service to use a health check that performs a simple HTTP request to your OWA virtual directory. As long as you get a proper "HTTP 200 (OK)" result back, the server is deemed operational and ready to accept new connections. For some reason, IIS is having some issues and is causing your web services virtual directory to stop functioning. Because the OWA virtual directory is still working as it should, health check completes successfully and the load balancer will continue sending new connections to that server, including requests for EWS. Obviously, because the web services virtual directory isn't working, the latter connections will throw an error to the client.

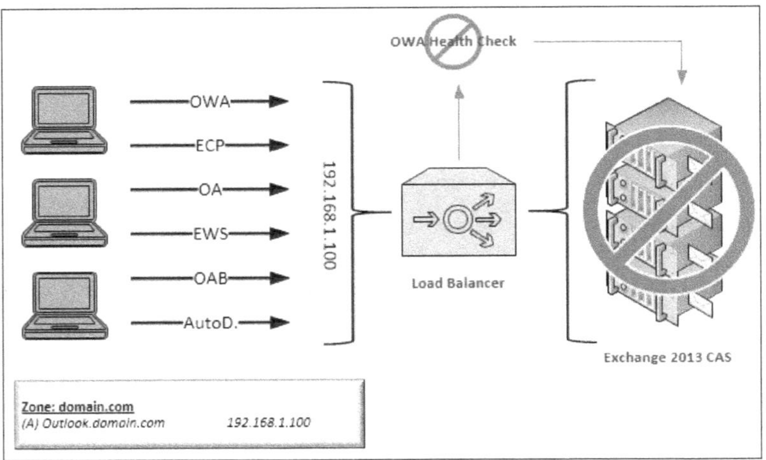

Load balancing at layer 4 using multiple IP addresses and a load balancer

Just like in the previous recipe, this one will cover load balancing at layer 4; but from a different angle. We will describe the principles and the idea behind this solution, however we cannot cover any device or model specific configuration steps.

Getting ready

To complete the following steps, you will need to use a virtual or hardware load balancer. The load balancer does not need to have any SSL offloading capabilities. In order for load balancing to work properly, you need to ensure that all Client Access Servers are configured with the same certificate.

How to do it...

Please note that depending on the model and make of the load balancer you are using, the terminology that is used might be different. Nonetheless, the same principles apply.

Execute the following tasks on your load balancer:

1. Create a new Virtual Service/Server (VS).
2. Configure the VS to perform the following:
    1. Accept requests for a single IP address on port `443` (the one from the example is `192.168.1.100`).
    2. Perform a health check on one of the virtual directories (for example, the "/OWA" virtual directory).
    3. Include all the CAS servers between which you want to load balance traffic.
    4. Use a load balancing mechanism between the different Client Access Servers. This could for instance be "round robin" or "least connections".
3. Repeat step 1 and step 2 for every Exchange workload that you will be load balancing. Use a different IP address for each workload and choose an appropriate health checking mechanism.

In the end, the configuration of your load balancer should match the following:

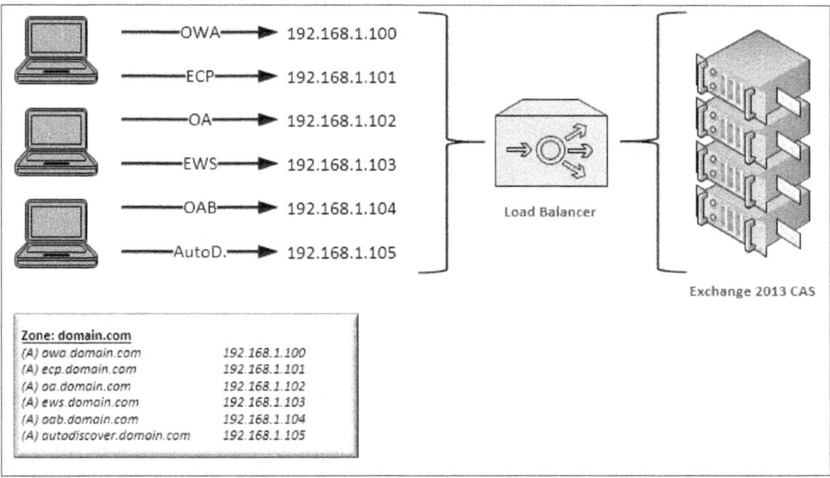

How it works...

Basically, how the load balancer treats traffic is no different than what and how it did to the previous module, where only a single IP address was used. However, to overcome the issue of having only a single health check, multiple virtual services—each with their own health check—are created. That way, you have a more granular control over when traffic should be sent to a server or not.

When taking a look back at the previous example, the load balancer had no clue that **Exchange Web Services** (**EWS**) weren't working as expected, because the health check was configured to only check the OWA virtual directory. When configured with multiple IP addresses and a health check per workload, a server on which EWS has failed will be taken offline, but only for EWS. If other health checks for that server are still completing successfully, it will keep on receiving traffic for those workloads.

As a result, you don't immediately lose an entire server's capacity when only a single workload fails. On the other hand, one might argue that it doesn't happen all too often that only a single workload fails.

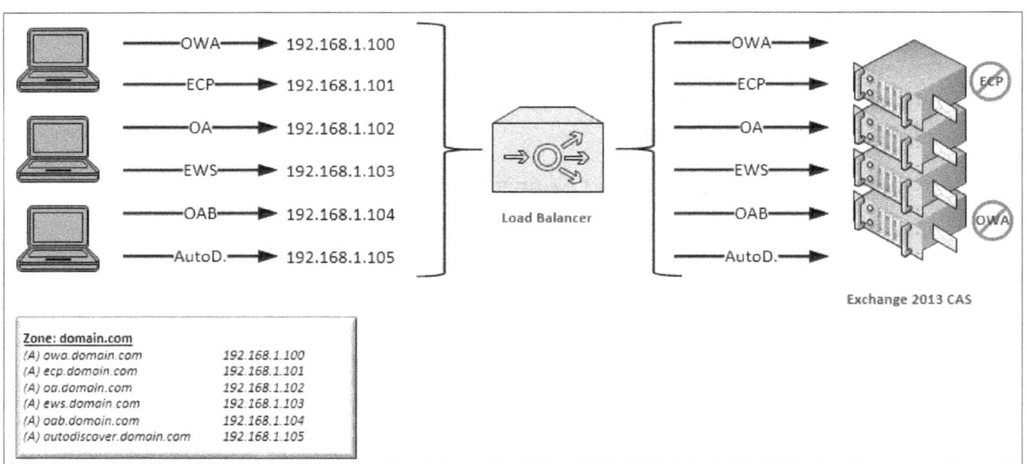

This higher degree of intelligence comes with a downside: you'll have to use multiple IP addresses. If you are publishing Exchange directly onto the Internet without a Reverse Proxy, that would mean that you'd have to use multiple external IP addresses as well. This could potentially be a problem because external **IPv4** addresses are becoming increasingly more scarce (and expensive) and **IPv6** hasn't been adopted that well, just yet.

Another downside of this approach is that you will have to add more entries on the certificate, resulting in an overall higher cost for the certificate. It also adds some more complexity in the environment as you will now have to manage many more namespaces.

Load balancing at layer 7 using a load balancer

Although from a high level perspective the configuration steps to setup load balancing at layer 7 are very similar to setting up load balancing at layer 4, its differences—the idea behind the setup and the way it works—are important enough to dedicate a recipe to it.

In the following recipe we will talk about the specifics, and explain how you would be able to configure a load balancing device to handle traffic at layer 7. Just like the previous recipes, we won't be able to provide you with model-specific guidance as there are way too many different vendors and models out there. Instead, the purpose is to cover the principles so that you'd be able to translate those into the proper configuration for the device model you are using.

Getting ready

To complete the following steps, you will need to use a virtual or hardware load balancer. The load balancer should be able to decrypt and re-encrypt SSL traffic. In order for load balancing to work properly, you need to ensure that all Client Access Servers are configured with the same certificate.

How to do it...

Execute the following tasks on your load balancer:

1. Create a new Virtual Server/Service (VS)
2. Configure the VS to perform the following:
    1. Accept requests from a single IP address on port 443 (the one from the example is 192.168.1.100).
    2. Decrypt and re-encrypt SSL traffic (layer 7).
    3. Configure one, preferably multiple health checks. To configure more health checks, your load balancer needs to support sub-virtual services or a mechanism also referred to as content-switching.
    4. Include all the Client Access Servers between which you want to load balance traffic. Depending on how your load balancer treats the multiple health checks, you might need to define an array per subvirtual service or a global one.
    5. Select a load balancing mechanism between the different Client Access Servers. This could for instance be "round robin" or "least connections".

In the end, the configuration of your load balancer should match the following:

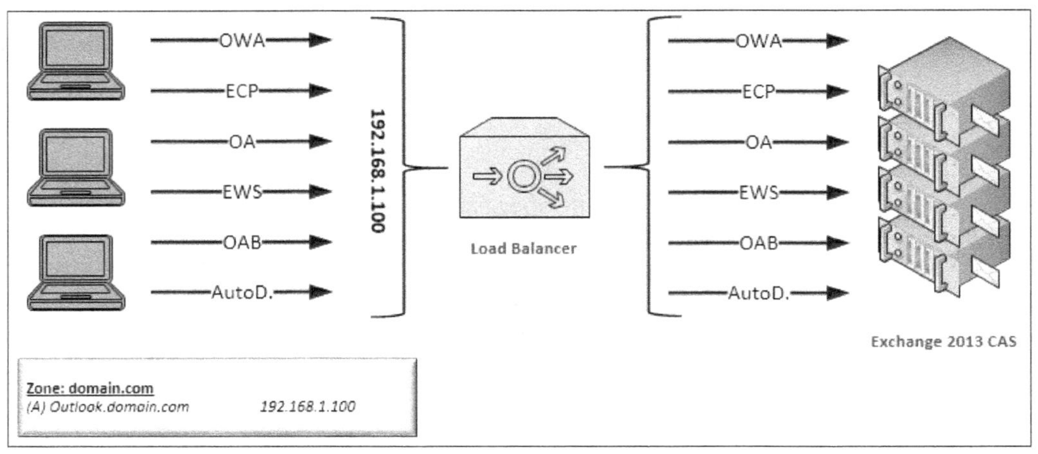

How it works...

One could say that this method of load balancing is combining the best of both previous examples: using a single IP address and a health check per workload. The reason that this is now possible is because the load balancer is now decrypting traffic, essentially allowing it to "read" what the traffic's destination is.

As traffic enters the virtual service, it is decrypted and analysed. This will reveal its destination to the load balancer. To determine where traffic should be routed to, the load balancer will take a look at the URL that the client is trying to connect to. If the client is for example, a smartphone trying to synchronize using ActiveSync, the URL would look like `https://host.domain.com/Microsoft-Server-ActiveSync`.

Because the load balancer now exactly knows where to route the traffic to, it can forward traffic to the appropriate "sub-virtual directory" for ActiveSync. This virtual directory could for instance be configured with its own health check and load-balancing mechanism that is different from other workloads.

The price you pay for this additional flexibility comes in the usage of more resources on the load balancer. Because traffic is decrypted and re-encrypted the CPU of the load balancer needs to do some over time. Depending on the size of your environment, this could potentially forcing you into buying a higher-sized model of your load balancer, easily costing a few thousand dollars more. At that point, one might wonder if paying that additional sum is worth it, given you could reach the same level of flexibility with only layer 4 load balancing.

There's more...

One constant in all of the previous load balancing scenarios, is the fact that your load-balancing mechanism (also referred to as scheduling method) can be pretty much anything you want. Because you are not using any affinity, this means that each subsequent request from a client might potentially end up at another Client Access Server. Although this isn't much of a problem since the Client Access Server will merely 'proxy' traffic to the appropriate mailbox server, it is still responsible for authenticating traffic.

Does this mean that every (new) connection is re-authenticated? Yes. And also that isn't much of a problem. When a Client Access Server authenticates a user for the first time, that user will receive an authentication cookie. To ensure that only appropriate Exchange Servers can read the content of that cookie, it will be encrypted using the certificate from the Client Access Server. When a user hits another CAS during the same session, the client will present this authentication cookie (instead of prompting the user for credentials). Assuming that you have configured the same certificate on all Client Access Servers, this 'new' CAS will be able to decrypt the cookie and authenticate the connection without any further actions.

As you might've guessed, it's extremely important that you configure the same SSL certificate on all Client Access Servers in the array if you want it to work properly.

Creating a highly available mailbox server infrastructure

In contrast to creating high availability for your Client Access Server infrastructure, doing it for your mailbox servers is quite different. Since Exchange's early days, you had to create a cluster (with shared storage) if you wanted Exchange to be somewhat highly available. At that time, the clustering components upon which Exchange relied were notorious for their difficulty to set up, maintain, and troubleshoot.

Over time, Microsoft made significant changes to the failover clustering component in Windows, improving the overall experience. Not only for the administrator, but also from an end user's perspective. Even today with Windows Server 2012, Microsoft keeps on improving dramatically.

Creating a cluster might ensure you servers are highly available, they usually don't care what the state of the data is. In the past, Exchange clusters relied heavily on the underlying storage to provide high availability. At the same time, it was that storage that created a single point of failure as only a single copy of the data would be used between multiple Exchange servers.

With the launch of Exchange 2007, Microsoft drastically changed how Exchange would be clustered and introduced a software-level replication mechanisms like CCR, SCR, and LCR that would be able to copy data between two Exchange servers, at nearly real-time.

Since then, Microsoft has been developing and improving Exchange along the same path. When Exchange 2010 was launched, the **Database Availability Group** (also referred to as **DAG**) was also born. The DAG was a huge leap forward how replication was performed and maintained improving the overall experience, flexibility and resiliency of Exchange.

Today, in Exchange 2013, we can see that—although the principles of the DAG remain untouched—it has further evolved, building on the feedback Microsoft received on Exchange 2010 and their experience running a cloud-based service such as, Office 365.

Configuring a DAG

The following recipe will describe the process of setting up a DAG.

Getting ready

In order to complete the following steps, you need to launch the Exchange Management Shell or open the Exchange Admin Center. You will also need at least two servers running the mailbox server role.

How to do it...

If your mailbox servers are running on Windows Server 2012, you will have to manually pre-create the **Cluster Name Object** (**CNO**) first:

1. Open **Active Directory Users and Computers**.
2. Navigate to and right-click on the OU where you want the CNO to be created.
3. Navigate to **New** | **Computer**.

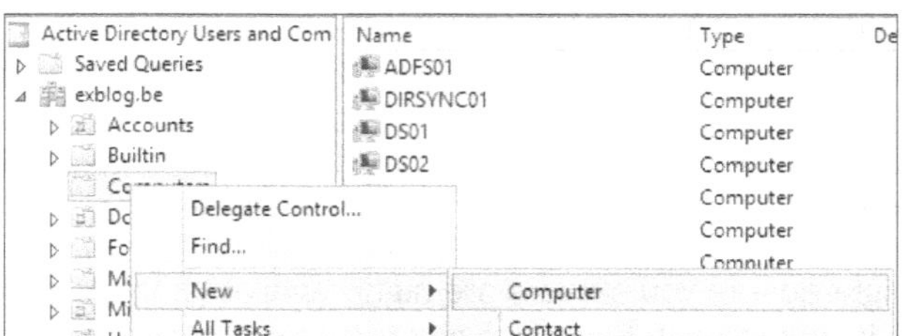

4. Enter a name for the CNO ("`DAG01`") and click on **OK**.

5. Right-click on the new CNO and select **Disable Account**. Click on **OK** to confirm.

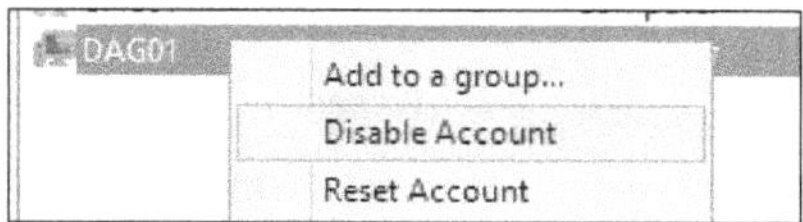

Next, the Exchange Trusted Subsystem should get appropriate permissions on the CNO:

1. Open **Active Directory Users and Computers** and make sure you select **Advanced Features** under **View** first.
2. Then, right-click on the CNO and select **Properties**.
3. Click on the **Security** tab and click on **Add**.

4. Type in **Exchange Trusted Subsystem** and click on **Check Names**. Click on **OK** to confirm.

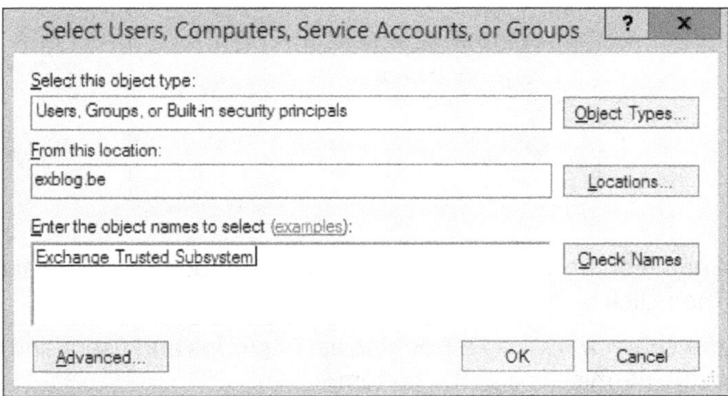

5. Select **Exchange Trusted Subsystem** and then check **Full Control** in the permissions at the bottom of the window.

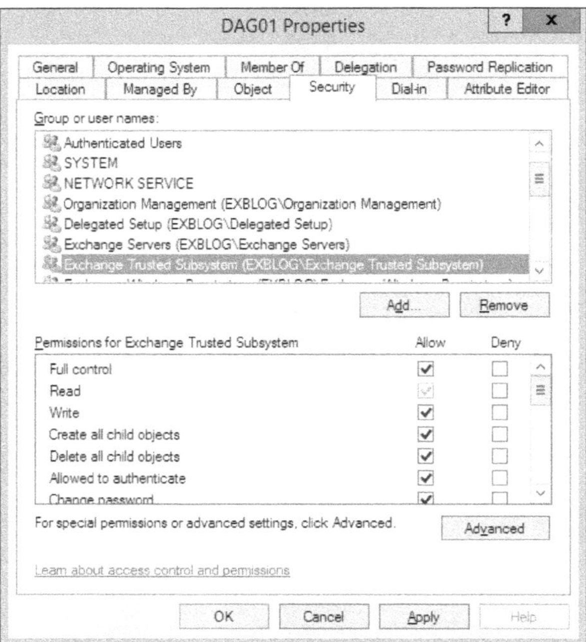

6. Click on **Add** again.
7. Click on **Object Types** and uncheck everything except for **Computers**. Click on **OK**.

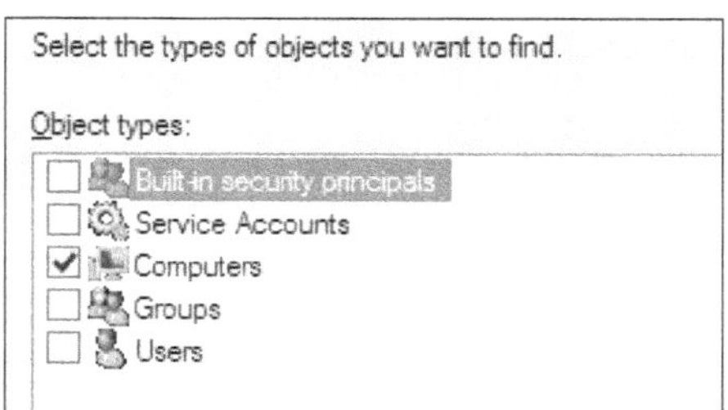

8. Enter the name of the first mailbox server to be added to the DAG and click on **Check Names**. Then click on **OK**.
9. Click on the server from step 8 from the list of groups and users and select **Full Control** in the permissions at the bottom.

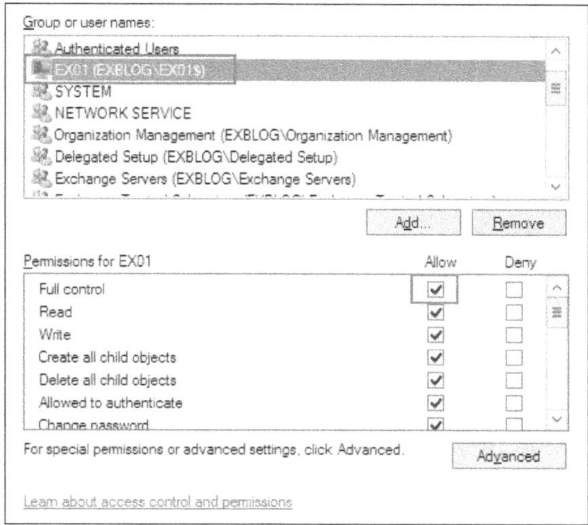

10. Click on **OK** to confirm.

Now that the CNO has been pre-created, we can go ahead and create the DAG:

1. Log in to the Exchange Admin Center and navigate to **servers** | **database availability groups**.
2. Click on the plus-sign (**+**) to start the **new database availability group** wizard.
3. Enter a name for the dag. For example: `DAG01`.
4. Type in the name of the witness server, in this example we will be using one of the Client Access Servers `EX02.domain.com`.
5. Type in the name of the witness directory. For example `c:\FSW`.
6. Add the IP address for the DAG (`192.168.20.200`)
7. Click on **save**.

Alternatively, you can use the Exchange Management Shell as well, by running the following command:

```
New-DatabaseAvailabilityGroup -Name "DAG01" -WitnessServer
  EX02.domain.com -WitnessDirectory "C:\FSW" -
  DatabaseAvailabilityGroupIPAddresses "192.168.20.100"
```

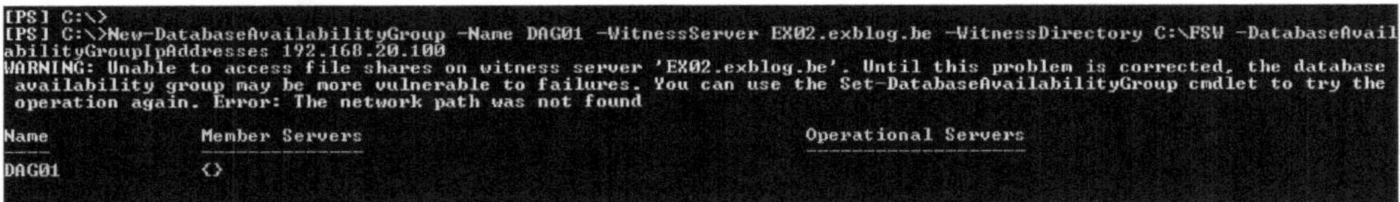

All that is left to do, is to add mailbox servers to the DAG.

Through the EAC.

1. Log in to the Exchange Admin Center and navigate to **servers** | **database availability groups**.
2. Click on the Manage DAG membership button.

3. In the **manage database availability group membership** window, click on the plus-sign (**+**) and select the mailbox servers you wish to add to the DAG. Click on **Add** and then on **OK** to confirm.

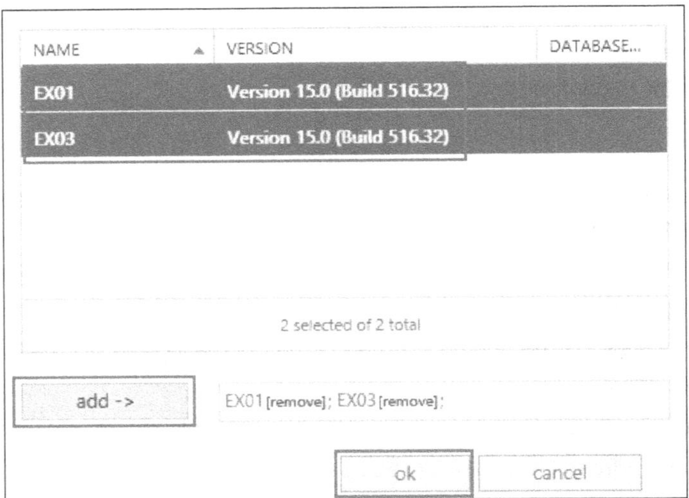

4. Click on **save**.
5. Or using the Exchange Management Shell:

```
Add-DatabaseAvailabilityGroupServer -Identity DAG01 -MailboxServer
EX01
```

Remember that if your mailbox servers are running in a different subnet, you have to assign an IP Address to the DAG for every subnet.

How it works...

As briefly explained in the introduction, a DAG uses a subset of Windows' failover clustering components. In fact, the DAG is a cluster that is using the "Node Majority and File Share Witness" quorum model. In general, a cluster requires more than half of the nodes to be up and running, also referred to as "having quorum".

Quorum is designed to prevent so-called "split-brain" situations. A split-brain is a situation in which two or more nodes in a cluster are bringing up the same resource online. A split-brain situation could potentially occur when your network becomes partitioned, for instance due to an outage, and knocks out communication between some or all nodes of your cluster.

If a cluster "loses quorum", meaning that more than half of the servers in the cluster become unavailable, all remaining nodes in the cluster will go offline to prevent split-brain. The result, however, is that the service that is hosted by the cluster becomes unavailable.

To make things more complicated, Windows Server 2012 introduced something that is called "dynamic quorum". Dynamic quorum, as the name suggests, will dynamically adjust the number of votes in the cluster after a node outage. Because the number of votes can change, so will the number of "votes" you need to have quorum. In the end, dynamic quorum should allow you to have a cluster running with a single node.

If you will, Exchange 2013 can take advantage of this feature. While the idea of increased availability might sound tempting, the purpose of a DAG shouldn't be to end up with a single server. Besides, if more than half of your servers are going down, you've probably got other things to worry about.

As described through the different tasks, the process of creating a DAG contains a few steps. First, when you run the **New DAG** wizard or execute the `New-DatabaseAvailabilityGroup cmdlet` a "placeholder" object is created in AD.

This object holds all the configuration data of the DAG with exception of the cluster-specific configuration settings which are stored in the cluster database. At this time, the cluster isn't created yet.

Along with the AD object, a **Cluster Name Object** or **CNO** is (or should manually be) created. The CNO is a (disabled) computer account which plays an important role in the internal operations of the cluster.

Lastly, the cluster is effectively created when the first mailbox server is added to the DAG. This happens while issuing the `Add-DatabaseAvailabilityGroupServer cmdlet`, mailbox servers that do not have the necessary failover clustering components on the system prior to running the `cmdlet`, will get them automatically installed.

As mailbox servers are added to or removed from the DAG, all necessary configuration changes are automatically made at the cluster level which makes that you should never have to use the built-in Failover Clustering management tools to manage a DAG.

Managing a DAG

The purpose of a DAG is to host one, preferably more, copies of a mailbox database. In the following examples, we will have a look at the different tasks you, as an Administrator, might have to perform.

Getting ready

To execute the following steps, you need access to the Exchange Admin Center or launch the Exchange Management Shell.

How to do it...

We will cover various task related to DAG in this section:

Adding database copies

Through the EAC:

1. Login to the EAC and navigate to **servers** | **databases**.
2. Select the database for which you want to add a new copy and select **add database copy**.

If you don't see the **add database copy** link, click on the three dots (**...**) to show more options.

3. In the **add mailbox database copy window**, select the mailbox server on which you want to create a new copy.
4. Set the **Activation preference number** to **2**.
5. Click on **save**.

To add a database copy using the Exchange Management Shell, run the following command:

```
Add-MailboxDatabaseCopy -Identity DB01 -MailboxServer EX03 -
  ActivationPreference 2
```

Moving database paths

As long as databases are replicated within the DAG, you cannot move the database files to another path. First, you need to remove existing database copies. However, we will only delete the "logical" element from Exchange and not the physical files and folders on the server. The files and folders on the different servers should be copied manually into their new location in order to avoid complete reseeding of the database.

In this example, we will remove the database copy we created earlier:

1. Login to the EAC and navigate to **servers** | **databases**.
2. Locate the database copy that you want to remove and select it.
3. From the right side of the EAC, click on **Remove**.
4. Verify this is the database copy you want to remove and click on **yes** to confirm.
5. Click on **OK** when the warning shows.

To remove a database copy from the Exchange Management Shell, run the following command:

```
Remove-MailboxDatabaseCopy EX03\DB01 -Confirm:$false
```

Although you could go ahead and manually delete the files, this would require you to re-seed the entire database afterwards. It might be a better option to keep the files and move them into the new location manually.

Once all but the active copies have been removed, the database can be moved into a new location. During the move, the database will be dismounted. You cannot use the EAC to initiate a database move, so you will have to run the following command:

```
Move-DatabasePath DB01 -EdbFilePath D:\Newlocation\DB01.edb -
  LogFilePath D:\Newlocation\Logs -Confirm:$false
```

If you haven't dismounted the database prior to executing the command, you will be asked to temporarily dismount it. Confirm this by pressing *Y*.

Once the files have been moved, use the procedure outlined before to re-add the database copies to other servers in the DAG.

Checking replication status

As part of the maintenance tasks involved with running a DAG, you need to keep an eye on the health of your database copies. One way of doing that is to verify that all copies are replicated correctly and are in a healthy state.

Through the EAC:

1. Login to the EAC and navigate to **servers** | **databases**.
2. Select the database for which you want to check the status.

3. Verify the status on the right-hand side of the screen:

I personally prefer the Exchange Management Shell because it gives a more compact and better formatted overview of the database copies on a server:

```
Get-MailboxDatabaseCopyStatus -Server EX03
```

Testing Replication Health

When the `Get-MailboxDatabaseCopyStatus` command shows one or more databases being out of sync, you might have a replication issue. A good point to start with is to run the `Test-ReplicationHealth` command. The purpose of the command is to test the different aspects that come into play for replication and report on possible issues. Some of the elements the command will take a look at are:

- Cluster Service health
- Network components health
- Active Manager
- Replication pipeline
- The command can be used against the local or a remote computer:

  ```
  Test-ReplicationHealth -Identity <MailboxServer>
  ```

How it works...

The principle of a DAG is simple: multiple servers in a failover cluster host one (or more) copies of a mailbox database. These copies can be activated when the current (active) copy fails, becomes corrupted or is unavailable because the server on which it is hosted failed.

To keep copies between different servers in sync, log files are copied from the server hosting the active mailbox database to the server(s) with a passive copy of that database. When the log file reaches a server hosting a passive copy, it's replayed into that passive database copy to bring it up-to-date. This all happens automatically when you configure a new database copy.

After the initial setup of a mailbox database copy, referred to as the seeding of a new database, transactions logs are copied in their entirety to catch up with the active copy. Once the new (passive) mailbox database copy is up-to-speed however, the replication process switches to "block mode" which means that instead of the full transaction logs, blocks of data that have been written to the transaction logs on the active database are immediately copied to the passive copy. That way, the time difference between the active database and passive copies is greatly minimized because the server hosting the passive copy doesn't have to wait for a new transaction log file to be rolled on the server with the active database. Sometimes, you might see that replication from the active copy to the passive copy switches back to file-level copying. This can happen when the replication between the active copy and passive copy encountered some problems or when the passive copy couldn't keep up.

When an error occurs and the current active copy becomes unusable or unavailable, active manager will search for a suitable passive copy on one of the servers in the DAG which it can activate. The process to select a passive copy is called best copy selection. In short, active manager will use a number of criteria to determine the state of a passive copy. The passive copy with the best state, which is the copy that is equal or as equal as possible to the active copy, will be activated. If multiple valid passive copies are found, the copy with the lowest preference number (and thus the highest preference) is mounted.

Once the failed server or database is brought back online, it will function as a passive copy and bring itself up-to-date again. Once that has completed successfully, Active Manager will then be able to use that copy to failover to in case something happens with the current active copy.

Because it is crucial that passive copies are in sync with the active copy, it's important to monitor the health of the copies as described earlier. If the output of the `Get-MailboxDatabaseCopyStatus cmdlet` shows a `CopyQueueLength` or `ReplayQueueLength` that is too high, your passive copy might be unusable and active manager might not be able to (automatically) failover to it. Ideally, both numbers should be 0. An elevated value for the `ReplayQueueLength` command will affect the amount of time it takes to mount (activate) the passive copy. The `CopyQueueLength` command on the other hand indicates the number of transaction logs that still need to be copied from the active copy. If that number is too high, active manager might not be able to automatically mount the passive copy, and although Exchange has all sorts of mechanisms to prevent it, data loss might still occur.

There's more...

There are some very interesting (and very good) reporting scripts out in the wild that might help you to better follow-up on the health of your database copies.

There is one script in particular, written by Exchange Server MVP Paul Cunningham, that I like a lot. Have a look at it on the following page:

`http://exchangeserverpro.com/get-daghealth-ps1-database-availability-group-health-check-script`

Configuring transport high availability

While shadow Redundancy is the mechanism used to provide high availability for messages in transit and the DAG is the primary mechanism for mailbox high availability, safety net (formerly known as the transport dumpster) is designed to keep a copy of messages that were processed successfully by a server for a configurable amount of time.

First released in Exchange 2007, the "transport dumpster" underwent some significant changes in Exchange 2010. These changes allowed the transport dumpster to help protecting database copies in a DAG by keeping messages that weren't replayed into passive database copies yet. Although its purpose hasn't changed much in Exchange 2013 "safety net", has been improved greatly yet again.

How to do it...

Actually, there isn't much to configure. By default both shadow redundancy and safety net are enabled. The process of resubmitting messages from safety net to a mailbox database is also fully automatic, requiring no intervention of an administrator. Isn't that great?!

On the other hand, there are some configurable settings for safety net that allow you to control the number of days messages are kept in safety net. This could be useful when you are working with lagged mailbox database copies.

Configuring safety net parameters

To change the amount of days that messages should be kept by safety net to 4 days, run the following command from the Exchange Management Shell:

```
Set-TransportConfig -SafetyNetHoldTime 4.00:00:00
```

How it works...

Shadow Redundancy

After a message enters the organization and is forwarded by the frontend transport service to one of the mailbox servers, Exchange will automatically create a copy of that message on another mailbox server in the organization. This process is referred to as Shadow Redundancy and should avoid messages from getting lost when a transport services (or the server hosting the transport service) goes down for whatever reason.

When this shadow copy of a messages is created, Exchange will automatically take into account the organization's topology and tries to create the copy so that the highest level of availability is achieved.

For example, when a DAG spans multiple sites, Exchange will try creating the shadow copy on a mailbox server located in one of the other sites. That way, not only redundancy for the message is achieved, but also what is called "geo-redundancy": if one data center fails, the other still has a copy of the messages. The process itself contains many more steps than what I outlined. However, you should have a firm idea of what the intent of Shadow Redundancy is by now.

If you need more details on how the shadow copy is exactly created (and what the logic behind it is), have a read through the following article: `http://technet.microsoft.com/en-us/library/dd351027(v=exchg.150).aspx`.

Safety net

One could say that safety net kicks in where shadow redundancy has left of. Once messages are processed successfully, they are stored in a safety net; creating a "bucket" of messages that have been sent/received over a certain amount of days. By default, safety net will keep messages for two days. But as we explained earlier, the amount of days is configurable and becomes important when you are working with lagged mailbox database copies.

Although its intent is not for an administrator to manually resubmit messages, safety net is there to resubmit messages to a mailbox database whenever the latter requests it. In fact, there are two scenarios in, which safety net might be queried for messages:

- After the (manual) failover of a mailbox database
- When a lagged mailbox database copy is activated (brought up-to-date)

In the first scenario, sometimes it happens that the passive copy that gets activated wasn't fully up-to-date. In an attempt to bring that database to the same level as the former active database, active manager—a component of the mailbox replication service, which manages DAGs and mailbox databases. It will also try different things amongst which is requesting missing data from the (former) active copy. However, in case that the former active copy is unrecoverable or otherwise unavailable, active manager will request the resubmission of the missing messages from safety net as the latter will contain all messages that were received over the past x-amount of time.

The same applies in the second scenario where a lagged mailbox database copy is activated. Normally, when a lagged mailbox database copy is activated, the replicated log files are replayed against the database to bring it up-to-date. Sometimes, you might not be able to replay these transactions logs because they are missing, have become corrupt or simply because you choose to. In that case, during the activation of the database all missing messages are requested from safety net. Of course, this requires that safety net is configured to keep messages for the same or longer period that the lag time of the lagged mailbox database copy. Keep in mind that this could mean that you'd have to keep messages in safety net for 14 days or more because that's the maximum configurable lag time of a database copy. Needless to say, you should plan where to store safety net accordingly as it might end up using quite a large amount of disk space.

Configuring redundant inbound mail delivery

Exchange is able to receive messages from the Internet with only very little configuration. However, none of the configuration steps you take would matter without "letting others know" where your mail server can be reached at. You could compare it to making the address of your post-office publicly available so that others know where to send messages addressed to you to.

Getting ready

In order to configure MX records for your domain(s), you will need access to the configuration tool of your DNS provider. The tool that you will be using will depend on the provider.

How to do it...

Log in to the administration tool of your public DNS zone and create a new MX record with the following values:

Type	Host	Preference	TTL (in seconds)
MX	<A, AAAA>	10	3600

The hostname value should either be an A-record in case you have a public IPv4 address or an AAAA-record in case it's IPv6 pointing to the external IP address of your Exchange infrastructure. The entry point into your organization could be a cloud-based message hygiene solution like Exchange Online Protection, an on-premise message hygiene solution like the Exchange 2010 Edge Transport server or even a direct connection to one of your Client Access Servers.

The value of the hostname of your MX record should not point to a CNAME record. The RFC documentation (2181 (SMTP)) around this is pretty clear:

> *The domain name used as the value of a NS resource record, or part of the value of a MX resource record must not be an alias. Not only is the specification clear on this point, but using an alias in either of these positions neither works as well as might be hoped, nor well fulfills the ambition that may have led to this approach. This domain name must have as its value one or more address records. Currently those will be A records, however in the future other record types giving addressing information may be acceptable. It can also have other RRs, but never a CNAME RR.*

Although some messaging systems won't care, it's better to follow the standards than to find out that you're having problems later down the road.

How it works...

Simply put, when an e-mail is sent to an external recipient, the server sending the message will determine where to send the e-mail to by looking up any configure **Mail Exchange** (**MX**) records in the recipient e-mail domain's public DNS zone.

A MX records represent the server that is (or servers that are) responsible for receiving e-mail for that domain. When querying for an MX record, three values are returned: the host, its preference and the time-to-live of the record. The preference value is of importance only when multiple MX records are defined for the same domain.

Consider the following screenshot:

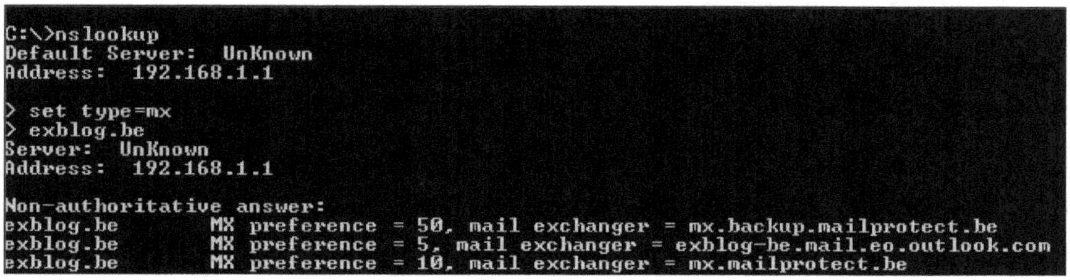

```
C:\>nslookup
Default Server:  UnKnown
Address:  192.168.1.1

> set type=mx
> exblog.be
Server:  UnKnown
Address:  192.168.1.1

Non-authoritative answer:
exblog.be       MX preference = 50, mail exchanger = mx.backup.mailprotect.be
exblog.be       MX preference = 5, mail exchanger = exblog-be.mail.eo.outlook.com
exblog.be       MX preference = 10, mail exchanger = mx.mailprotect.be
```

In case multiple MX records are found with different preference values, the sending server will attempt to deliver e-mail to the host that has the lowest value (and thus the highest priority) first. Only in specific cases where e-mail cannot be delivered to the preferred host, will the sending server fall back and attempt to send messages to a host with a higher preference value.

If multiple MX records exist with the same preference value, the sending server will randomly pick one of these records with the same value. If, for some, reason the sending server cannot connect to the first host, it will fall back and try connecting to one of the other—equally preferred hosts.

There's more...

Having multiple MX records does not necessarily guarantee redundant inbound mail delivery unless you also have multiple gateways or edge transport servers capable of accepting messages.

Another option is to use a cloud-based service which, in case of an outage of your messaging environment, will temporarily store messages and redeliver them after your on-premises environment comes back online.

Performing maintenance in a highly available environment

Setting up a highly available environment is one thing, being able to support and maintain it another. To be quite honest, 80 percent of setting up a highly available messaging solution is all about planning; 20 percent of the effort is required to set it up. Maintaining the solution afterwards, requires 100 percent attention and effort. Exchange has come a long way and supporting high availability is no more than a fraction of what it used to be. In the following recipe we'll dive a little deeper into the maintenance mode of Exchange and explain how you can (temporarily) take an Exchange server out of service allowing you to troubleshoot, update or otherwise perform any action on it.

Getting ready

To complete the following steps, you will need to open the Exchange Management Shell.

How to do it...

We will cover the many tasks in accordance with the maintenance.

Starting maintenance on Mailbox or multi-role servers

First, we need to make sure that the transport component on the server does not accept any new messages:

```
Set-ServerComponenState $env:COMPUTERNAME -Component HubTransport
  -State Draining -Requester Maintenance
```

Next, any messages that are still queued on the server should be moved (redirected) to another Exchange server. Please note that the value for the Target server should be a FQDN:

```
Redirect-Message -Server $env:COMPUTERNAME -Target <fqdn>
```

If the server is part of a DAG, you should "pause" the cluster node and make sure that it will not be used as a failover target by other Exchange servers while in maintenance:

```
Suspend-ClusterNode $env:COMPUTERNAME
Set-MailboxServer $env:COMPUTERNAME -
DatabaseCopyActivationDisabledAndMoveNow $True
Set-MailboxServer $env:COMPUTERNAME -DatabaseCopyAutoActivationPolicy
Blocked
```

If your mailbox servers are located across multiple Active Directory sites, it is important that you either wait for Active Directory replication to occur or force it to happen immediately. Otherwise, if you immediately start doing work after running these cmdlets, the remote Exchange servers might not yet be aware of the change that this server should not be used as a failover target.

Lastly, if the server is a multi-role server, you will also need to run the following command to put the remainder of the Exchange services into maintenance mode.

```
Set-ServerComponentState $env:COMPUTERNAME -Component
  ServerWideOffline -State Inactive -Requester Maintenance
```

To verify this has worked, run the following commands:

```
Get-ServerComponentState $env:COMPUTERNAME
Get-MailboxServer $env:COMPUTERNAME
Get-ClusterNode $env:COMPUTERNAME
```

The examples above use the environment variable `$env:COMPUTER` because it contains the local server's name. These cmdlets can also be executed remotely by using the remote server's name or FQDN.

Starting maintenance on Client Access Servers

```
Set-ServerComponentState $env:COMPUTERNAME -Component
  ServerWideOffline -State Inactive -Requester Maintenance
```

Stopping maintenance

Stopping maintenance mode is simply reverse-executing the actions you performed to put a server into maintenance mode, with the exceptions that there is no need to redirect messages from one server to another.

For a mailbox or multi-role server:

```
Set-ServerComponentSate $env:COMPUTERNAME -Component
  ServerWideOffline -State Active -Requester Maintenance
Resume-ClusterNode $env:COMPUTERNAME
Set-MailboxServer $env:COMPUTERNAME -
  DatabaseCopyActivationDisabledAndMoveNow $False
Set-MailboxServer $env:COMPUTERNAME -
  DatabaseCopyAutoActivationPolicy Unrestricted
Set-ServerComponentState $env:COMPUTERNAME -Component HubTransport
  -State Active -Requester Maintenance
```

For a Client Access Server:

```
Set-ServerComponentSate $env:COMPUTERNAME -Component
  ServerWideOffline -State Active -Requester Maintenance
```

How it works...

Exchange 2013 contains a feature called "managed availability", which could be seen as a sort of in-product monitoring platform that keeps an eye on the health of the system. As such, managed availability regularly executes probes (health checks, if you will) to determine whether a service or component is working as expected.

If a problem is detected, managed availability can take a bunch of corrective measures ranging from anything like simply restarting a service to forcibly rebooting a server (also referred to as bug checking the server).

Although regular Exchange cumulative updates should automatically put a server into maintenance mode, they won't take any actions like moving databases or suspending a cluster node, just like other 3rd-party applications probably won't do. Therefore, managed availability might mistakenly assume the server is behaving badly and try to take corrective actions while you are working on the server. I can imagine you wouldn't want your server to spontaneously reboot while doing some application updates, right?

To prevent managed availability from stepping in, there are several tasks to complete depending on what Exchange server roles you are running on the machine. The Client Access Server is obviously the easiest one, as you will only have to put the Exchange components into a temporary offline state by means of a single command.

A mailbox server and notably a mailbox server that is part of a DAG requires some additional attention. First, you need to ensure no messages are left on the server. Next, you need to make sure the server cannot be used a failover target while you are performing maintenance. To achieve this, you will have to move all active mailbox database copies to another server in the DAG, pause the server node in the DAG, make sure that other servers know they cannot use it as a failover target and mark the remaining components as offline.

There's more...

Michael has put together a handy script that will automatically put a server into maintenance mode, taking into account whether the server is a standalone or multi-role server.

Check it out here at `http://michaelvh.wordpress.com/2013/04/08/script-putting-exchange-server-2013-into-maintenance-mode/`.

7

Transitioning to Exchange Server 2013

In this chapter, you will learn how to migrate from an existing on-premise Exchange 2007 or Exchange 2010 environment to Exchange 2013. As part of this process, you will learn the following tasks:

- Installing Exchange 2013 in an existing Exchange organization
- Performing Exchange 2013 post installation configuration
- Moving mailboxes to Exchange 2013
- Moving Public Folders to Exchange 2013
- Post migration steps
- Performing maintenance in a co-existence scenario

Introduction

Over the years, Exchange has become the most popular enterprise messaging solution, world-wide. Although many companies are running other solutions such as Lotus Notes or Zarafa, it is likely that you are already running a version of Exchange in your organization.

In the past, moving from one version of Exchange to another was sometimes a daunting task. Although an upgrade to Exchange 2013 still needs proper planning, one could argue it is less complicated than moving from Exchange 2003 to Exchange 2010. However, there is still the element of Public Folder migrations that you need to keep in mind. This is, without any doubt, one of the most challenging tasks when transitioning to Exchange 2013.

There are only a few supported "upgrade paths" to Exchange 2013. If you are still running Exchange 2003, you will need to perform a "double-hop" migration. This means that you will first have to migrate to Exchange 2007 or Exchange 2010 before you can move to Exchange 2013. This is because Exchange 2013 does not support transitioning directly from Exchange 2003. In fact, Exchange 2013 setup will prevent you from installing Exchange 2013 as long as there are still Exchange 2003 servers in the organization.

The following table outlines the different transitioning options for Exchange 2013:

Source Platform	Approach
Exchange 2003	Perform a double-hop migration by moving to Exchange 2007/2010 first before transitioning to Exchange 2013. Alternatively, a cross-forest migration is also an option.
Exchange 2007 SP3 UR10	Transition directly to Exchange 2013.
Exchange 2010 SP3	Transition directly to Exchange 2013.

Transitioning from Exchange 2007 or Exchange 2010 is fully supported, as long as you make sure that both the existing environment as Exchange 2013 are running the correct service packs/coexistence updates.

- For Exchange 2007 this would be Service Pack 3, Update Rollup 10
- Exchange 2010 requires at least Service Pack 3
- Exchange 2013 must be running at least **Cumulative Update 1** (**CU1**)

Please note that these requirements apply to all the servers in the organization.

Although the installation of Exchange 2013 itself is no different from when you install it in a clean environment, the difference is in the configuration. There are some caveats to watch out for; especially with regards to coexistence.

The following section will guide you through each of these configuration steps, allowing you to successfully move from your current Exchange environment to Exchange 2013.

Installing Exchange 2013 in an existing Exchange organization

Getting ready

In the following few topics we will show you how to install and configure Exchange 2013 in an existing Exchange 2010 organization. In order to keep things practical, the examples in this chapter are built upon a fictional scenario:

The organization is called "Exblog" and is currently running a single Exchange 2010 Service Pack 3 multi-role server (EX2010-01). The organization is preparing to move to two new Exchange 2013 servers: EX2013-01 will take on the Client Access Server server role and EX2013-02 will have the mailbox server role installed. Although a single Exchange 2013 server could be used, we are splitting CAS and mailbox across two servers to clearly distinct actions that apply to the one or the other.

Users are currently spread over two mailbox databases, `DB01` and `DB02`. A single **Public Folder Database** (**PF01**) contains Public Folders for each of the departments. These Public Folders will also be migrated. Users currently connect to the environment through a single namespace `webmail.exblog.be`. This namespace will be re-used in Exchange 2013.

The following diagram depicts how the organization's architecture will look like once Exchange 2013 is installed:

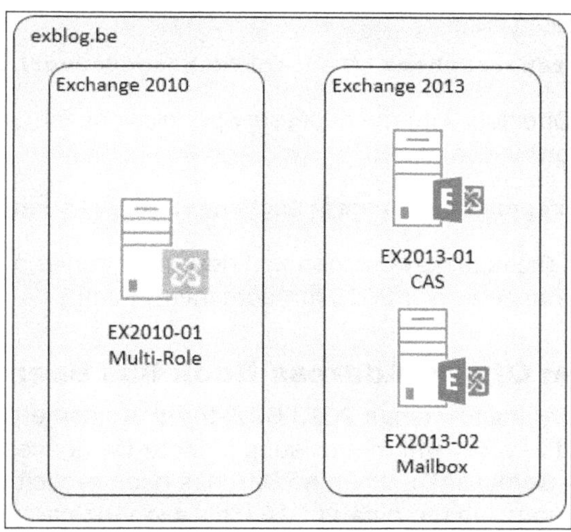

In order to complete the following steps, you will need to have previously downloaded the Exchange 2013 CU2 installation bits and have Schema, Enterprise, and Domain Admin permissions as well as be member of the Organization Management group in Exchange.

How to do it...

This chapter focuses mainly on how to configure coexistence between Exchange 2013 and previous Exchange versions. However, this does not mean that you don't need to perform the basic configuration as described in the previous chapters.

Preparing the existing Exchange Organization

Prepare your Exchange organization by installing Exchange 2010 Service Pack 3 on every server in the environment. Note that this will also require you to extend the Active Directory schema (using the bits of Service Pack 3).

Preparing Active Directory

Once the existing Exchange 2010 organization has been brought up to date to at least Service Pack 3, we need to prepare our Active Directory for Exchange 2013.

We will need to perform the following operations:

1. Extend the AD Schema, this time with the Exchange 2013 CU2 extensions. You can do this by executing the following command from the command-line. Make sure that you browse to the repository where your Exchange 2013 CU2 binaries are located first:

   ```
   Setup.exe /PrepareSchema /IAcceptExchangeServerLicenseTerms
   ```

2. Prepare Active Directory with the necessary permissions for Exchange 2013 by running the following command:

   ```
   Setup.exe /PrepareAD /IAcceptExchangeServerLicenseTerms
   ```

How you should perform these tasks has been well described earlier on. Have a look at *Chapter 2, Installing Exchange Server 2013* for more information.

Check whether an Offline Address Book has been defined

Before moving on to installing Exchange 2013 CU2, there are some things that need to be checked. First, you need to verify whether existing Mailbox Databases have been configured with an **Offline Address Book** (**OAB**). When no OAB has been explicitly configured, Exchange will automatically revert to using the default OAB. This scenario can potentially have a large impact, particularly in large environments or in environments with constrained bandwidth: during the installation of Exchange 2013 a new default OAB gets automatically created. Clients, whose mailboxes are stored on a mailbox database without explicitly configured OAB, will automatically detect this new OAB and perform a full OAB download. Depending on the size of your organization, having every client download the full OAB might have a negative impact on the performance of your Exchange server as well as the usage of your available bandwidth.

To check the OAB settings, execute the following steps:

1. Open the Exchange 2010 Management Shell.

2. Run the following command: `Get-MailboxDatabase | ft Name,OfflineAddressBook`.

```
[PS] C:\Windows\system32>Get-MailboxDatabase | ft name,OfflineAddressBook -AutoSize

Name OfflineAddressBook
---- ------------------
DB01
DB02
```

If the output shows that one or more databases has no Offline Address Book configured, proceed to the following step. If not, skip to "Installing Exchange 2013 CU2".

Configuring an OAB for a mailbox database

1. Open the Exchange 2010 Management Shell.
2. Run the following command to manually configure mailbox databases missing the OAB value to the current default Offline Address Book:

```
Get-MailboxDatabase | where{$_.OfflineAddressBook -eq $Null} |
  Set-MailboxDatabase -OfflineAddressBook (Get-
  OfflineAddressBook | where{$_.IsDefault -eq $True})
```

To verify that this has worked, run the following command:

```
Get-MailboxDatabase | ft Name,OfflineAddressBook
```

```
[PS] C:\Windows\system32>Get-MailboxDatabase | ft name,OfflineAddressBook -AutoSize

Name OfflineAddressBook
---- ------------------
DB01 \Default Offline Address Book
DB02 \Default Offline Address Book
```

Once you have successfully completed the preceding steps, you are ready to install Exchange 2013 CU2. Before proceeding to the next step, make sure to install the required prerequisites as described in *Chapter 2, Installing Exchange Server 2013*.

Installing Exchange 2013 CU2

Install at least one Exchange 2013 Mailbox and one Client Access Server. Both server roles can be combined on a single multi-role server if you like. To install the mailbox Server role (`EX2013-01`), run the following command:

```
setup.exe /mode:install /roles:m /IAcceptExchangeServerLicenseTerms
```

To install the Client Access Server role (EX2013-02), run the following command:

```
setup.exe /mode:install /roles:c /IAcceptExchangeServerLicenseTerms
```

For more details on how to install Exchange 2013, have a look at *Chapter 2, Installing Exchange Server 2013* and *Chapter 3, Configuring the Client Access Server Role*.

Once you have installed both server roles, proceed to the next topic.

Performing Exchange 2013 post installation steps

Once Exchange 2013 is installed, there are a number of steps you have to go through to configure coexistence between legacy Exchange version and Exchange 2013.

Getting ready

The following steps require you to have access to both the Exchange Management Shell and Exchange Admin Center.

Remember that for version-specific configuration steps, you will have to revert to using the tools for that version. This means that you will have to make changes to Exchange 2010 using the Exchange 2010 native tools.

How to do it...

Accessing the Exchange Admin Center

The first thing you'd probably want to do is login into the Exchange Admin Center. By default, the EAC can be reached via the FQDN of one of your Client Access Servers:

1. Open a web browser and navigate to the following URL: `https://ex2013-02.exblog.be/ecp`. For now, you can safely ignore the certificate warning.
2. Login to the EAC using your admin credentials.

By default, Exchange 2013 will proxy requests over to Exchange 2010 as long as your mailbox is still located there. As a result, you will see the Exchange 2010 Control Panel instead of the Exchange 2013 Admin Center.

To work around this issue, you have two options:

1. Move your (admin) mailbox to Exchange 2013.
2. Append `?ExchClientVer=15` to the ECP URL, like this `https://ex2013-02.exblog.be/ecp?ExchClientVer=15`.

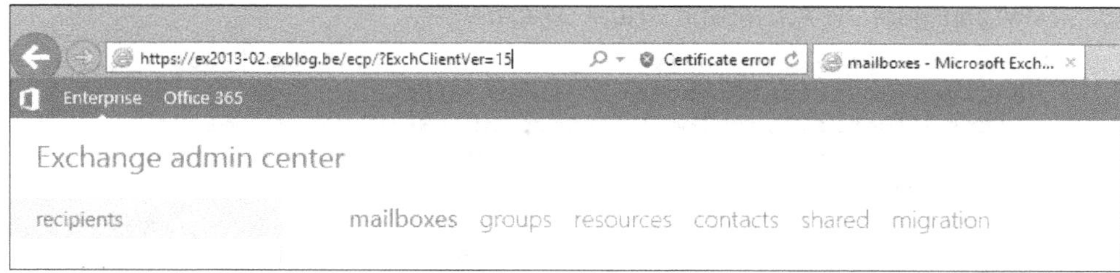

The problem outlined in the preceding section will only occur when your admin account also has a mailbox. In case it does have a mailbox, note that although moving your mailbox to Exchange 2013 might solve the problem with EAC, it will likely also prevent Outlook from connecting to your mailbox until you've completely configured Exchange 2013. Unless you have already configured coexistence between both environments, you should avoid moving mailboxes to Exchange 2013.

Configuring virtual directories

Just as explained in *Chapter 3, Configuring the Client Access Server Role*, the virtual directories in Exchange 2013 have to be configured accordingly. In this example, all virtual directories will be configured to use a single namespace: `webmail.exblog.be`. For more information on namespace planning and configuring certificates, have a look at *Chapter 3, Configuring the Client Access Server Role*.

1. Open the Exchange Management Shell.
2. Configure the OWA Virtual Directory by running the following command:

```
Get-OwaVirtualDirectory -Server EX2013-02 | Set-
  OwaVirtualDirectory -InternalUrl
  https://webmail.exblog.be/owa -ExternalUrl
  https://webmail.exblog.be/owa
```

3. Next, configure the ECP Virtual Directory:

```
Get-EcpVirtualDirectory -Server EX2013-02 | Set-
  EcpVirtualDirectory -InternalUrl
  https://webmail.exblog.be/ecp -ExternalUrl
  https://webmail.exblog.be/ecp
```

4. Then, configure the Offline Address Book Virtual Directory:

```
Get-OABVirtualDirectory -Server EX2013-02 | Set-
  OABVirtualDirectory -InternalUrl
  https://webmail.exblog.be/OAB -ExternalUrl
  https://webmail.exblog.be/OAB
```

5. Now, configure the ActiveSync Virtual Directory:

   ```
   Get-ActiveSyncVirtualDirectory -Server EX2013-02 | Set-
     ActiveSyncVirtualDirectory -InternalUrl
     https://webmail.exblog.be/Microsoft-Server-ActiveSync -
     ExternalUrl https://webmail.exblog.be/Microsoft-Server-
     ActiveSync
   ```

6. Finally, configure the Web Services Virtual Directory:

   ```
   Get-WebServicesVirtualDirectory -Server EX2013-02 | Set-
     WebServicesVirtualDirectory -InternalUrl
     https://webmail.exblog.be/EWS/Exchange.asmx -ExternalUrl
     https://webmail.exblog.be/EWS/Exchange.asmx
   ```

Once these virtual directories have been configured, you're ready to move on to the next step.

Configuring Autodiscover

Although the Autodiscover service also has a virtual directory, the URL on which it can be reached isn't configured through it. Instead, the `AutodiscoverServiceInternalUri` is a property of the Client Access Server that you have to configure as follows:

```
Set-ClientAccessServer EX2013-02 -AutodiscoverServiceInternalUri
  https://autodiscover.exblog.be/Autodiscover/Autodiscover.xml
```

Configuring certificates

Since we are not making any changes to the namespace, we can easily re-use the certificate that was used in Exchange 2010. As described in *Chapter 2, Installing Exchange Server 2013*, this certificate should have at least the following namespaces on it:

- `Autodiscover.exblog.be`
- `Webmail.exblog.be`

First, let's export the certificate from Exchange 2010:

1. Open the Exchange Management Shell on `EX2013-02` and run the following command:

   ```
   Get-ExchangeCertificate -Server EX2010-01
   ```

2. Copy the thumbprint of the certificate that has to be exported.
3. Now, run the following commands:

   ```
   $cert = Export-Exchangecertificate -ThumbPrint <thumbprint>
     -BinaryEncoded:$true -Password (get-credential).password
   Set-Content -Path c:\certexport.pfx -Value $cert.FileData -
     Encoding Byte
   ```

Next, the certificate has to be imported and enabled in Exchange 2013:

1. Copy the certificate from `EX2010-01` to `EX2013-02`.
2. From the Exchange Management Shell on `EX2013-02`, run the following commands:

   ```
   Import-ExchangeCertificate -FileData ([byte[]]$(Get-Content
     C:\certexport.pfx -ReadCount 0 -Encoding Byte)) -Password
     (Get-Credential).password
   ```

3. Lastly, enable the new certificate for IIS and SMTP:

   ```
   Enable-ExchangeCertificate <ThumbPrint> -Services IIS,SMTP
   ```

4. Type *Y* and press *Enter* if you are prompted with a warning about replacing the default SMTP certificate.

Note that you only need to configure certificates on the Client Access Server. For more information on configuring certificates, have a look at *Chapter 4, Configuring MBX*.

Configuring Outlook Anywhere

Because of the change of how Outlook connects to Exchange, Outlook Anywhere is by default enabled in Exchange 2013. In Exchange 2010 and 2007 it was an optional feature that had to be enabled, thus the chances are that you aren't using it yet.

By enabling Outlook Anywhere on Exchange 2007 or 2010, you enable Exchange 2013 to proxy requests for mailboxes that are still hosted on either Exchange 2007 or 2010. This will happen whenever a user connects to Exchange 2013 using Outlook Anywhere.

1. Open the Exchange 2007 or 2010 Management Shell.
2. Type the following command(s):

   ```
   Enable-OutlookAnywhere -Server EX2010-01 -ExternalHostName
     webmail.exblog.be -ClientAuthenticationMethod NTLM -
     IISAuthenticationMethods NTLM
   ```

If Outlook anywhere was already enabled previously, you will only need to modify the IIS authentication method:

```
Get-OutlookAnywhere -Server EX2010-01 | Set-OutlookAnywhere -
  IISAuthenticationMethod NTLM
```

You'll need to configure the proper hostnames and choose appropriate authentication mechanisms.

Configuring a Legacy Namespace (Exchange 2007 only)

Transitioning from Exchange 2007 is not all too different from migrating from Exchange 2010. If you performed upgrades before, you might remember that upgrades from Exchange 2003 and 2007 to Exchange 2010 required you to configure a so-called legacy namespace.

Because Exchange 2013 cannot proxy OWA requests for mailboxes on Exchange 2007, the legacy namespace is also required here. It will allow Exchange 2013 to redirect clients to Exchange 2007 when they login into OWA through Exchange 2013.

1. Open the Exchange Management Shell on the Exchange 2007 server.
2. Execute the following command:

```
Get-OWAVirtualDirectory -Server EX2007 | Set-
  OWAVirtualDirectory -InternalUrl
  https://legacy.exblog.be/OWA -ExternalUrl
  https://legacy.exblog.be/OWA
```

Unfortunately, this redirection is not completely transparent to the user. When logging in through Exchange 2013, your clients will have to authenticate a first time. Exchange 2013 will then redirect them to Exchange 2007 which will prompt them for credentials again, unless you've configured integrated authentication for OWA. In that case, only non-domain-joined clients would have to enter their credentials.

If the legacy namespace isn't included in the certificate for Exchange 2007, you should not forget to request and install a new certificate. Failure to do so might cause a certificate warning whenever users access OWA on Exchange 2007.

As a result of this requirement, some companies decide to use a completely new namespace in Exchange 2013, which would relieve you from requesting a new certificate which can—in some cases be relatively expensive. Another option is to use a relatively cheap wildcard certificate to fulfill this requirement.

Pointing DNS to Exchange 2013

The finale stage of the installation and configuration consists in switching the namespace (`webmail.exblog.be`) from Exchange 2010 to Exchange 2013.

As from the moment you switch DNS, all traffic will flow through Exchange 2013 which will then proxy or redirect request for legacy versions of Exchange.

To point the internal URLs to Exchange 2013, execute the following steps:

1. Open the DNS management console on one of your domain controllers.
2. Navigate to the internal DNS zone (`exblog.be`).

3. Double-click on the webmail host record.
4. Modify the FQDN for the target host to `EX2013-02.exblog.be`:

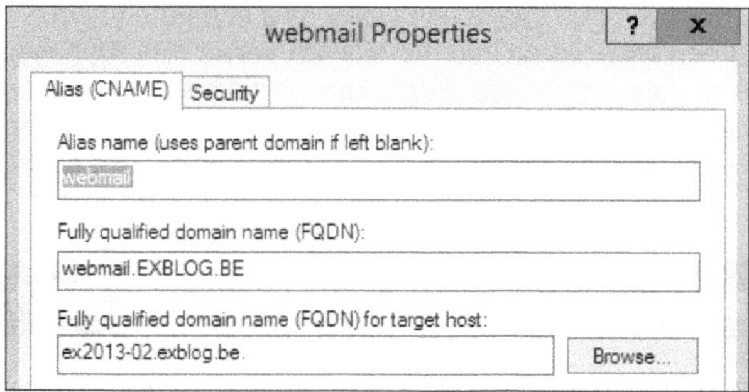

5. Click on **OK**.
6. Repeat steps 3 to step 5 for the Autodiscover host record.

There's more...

Exchange 2013 doesn't contain an Edge server role. Luckily this doesn't mean you cannot use an existing Exchange 2007 or Exchange 2010 Edge Transport server.

Exchange 2013 will not be able to use an existing Edge subscription. Instead, you will have to create a new Edge subscription:

1. Login to the existing Edge Transport server and open the Exchange Management Shell.
2. Run the following command:

```
New-EdgeSubscription -FileName c:\EdgeSubscription.xml
```

3. Copy the xml file to the Exchange 2013 mailbox server you want to subscribe to the Edge Transport server.
4. Open the Exchange Management Shell on the Exchange 2013 server and run the following command:

```
New-EdgeSubscriptions -FileData ([byte[]]$(Get-Content -Path
  "C:\EdgeSubscription.xml" -Encoding Byte -ReadCount 0)) -
  CreateInternetSendConnector $true -
  CreateInboundSendConnector $true
```

5. Lastly, run the following command to force a synchronization:

```
Start-EdgeSynchronization
```

> The Exchange 2007 and 2010 Edge Transport server works a tad differently from Exchange 2013. As such, it expects to connect to a Hub Transport server. However, this role doesn't exist as a separate role anymore and has largely been assimilated into the Mailbox server role. This means that when you are configuring a legacy Edge Transport server, you are bypassing the Exchange 2013 Client Access server. As a result, you also won't be able to import the Edge subscription file on a standalone Client Access Server.

Moving mailboxes to Exchange 2013

The process of how to migrate mailboxes between Exchange 2007, Exchange 2010 and Exchange 2013 is identical to moving mailboxes between databases in Exchange 2013 (see *Chapter 5, Configuring External Access* for more details). Depending on how many users you have to move, you might want to take a different approach though.

Getting ready

To execute the following steps, you will need access to the Exchange Admin Center and Exchange Management Shell.

How to do it...

We will cover certain number of tasks in this section.

Determining migration batches

Depending of the size of your organization, you will either move users all at once or in several batches over several days, weeks, possibly even months.

The first thing you should do however, is test your Exchange 2013 environment by conducting a pilot. The pilot involves moving a small set of regular users that will be moved to Exchange 2013 ahead of the rest and validate that everything is working as it should.

Picking the right people for the pilot is not always easy and should reflect - if possible - all types of profiles: users that rarely use e-mails, heavy e-mail users, c-level management, and personal assistants and so on. Especially personal assistants in particular tend to make good test users. Usually they regularly use features in Outlook that not many others use in the same way such as, accessing someone else's mailbox, working with multiple calendars, and leveraging send-as or send-on-behalf permissions.

When moving people, it's always a good idea to move groups of people that work together, like a department, at the same time. Although this is not a hard requirement when moving from Exchange 2007 or Exchange 2010, it might ease things from a supportability point-of-view.

In order to save some time further down the road, it's handy that you create a CSV file per batch that contains the following information:

- User's display name
- Exchange alias
- Primary e-mail address

Creating migration batches

The following command will create a migration batch for the users specified in a file called users.csv, to a mailbox database called `DB03`:

```
New-MigrationBatch -Name MigBatch1 -CSVData
  ([System.IO.File]::ReadAllBytes("C:\temp\users.csv")) -Local -
  TargetDatabase DB03 -AutoStart -AutoComplete
```

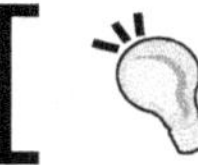

Make sure to specify the full path to where the CSV file is located otherwise the command will fail.

The CSV file should be in the following format:

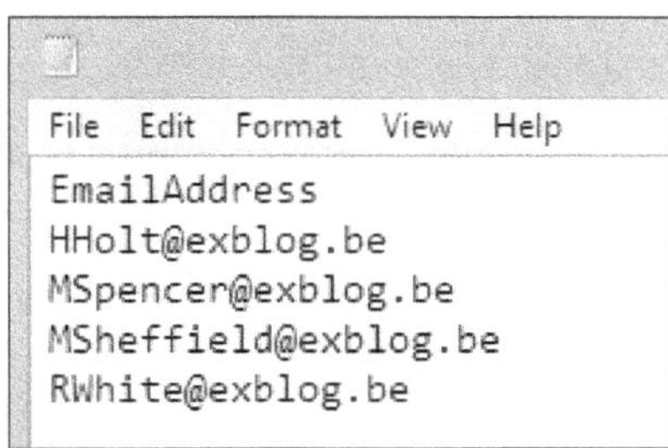
File Edit Format View Help

EmailAddress
HHolt@exblog.be
MSpencer@exblog.be
MSheffield@exblog.be
RWhite@exblog.be

Alternatively, you can do the same from the Exchange Admin Center:

1. Navigate to **recipients** | **migration**.
2. Click on the plus-sign (**+**) and select **Move** to a different database, which will start the **New migration batch** wizard.
3. Click on **Specify the users with a CSV file** and then click on **Browse...** to select it. Once you've located the file, click on **Open** to confirm.
4. In the **New Migration Batch** window, click on **next**.
5. Enter a descriptive name for the migration batch.
6. Select **Move archive mailbox along with primary mailbox**.
7. Click on **browse...** under **Target database** and select the database you want to move the user to. If you don't specify a database, Exchange will choose one itself.

8. Click on **next**.
9. Click on **browse...** and select the recipient that should receive the migration reports by e-mail.
10. Select **Automatically start the batch** and **Automatically complete the migration batch**.
11. Click on **new**.

Executing the preceding steps will create a migration batch and almost immediately start moving mailboxes over to Exchange 2013. If you want to create migration batches ahead of time, have a look at the following topic for more information.

Scheduling migration batches

Although mailbox moves can easily be executed during the day, most companies still prefer to move data at night when there's less load on the systems. In such cases, it is nice that you can schedule migration batches ahead of time so that they kick-off automatically at a later timeframe. Scheduling batches and executing them is a two step process:

1. Create a new migration batch without auto-starting it.
2. Manually (or via a script) start the migration batch.

The only difference from creating a "regular" migration batch is that you now select **Manually start the batch later** at the end of the **New Migration Batch** wizard.

Via the Exchange Management Shell, you don't add the AutoStart parameter:

```
New-MigrationBatch -Name Batch1 -CSVData
  ([System.IO.File]::ReadAllBytes("C:\temp\users.csv")) -Local -
  TargetDatabase DB03 -AutoComplete
```

This command should create a new `MigrationBatch` in the `Created` state. To verify that it was created successfully, run the following command:

```
Get-MigrationBatch
```

```
[PS] C:\>Get-MigrationBatch

Identity                  Status          Type                      TotalCount
--------                  ------          ----                      ----------
migbatch1                 Created         ExchangeLocalMove         1
```

The migration batch will remain in `Created` state until you manually (or via a script) start the migration batch:

```
Start-MigrationBatch -Identity "MigBatch1"
```

You could also use the EAC to start the migration batch:

1. Navigate to **recipients** | **migration**.
2. Select the migration batch you want to start from the list of existing batches.

3. Click on the play-button from the top menu to start the batch.
4. Click on **Yes** to confirm.

If you want the Migration Batch to start automatically at a later time, for instance at night, you should create a Scheduled Task. Start by creating new Exchange script which includes the command to start the batch:

```
Start-MigrationBatch -Identity "MigBatch1"
```

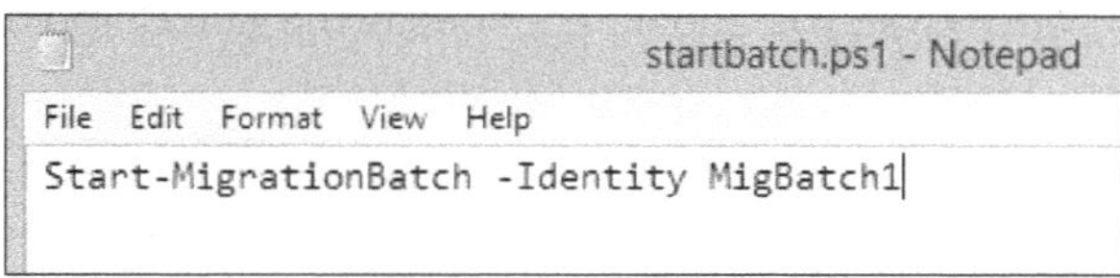

Save the file a `startbatch.ps1` for instance in `C:\Scripts`.

Next, schedule the script through Windows' task scheduler:

1. Open the **Task Scheduler**.
2. Click **Create Basic Task...**.
3. Enter a name for the task. For example, `Migration Batch 1` and click on **Next**.
4. Select **One time** and click on **Next**.
5. Specify the date and time when the script should run and click on **Next**.
6. Select **Start a program** and click on **Next**.
7. Type the following under `Program/script`:

```
PowerShell.exe -command ". 'C:\Program
  Files\Microsoft\Exchange Server\V15\bin\RemoteExchange.ps1';
  Connect-ExchangeServer -auto; C:\Scripts\StartBatch.ps1"
```

8. Click on **Next**. When prompted to confirm you want to run `PowerShell.exe` with specified arguments, click on **Yes**.
9. Click on **Finish**.

The task scheduler will run the script at the configured date and time, which will automatically resume the Migration Batch. Because the `AutoComplete` parameter was specified, the batch will also complete automatically meaning that the user will also be switched over to Exchange 2013.

There's more...

When creating a new migration batch, the `AllowIncrementalSync` parameter is set to `$True` by default. This means that when a migration batch is started, but not completed, data is synchronized from the source mailbox to the target once every 24 hours.

This feature is especially useful in migrations where you want to copy as much data as possible ahead of time so that the last step, including the actual switch-over process completes faster.

Synchronizing data ahead of time

If you want to create migration batches way ahead of time, for instance a few weeks before performing the actual switch-over, you should not specify the AutoComplete-parameter when creating a new batch:

```
New-MigrationBatch -Name MigBatch1 -CSVData
  ([System.IO.File]::ReadAllBytes("C:\temp\users.csv")) -Local -
  TargetDatabase DB03 -AllowIncrementalSyncs
```

When you are ready to execute the switch-over, run the following command. It will run a final synchronization and complete the migration batch:

```
Complete-MigrationBatch -Identity MigBatch1
```

Moving Public Folders to Exchange 2013

Unlike earlier migrations where you could migrate Public Folders ahead of the users, in Exchange 2013 all of your users—who needs access to Public Folders—need to be moved to Exchange 2013 prior to moving the Public Folders. This because Exchange 2010 users cannot access Public Folders hosted on an Exchange 2013 server.

Getting ready

In order to execute the following steps, you need to access the Exchange Management Shell.

How to do it...

In this section we will cover the tasks related to Public Folders:

Gathering Public Folder statistics

In this first step, we'll gather some statistics about the existing Public Folders. This information will allow us to later on verify whether all existing data was copied over to Exchange 2013 successfully.

Run the following commands from the Exchange Management Shell in Exchange 2007/2010 and store the CSV files in a location for later user.

First, let's save the current Public Folder tree-structure:

```
Get-PublicFolder -Recurse | Export-CSV
  C:\MigrationDocuments\PFStructure_2010.csv
```

Next, let's have a look at the items per folder:

```
Get-PublicFolder -Recurse | Get-PublicFolderStatistics | Export-CSV
  C:\MigrationDocuments\PFStats_2010.csv
```

Last but not least, let's save the current client permissions for each Public Folder:

```
Get-PublicFolder -GetChildren | Get-PublicFolderClientPermission |
  Select Identity,User -ExpandProperty AccessRights | Export-CSV
  C:\MigrationDocuments\PFPermissions_2010.csv
```

Preparing Exchange 2007/2010 for the migration

Before attempting to migrate Public Folders, you need to make sure there is no trace of a previous (successful) migration attempt.

To verify this, run the following commands from the Exchange Management Shell:

```
Get-OrganizationConfig | FT PublicFoldersLockedForMigration,
  PublicFolderMigrationComplete -AutoSize
```

Both values should be set to `False`. If not, run the following command to reset the values:

```
Set-OrganizationConfig -PublicFoldersLockedForMigration $False -
  PublicFolderMigrationComplete $False
```

Preparing Exchange 2013 for the migration

Just as in Exchange 2007/2010 there should be no trace of a previous migration attempt in Exchange 2013. To verify if there are any existing migration requests, run the following command:

```
Get-PublicFolderMigrationRequest
```

If existing requests are found, remove them:

```
Get-PublicFolderMigrationRequest | Remove-
  PublicFolderMigrationRequest -Confirm:$false
```

To verify that the preceding command worked, run the following commands:

```
Get-Mailbox -PublicFolder
Get-PublicFolder
```

The `Get-PublicFolder` command should return an error stating the following:

No active public folder mailboxes were found. This happens when no public folder mailboxes are provisioned or they are provisioned in 'HoldForMigration' mode. If you're not currently performing a migration, create a public folder mailbox.

Generating the CSV files for migration

The first step in the migration consists of exporting existing Public Folder data to the CSV files. These files will be used to map existing Public Folders to new Public Folder mailboxes.

1. Navigate to `C:\Program Files\Microsoft\Exchange Server\V15\Scripts` and copy the following two files to one of your legacy Exchange servers:
   - `Export-PublicFolderStatistics.ps1`
   - `Export-PublicFolderStatistics.strings.psd1`
2. Open the Exchange Management Shell on the legacy Exchange server (`EX2010-01`).
3. Type `cd $exscripts`.
4. Run the following command:

   ```
   Export-PublicFolderStatistics.ps1 -PublicFolderServer EX2010-
     01.exblog.be -FilePath "C:\MigrationDocuments\PFStats.csv"
   ```

Next, we need to use the results from this file to generate another CSV file that will "map" the existing Public Folders to new Public Folder mailboxes, based on a maximum size for the Public Folder mailbox:

1. Copy the `PFStats.csv` file to the same folder on `EX2013-02`.
2. Open the Exchange Management Shell on `EX2013-02` and type `cd $exscripts`.
3. Run the following command:

   ```
   PublicFolderToMailboxMapGenerator.ps1 -MailboxSize 5242880
     -ImportFile c:\MigrationDocuments\PFStats.csv -ExportFile
     C:\MigrationDocuments\PFMap.csv
   ```

Changing Public Folder names

The preceding script will, by default, give all Public Folders a name such as `Mailbox1`, `Mailbox2`, `Mailbox3`, and so on. It's not unthinkable, you might want to change this into a more appealing name conform your companies guidelines.

To do so, open the `PFMap.csv` file and edit it accordingly by renaming `Mailbox1` into for example, `PFMBX01`. Repeat, if necessary, for other Public Folder mailboxes as well:

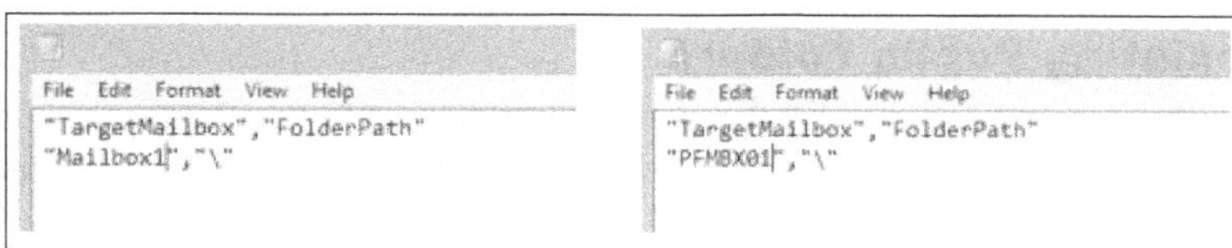

Creating Public Folders

Unfortunately, Exchange 2013 will not automatically create Public Folders based on the output from the `PublicFolderToMailboxMapGenerator.ps1` script. As a result, you will need to manually create the Public Folders from the `PFMap.csv` file.

The first Public Folder that you create, will become the master hierarchy mailbox. You should also treat it a little differently from the rest by adding the `-HoldForMigration` parameter:

```
New-Mailbox -PublicFolder -Name PFMBX01 -HoldForMigration
```

All subsequent Public Folder mailboxes can be created as follows:

```
New-Mailbox -PublicFolder -Name PFMBX02
New-Mailbox -PublicFolder -Name PFMBX03
```

Initiating the Public Folder move request

Once you've completed the preceding steps, run the following command to kick of the Public Folder move request:

```
New-PublicFolderMoveRequest -SourceDatabase (Get-PublicFolderDatabase
  -Server EX2010-01) -CSVData (Get-Content
  C:\MigrationDocuments\PFMap.csv -Encoding Byte)
```

To follow up on the status of the move request, run the following command:

```
Get-PublicFolderMigrationRequest
```

For more detailed information, you can run the following command, similar to querying detailed information for mailbox move requests:

```
Get-PublicFolderMigrationRequest | Get-
  PublicFolderMigrationRequestStatistics
```

Once the status of the migration request has reached `AutoSuspended`, you can move to the next step:

Locking existing Public Folders

Now that everything is in place to start the actual migration of Public Folder data, the existing Public Folders (in Exchange 2007/2010) will have to be locked down to prevent users from making changes to them.

When executing the following commands, logged on users will be logged of and the Public Folders will be marked as read-only:

```
Set-OrganizationConfig -PublicFoldersLockedForMigration $True
```

> Please note that if you have multiple Public Folder databases, it might take a while before all databases replicated the `PublicFoldersLockedForMigration` flag. If you want to speed up things, restart the `MSExchangeIS` service.

Completing the Public Folder migration request

The following step is to resume the previously created Public Folder migration request.

```
Get-PublicFolderMigrationRequest | Set-PublicFolderMigrationRequest -
  PreventCompletion:$false
Get-PublicFolderMigrationRequest | Resume-
  PublicFolderMigrationRequest
```

During this step of the migration, the Public Folders will remain inaccessible to your users. Make sure to plan accordingly for this downtime. The following screenshot displays the error a user when trying to access a Public Folder in Outlook during this period:

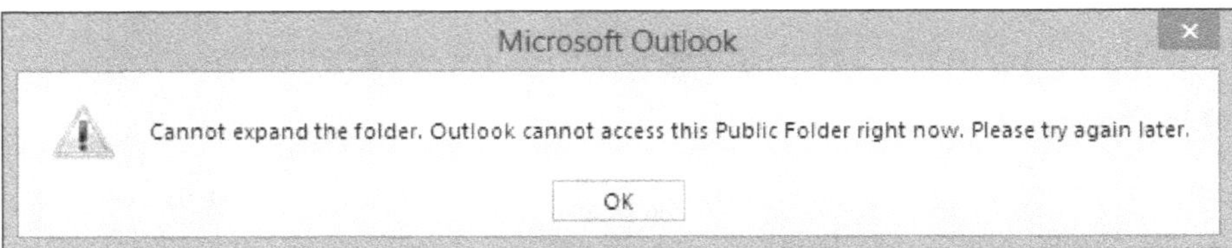

Verifying the migration

In the very first step of the migration, we gathered some statistics on the legacy Public Folders. We will now do the same for the Public Folders on Exchange 2013:

```
Get-PublicFolder -Recurse | Export-CSV
  C:\MigrationDocuments\PFStructure_2013.csv
Get-PublicFolder -Recurse | Get-PublicFolderStatistics | Export-CSV
  C:\MigrationDocuments\PFStats_2013.csv
Get-PublicFolder -GetChildren | Get-PublicFolderClientPermission |
  Select Identity,User -ExpandProperty AccessRights | Export-CSV
  C:\MigrationDocuments\PFPermissions_2013.csv
```

Once all of the information has been exported, you'll need to compare the files created earlier against the once that were just created for Exchange 2013. If everything went well, they should both have matching data for each Public Folder.

Finalizing and cleaning up

If everything went as expected, you are now ready to finalize the migration and clean up the Public Folders from the legacy Exchange server environment.

To finalize the migration in Exchange 2013, run the following commands. The first command will mark the migration as completed:

```
Set-OrganizationConfig -PublicFolderMigrationComplete:$true
```

Next, configure the mailboxes in your organization to use one of the Public Folder mailboxes as their default Public Folder mailbox:

```
Set-Mailbox -Identity <user> -DefaultPublicFolderMailbox "PFMBX01"
```

Cleaning up the legacy environment, consists of removing the remaining Public Folder databases:

```
Remove-PublicFolderDatabase -Identity <legacyDatabase>
```

Before you'll be able to delete existing Public Folder databases from Exchange 2007 or 2010, existing Public Folders have to be removed first.

Have a look at the following pages for more information on how to remove Public Folders and Public Folder databases from an Exchange 2007 or 2010 environment:

- http://technet.microsoft.com/en-us/library/dd876883(EXCHG.140).aspx
- http://technet.microsoft.com/en-us/library/cc164367(EXCHG.80).aspx

There's more...

Performing delta synchronizations

After a Public Folder Migration Request completes copying data, it will automatically suspend itself and go into the so-called `AutoSuspended` state. That way the actual switch-over, which requires downtime, happens in a much shorter time as only the changes between the time you've created the migration request and the time that you're completing the request have to be copied over.

Sometimes, especially in larger environments that heavily rely on Public Folders, a lot of data might have been added between those two moments. This would cause the completion phase to take more time, resulting in a longer downtime for your clients.

To overcome this issue, you can regularly resume the migration request without specifying– the `PreventCompletion:$false` parameter first. That way, you prevent all changes from accumulating and taking up more time during the completion.

```
Get-PublicFolderMigrationRequest | Resume-
  PublicFolderMigrationRequest
```

Rolling back a migration

Sometimes things can happen that might require you to roll-back a migration. For instance, this could happen when a line-of-business application is behaving badly after migrating to Exchange 2013 and forcing you to move one or more users back to Exchange 2007 or 2010.

Start by unlocking the Public Folders:

```
Set-OrganizationConfig -PublicFoldersLockedForMigration:$false
```

```
Set-OrganizationConfig -PublicFolderMigrationComplete:$false
```

Next, if you want your Exchange 2013 users to be able to access Public Folders in Exchange 2007 or 2010, you also need to remove all Public Folders from Exchange 2013:

```
Get-Mailbox -PublicFolder | Remove-Mailbox -PublicFolder
```

Public Folder migrations are a one way process. This means that you can copy Public Folders from a legacy Exchange version to Exchange 2013, but you cannot copy Public Folders from Exchange 2013 back. As a result, when rolling back a migration, you are "throwing away" any changes made to the Public Folders in Exchange 2013.

Post migration steps

Getting ready

Once all mailboxes and Public Folders have been moved over, you are almost ready to start decommissioning your older Exchange 2007 or 2010 server.

However, there are still some small steps that you need to take prior to removing them from the environment.

How to do it...

This section comprises of task related to the post migration steps.

Configuring send connectors

Send connector are used to send e-mails either to the Internet or other messaging systems. When installing Exchange 2013, it will not automatically add the Exchange 2013 transport servers to the list of server allowed to use the send connector.

Prior to removing Exchange 2010, these settings need to be updated so that the Exchange 2013 servers are also part of the `SourceTransportServers` list:

```
Set-SendConnector -Identity "Internet" -SourceTransportServers
  @{Add="EX2013-01"}
```

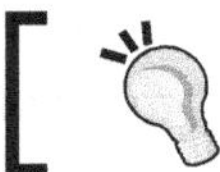

Make sure to repeat this step for each send connector.

Performing maintenance in a co-existence scenario

Getting ready

To perform the following steps, you must login to the Exchange Management Shell on an Exchange 2010 server.

How to do it...

To take an Exchange 2010 "out-of-service" so that Exchange 2013 wouldn't proxy any new requests to it, run the following command from Exchange 2010:

```
Set-ClientAccessServer -Identity EX2010-01 -IsOutOfService $true
```

How it works...

In a coexistence scenario, Exchange 2013 will be the ingress point for all client connectivity. The Exchange 2013 Client Access Server will be based on the location of the user's mailbox—proxy the request over to the appropriate mailbox or Client Access Server.

In case of coexistence with Exchange 2010, the Exchange 2013 CAS will always proxy request to the Exchange 2010 Client Access Server. In order to know where it needs to send the request to, Exchange 2013 will "construct" a URL from the Exchange 2010's server fully qualified domain name instead of using one of the pre-configured URLs.

For example: if Exchange 2013 needs to proxy a request for OWA to Exchange 2010, it will connect to `https://exchange2010servername.domain.com/owa` instead of the `InternalUrl` or `ExternalUrl` value of the OWA virtual directory of that server. This prevents issues where one of the URLs would be the same as the ones for Exchange 2013.

In order to know what Exchange 2010 Client Access Servers are available to send requests to, managed availability will actually poll each Exchange 2010 server, every 10 seconds, to determine whether the server is available or not.

By putting an Exchange 2010 Client Access Server out of service, you don't really take down the service, instead you make it appear offline to Exchange 2013 so that it won't proxy requests over to it. This can be useful when for example you are patching the server, but also when you don't want a server to receive those connections.

There's more...

Have a look at *Chapter 6, Implementing and Managing High Availability*, for additional information on how to put an Exchange 2013 server into maintenance mode.

8
Configuring Security and Compliance Features

In this chapter, you will learn how to configure and use Exchange's built-in security and compliance features such as archiving, Transport rules, Data Loss Prevention, and rights management. As part of this chapter, you will learn the following:

- Configuring personal archives
- Enabling In-Place Hold for a mailbox
- Performing discovery searches
- Configuring Transport rules
- Creating Data Loss Prevention policies
- Using Mailbox Audit logging

Introduction

In many companies, e-mail is the most commonly used way of communicating with one another. As a result, a lot of a company's intellectual property is sent with and stored within Exchange. Not taking measures to secure the environment would pose a potential threat to your data as it could leave the door open for possible data leakage.

If you're dealing with personal or financial information of third-parties, leaking data, whether it is accidentally or on purpose, could have serious legal consequences. Microsoft realizes that in this modern world of digital communication, Exchange needs to be able to handle all sorts of threats. That is why over the past few years Microsoft has invested a lot of time and effort in developing and improving native protection features that can help you secure your data against different types of threats.

To meet regulatory requirements towards data retention, **In-Place archiving** and **In-Place Hold** allow you to control how long to keep data: for a specific amount of time or, if necessary, indefinitely. Transport rules and Data Loss Prevention help identifying potential risky transactions and take appropriate actions before evil is done. Integrated Rights Management on the other hand, helps ensuring your data remains safe, regardless of its location. It also helps securing data so that only authorized persons can access, modify, or otherwise handle it.

Last but not least, features such as mailbox audit logging help keeping an eye on the environment so that you'd be able to determine if some user or administrator might have gone rogue.

All in all, even though these features all together are not able to secure your environment completely, they do offer a comprehensive, but foremost built-in feature set that will satisfy most of your requirements and needs.

Configuring In-Place Archiving

Over the years, many companies have grown accustomed to using PST files to offer users an archive-like experience. Especially, the ease of use and neat integration within Outlook made it a very popular feature. On the other hand, PST files also have some severe drawbacks. First of all, as they should only be stored locally on the computer, it's very difficult to make them highly available. To work around this problem, many companies have wrongly stored PST files on a network share. However, this is not supported and can easily render a PST file corrupt. Not to mention the slowness it brings upon Outlook and the fact they're not available through OWA. All in all, enough reasons to try to avoid them.

Because PST files should be stored locally on the computer, you as an administrator have little or no control over them, meaning that you cannot easily control access to them nor can you apply policies on them. As a result, PST files can be a liability to the security of your data as you've got no means to protect them from data loss or theft.

In-Place Archives are Exchange's answer to PST files. Not only are these archives stored on the Exchange server (and also available through OWA!), but at the same time they can help to alleviate the load on the client by reducing the OST file size. Archives are also a great way to store infrequently needed e-mails for longer periods of time without cluttering or over-growing the primary mailbox. This could, for instance, be the case when a compliancy rule dictates that your company is required to keep data for a certain amount of time.

An administrator could, for instance, control how long messages are kept and, in combination with retention policies, make sure messages are deleted once they've passed their retention time.

And then there are the architectural benefits, archives can potentially bring. By combining the power of Office 365 and your on-premises archives, you can offload the archives to Office 365 which helps reduce your on-premises data footprint and the costs associated therewith.

How to do it...

In this section we will learn how to configure In-Place Archiving

Enabling an in-place Archive for a mailbox

For enabling an In-Place Archive for a mailbox, execute the following steps to create an archive through the **Exchange Admin Center** (**EAC**):

1. Login to the EAC and navigate to **recipients** | **mailboxes**.
2. Select the mailbox for which you want to enable an archive.
3. Click on **Enable under In-Place Archive** at the right-hand side of the screen.
4. In **create in-place archive-wizard**, click on **browse...** and select a mailbox database.

The archive does not have to be stored within the same database as the user's primary mailbox. If you do not select a database, Exchange will select a random database itself.

5. Click on **OK**.

Alternatively, you can also create an archive through the Management Shell. The following command will create an archive for a user named "Andrew Dunn":

```
Enable-Mailbox -Identity ADunn -Archive
```

To specify in which database an archive should get created, run the following command:

```
Enable-Mailbox -Identity ADunn -Archive -ArchiveDatabase MDB01
```

After you've enabled the archive, you will see that the EAC will now change the mailbox type from **User** to **User (Archive)**. To check the Archive details through the Exchange Management Shell, run the following command:

```
Get-Mailbox ADunn | fl *archive*
```

Creating policy tags

Execute the following steps to create a new **Default Policy Tag** (**DPT**) using the EAC:

1. Login to the EAC and navigate to **compliance management** | **retention tags**.
2. Click the plus-sign (**+**) and select **applied automatically to entire mailbox (default)**.

To create a new personal tag, select **applied by users to items and folders (personal)** instead.

3. Enter a name for the Default Policy Tag, for example, `Default Tag 1 Year to Archive`.
4. Select **Move to Archive** as the retention action.
5. Specify a retention period in days. Enter `180`, the equivalent to about six months.
6. It's highly recommended, but not required, to enter a description for this policy tag. Click on **save** to confirm.

Creating a default policy tag through the EAC is done by using the following command. This command will create a default policy tag that will move items to the archive after one year:

```
New-RetentionPolicyTag -Name "DPT 1 Year to Archive" -Type All -
AgeLimitForRetention 365 -RetentionAction MoveToArchive
```

Creating personal tags is done slight differently. The following command will create a personal tag that moves items to the archive after a period of 180 days:

```
New-RetentionPolicyTag -Name "Move to archive 6 Months" -Type Personal -
AgeLimitForRetention 180 -RetentionAction MoveToArchive
```

To disable archiving for the item or folder to which the following tag is applied, use this command:

```
New-RetentionPolicyTag -Name "Never move to archive" -Type Personal -
RetentionEnabled $false -RetentionAction MoveToArchive
```

Applying personal tags

Personal tags can be applied either using Outlook (2010 or newer) or through Outlook Web App. They can be applied to items or folders:

1. Open Outlook or Outlook Web App.
2. Right-click on the folder or message you want to assign a tag to and click on **Assign Policy**.
3. Select the appropriate personal tag. For instance, **Personal 1 year move to archive (1 Year)** in OWA or **1 year in Outlook**.

The screenshot for Outlook Web App is as follows:

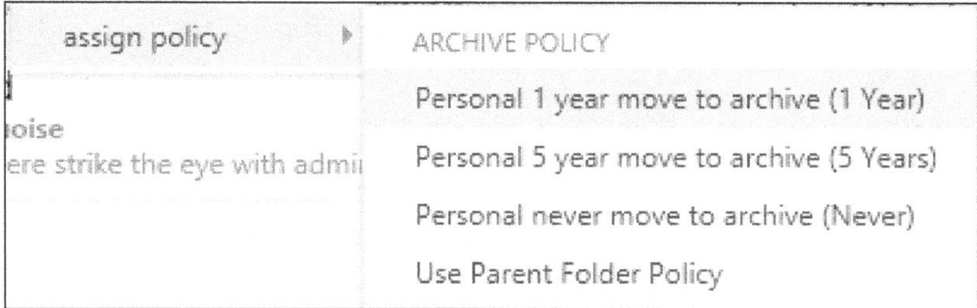

The screenshot for Outlook 2013 is as follows:

Creating retention policies

A retention policy is a collection of one or more linked retention policy tags. By assigning a retention policy to a user's mailbox, you effectively make the tags linked to that policy available to the user.

For more information on the difference between a default policy tag, a retention tag, and a personal tag, have a look at the following *How it works...* section.

The following command will create a new retention policy called `NewArchivePolicy` and link the **Personal 1 year move to archive (1 Year)** retention policy to it:

```
New-RetentionPolicy -Name "NewArchivePolicy" -RetentionPolicyTagLinks
"Personal 1 year move to archive"
```

It is also possible to specify multiple retention tags at once. For example, the following command will create a retention policy called `NewArchivePolicy` and link two retention policy tags to it: **Personal 1 year move to archive (1 Year)** and **Personal never move to archive**:

```
New-RetentionPolicy -Name "NewArchivePolicy" -RetentionPolicyTagLinks
"Personal 1 year move to archive","Personal never move to archive"
```

> Note that although a retention policy can have multiple retention tags linked to it, it can only contain a single default policy tag.

To create a retention policy through the EAC, execute the following steps:

1. Login to the EAC and navigate to **compliance management** | **retention policies**.
2. Click on the plus sign (**+**) to start the **new retention policy** wizard.
3. Enter a name, for example, `NewArchivePolicy`.
4. Click on the plus sign (**+**) to select one or more existing retention tags. Click on **add** and then **Ok** to add them to the policy.
5. Click on **Ok** again to create the policy.

Adding retention policy tag links to an existing retention policy

The following command would not have the desired result as it would override and therefore remove the existing retention tag links from the policy:

```
Set-RetentionPolicy "NewArchivePolicy" -RetentionPolicyTagLinks "6 Months move to archive"
```

Instead, we need to work around this problem by capturing the existing links into a variable and adding the new retention tag link to that variable before applying it to the retention policy:

```
$RetentionTags = (Get-RetentionPolicy "NewArchivePolicy").RetentionPolicyTagLinks

$RetentionTags+= "6 Months move to archive"

Set-RetentionPolicy "NewArchivePolicy" -RetentionPolicyTagLinks $RetentionTags
```

Modifying a retention policy through the EAC offers the benefit that it doesn't require the workaround as it will automatically leave the existing links in place:

1. Login to the EAC and navigate to **compliance management** | **retention policies**.
2. Double-click on the retention policy you want to modify. For example. **NewArchivePolicy**.
3. Click on the plus sign (**+**) to select one or more new retention tags.
4. Select the appropriate retention tags from the **select retention tags** window. Then, click on **add** and **Ok** to add them to the policy.
5. Click on **save** to save the changes to the policy.

Assigning retention policies

Before a retention policy becomes effective, it has to be assigned to a user's mailbox. The following command will apply the **NewArchivePolicy** retention policy for Andrew Dunn's mailbox:

```
Set-Mailbox Adunn - RetentionPolicy NewArchivePolicy
```

Alternatively, you could also do it through the EAC:

1. Log in to the EAC and navigate to **recipients** | **mailboxes**.
2. Double-click on the mailbox of the user you want to assign the retention policy to.
3. Navigate to **mailbox features**.
4. Select the retention policy you created earlier from the drop-down list under **Retention policy**.
5. Click on **save**.

Configuring the Managed Folder Assistant (MFA)

The Managed Folder Assistant is, amongst other things, responsible for applying retention policies. It inspects the items in the mailbox and evaluates whether they are subject to one of the retention tags from the retention policy that is applied to the mailbox. In case an item is subject to one of the tags, that item gets "stamped" and the MFA will then apply the action specified by the tag.

The MFA is a so-called throttle-based assistant: it runs continuously in the background, so there is no need to schedule it. By default, the MFA is configured to process all mailboxes on a daily basis. In Exchange, this is referred to as the MFA's work cycle, which is thus set to `1`.

Using the following command, you can modify the work cycle, for example set it to `2` days:

```
Set-MailboxServer "EX2013-01" -ManagedFolderWorkCycle 2
```

Usually, there is no need to modify the default value of one day. However, if you are, for example, having performance issues, (temporarily) increasing the amount of days in the work cycle might help alleviating the system.

Enabling or disabling retention hold

When a user leaves the office for a period of time (for example, on an extended leave), it might well be that one or the other retention tag is applied to items before the user has had the chance to access them.

In such case, you can configure what's called a **retention hold** on a mailbox. which will temporarily suspend the processing of retention policies on the mailbox. The following command will enable retention hold for Andrew Dunn's mailbox:

```
Set-Mailbox Adunn -RetentionHoldEnabled $True
```

Disabling the retention hold is as simple as running the following command:

```
Set-Mailbox ADunn -RetentionHoldEnabled $False
```

How it works...

As explained earlier, retention tags are used to apply retention settings to an entire mailbox, its folders, or items within that mailbox. There are three types of retention tags:

- **Default Policy Tag**: It is applied to all untagged items
- **Retention Policy Tag**: It is applied to default folders like the `Inbox`, `Sent Items`, `Calendar`, and so on
- **Personal Tag**: It is applied by the user on a per-folder or per-item base

> Not all available retention actions can be associated with all of the retention types mentioned in the preceding section. For instance, a retention policy can only be associated to (permanently) delete items whereas Personal Tags can also be associated with an action to move items to the archive (**MoveToArchive**).

Although a tag typically consists of multiple properties including its name or a description, the following three tags are the ones we're particularly interested in as they define the core functions of the tag itself:

- **Retention time**: Defines the amount of time to keep an item
- **Retention action**: Defines what to do with the item after the retention time
- **Type**: Defines on which type of items a tag can be applied

A default policy tag is a tag for which the type has been set to **All**. When a retention policy contains a default policy tag, all (untagged) items in a mailbox are subject to the settings from that specific tag. This also means that once the MFA has processed the mailbox for the first time, the retention action associated with that tag is executed on all the items.

If a retention policy contains multiple retention tags, for example, a mixture of personal tags, the user can manually choose to override the default settings which are applied by the default policy tag, by manually assigning one of the personal tags from the retention policy to one or more items or folders.

Personal tags are tags for which the type has been set to **Personal**. Unlike the default policy tag, which can only have one per retention policy, you can link multiple personal tags to a retention policy. It is best practice not to overload a user with different retention tags to choose from. Therefore, it is a good idea to limit the total amount of personal tags in a retention policy to four or maybe five.

Although regular retention policy tags are very useful, they cannot be used to move items into an archive. Instead, they can only be used to automatically organize a user's mailbox by deleting items after a specified amount of time.

When the MFA processes items, it will always take into account the tag that is applied closest to the item. This means that a tag that is applied to an item has a higher priority than tags applied to folders or the default policy tag.

There's more...

When the MFA passes through a mailbox, it will use a variety of rules to check if an item is past its retention age so that it can take the appropriate retention action. Depending on the type of the item (message, task, calendar entry, and so on), the MFA will determine the age differently. To find out more about this process, have a look at the following web page:

`http://technet.microsoft.com/en-us/library/bb430780(v=exchg.150).aspx`

Delegating access to an archive

You cannot explicitly grant someone access to an archive, or items and folders within that archive. Additionally, if someone has only limited access to some or all of a user's primary mailbox folders, they will have no permissions on the archive whatsoever.

In order to provide someone with access to the archive, they have to be granted full mailbox access on the primary mailbox, which will automatically grant them access to the Archive as well. Using the Auto-Mapping feature, the archive will then automatically show up in the delegate's Outlook. As the name of the feature might have given away already, Auto-Mapping will ensure that mailboxes (and archives) that a user has access to will automatically show up in Outlook.

Exchange Online Archiving (EOA)

For those who are looking to implement archives, but lack the available storage space to keep the data, Exchange Online Archiving is be an interesting alternative. Exchange Online Archiving is a feature that enables you to keep your primary mailbox on-premises while storing the archive mailbox in Office 365. Because this feature leverages a hybrid configuration, logon operations of the archive are fully transparent to the end user.

For more information on Online Archiving, have a look at the following URL:

`http://office.microsoft.com/en-us/exchange/microsoft-exchange-online-archiving-archiving-email-FX103763589.aspx`

Enabling In-Place Hold for a mailbox

Sometimes companies are required to keep part of their data for a certain amount of time. This is often the case when the company is subject to one (or more) regulatory requirements or possibly under investigation.

One way to go about this is to kindly ask users not to delete items from their mailbox or maybe move them into a special container. Using Outlook rules you might even be able to automate part of this task. The problem is that this doesn't ascertain that all data is preserved as it cannot prevent user from accidentally deleting something. It also does not prevent tampering with items or just a user's bad intent. Let's just hope the latter doesn't happen all that often!

In-Place Hold, being a server-side feature, allows for easy preservation of data from one or more mailboxes. Items can be kept indefinitely, based on a query or on a period of time (time-based); all without requiring the user's interaction.

Getting ready

Before starting the following tasks, make sure you have the appropriate permissions (member of the Discovery Management role group).

How to do it...

The following command will create an indefinite In-Place Hold for Andrew Dunn's mailbox:

```
New-MailboxSearch "Hold-1" -SourceMailboxes "ADunn" -InPlaceHoldEnabled
$true
```

Similarly, disabling the In-Place Hold is done as follows:

```
Set-MailboxSearch "Hold-1" -SourceMailboxes "ADunn" -InPlaceHoldEnabled
$false
```

Disabling the In-Place Hold doesn't necessarily remove the mailbox search that you created.

By default, a user won't notice that his or her mailbox is enabled for an In-Place Hold (also referred to as a legal hold). Luckily, you can use the retention comment and retention URL parameters to configure a message and a link, which will be shown in Outlook. The link can be used to point to a company-internal web page that contains more information about legal hold.

The following command will configure a comment and URL for Andrew Dunn's mailbox:

```
Set-Mailbox ADunn -RetentionComment "Your mailbox has been placed on a
legal hold" -RetentionUrl "http://companyweb/legalhold"
```

After a restart of the Outlook client, the user would see the following settings in Outlook's backstage. Clicking on **More Information** would take the user to the URL you configured before as shown in the following screenshot:

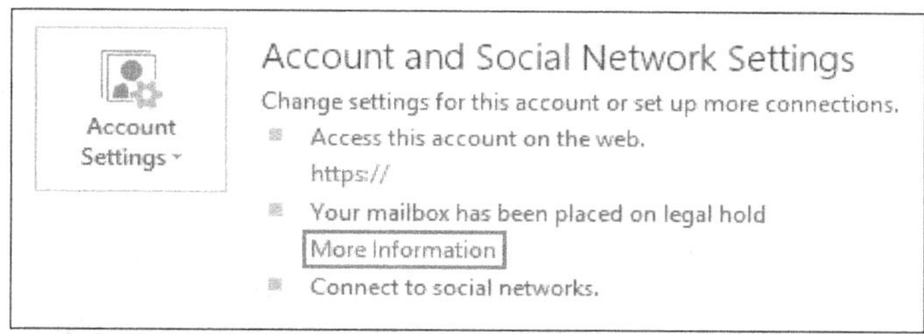

Alternatively, you can also perform the following actions through the EAC:

1. Log in to the EAC and navigate to **compliance management** | **in-place eDiscovery & hold**.
2. Click on the plus sign (**+**) to open the **new in-Place eDiscovery & hold** wizard.
3. Enter a name for the hold, for example, `Hold-1`. It's always a good idea to enter a description, especially when the name of the hold isn't very descriptive.
4. Click on **Next**
5. Select **Specify mailboxes to search** and click on the plus sign (**+**) to select one or more mailboxes. Click on **add** and then **Ok** to effectively add the mailboxes to the hold.
6. Click on **Next**.
7. Leave the default (**Include all user mailbox content**) and click on **Next**.
8. Check the box next to **Place content matching the search query in select mailboxes on hold** and make sure to select **Hold indefinitely**.
9. Click on **Finish** to enable the In-Place Hold.

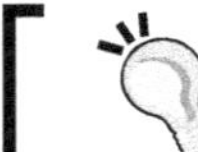

You cannot use the EAC to configure a retention comment or retention URL.

After creating a Mailbox Search, it should automatically start. In a coexistence scenario with Exchange 2010, you might notice that the search remains in a queued state. This is probably because the Discovery Search System mailbox (`SystemMailbox{e0dc1c29-89c3-4034-b678-e6c29d823ed9}`) is still hosted on Exchange 2010.

To get the Mailbox Search running, move that mailbox to Exchange 2013 and stop/restart the Mailbox Search.

How it works...

In-Place Hold preserves items from a mailbox by storing them in the hidden folder under the mailbox hierarchy, called the Recoverable Items folder also known as the **dumpster**.

Under normal circumstances, whenever an item is deleted from the mailbox it is first moved to the Deleted Items folder. *Shift* + deleting or deleting an item from the Deleted Items folder will move that item into the Deletions folder of the Recoverable Items folder. The deleted item will remain there until it's past the deleted items retention period. By default, this period is 14 days which means that after the initial 14 days, items will get purged from the deleted items folder gradually.

When an In-Place Hold is enabled, the deleted items retention period is ignored (as is the storage quota for the recoverable items) and items are moved into one or more subfolders of the Recoverable Items folder:

- DiscoveryHold
- Versions

Unlike the Deletions subfolder, which allows user interaction through the Recover deleted items feature, these folders are completely invisible to the user.

Deleted items are moved from the user's mailbox into the DiscoveryHold folder. There, the item will remain until the period defined by the hold has passed. If no time-based query was defined, the item will be kept indefinitely. This means that it will remain in the folder until the In-Place Hold is removed.

Putting a mailbox on an In-Place Hold not only means that items should be kept after they are deleted, but also should prevent tampering of items. In a nutshell, Exchange uses a mechanism that is called copy-on-write, which will create a copy of the original item every time the item is being changed.

For an overview of what actions trigger the copy-on-write process, have a look at the following URL:

`http://technet.microsoft.com/en-us/library/ff637980(v=exchg.150).aspx#RIF`

There's more...

There is more in store, which is explained in the following sections.

Time and query based hold

Next to the indefinite In-Place Hold as described earlier, you can also use a time and query based approach to place items in a mailbox in hold. This can be particularly useful if there are only a specific set of items you are looking for or if you know upfront the amount of time that a mailbox needs to be placed on hold.

To configure a time-based hold, execute the following steps:

1. Log in to the EAC and navigate to **compliance management** | **in-place eDiscovery & hold**.
2. Click on the plus sign (**+**) to open the **new in-Place eDiscovery & hold** wizard.
3. Enter a name for the hold, for example, `Time-hold-2`. It's always a good idea to enter a description, especially when the name of the hold isn't very descriptive.
4. Click on **Next**.
5. Select **Specify mailboxes to search** and click on the plus sign (**+**) to select one or more mailboxes. Click on **add** and then **Ok** to effectively add the mailboxes to the hold.
6. Click on **Next**.
7. Select **Filter based on criteria**.
8. Check the box next to **Specify start date and Specify end date** and configure dates accordingly. Then click on **Next**.
9. Check the box next to **Place content matching the search query in select mailboxes on hold** and make sure to select **Hold indefinitely**.
10. Click on **Finish** to enable the In-Place Hold.

Litigation hold

Although, we showed you how to configure a litigation hold, the use of this feature is highly deemphasized as Microsoft has decided to deprecate the feature. It's recommended that you use In-Place eDiscovery and hold to configure an indefinite In-Place hold for a mailbox.

eDiscovery in SharePoint 2013

New in SharePoint 2013 is the eDiscovery Center, which when configured, allows to use SharePoint to perform eDiscovery searches in Exchange 2013. Compared to Exchange 2013, the eDiscovery Center offers much more functionality and has the ability to perform searches over different content stores like Exchange, SharePoint, and Lync.

How to configure this integration is beyond the scope of this book. If you're interested in knowing more about this feature, the following TechNet article is worth reading. It explains how to set up, configure, and integrate eDiscovery:

`http://technet.microsoft.com/en-us/library/fp161514.aspx`

Retrieving Discovery Search results

Creating a Discovery Search, for example, to put a mailbox on an In-Place hold, is one thing; getting the results is another. Not that fetching the results is a difficult thing to do, but there are some things to look out for.

Getting ready

In order to complete the following tasks, you need to be at least a member of the Discovery Management role group.

How to do it...

When you create a new Mailbox Search, it will automatically be started. Before being able to modify properties of an existing search, for instance, like which mailboxes you want to include, the search has to be stopped and re-started.

The following command will stop the active mailbox search called `Hold-2`:

```
Stop-MailboxSearch -Identity "Hold-2"
```

Unsurprisingly, starting a search is done as follows:

```
Start-MailboxSearch -Identity "Hold-2"
```

Alternatively, you can also achieve the same results using the EAC:

1. Log in to the EAC and navigate to **compliance management** | **In-place eDiscovery & hold**.
2. Select the search you want to stop and then click on the stop button.
3. To resume, click on the resume button.

Retrieving search results

When you are ready to retrieve the results of a specific Mailbox Search, you can easily copy the results to one of the Discovery Search mailboxes in your organization. From there, anyone who has access to that mailbox can also access the search result. During the Exchange installation, a first Discovery Mailbox is automatically created for you.

To export the results of a previously created Mailbox Search, perform the following steps:

1. Log in to the EAC and navigate to **compliance management** | **in-place eDiscover & hold**.
2. Click on the magnifier and select **Copy search results**.
3. A new window will pop up. Select **Send me mail when the copy is completed**.
4. Click on **browse...** and select the Discovery mailbox where the results should be copied to.
5. Click on **Copy**.

The copy might take a while, depending on the amount of e-mails that have to be copied to the Discovery Search mailbox. However, because you selected an e-mail to be sent when the copy is complete, you are now free to do other things.

Once the copy is complete, you should receive an e-mail similar to the following screenshot:

Percent Complete:	100%
Started by:	Michael Van Horenbeeck
Stopped by:	N/A
Start Time:	10/05/2013 18:41:53
End Time:	10/05/2013 18:42:03
Mailboxes to search:	(1) /o=Exchange/ou=Exchange Administrative Group (FYDIBOHF23SPDLT)/cn=Recipients/cn=Andrew Dunn943
Mailboxes searched successfully:	(1) adunn@exblog.be
Mailboxes not searched successfully:	(0) None
Exclude Duplicate Messages:	False
Resume:	False
Include Keyword Statistics:	False
Size:	200.8 KB (205,600 bytes), Estimated size was: 205600
Items:	25, Estimated number of items was: 25
Results:	/o=Exchange/ou=Exchange Administrative Group (FYDIBOHF23SPDLT)/cn=Recipients/cn=DiscoverySearchMailbox (D919BA05-46A6-415f-80AD-
Errors:	None
Keyword Hits:	No keyword statistics for copy search.

If you then log on to the relevant Discovery Search mailbox, you will find that the search result have been copied into a separate folder which has the name of the search you defined earlier:

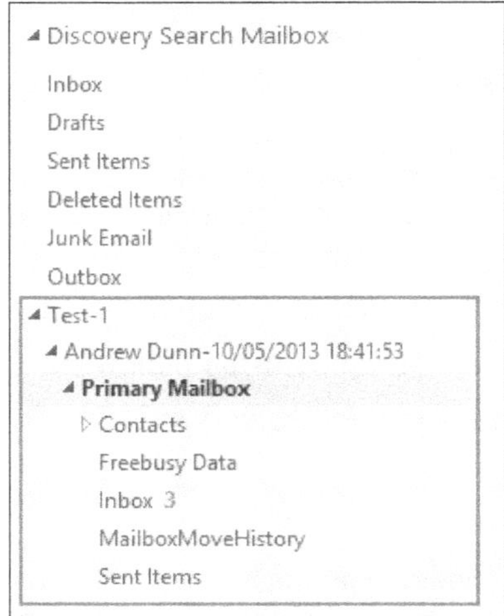

There's more...

There is more in store, which is explained in the following sections.

Searching and deleting e-mails

Using the `Search-Mailbox` command, it is possible to search for messages and delete them at the same time. This can be particularly useful when trying to remove specific message, but be warned that when using the `-DeleteContent` switch, you cannot preview the results.

As a workaround for this limitation, you could preview the results before taking the action to delete them. The following command will search Andrew Dunn's mailbox for items that have a subject that contain the words "Sales Figures". Because the `-LogOnly` parameter has been used, only a log will be generated. The actual message will not be copied into the Search Admin's mailbox:

```
Search-Mailbox -Identity ADunn -Keywords "Subject:'Sales Figures'" -
TargetMailbox "SearchAdmin" -TargetFolder "SearchAndDelete" -LogOnly -
LogLevel Full
```

If you reviewed the results and are happy to remove the items, run the following command:

```
Search-Mailbox -Identity ADunn -Keywords "Subject:'Sales Figures'" -
DeleteContent
```

Unsearchable items

Sometimes a mailbox might contain items which couldn't be indexed when they were received. This could be the case when a message contains a large amount of attachments or when a compress attachment (for example a ZIP file) contains multiple other compressed attachments.

Because the `Search-Mailbox` command relies on the content index to perform its search, you might want to include the `-IncludeUnsearchableItems` parameter in some searches. When doing so, Exchange will also search items that have not been indexed before.

Configuring Transport rules

Transport rules were first introduced in Exchange 2007. They allow you to look for specific conditions in messages flowing through the Hub Transport component (now part of the Mailbox Server role) and based upon that, take a variety of actions such as applying Rights Management templates, redirecting messages, or silently dropping the messages.

Getting ready

In order to execute the following steps, make sure that you have the appropriate permissions (that is, Organization Management or Records Management) and log in to the EAC or the EMS.

How to do it...

Transport rules are very powerful and mistakes can be costly. Although creating Transport rules isn't a hard thing to do, you should be wary of the results and always test them before taking them into production.

Creating Transport rules

The following command will create a new Transport Rule that will append a disclaimer to the message if it's sent by one of the members of the Sales DL:

```
New-TransportRule -Name "SalesDisclaimer" -From "Sales@exblog.be" -
SenderAddressLocation HeaderOrEnvelope -ApplyHtmlDisclaimerText "This is
the Sales Disclaimer" -ApplyHtmlDisclaimerFallbackAction Ignore
```

As the syntax of the command might have given away, it is also possible to include HTML code in the disclaimer. Although, using the EMS can be quicker in many ways, creating Transport rules is far easier using the EAC.

The EAC is a convenient way to visually build rules (or a set of rules) without getting tangled in the many parameters.

To create the same preceding Transport rules, only this time using the EAC, use the following steps:

1. Log in to the EAC and navigate to **mail flow** | **rules**.
2. Click on the plus sign (+) and select **Apply disclaimers...**.
3. Enter a name, for example, `SalesDisclaimer`.
4. Select **The sender is...** under ***Apply this rule if...**.
5. Select the appropriate sender(s) from the **Select Members** window and click on **Ok** to confirm.
6. Click on **Enter text...** next to the **Append the disclaimer...**drop-down list.
7. Specify a disclaimer, for instance, type `This is the Sales Disclaimer` and click on **Ok** to confirm.
8. Leave the other settings at their default and click on **Save** to create the Transport rule.

Enabling/disabling Transport rules

If the need arises to temporarily disable a Transport rule, without deleting it, being able to disable, and re-enable it afterwards can be handy.

The following command will disable the `SalesDisclaimer` Transport rule:

```
Disable-TransportRule "SalesDisclaimer".
```

Enabling is as easy as running the following command:

```
Enable-TransportRule "SalesDisclaimer"
```

Testing Transport rules

Next to building and testing Transport rules in a test environment, you can also configure a new rule to run in a sort of "monitoring" mode by configuring the rule not to be enforced but to **Test without Policy Tips**.

When this option is selected, Exchange will evaluate the rule and log the action in the message tracking logs, but it will not apply the configured action. This is a great way to test the impact of a rule before actually enforcing it.

To configure a new or modify an existing rule for testing, simply select the **Test without Policy Tips** option in the rules wizard as shown in the following screenshot:

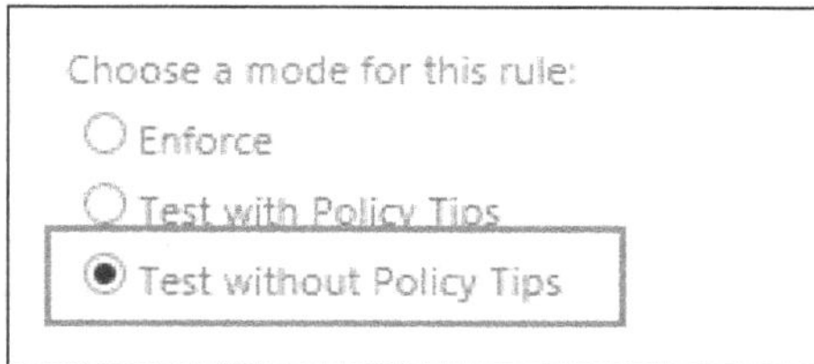

> If you configure a rule that contains a policy tip, selecting **Test with Policy Tips** would display the tip to the user without applying the action configured in the rules. Just like the option to test without policy tips, the results of the transport rule will be logged in the message tracking logs.

How it works...

Transport rules are very flexible and offer a wide variety of possibilities. Basically, a Transport rule is built upon two concepts: predicates and actions.

One or more predicates are used to define conditions and if necessary also exceptions to those conditions. Very much like the preceding example where the condition was that the message had to be sent from the Sales DL. In that example, the predicate that was used was the `From` predicate.

Exchange 2013 offers a huge list of predicates that can be used. For a complete overview of this list, have a look at the following article:

`http://technet.microsoft.com/en-us/library/dd638183(v=exchg.150).aspx`

Then, there's also the actions. The configured action is what the transport rule agent will actually execute if a given condition or set of conditions is met. Just like the predicates, the list of available actions is huge. For a full overview, have a look at the following article:

`http://technet.microsoft.com/en-us/library/aa998315(v=exchg.150).aspx`

When a message flows through Transport, the Transport rule agent will, once the message's destination has been resolved, start processing the rules. First, it will take a look at the message type (internal traffic, external traffic, and so on) as the message type might slightly change the way the messages should be treated. For instance, the Transport agent can only process encrypted messages in a limited way as it has only access to the envelope headers of the message. This means that rules that require access to the content of the message won't be processed.

After that, the Transport agent will start processing the rules, looking at a variety of elements including the message scope, the priority, conditions of the rule, exceptions, and so on all the way up to the action defined in the rule; of course, only if the condition (or exceptions to it) are met.

By default, the Transport agent will continue processing additional rules. However, if a condition is met and the "stop processing more rules" switch is enabled in the transport rule, the Transport agent will stop processing. If not, it will continue processing transport rules until it has processed them all or it finds a rule for which the condition matches and the switch is enabled.

There's more...

Although, at first sight, transport rules in Exchange 2013 might seem the same as in 2010, a lot of the changes were made under the hood. First and foremost, transport rules now support **Data Loss Prevention** (**DLP**), which you can read about later in this chapter. There are also a few new predicates and actions compared to Exchange 2010. The biggest change, however, is when Transport rules are applied in the Transport chain.

In Exchange 2010, transport rules were applied at the `onRoutedMessage` event. Now, they are invoked on the `onResolvedMessage` event. This change allows for additional actions, for example, forcing TLS or influencing how messages are routed to their destination by forcing the use of a specific connector.

Supported file types

By default, Transport rules support a wide variety of file types, including but not limited to the following: Office 2007, 2010, and 2013, Word, Excel, OneNote, PowerPoint, and OneNote files, Office 2003 Word, Excel and PowerPoint, PDF, HTML, XML, JPG, TIFF, and many more.

It is possible to add supported file types by registering third-party iFilters. How to install these iFilters will greatly depend on the iFilter itself, however, the process of registering it with Exchange 2013 will roughly be the same as the following:

1. Add the iFilter's unique CLSID to the Exchange Server's registry (`HKLM\Software\Microsoft\ExchangeServer\v15\HubTransportRole\CLSID`).
2. Add the file type's extension to the registry: (`HKLM\Software\Microsoft\ExchangeServer\v15\HubTransportRoles\filters`).
3. Restart the MSExchange Transport and Microsoft Filtering Management service.

Working with Data Loss Prevention policies

Data Loss Prevention is another great feature in Exchange 2013 that can help you prevent accidental or malevolent leakage of company's internal or other sensitive data.

Getting ready

In order to work with DLP policies, you must be granted appropriate permissions (Organization Management or Compliance Management).

How to do it...

The following steps will create a new DLP policy, based on a template, which will search for US social security numbers and health information. It will then place the policy in a testing mode which will generate reporting information, but will not enforce any actions to messages that match the conditions defined in the template:

1. Log in to the EAC and navigate to **compliance management** | **data loss prevention**.
2. Click on the plus sign (**+**) and select **New DLP policy from template.**
3. Enter a name for the policy, for example, `DLP-HIPAA`.
4. Enter a description of the purpose of this new policy.
5. From the list of templates, select **U.S. Health Insurance Act (HIPAA).**
6. Click on **More options...** and select **Test DLP policy without Policy Tips**.
7. Click on **save** to create the policy.

Note that there are three operational modes to choose from:

- **Enforce**, which will activate the DLP policy and start executing the action(s) linked to the policy.
- **Test DLP policy with Policy Tips**, which will not execute the action(s) defined in the policy, but will generate policy tips (if configured) to the user.
- **Test DLP policy without Policy Tips**, which will only report on the number of positive matches. It will not execute any actions or generate policy tips.

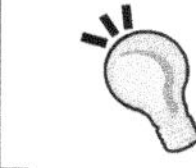

It's always a good idea to test drive a new DLP policy before enforcing it. This will allow you to evaluate the effectiveness of the policy and whether or not it's behaving as you expected.

Creating a custom DLP policy

First, we need to create an empty DLP policy which will serve as a sort of placeholder, which we will configure afterwards:

1. Log in to the EAC and navigate to **compliance management** | **data loss prevention**.
2. Click on the plus sign (**+**) and select **New custom DLP policy**.
3. Enter a name for the policy, for example, `DLP-Custom-CC`.
4. Provide a description for this policy.
5. Select **Test DLP policy with Policy Tips** and click on **save**.

Next, we're going to configure this policy to scan for credit card numbers, block any message that contains more than a single number, and generate a warning (policy tip) for the end user:

1. Double-click on the policy that was just created (**DLP-Custom-CC**).
2. In the properties window, navigate to **rules** and click on the plus sign (**+**) to add a custom rule.
3. Select **Block messages with sensitive information**.
4. In the **new rule** wizard, click ***Select sensitive information types...**.
5. Click on the plus sign (**+**) and select **Credit Card Number** from the list of available information types. Then click on **add** and **ok**.

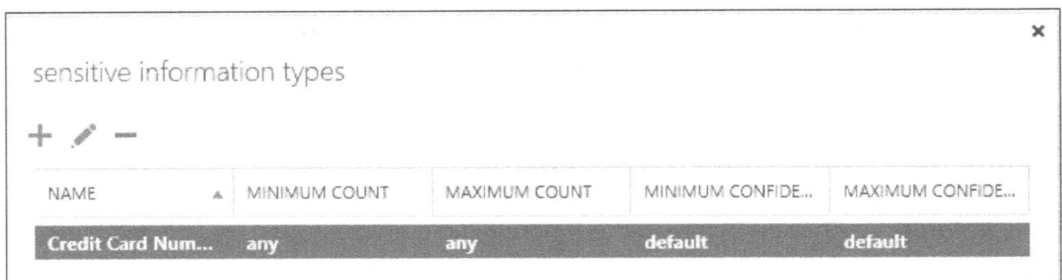

6. Click on **ok** in the **sensitive information types** window.
7. Back in the **new rule** wizard, click on ***Select one...** next to **Generate incident report and send it to...**.

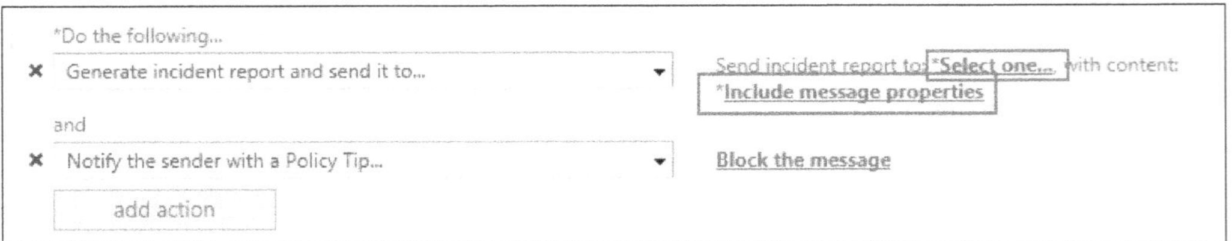

8. Select the mailbox of a user who you want to be notified when the policy blocked a message and click on **ok**.
9. Now, click on ***Include message properties** and select all the information you want to include in the incident report. For example, select **sender**,**recipients**, and **original mail**. Then click on **ok**.
10. Under **Audit this rule with severity level** select **high**.
11. Click on **save**.
12. Click on **save** once more to create the policy.

Creating custom policy tip messages

Depending on what actions you define in a DLP policy, one of the default policy tips will be generated by the Exchange 2013 server. By default, these policy tips are only in English and the text is relatively generic.

By creating custom policy tip messages, you can modify the text, add support for multiple languages, and define a URL that people will see whenever they're about to send a message that violates one of the DLP policies.

Depending on what actions you define, a different policy tip is shown:

DLP Policy Action	Policy Tip
Notify the sender	Notify the sender
Block the message unless it's a false positive	Allow the sender to override
Block the message, but allow the sender to override and send	
Block the message	Block the message
Block the message, but allow the sender to override with a business justification and send	Link to compliance URL

The steps for creating custom policy tip messages are as follows:

1. Log in to the EAC and navigate to **compliance management** | **data loss prevention**.
2. Click on the **Policy Tips** button
3. Click on the plus sign (**+**) to add a custom policy tip.
4. Under **Policy Tip**, select **Notify the sender**.
5. Select **English** as the Locale.
6. Create a custom policy tip text, for example, `It looks like this message or its content violates on of the company-define compliancy rules. Please verify that you are allowed to send this information outside the organization.`

How it works...

A DLP policy could be seen as a pre-created set of conditions which contain transport rule predicates, actions, and exceptions that can be used to recognize common patterns in a message or its attachments and as such can be used to scan for sensitive data. For instance, you could be looking for credit card numbers, social security numbers, driver's licenses, and so on.

Given that DLP policies are an extension to transport rules, they work the same way and also offer a variety of actions that you can take when a match is found. When the transport service invokes the Transport rules, the content scanning engine will scan the contents of the message (and supported attachments), and use a complex set of algorithms to match data against one of the rules. If a match is found, the configured actions from the policy are executed.

Additionally, DLP allows you to generate a so called policy tip. These are notifications a user will see in Outlook 2013, similar to how MailTips work.

Unfortunately, policy tips are only supported by Outlook 2013. When using older versions of Outlook, the DLP policy action will be executed, but the user will not get a policy tip, even if one is configured.

Amongst the actions that can be taken, you not only have the option to block a message, but also to allow a user to override the block. This override is either authoritative or you can configure it to send a request to the user's manager for approval.

Exchange 2013 offers some built-in DLP policies that you can use to speed up the configuration. These templates contain some very common information types, though it's not unthinkable that your company uses specific data that you'd want to protect as well.

In such case, you can create your own custom DLP policy that will use a regular expression to match your specific need. Additionally, third-party developers could also create templates that can be imported into Exchange 2013 quite easily.

Using mailbox audit logging

It's not uncommon to see that mailboxes contain sensitive information or company-internal documents that possibly include personal, financial, or other private records of third-party individuals or companies.

Especially in larger environments it's difficult to keep track of who has access to what, even more so it's almost impossible to track who exercised the permissions that he or she was granted.

Mailbox audit logging will exactly do that: keep track of who accesses a mailbox. Not only will it do that for users or delegates, but also for administrators. The latter would not only happen when an Administrator opens another user's mailbox, but also when administrative tasks are executed like In-Place eDiscovery or Mailbox Export Requests.

How to do it...

Mailbox audit logs are enabled on a per-mailbox basis, allowing granular control over which mailboxes you want to monitor and which ones not.

The following command will enable mailbox audit logging for Andrew Dunn's mailbox:

```
Set-Mailbox ADunn -AuditEnabled $True
```

Unsurprisingly, setting `-AuditEnabled` to `$False` will disable the audit logging for that mailbox again.

Auditing for specific events

When executing the preceding command, most mailbox actions will be logged. In some cases you might want to turn down the volume of entries generated and only monitor for specific events.

The following command will enable mailbox audit logging for Andrew Dunn's mailbox, and specifically monitor for delete operations executed by admins:

```
Set-Mailbox ADunn -AuditAdmin MoveToDeletedItems,SoftDelete,HardDelete -
AuditEnabled $true
```

Next to configure audit logging specifically for Administrators, you can also look for events caused by mailbox Owners (`-AuditOwner`) or Delegates (`-AuditDelegate`).

For more information on what values you can configure for these parameters, have a look at the following cmdlet reference page:

`http://technet.microsoft.com/en-us/library/bb123981(v=exchg.150).aspx`

Configuring an audit log age

If you don't configure an audit log age when enabling audit logging, it will be set to 90 days by default. Sometimes, this might prove not to be enough, or perhaps just the opposite!

The following command will configure the audit log to purge all entries after 45 days:

```
Set-Mailbox ADunn -AuditLogAgeLimit 45 -Confirm:$false
```

Searching the audit logs

Basically, there are two ways to search the entries in the audit logs. Firstly, you can launch an immediate search using the `Search-MailboxAuditLog` cmdlet. Alternatively, you can use the `New-MailboxSearch` cmdlet to execute the search and receive the results via e-mail.

The following command will search the audit logs of ADunn and look for logon events from Administrators and output the results on screen:

```
Search-MailboxAuditLog -Mailboxes Adunn -LogonTypes Admin
```

Because this command could possibly return a huge amount of entries, it's best that you either specify a start-date and an end-date between which the search should look for events or limit the amount of results using the `-ResultSize` parameter.

For example:

```
Search-MailboxAuditLog -Mailboxes Adunn -LogonTypes Admin -StartDate
01/02/2013 -EndDate 20/02/2013 -ResultSize 250
```

Using the `New-MailboxAuditLogSearch` cmdlet, we can search for the same entries, but receive the results via mail. You could use this to create a script that creates a daily or weekly digest.

```
New-MailboxAuditLogSearch "Admin access for Andrew Dunn's Mailbox" -
Mailboxes "ADunn" -LogonTypes Admin -StatusMailRecipients admin@exblog.be
```

Generating audit reports

Exchange 2013 offers a few built-in reports that you can use to quickly gather results from the audit logs. These reports can be located in the EAC under **compliance management** | **auditing**.

To generate the **non-owner mailbox access report**, complete the following steps:

1. Log in to the EAC and navigate to **compliance management** | **auditing**.
2. Click on **Run a non-owner mailbox access report**.
3. Select a start and an end date.
4. Click on **select mailboxes...** to select the mailboxes for which you want to search the mailbox audit logs.
5. Under **Search for access by**, select **all non-owners**.
6. Click on **Search**.

How it works...

When mailbox audit logging is enabled, the Exchange server will audit for the events that were configured when enabling audit logging. When an action is executed that matches one of the monitored actions, an entry is written into the Audits folder in the user's mailbox. The Audits folder is a hidden folder, which the user cannot access. Because it's part of the mailbox, moving a mailbox will also move the logs with it.

Similarly, removing a mailbox will also remove the audit logs. So, if you are required to keep historical data of the mailbox audit logs, you mustn't immediately remove a user's mailbox when he or she leaves the company!

There's more...

In some cases, you would want certain accounts to be excluded from audit logging. This could be the case, for example, with service accounts that legitimately and frequently access a user's mailbox. By allowing these accounts to bypass the audit logging, you also turn down the noise in the audit logs.

To configure mailbox audit logging bypassing for a service account named `svc_App1`, execute the following command:

```
Set-MailboxAuditBypassAssociation -Identity "svc_App1" -
AuditByPassEnabled $True
```

Unlike configuring mailbox audit logging, bypassing isn't done on a per-mailbox basis but rather globally. This means that when an account is configured to bypass audit logging, it won't show up in any of the enabled audit logs.

9
Performing Backup, Restore, and Disaster Recovery

In this chapter, we will cover:

- Understanding backups
- Defining backup objectives
- Creating a new backup job with Windows Server Backup
- Restoring an Exchange Server Database
- Recovering a failed Exchange server

Introduction

In *Chapter 1, Planning an Exchange Server 2013 Infrastructure*, we touched briefly on the subject of backups and disaster recovery. So it's high time for us to dig a bit deeper.

When designing an Exchange infrastructure, one of the topics lying on the discussion table always includes backups. Now, what is it that turns this subject into an object for discussion?

Well in my opinion this is because everyone knows that taking backups is critical, yet a lot of organizations don't always follow the best practices. One particular thing that frequently pops up is the question whether or not backups are regularly tested. Because after all, what is the point in taking backups if you never performed a restore? How about finding out your backups are invalid, right at the moment when you need to restore them? Not particularly a situation I'd like to see myself end in.

Ask yourself the same question. Do you test your backups regularly? If you honestly answered "No we don't even have such a plan", no worries, we will guide you through the process of establishing such a plan. You might need it one day.

Another discussion that sometimes is hard to tackle is, whether you should rely on incremental backups on a daily basis, or perform full Exchange database copies. And then there's the question whether you should be backing up to disk, to tape, or maybe a combination of both.

There is no one right answer as to how you should treat backups in Exchange. The truth is that no matter what solution you have in mind, you'll often be forced to work with the backup devices and software that's already at hand. Although it might not always be possible to do so, we suggest you to try to integrate Exchange backups in your overall backup strategy. There's no point in creating a totally different approach only for Exchange. On the contrary, it makes your backup harder to manage in the long run. Of course there are situations when you have no other option than to architect a new backup solution. This could, for instance, be the case where your current solution cannot handle the additional capacity or when it does not provide the bandwidth to backup Exchange in a timely manner.

- Backups in Exchange 2013 are relatively simple, at least when compared to previous versions like Exchange 2010. Although, the **Volume Shadow Services** (**VSS**) architecture in Exchange 2013 has been redesigned, it now includes two Exchange VSS writers instead of one, the principles remain the same.
- There are many backup applications that currently support Exchange 2013. Amongst them are Microsoft's own Windows Server Backup, System Center Data Protection Manager 2012, and a bunch of third-party vendors.
- Although Windows Server Backup does its job just fine, it's not intended as an enterprise-grade solution. As such it doesn't offer the same functionalities that other backup applications might have. However, it is a great tool for testing or quickly taking a single backup.

Defining backup objectives

Although backup operations have always been something that come naturally in many environments, it's not uncommon to get asked if taking Exchange backups is still necessary. After all, Exchange Server 2013 has built-in features that allow for multiple database copies replicated over different locations, which might give you the impression: taking backups is not really needed anymore. Although that idea certainly makes sense, database copies are not able to provide an historical point-in-time backup.

How to do it...

In short, your backup strategy should be based on your **Service Level Agreements** (**SLAs**). So the first step should be to find out or determine what the service levels are.

Traditionally, SLAs for backups are determined by the following objectives:

- **RTO** (**Recovery Time Objective**): This refers to the amount of time within which a service must be restored. This doesn't only contain the time it takes to restore the backup from its media, but also the time required to make the recovered data available and if applicable restore the service.
- **RPO** (**Recovery Point Objective)**: This value refers to the maximum period in which data loss is acceptable for the business. This time will heavily influence your overall backup strategy. A very short RPO time might require you to take several backups in a day that also need to be stored safely.
- **Backup Window**: This refers to the amount of time you have for taking backups. In most organizations, this is outside of business hours, although more and more environments are looking at implementing continuous backups, which are taken at multiple times throughout the day.

If your organization is happy with the idea, they might lose one week's worth of data (RPO), than why should you perform backups on a daily basis? Of course, it's very unlikely you'll ever come across a requirement like this; I cannot imagine a company being fine with losing that significant amount of data.

The combination of the aforementioned objectives will directly influence your backup strategy. Consider the following scenario:

The company you are designing an Exchange 2013 environment for has defined that, regardless of the kind of failure, no more than 4 hours of data should be lost. Also, the time it takes to recover the data should not exceed more than 4 hours by itself.

From this information, we can deduct the following objectives:

Objective	Value
RPO	4 hours
RTO	4 hours
Backup Window	Unknown

At first, these values might seem doable, but there's a very important piece of information that should not be overlooked "regardless of the kind of failure". This one sentence actually reveals that even a complete site failure (for instance, in case of a disaster) should not have an impact on the RPO or RTO times.

In reality, however, you'll often see that exceptional situations in which an entire site is lost due to extreme situations are exempted from the causes included in the RPO and RTO times. It's not uncommon to see that, for these situations, other timings are defined. If that's the case, your backup solution should not only account for the default RTO/RPO objectives, but also for the second set of objectives.

Now, back to the original example. The information doesn't directly reveal the backup window within which you need to operate. However, given that you cannot lose more than 4 hours of data, a backup cannot take more than 4 hours to finish as you cannot have two backup operations running against the same data set at the same time.

Taking that into account, another important aspect is deciding on what backup technology you are going to use. If your Exchange organization contains multiple very large databases, you might end up with a situation where your existing backup solution cannot guarantee the transfer rate to finish within the window. At this time, you have two options:

- You architect a new backup solution and buy the required equipment to meet the defined RPO/RTO objective
- You go back to the business and try to readjust the objectives

How it works...

Defining your backup strategy is dependent on the outcome of the precedingly mentioned terms. Talk to your business to get these values. Of course, it shouldn't be a surprise that if shorter timings are defined for these parameters, the more complex and more costly your backup environment will be.

To give you a more logical overview of the complexity of designing a backup strategy, the following table will help you in structuring the different aspects:

Strategy Phase	Description
Analyze	Identify the components to be restored (for example, databases, logfiles, full server restore)
	Identify business requirements (RPO, RTO)
	Investigate technical requirements (backup to disk, backup to tape, and so on)
Define	Hardware and software requirements
	Full backups, incremental backups
	Manual or automated restore process
	Communication during outage

Strategy Phase	Description
Configure	Install hardware and software for backup
	Backup all defined components
	Configure backup job reporting and alerting
	Handle backup storage (offsite, in vault)
Test	Perform regular backup and restore testing
	Calculate required amount for performing different types of restores
	Test offline full restore in case of major disaster

As long as you don't have a full answer to each and every topic in the preceding mentioned table, don't even consider thinking you have a good backup strategy!

There's more...

I'm often asked, which files and folders an Exchange backup should include. Depending on whether you are backing up a Mailbox Server or Client Access Server, there are some differences.

First, from a configuration point-of-view, it's always a good idea to include the following:

- System State backup (includes system configuration files, registry, IIS metabase)
- Customized Exchange configuration files (for example, `web.config`)
- Certificates (in case of a Client Access Server)

From a data point-of-view, the following items are important:

- Exchange databases
- Exchange transaction log files

Lastly, there's also **Active Directory** (**AD**) that needs a regular backup. Exchange 2013 is heavily dependent on Active Directory; therefore, taking regular backups of your Active Directory database is encouraged. Without having a fully operational Active Directory environment, no Exchange component restores are even possible.

It's not necessary to backup Active Directory as part of your data backups. Under normal circumstances, you would never need to use the AD backups. However, in situations where you have to revert to a disaster recovery, these backups will be required.

Creating a new backup job with Windows Server Backup

In this section, we explain how the backup configuration should be performed, by making use of the Windows Server 2012 built-in backup tool. We start by showing you how the backup component itself is installed locally on the Exchange Server 2013 machine, how the Exchange backup job configuration might look like, and how you can perform a backup test yourself, storing the backup files on a separate volume.

How to do it...

Windows Server 2012 built-in backup component is fully supported for Exchange Server 2013 backup operations. As this component is not installed by default, we first have to install this feature. Because Windows Server Backup cannot take Exchange backups from a remote computer, it needs to be installed locally. Installing Windows Server 2012 backup:

1. From the Windows Server 2012 Server Manager go to **Configure this local server**, choose option **2 Add roles and features** as shown in the following screenshot, which will launch the **Add Roles and Features Wizard**:

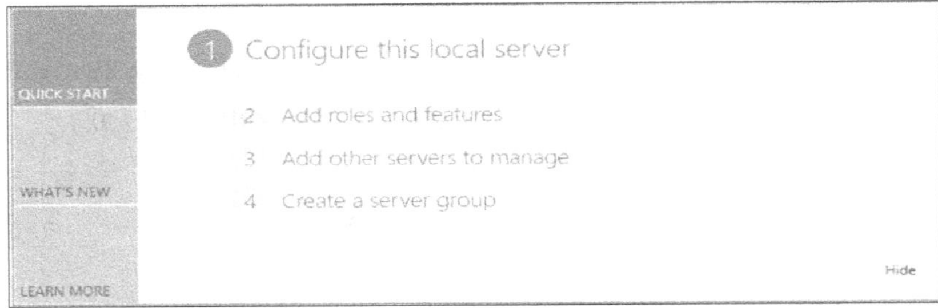

2. From this wizard, select **Role-based** or **Feature based** installation as the installation type. Select your local server from the server selection step.
3. On the **Server Roles** window, click on **Next** without selecting any roles as shown in the following screenshot:

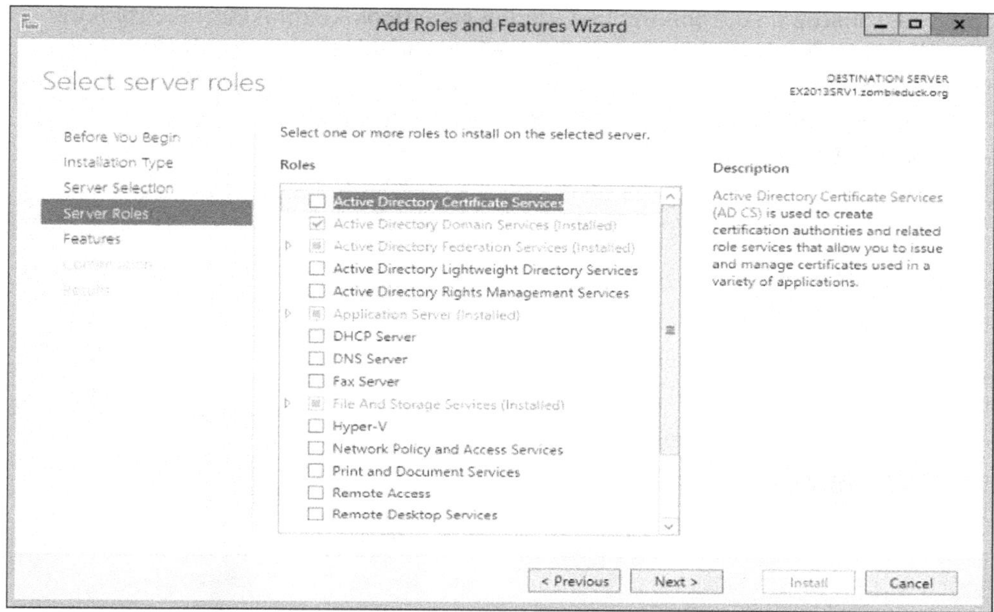

4. From the **Select Features** window, scroll down in the list of features, and select **Windows Server Backup**. Then click on **Next** as shown in the following screenshot:

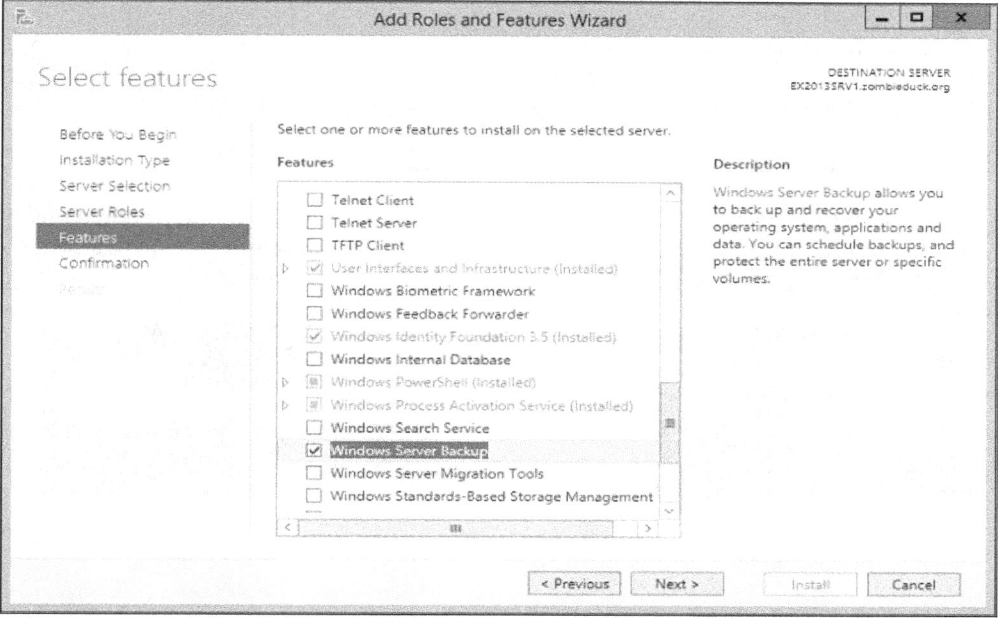

5. Press **Install** on the **confirm installation selections** window; this will install the Windows Server Backup components, which should on average take no more than a few minutes.
6. Once the installation is done, close the install feature window as shown in the following screenshot:

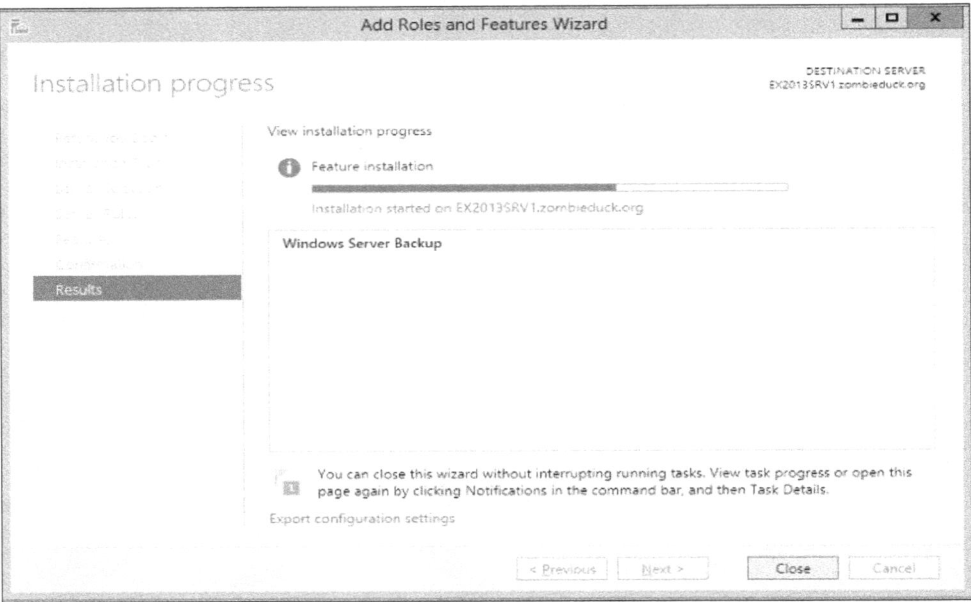

This completes the installation of the Windows Server Backup component.

Next, we will see the steps for configuring your Exchange Backup job:

1. From the Windows Server 2012 Start Screen, launch the charm bar / search and type `Windows backup`; this will show the **Windows Server Backup** tool icon as shown in the following screenshot. Click this icon to start the application.

2. From the **Action** pane, select **Backup Schedule**, which will launch **Backup Schedule Wizard** as shown in the following screenshot:

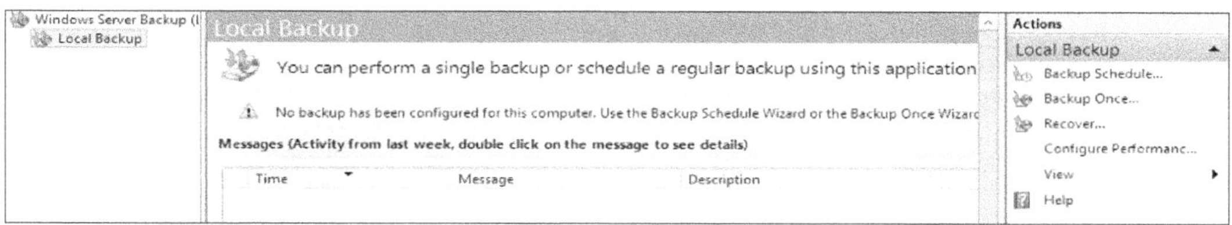

3. On the **Select Backup Configuration** window, select **Full Server** (this will include all Exchange Server components like Exchange databases, transaction log files, but also system state, system partition, and so on).
4. On the **Specify Backup Time** window, leave the default of 21:00h and click on **Next** (note that even Windows Server Backup allows for multiple backups per day, which are in fact similar to snapshots)
5. On **Specify Destination Type**, select **Backup to a shared network folder** as shown in the following screenshot; note that Windows Server Backup allows for different backup destinations, which are dedicated external hard disks, local volume in the server, or network share.

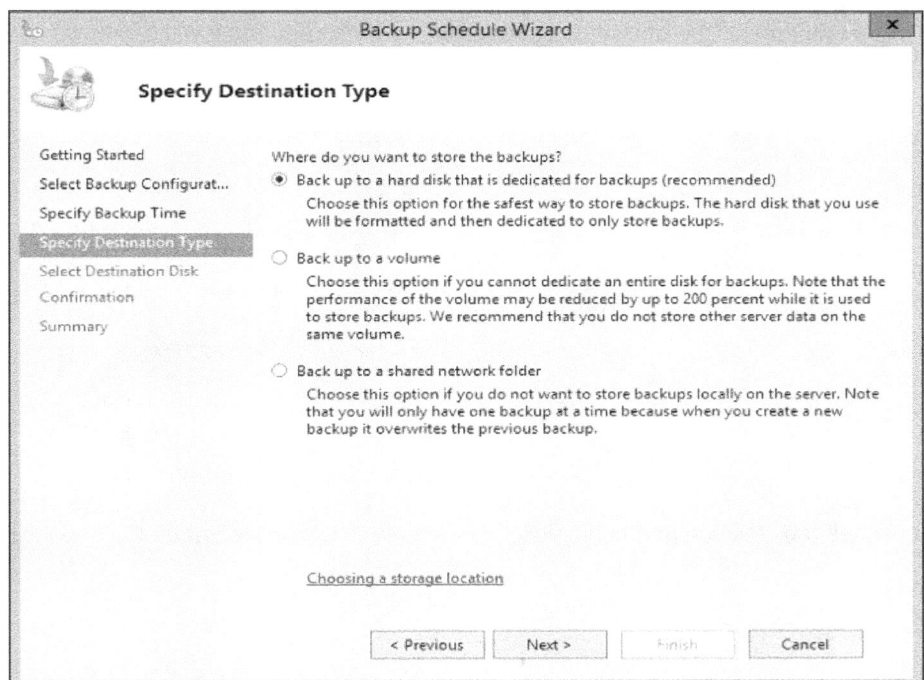

6. Note the warning popup shown in the following screenshot, which warns us about the fact that only the last backup file is stored at the remote location, and all previous backup files will be overwritten. This means, in this specific scenario, it is advised to move backup files to another location after the backup is completed successfully. That way you prevent to have no backup at all when, for example, the latest backup job should result in a corrupt backup file.

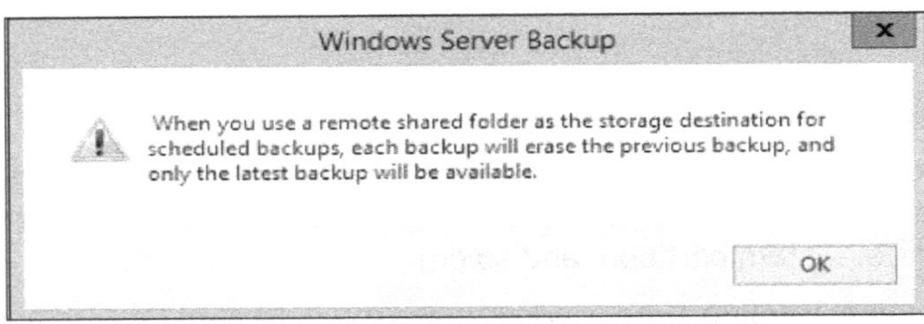

7. Enter the **Remote Destination Folder** as an UNC path. For example `\\sharename` or `\\ip-address\shared folder name`.
8. Enter the administrative user or backup user credentials in the credential popup window, and verify the settings of the backup job in the **Confirmation** window. The user that you enter here should have sufficient permissions to backup Exchange and have permissions to write in the destination folder.
9. At this moment, the backup job itself will be configured, and it will be shown in the **Scheduled backup** pane in the Windows Server Backup console as shown in the following screenshot:

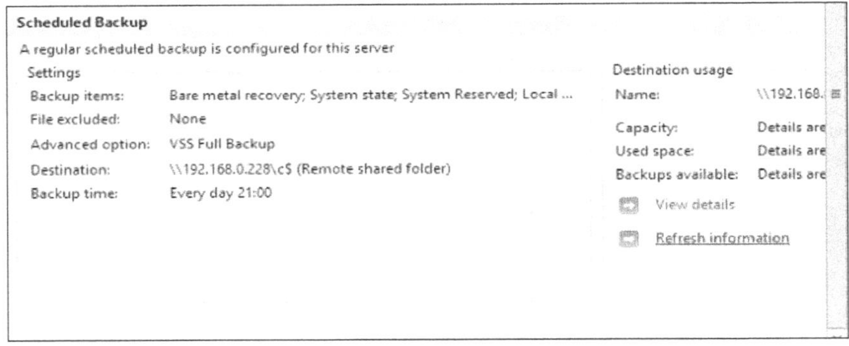

This concludes the creation and configuration of a sample Exchange Server Backup job.

Now, when a backup job has been configured, it is time to run this backup job as a test. Although we configured a scheduled time of 21:00h, we still have the possibility to manually start this backup job whenever we want. However, this is not possible from within the backup tool itself. We will need to use the **Task Scheduler** for this. The steps for running an Exchange backup are as follows:

1. From the Windows Server 2012 Start Screen launch the charm bar and type `task scheduler`. This will show the **Task Scheduler** icon; click on the icon to start this application.
2. From within the **Task Scheduler**, go to **Task Scheduler Library** | **Microsoft** | **Windows** | **Backup** in the left tree. This will show the configured backup jobs in the middle pane as shown in the following screenshot:

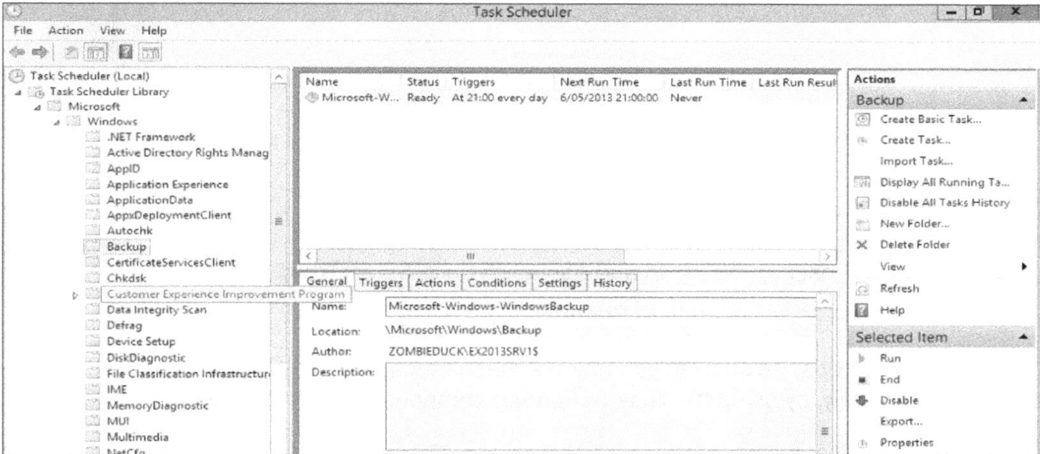

3. Select the backup job you have just configured and right-click on it. Select **Properties**.

4. Select the **Settings** tab; mark the option **Allow task to be run on command** and press **OK** to confirm as shown in the following screenshot. Close the pop-up window.

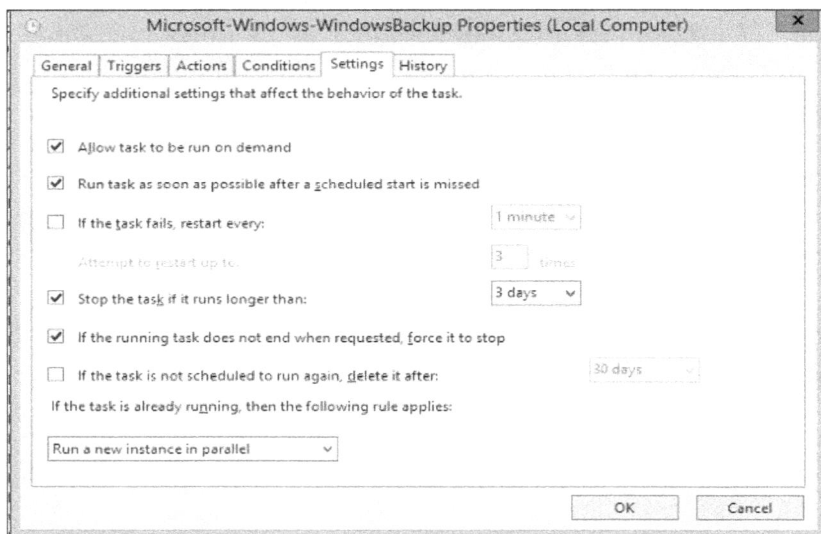

5. Select the backup job again and right-click on it. Select **Run**.
6. Note the state will change to **Running**.

In the preceding steps, we showed you how a scheduled backup job can be configured for running immediately, by using the **Task Scheduler** component of Windows Server.

While the job is still selected, click on the **History** tab. This will show all steps that have been taken so far by this job.

Notice **Event ID 200 Action Started**, at the time your backup job was launched, followed by **Event ID 110 Task Triggered** while the backup job itself was running. When the backup job is finished, **Event ID 201 Action Complete** will be reported as shown in the following screenshot:

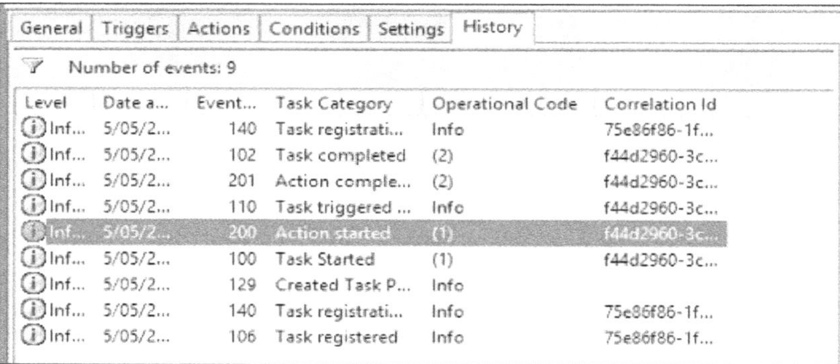

There's more...

Besides checking the Task Scheduler, there are other ways to find out what happened with your scheduled Exchange backup jobs. They are explained in this section.

Inspect the Event Viewer

At the scheduled time of backup, a series of Exchange Server events will be written into the Event Viewer, related to **Exchange VSS writer** and **ShadowCopy**. As in our given example, the following information is seen sequentially in the Event Log:

- The Microsoft Exchange VSS writer has successfully collected the metadata document in preparation for backup.
- The Microsoft Exchange VSS writer instance <instanceID> has successfully prepared for a full or a copy backup of database 'Mailbox database name'. The following database will be backed up.
- The Microsoft Exchange Replication Service VSS writer (InstanceID) successfully prepared for backup.
- Information Store - Mailbox Database ID Shadow Copy instance 2 starting. This will be a Full Shadow copy.

When the backup job is finished, it will also be logged in the Event Viewer. The page will look like the following screenshot:

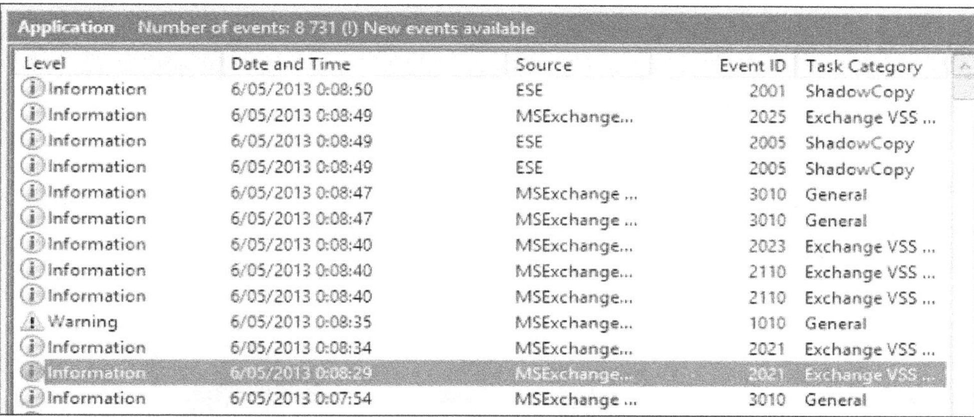

Application Number of events: 8 731 (!) New events available

Level	Date and Time	Source	Event ID	Task Category
Information	6/05/2013 0:08:50	ESE	2001	ShadowCopy
Information	6/05/2013 0:08:49	MSExchange...	2025	Exchange VSS ...
Information	6/05/2013 0:08:49	ESE	2005	ShadowCopy
Information	6/05/2013 0:08:49	ESE	2005	ShadowCopy
Information	6/05/2013 0:08:47	MSExchange ...	3010	General
Information	6/05/2013 0:08:47	MSExchange ...	3010	General
Information	6/05/2013 0:08:40	MSExchange...	2023	Exchange VSS ...
Information	6/05/2013 0:08:40	MSExchange...	2110	Exchange VSS ...
Information	6/05/2013 0:08:40	MSExchange...	2110	Exchange VSS ...
Warning	6/05/2013 0:08:35	MSExchange...	1010	General
Information	6/05/2013 0:08:34	MSExchange...	2021	Exchange VSS ...
Information	6/05/2013 0:08:29	MSExchange...	2021	Exchange VSS ...
Information	6/05/2013 0:07:54	MSExchange ...	3010	General

Inspect the Windows Server Backup tool

At any given moment, we can see the last results of the backup job, when the next job is scheduled and more:

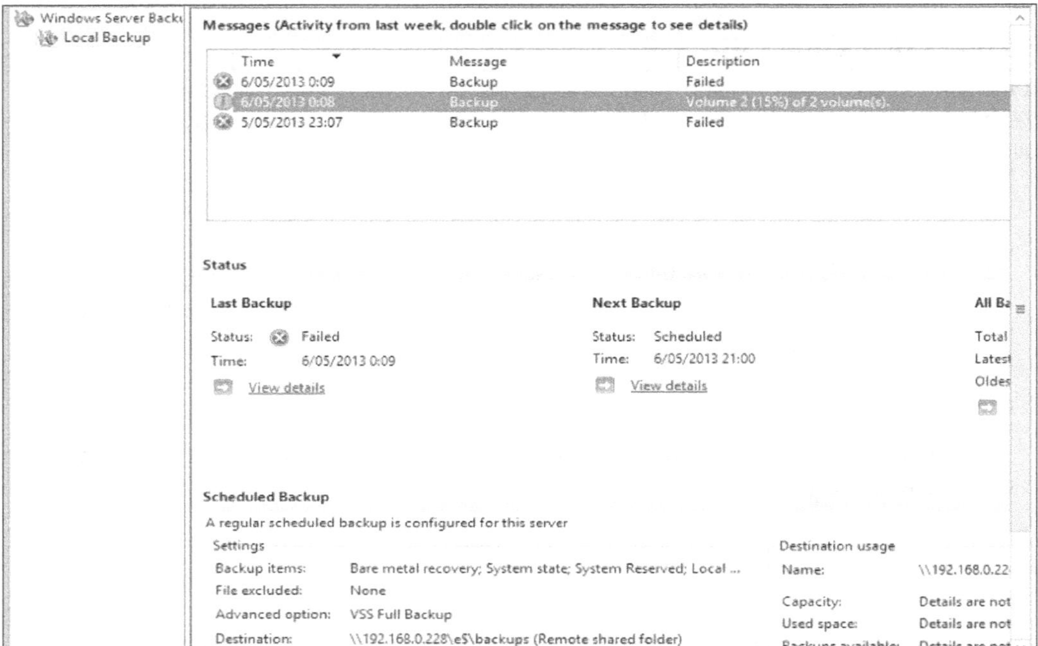

Investigating database properties

Another way to check if a database was backed up recently is to have a look at its properties using the following command:

```
Get-MailboxDatabase <dbname> -Status | ft name,BackupInProgress,LastFullB
ackup -Autosize
```

The output of the preceding command is shown in the following screenshot:

```
[PS] C:\Windows\system32>Get-MailboxDatabase -status | ft name,BackupInProgress,LastFullBackup -AutoSize

Name        BackupInProgress LastFullBackup
----        ---------------- --------------
DBMBX15-01              True 29/07/2013 21:00:41
DBMBX15-02              True 29/07/2013 21:00:43
DBMBX15-03              True 29/07/2013 21:00:49
```

Restoring an Exchange Server Database

Now, you know how to configure a backup job and verify that backups are indeed completed successfully, we can go to the next step, which includes executing the restore of an Exchange database.

Getting ready

In order to complete the following steps, you must have taken a backup following our preceding example.

How to do it...

Before technically explaining how a restore process is working, we need to draw your attention to the possible methodologies of restoring.

Exchange 2013 allows for two ways of restoring a full database:

- Restore to original location, thereby overwriting existing database
- Restore to alternate location, to allow for mounting into a recovery database

Performing a full Exchange 2013 database restore

In this exercise, we will walk you through the scenario of performing a full Exchange 2013 mailbox database restore.

As restoring to an alternate location is very common, that's exactly what we will walk you through:

1. From the **Windows Server Backup** tool, go to **Actions** | **Recover...**; this will start the Recovery Wizard.
2. Select the location where the backup is stored (in our scenario, this is **another location**). Click on **Next**.
3. Select **Remote Shared Folder** in the location type window and click on **Next**.
4. Enter the UNC path where the backup files are located. Then click on **Next**.
5. From the **Select Backup Date** window, browse to any of the available backups from the previous step (in our scenario, the only available backup we can choose from is the one previously generated, which might differ from your options if you have been testing with backups before).

6. In the **Select Recovery Type** window, it is very important you decide on what files you want to restore, as multiple options are possible:
    1. Files and Folders; Allows you to restore individual files and folders on file level (so no active Exchange Databases through VSS).
    2. Volumes: Will restore a full volume, for example C:\.
    3. Applications: Allow you to restore specific application items (like Exchange mailbox databases).
    4. System State: Will perform a full system state restore to the source server.
7. Select **Applications** from the recovery type window and click on **Next**.
8. In the **Select Application** window, make sure you select **Exchange** and click on **Next**.
9. In the specify recovery options window, we choose **Recover to another location,** and browse for this specific location, for example, to "C:\ExchangeRecovery" on the same source server. Then click on **Next**
10. In the confirmation window, you can see the two Exchange Mailbox Database instances that were running on our Exchange Server at the time of backup; these two database files will be restored to the given directory.
11. Click on the **Recover** button to complete the restore wizard; the actual file restore process will now be executed.
12. Once the restore process is complete, verify whether the restored transaction log files and Exchange database files are present in the restore directory you specified during step 9.

Setup and usage of an Exchange 2013 Recovery Database

As with the previous Exchange versions, Exchange 2013 still supports the use of recovery databases to restore individual or full mailbox data items into the active mailbox database. Without overwriting the full Exchange mailbox database, you have the option to mount the recovery database, extract specific information you need (for example, a specific user's mailbox), and restore this directly into the active Exchange mailbox database.

In a worse scenario where your main production database has been completely corrupted, one could start with a fresh empty Exchange mailbox database, creating new mailboxes in this database for the existing users (which will immediately allow for a working Exchange environment again, although mailboxes will be empty at first, but new mail coming in and out will be useful), and performing a restore of all data from a mounted recovery database into this new one. This procedure is also known as **dial tone recovery**.

We will be using PowerShell to create a new Recovery Database by using the following command

```
New-MailboxDatabase-Recovery-Name RecoveryDB -Server EX2013SRV1
-EdbFilePath "C:\ExchangeRecovery\RecoveryDB\RecoveryDB.EDB"
-LogFolderPath "C:\ExchangeRecovery\RecoveryDB"
```

The output of the preceding command is shown in the following screenshot:

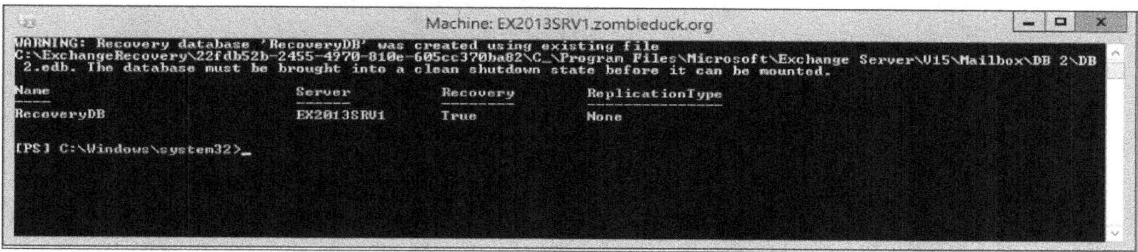

Note that the parameters **Name**, **EdbFilePath**, and **LogFolderPath** should be updated to reflect your own environment.

After the cmdlet has been executed successfully, this will be confirmed in the Shell as well, using the following output:

"A very important remark here is the fact that the Exchange database from the restore will always be in a dirty shutdown state, as is also clearly emphasized by the shell. So the first next thing is making sure our restored databases are back in a clean shutdown state."

To verify whether a database is in a **clean shutdown** state, you must use the ESEUTIL.exe tool which we will explain in a while.

Performing ESEUTIL /R on a restored Exchange database

As already mentioned, any restore of an Exchange database backup to an alternate location, will result in a **dirty shutdown** state of the database and its associated log files. As this will prevent the database from being mounted, we need to bring the database back into a clean shutdown state by using ESEUTIL /R.

The command line syntax for doing this looks similar to the following:

```
ESEUTIL.EXE /R <logfile> /l <logfilepath>
```

If we continue to work with our example scenario, the exact command would look like the following:

```
ESEUTIL.EXE /R E00 /L c:\recoverydb
```

The output of the preceding command is shown in the following screenshot:

```
Administrator: Command Prompt - eseutil /p "c:\ExchangeRecovery\Mailbox Da...

C:\>eseutil /r E00 /l c:\ExchangeRecovery

Extensible Storage Engine Utilities for Microsoft(R) Exchange Server
Version 15.00
Copyright (C) Microsoft Corporation. All Rights Reserved.

Initiating RECOVERY mode...
    Logfile base name: E00
            Log files: c:\ExchangeRecovery
         System files: <current directory>

Performing soft recovery...
                      Restore Status (% complete)

          0    10   20   30   40   50   60   70   80   90  100
          |----|----|----|----|----|----|----|----|----|----|
          ...................................................X
```

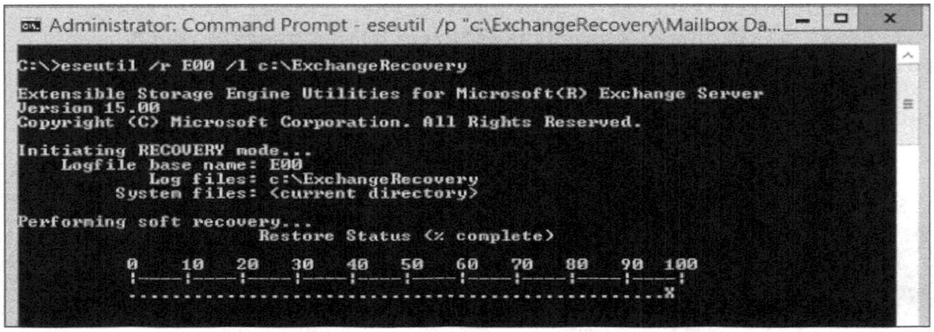

After the repair operation has been done, we will verify if the database is back in a clean shutdown state, by using the `ESEUTIL.EXE /MH` parameter:

```
ESEUTIL.EXE /MH c:\recoverydb\mailbox database
```

The output of the preceding command is shown in the following screenshot:

```
Administrator: Command Prompt

C:\>eseutil /mh "c:\ExchangeRecovery\Mailbox Database 0074851821.edb"

Extensible Storage Engine Utilities for Microsoft(R) Exchange Server
Version 15.00
Copyright (C) Microsoft Corporation. All Rights Reserved.

Initiating FILE DUMP mode...
         Database: c:\ExchangeRecovery\Mailbox Database 0074851821.edb


DATABASE HEADER:
Checksum Information:
Expected Checksum: 0x1f3bbb2d
  Actual Checksum: 0x1f3bbb2d

Fields:
        File Type: Database
         Checksum: 0x1f3bbb2d
   Format ulMagic: 0x89abcdef
   Engine ulMagic: 0x89abcdef
 Format ulVersion: 0x620,20
 Engine ulVersion: 0x620,20
Created ulVersion: 0x620,20
     DB Signature: Create time:05/07/2013 23:14:36.245 Rand:432686169 Computer:
         cbDbPage: 32768
           dbtime: 10089373 (0x99f39d)
            State: Clean Shutdown
     Log Required: 0-0 (0x0-0x0)
    Log Committed: 0-0 (0x0-0x0)
   Log Recovering: 0 (0x0)
  GenMax Creation: 00/00/1900 00:00:00.000
         Shadowed: Yes
       Last Objid: 38871
     Scrub Dbtime: 0 (0x0)
       Scrub Date: 00/00/1900 00:00:00
     Repair Count: 2
      Repair Date: 05/07/2013 23:14:36.245
 Old Repair Count: 0
  Last Consistent: (0x0,0,0)  05/07/2013 23:14:36.354
      Last Attach: (0x0,0,0)  05/07/2013 23:14:36.261
      Last Detach: (0x0,0,0)  05/07/2013 23:14:36.354
    Last ReAttach: (0x4C9,2,0)  03/12/2013 16:50:33.573
```

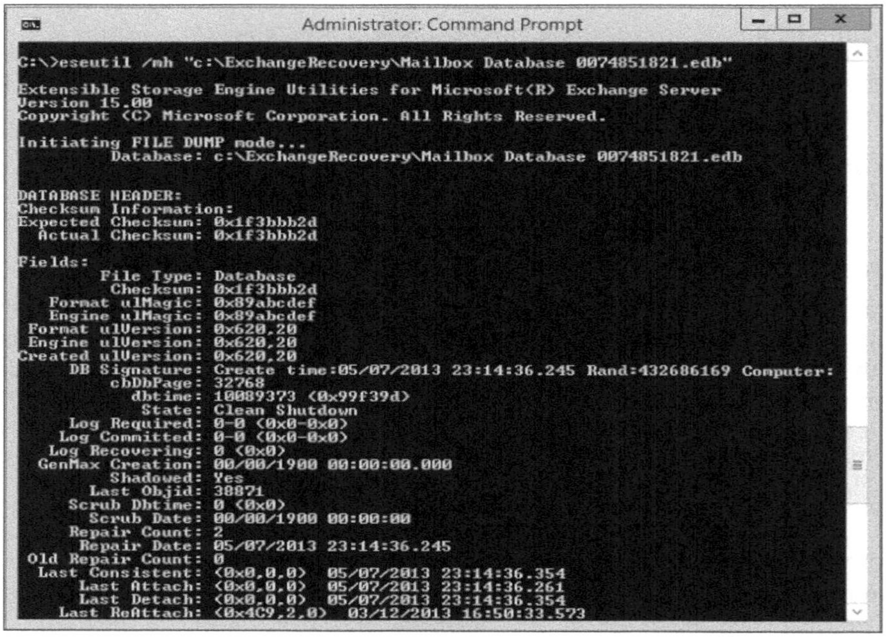

Restoring mailbox data from a Recovery Database into the active Mailbox Database

In this last step, we will actually restore mailbox data from the Recovery Database back into our (active) production database. In Exchange 2010, we used the `Restore-Mailbox` cmdlet for this purpose. However, since Exchange 2010 SP1 (and also Exchange 2013), the new cmdlet to be used is:

```
New-MailboxRestoreRequest -sourcedatabase (your recoveryDB) -
sourcestoremailbox (your mailbox user ID) -targetmailbox (the mailbox in
the active production database in which you want to restore)
```

For example:

```
New-MailboxRestoreRequest -sourcedatabase "RecoveryDB" -
sourcestoremailbox "User1" -targetmailbox "User1"
```

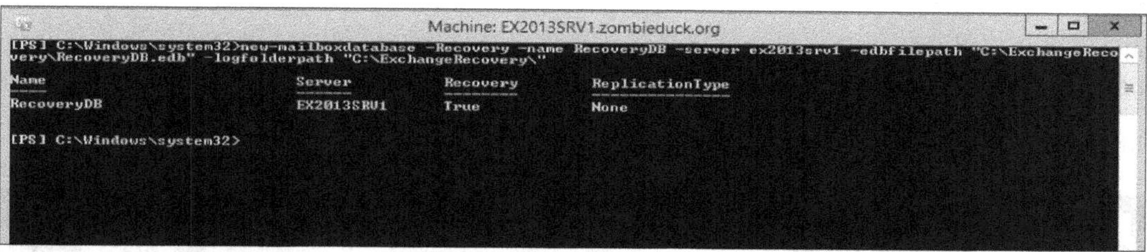

Note that this example will overwrite the current user's mailbox. If you only want to restore specific items from the user's mailbox, the cmdlet has a few parameter options for this such as, `ExcludeFolders` and `IncludeFolders` to reference specific subfolders of the inbox.

During the restore operation itself, we can follow the ongoing process by firing the `Get-MailboxRecoveryRequest` cmdlet. The output is as shown in the following screenshot:

```
cmdlet New-MailboxRestoreRequest at command pipeline position 1
Supply values for the following parameters:
SourceDatabase: recoverydb
SourceStoreMailbox: administrator
TargetMailbox: administrator

Name                    TargetMailbox                           Status
----                    -------------                           ------
MailboxRestore          zombieduck.org/Users/Administrator      Queued

[PS] C:\Windows\system32>Get-MailboxRestoreRequest

Name                    TargetMailbox                           Status
----                    -------------                           ------
MailboxRestore          zombieduck.org/Users/Administrator      Completed

[PS] C:\Windows\system32>_
```

How it works...

Performing a restore of an Exchange Server 2013 mailbox database or mailbox items is not an easy task to execute. Especially, if you are using the Windows Backup tool for this. Although, as we showed you in the scenario, the tool does the job, the different steps that are required in making it all work are a bit trivial.

To summarize, the restore process works as follows:

1. Install the Windows Server 2012 Windows Backup tool.
2. Configure and run a backup job.
3. Configure a Recovery Database.
4. Perform a restore from backup.
5. Launch `New-MailboxRestoreRequest` to actually restore a full mailbox or specific mailbox items from the Recovery Database back into production database.

There's more...

Instead of using the native built-in Windows Backup Tool, consider one of the long list of third-party backup software solutions available, of which a lot also have native support for Exchange Server.

Although the information is not officially published by Microsoft, Exchange MVP *Johan Veldhuis* has a very nice overview of backup solutions and their support state of Exchange 2013:

`http://johanveldhuis.nl/?p=2742&lang=en`

Recovering a failed Exchange server

Recovering data is one thing. Sometimes, however, servers fail beyond the point where they can easily be repaired, thus calling for a different approach to the restore process.

The following recipe will guide you through the process of recovering a server, after which you will be able to proceed with recovering data as described earlier.

Getting ready

In order to complete the following steps, we assume that you have executed the previous exercises up to the point where you have a valid backup that you can use to restore data.

How to do it...

When you get to the point that you deemed a server as irrecoverable and plan on rebuilding the server from scratch (on the same or new hardware), there is a series of actions you need to perform:

1. Reset the computer account in Active Directory.
2. Join the 'new' computer to the domain using the same name as the failed server.
3. Run `setup.exe /mode:recoverserver`.
4. Execute post-recovery actions like restoring server-specific settings and data.

Resetting a computer account in Active Directory

The following actions will reset the existing computer account in Active Directory. By doing so, you allow the replacement server to be joined with the same name afterwards.

1. Login to a Domain Controller or a domain-member server that has the Active Directory Remote Server Administration Tools installed.
2. Open **Active Directory Users & Computers**.
3. Navigate to the Organization Unit or container in which the computer account for the failed server resides.
4. Right-click on the computer account and select **Reset**.

Next up is joining the replacement server to the domain. Don't forget to use the same name as the failed server. So if your failed server's name was `EX2013-01`, the new server's name should also be `EX2013-01`.

After you have joined the computer to the domain, it's time to recover the server.

Recovering a failed exchange server using the /m:recoverserver switch

Before executing the following steps, you need to make sure that you have installed all the operating system prerequisites as outlined earlier in this book in *Chapter 2, Installing Exchange Server 2013*.

1. Login to the replacement server and open an elevated command prompt.
2. Navigate to the Exchange binaries folder. Please note that the binaries that you use must be of the same version as the ones that were installed on the failed server. If your failed server had Exchange 2013 CU2 installed, you should now also use the CU2 bits.
3. Run the following command:

   ```
   Setup.exe /mode:recoverserver /IAcceptExchangeServerLicenseTerms
   ```

4. Wait for the setup to complete and restart the server.

Depending on how your server was setup before, there are some specifics that you need to take into account.

First, there's the location where Exchange was previously installed. If that location is different from the default (`C:\Program Files\Microsoft\Exchange Server\v15`), you have to specify the `/TargetDir` parameter when executing the `setup.exe` command. The `/TargetDir` parameter should specify the path where Exchange was installed on the failed server.

If you are recovering a server that was part of a Database Availability Group, there are some additional steps to run, before running the `setup.exe` command:

1. Remove any existing Mailbox Database copies that still refer to the failed server using the `Remove-MailboxDatabaseCopy` command.
2. Remove the failed server as a member from the DAG using `Remove-DatabaseAvailabilityGroupServer`.

Assuming your failed server's name was `EX2013-01` and it had two database copies (DB01 and DB02), you would run the following commands:

```
Remove-MailboxDatabaseCopy EX2013-01\DB01
Remove-MailboxDatabaseCopy EX2013-01\DB02
Remove-DatabaseAvailabilityGroupServer -Identity DAG01 -MailboxServer EX2013-01 -ConfigurationOnly
```

Notice the use of the `-ConfigurationOnly` switch. We need to add this switch because our failed server isn't online and cannot be reached. However, if you are trying to remove a server that is still online, you wouldn't have to add the switch.

Executing post-installation tasks

Once your server has rebooted after the Exchange setup wizard has run, there are some additional steps you have to take before your server is fully operational. These steps include restoring the server's previous configuration either by restoring it from backup or manually reconfiguring it.

Amongst other items, these steps include configuring:

- Certificates
- Registry settings/changes
- Custom entries or changes to configuration files
- Local permissions

If your server was a member of the Database Availability Group before, you should add it to the DAG again. For more information on how to do this, have a look at *Chapter 6: Implementing and Managing High Availability*.

How it works...

Like previous versions, Exchange 2013 stores a lot of its configuration data in Active Directory. As a result, the Exchange setup wizard is able to determine most of its configuration during the installation. By using the same computer name as the failed server, the setup wizard (`setup.exe`) looks up relevant configuration information for that Exchange server in Active Directory and uses it to reconfigure the server with those settings. The benefit is clearly that you, the admin, don't have to redo that part of the configuration. It's only part of the configuration because the setup wizard has no clue about settings that were stored locally on the server (for example, certificates). These changes will have to be made manually.

Given that some of the locally stored configuration items are quite important, it's obvious that you should document your changes well, if possible use some sort of change management process to keep changes under control throughout the lifetime of your Exchange servers. That way, you'll always be able to re-apply changes to the replacement server that you made on the failed server previously.

10
Implementing Security

In this chapter, we will cover:

- Configuring Role-Based Access Control (RBAC)
- Configuring administrator audit logging
- Configuring anti-spam and anti-malware features

Introduction

In the previous chapters we already discussed some of Exchange's built-in security and compliance features like mailbox audit logging, DLP, Transport rules, personal archives, and so on. This chapter, although also dedicated to security, takes a look at the security features that can be used to protect Exchange (and its configuration) rather than its data, something that the aforementioned features are mainly used for.

Configuring role-based access control

In the early days, securing access to Exchange was relatively easy: either you had permissions to make configuration changes or you did not. The problem with this model is that you don't have a very granular way of deciding who can do what. In smaller environments where there's a single person or team managing everything from AD to Exchange, this approach would probably work pretty well. However, larger environments often have different teams managing different parts of the infrastructure. Especially when the AD admin isn't the one who also manages Exchange, having too many permissions could become a problem.

Previously, when the management of Active Directory and Exchange were split across different persons or teams, one had to use delegation of permissions in Active Directory to make this work. For those who have worked with delegation in Active Directory: it isn't very easy and requires a lot of planning to set up and work to maintain.

This is where role-based access control comes into play. Originally introduced in Exchange Server 2010, RBAC continues to be important in Exchange 2013 as well.

RBAC is all about a simple catchphrase: "who can do what and where". In essence, RBAC allows you to determine who (users) can execute what actions (cmdlets) against specific parts of Exchange's configuration (assignments). RBAC uses management roles, role groups, and role assignments to make all this happen.

A management role is a collection of one or more tasks, represented by a collection of one or more cmdlets. For instance, there is a built-in role called **Migration** which contains the cmdlets to configure and execute mailbox moves. To control who has access to these cmdlets and where these can be used, a management role assignment is used. This assignment ties a user (or group) to a specific management role. Along with the definition of the who and the what, a role assignment includes a write scope which defines where or against what objects the cmdlets can be used.

How to do it...

First, let's get familiar with the RBAC. Exchange 2013 has 14 built-in role groups, which you can discover by running the following command from the Exchange Management Shell:

```
Get-RoleGroup
```

The output of the preceding command is shown in the following screenshot:

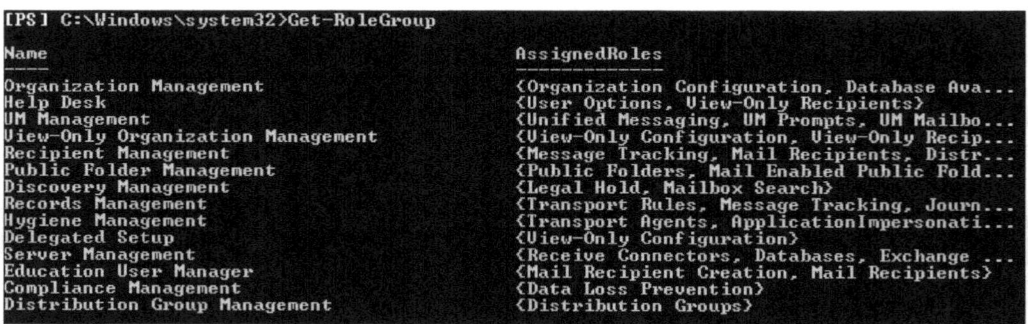

```
[PS] C:\Windows\system32>Get-RoleGroup

Name                                    AssignedRoles
----                                    -------------
Organization Management                 {Organization Configuration, Database Ava...
Help Desk                               {User Options, View-Only Recipients}
UM Management                           {Unified Messaging, UM Prompts, UM Mailbo...
View-Only Organization Management       {View-Only Configuration, View-Only Recip...
Recipient Management                    {Message Tracking, Mail Recipients, Distr...
Public Folder Management                {Public Folders, Mail Enabled Public Fold...
Discovery Management                    {Legal Hold, Mailbox Search}
Records Management                      {Transport Rules, Message Tracking, Journ...
Hygiene Management                      {Transport Agents, ApplicationImpersonati...
Delegated Setup                         {View-Only Configuration}
Server Management                       {Receive Connectors, Databases, Exchange ...
Education User Manager                  {Mail Recipient Creation, Mail Recipients}
Compliance Management                   {Data Loss Prevention}
Distribution Group Management           {Distribution Groups}
```

Alternatively, you can also use the Exchange Admin Center:

1. Log in to the EAC and navigate to **permissions** | **admin roles** as shown in the following screenshot:

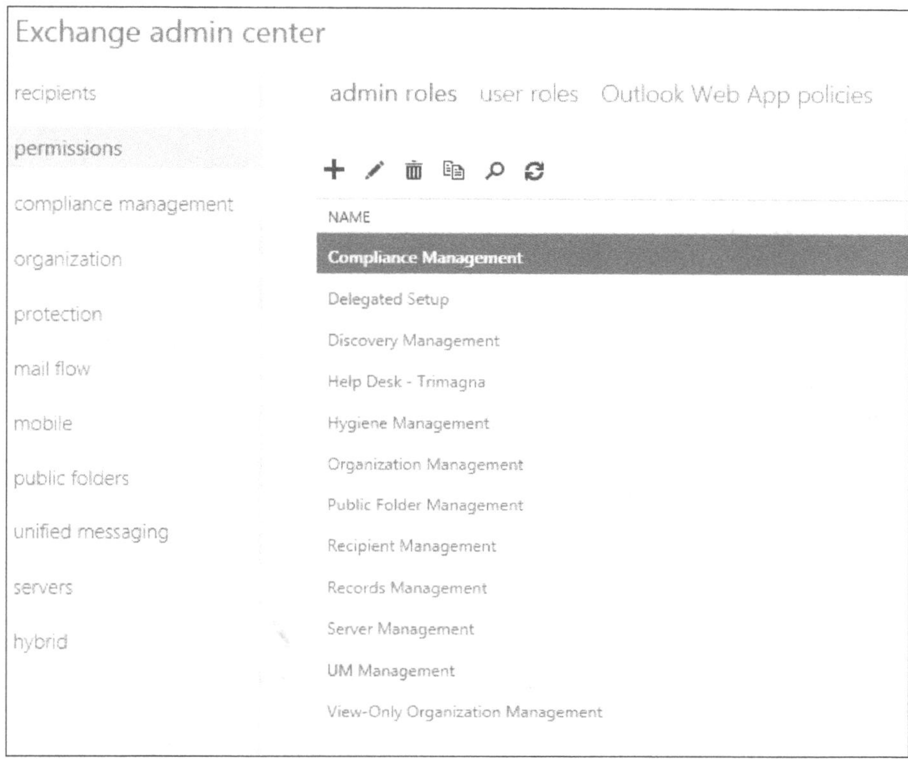

2. When selecting a role group from the middle pane, the details of that role group are automatically displayed in the action pane, as seen in the following screenshot:

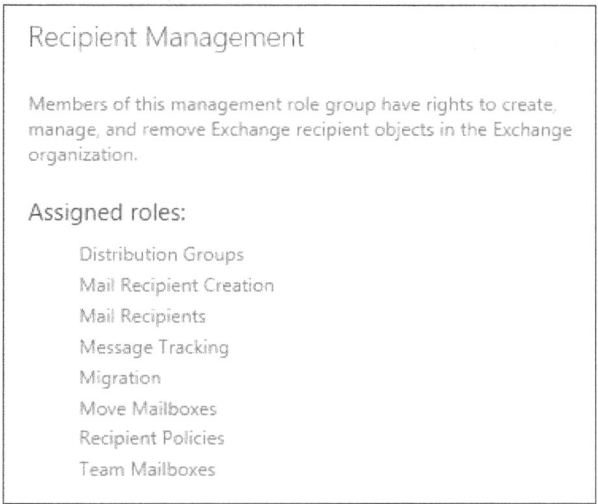

3. Opening the properties of a role group will reveal the following information:

    - Name
    - Description
    - Write scope
    - Roles assigned to this role group
    - Members

Adding members to a role group

As already mentioned, Exchange 2013 provides 14 pre-configured role groups, which can be used immediately after the Exchange installation. You only have to add members to these role groups before you can start using them. Adding members is as easy as adding a user to the security group for the role group.

This can be done either through the EAC or via the `Add-RoleGroupMember` cmdlet. The following command will add the user `MHolt` to the built-in `Recipient Management` role group:

```
Add-RoleGroupMember -Identity "Recipient Management" -Member MHolt
```

Creating a custom role group and limit the write-scope to an organizational unit

There are two ways in which you can create new role groups. Either you start from an existing role group or you can create a new role group from scratch.

Let's start by creating a new role, based on the existing role group `Recipient Management`:

1. Log in to the EAC and navigate to **permissions** | **admin roles**.
2. Select **Recipient Management** and click on the copy sign to start the new role group wizard as shown in the following screenshot:

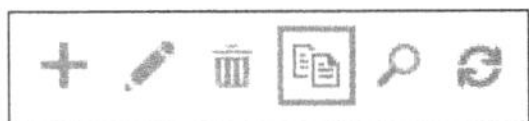

Notice that the input fieds are pre-populated with the settings from the existing role group, as seen in the following screenshot:

new role group

*Name:

Copy of Recipient Management

Description:

Members of this management role group have rights to create, manage, and remove Exchange recipient objects in

The name of the new role group is automatically changed to **Copy of...**, but all other information is retained. The first thing you need to do is to change the name and description to match the purpose of your new role group. Especially when you will be creating several role groups, it's a good idea to make the description as clear as possible so that no confusion exists about what the role group should be used for.

Since we are creating a copy of the `Recipient Management` role group, it's a good idea to reflect this and its purpose in the name. Assuming that we are limiting the scope to an OU called `Antwerp`, you could do the following:

1. Edit the **Name** and **Description** field as shown in the following screenshot:

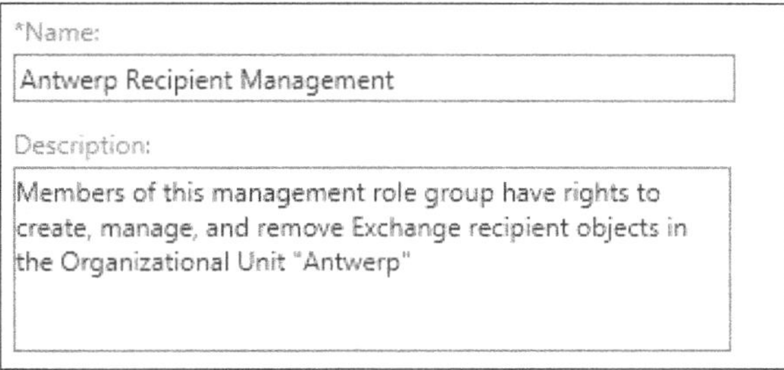

2. Next, we need to configure the organization unit to which we want to scope this new, custom, role group. Under **Write scope**, select **Organizational unit:** and type the path to the organizational unit as shown in the following screenshot:

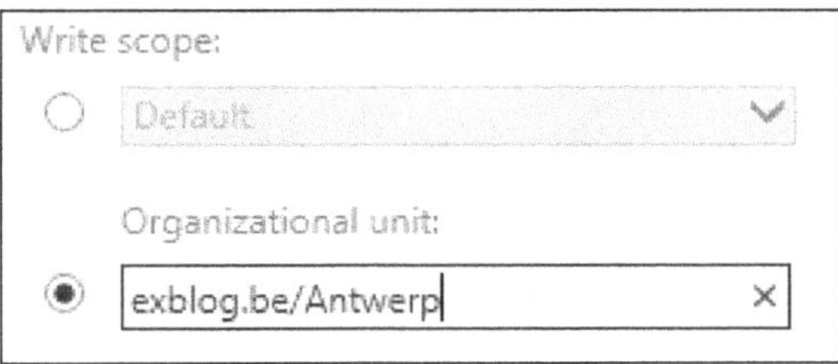

3. Assuming that we do not want to remove any of the management role (tasks) from the role group, all that is left to do is to add members to this role group. Click on the plus sign (**+**) under **Members**. Select the member(s) you want to add and click on **Ok**.
4. Click on **Save** to create the role group.

As you can see, creating a custom role group is not difficult. That is, if the management roles that are assigned to one of the pre-configured role groups are sufficient for your needs.

Sometimes you might not want a new role group to have the exact same permissions as its parent role group. Removing permissions from a role group is relatively easy.

If we return to our previous example, before clicking on **save**, you can remove one or more roles from the role group by selecting them and clicking on the minus button (-) as shown in the following screenshot:

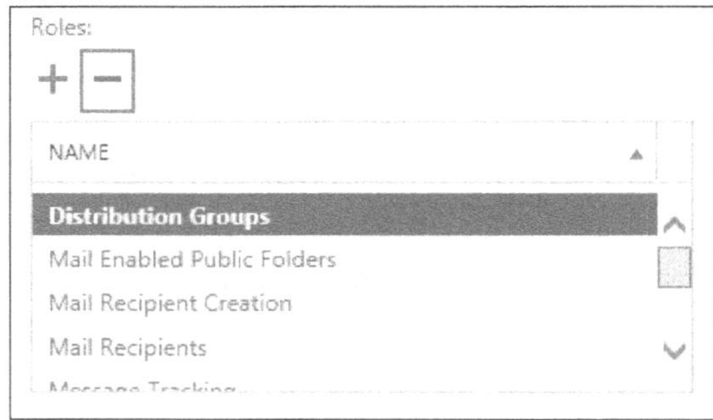

This all works great for as long as any of the existing role groups (or Management Roles) contain the permissions you're planning to use. Sometimes, however, you might find yourself in a situation where none of the built-in management roles or role groups have the exact set of permissions that you're looking for.

In that case, you'll need to create both a new management role and a new role group.

Although, you can assign management roles directly to a user, it's better to assign them to a role group first and then add users to that role group. This prevents you from having to assign a management role multiple times to different users as you can just add them to the role group instead.

Creating a role group from scratch

In this exercise, we will create a custom role group that has permissions to administer Exchange Databases, Database Copies, and Database Availability Groups:

1. From within the EAC, click on the plus sign (**+**) to create a new role group.
2. Enter `Database and DAG Admins` in the **Name** field.

3. Enter `This group has the required permissions to administer Exchange Databases and Database Availability Groups in the Exchange Organization` in the **Description** field.
4. In the roles topic, click on the plus sign (**+**); this will open a new window from which you can select existing management roles. From here, select **Database Availability Groups**, **Database Copies**, and **Databases** as shown in the following screenshot:

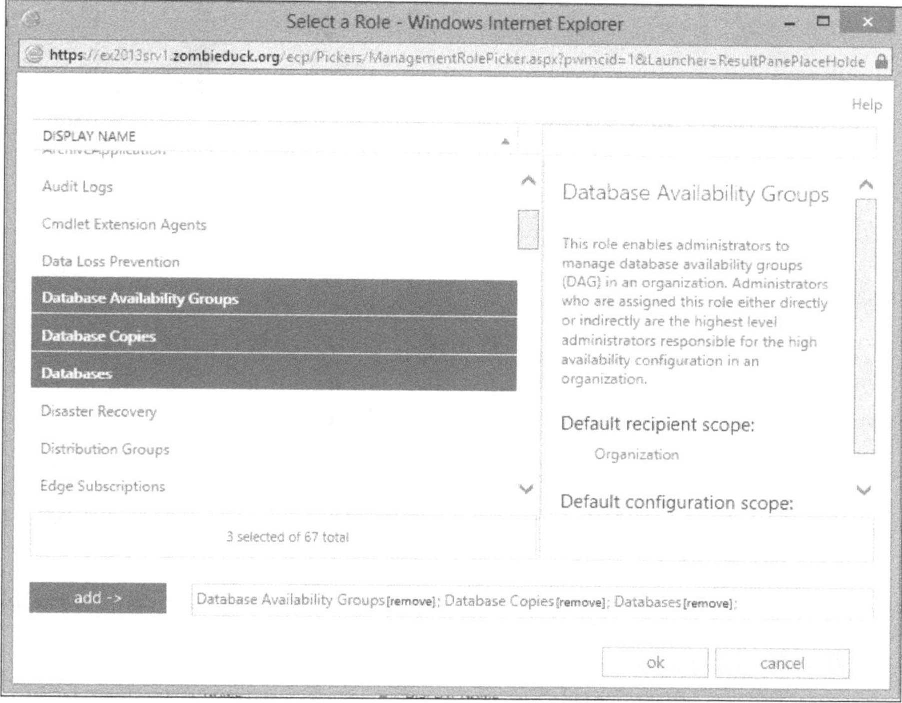

5. Add members to the role group. How to do this has already been explained in the previous exercise. If you want, you can create the group without adding users and add them at a later time.
6. Click on **Ok** to create the role group.

Creating a new management role assignment with a limited scope

As discussed earlier, creating a role group that contains any of the built-in management roles is great as long as these management roles reflect what you are trying to accomplish. Let's assume that in the previous example, you want to limit the databases that one can manage. For instance, you want a member of the role group only to be able to manage databases DB01 and DB02.

From the previous exercise we already know that the Databases Management Role is the one that we will be using. However, because we want to limit its scope to two databases, we cannot use the GUI to add it to the role group. Instead, we will have to revert to PowerShell to create a new management scope and then use that scope in the role assignment which ties the management role to the role group as shown in the following screenshot:

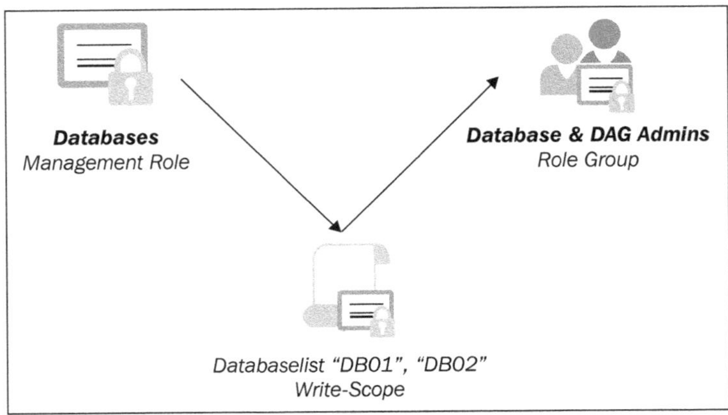

The following command will create a new management scope, called `DB01-DB02`:

```
New-ManagementScope -Name "DB01-DB02" -DatabaseList "DB01","DB02"
```

Next, this scope has to be used to link the `Databases Management` role to our `Database & DAG Admins` role group:

```
New-ManagementRoleAssignment -Role Databases -SecurityGroup  "Database &
DAG Admins" -CustomConfigWriteScope DB01-DB02
```

There are many different ways in which you can limit the scope of a management assignment. Listing all of them would take too long, but I encourage you to have a look at the following TechNet article to get you started: `http://technet.microsoft.com/en-us/library/dd335137(v=exchg.150).aspx`.

To find out what the name of the security group is from the role group you created earlier, open **Active Directory Users & Computers** and navigate to the **Microsoft Exchange Security Groups** container as shown in the following screenshot:

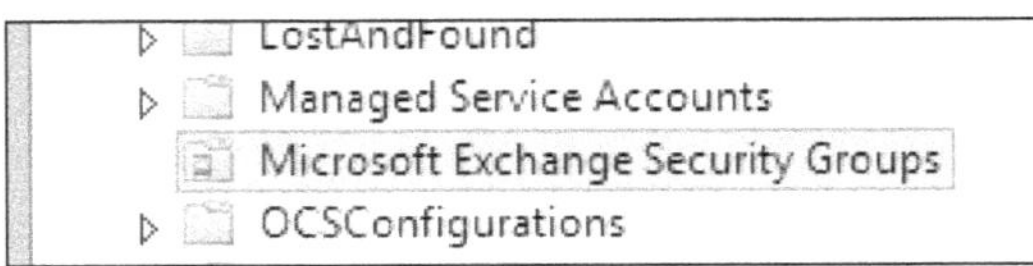

There's more...

Although the article dates back to November 2009, the Exchange Product Team has a very detailed description on how the RBAC permissions model works:

`http://blogs.technet.com/b/exchange/archive/2009/11/16/3408825.aspx`

Configuring administrator audit logging

As part of the Exchange native data protection features in *Chapter 8, Configuring Security and Compliance Features*, we talked about a mechanism called mailbox audit logging which tracks access to a specific mailbox.

Wouldn't it be cool to do the same level of inspection logging on the overall Exchange Organization? Administrator audit logging can be used to create a log of every change a regular user or an Exchange Administrative user makes to the Exchange Organization. By inspecting the log, you can track who made what changes and when they were made.

How to do it...

By default, Adminstrator audit logging is enabled in Exchange 2013, for all administrative cmdlets that are run within Exchange 2013. If the audit logging has been disabled and you want to turn it on again, use the following cmdlet:

```
Set-AdminAuditLogConfig -AdminAuditLogEnabled $False
```

Although, we wouldn't recommend this, you have the option to disable audit logging. This is achieved by running the following PowerShell cmdlet:

```
Set-AdminAuditLogConfig -AdminAuditLogEnabled $False
```

Configuring the auditing of specific events

By default, all administrative actions are logged in the Administrator audit logging. However, it is possible to update the list of events that should be taken into account in the auditing logging. So instead of logging every action, you can specify to only log certain activities:

```
Set-AdminAuditLogConfig -AdminAuditLogCmdlets <parameter>
```

For a detailed list of all parameters you can define for logging, along with some examples, have a look at the following Microsoft Exchange 2013 TechNet article:

`http://technet.microsoft.com/en-us/library/dd298169(v=exchg.150).aspx`

Configuring the audit log age

By default, the Administrator audit Logging keeps track of all changes for a period of 90 days. Although this should be enough in most organizations, the following command will extend that period to 180 days:

```
Set-AdminAuditLogConfig -AdminAuditLogAgeLimit 180:00:00:00
```

In case you were wondering where the 180.00:00:00 comes from; the time notation happens in the following format: days.hours:minutes:seconds.

Generating the audit log reports

Exchange 2013 has a few built-in reports available, which you can consult from the EAC:

1. From within the EAC, go to **compliance management** | **auditing**.
2. Click on **Export the Administrator audit log...**.
3. From the pop-up window, enter the start and end date you want to use for the logging; also specify the user account that you want to send the logging report to.
4. Click on **Export**; this will send the auditing report to the user you selected in step 3. The e-mail subject will be `Admin Audit Log Search "SearchID" - Requested by user - Completed Successfully.`

Note that it can take a while before the report is delivered to the user.

5. The audit log file itself is called **SearchResult.xml** as shown in the following screenshot:

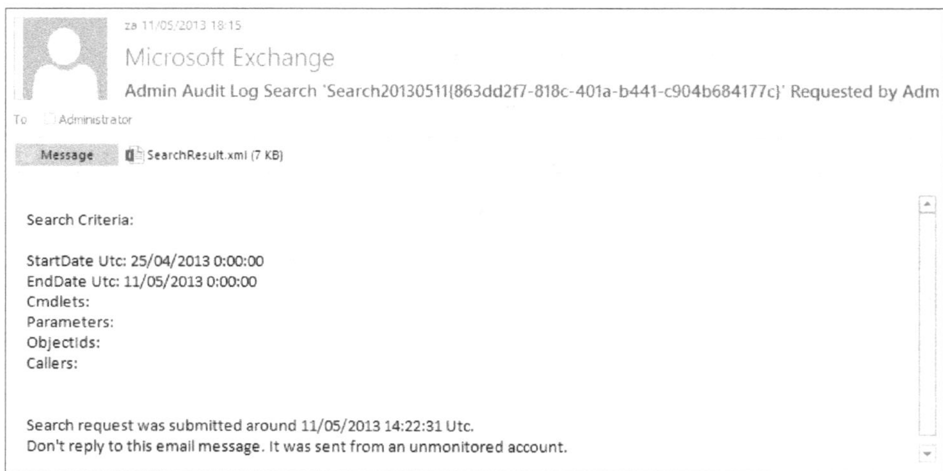

6. The contents of the log file itself look similar to the following sample output:

```
OriginatingServer="EX2013SRV1 (15.00.0516.025)">
    <CmdletParameters>
      <Parameter Name="Identity" Value="recoveryDB" />
    </CmdletParameters>
  </Event>
  <Event Caller="exblog.be/Users/Administrator" Cmdlet="Mount-
  Database" ObjectModified="RecoveryDB" RunDate="2013-
  05-07T23:19:12+02:00" Succeeded="true" Error=""
  OriginatingServer="EX2013SRV1 (15.00.0516.025)">
    <CmdletParameters>
      <Parameter Name="Identity" Value="recoverydb" />
    </CmdletParameters>
  </Event>
  <Event Caller="exblog.be/Users/Administrator" Cmdlet="Remove-
  MailboxDatabase" ObjectModified="RecoveryDB" RunDate="2013-
  05-06T23:03:20+02:00" Succeeded="true" Error=""
  OriginatingServer="EX2013SRV1 (15.00.0516.025)">
    <CmdletParameters>
      <Parameter Name="Identity" Value="recoverydb" />
      <Parameter Name="Confirm" Value="True" />
    </CmdletParameters>
  </Event>
  <Event Caller="exblog.be/Users/Administrator" Cmdlet="New-
  MailboxDatabase" ObjectModified="RecoveryDB" RunDate="2013-
  05-06T23:04:13+02:00" Succeeded="true" Error=""
  OriginatingServer="EX2013SRV1 (15.00.0516.025)">
    <CmdletParameters>
      <Parameter Name="Recovery" Value="True" />
      <Parameter Name="Name" Value="RecoveryDB" />
      <Parameter Name="Server" Value="ex2013srv1" />
      <Parameter Name="EdbFilePath" Value="C:\ExchangeRecovery\
      RecoveryDB.edb" />
      <Parameter Name="LogFolderPath" Value="C:\ExchangeRecovery"
      />
    </CmdletParameters>
  </Event>
```

7. From the preceding example, we can see that the following actions were executed:

    - On May 7th, 11.19PM, the Administrator account ran a cmdlet (by using GUI or EAC) to mount a database called `recoveryDB`
    - On the same date, a few minutes before, the same user ran a cmdlet to remove the Exchange database
    - Followed by a cmdlet to create a new Exchange database

How it works...

By using administrator audit logging, a log entry is created every time a cmdlet is executed on the Exchange 2013 environment (by default commands starting with `Get`, `Test`, and `Search` are not logged).

The log contains the cmdlet name, the specified parameters and their values, the object that was changed, who executed the cmdlet, when it was run, and on what server.

The logging information is stored in a hidden folder in a dedicated arbitration mailbox.

The reports are created only on demand and can be retrieved through the EAC, the `Search-AdminAuditLog`, or `New-AdminAuditLogSearch` cmdlets.

For example, for running a log report of all changes from the last day, use the following shell command:

```
Search-AdminAuditLog -Startdate ((get-date).AddDays(-1)) -EndDate (get-date)
```

The audit logging log file is an XML file which contains multiple log entries. By specifying certain parameters in the aforementioned commands you can narrow down the results.

For example, specifying the `-Cmdlets` parameter with the `New-AdminAuditLogSearch` cmdlet will only return results specific for the cmdlet you specified.

By default, the `SearchResult.xml` file is limited to a size of 10 Mb. If the resulting log file is larger, you will still receive the e-mail, but not the attachment itself. In that case, you should modify the search parameters to narrow down the results.

Configuring anti-spam and anti-malware features

Spam e-mail and the fight against it is nothing new. In fact, it has been around pretty much ever since the first e-mail system was created a few decades ago. Although, at first the impact of spam e-mail was limited, the amount of spam that organizations have to deal with has grown exponentially up to the point that more than 90 percent of messages sent worldwide each day are considered spam. One of the reasons why spam has become this popular, is of course, the fact that use of e-mail is widespread both for business and private conversations.

Often, spam is associated with unwanted advertisements. Although, that's how it all started, nowadays spam is much more than that; it's considered to be a collective noun for all unsolicited e-mail including advertisements or e-mails containing malicious code like viruses or malware.

Getting ready

Protecting Exchange against spam and malware is trivial to guarantee the health of the system and the clients. In the following exercises we will be configuring Exchange's built-in anti-spam and anti-malware features.

In order to complete these steps, you must have access to the Exchange Admin Center or Management shell.

How to do it...

Given that the Transport-related components are part of the Mailbox Server role, the following steps should be executed against a Mailbox Server. Don't forget to repeat these steps for each Mailbox Server in your organization for which you want to enable the built-in agents.

Installing anti-spam agents

Just like in Exchange 2010, installing the anti-spam agents is done by running a PowerShell script from the built-in Exchange 2013 `Scripts` folder:

1. From within the Exchange shell, browse to the Exchange 2013 `Scripts` folder.
2. From this folder, run the following script:

   ```
   install-AntiSpamAgents.ps1
   ```

   The output will be as follows:

   ```
   [PS] C:\Program Files\Microsoft\Exchange Server\V15\Scripts>.\install-AntispamAgents.ps1
   WARNING: Please exit Windows PowerShell to complete the installation.
   WARNING: The following service restart is required for the change(s) to take effect : MSExchangeTransport
   WARNING: The following service restart is required for the change(s) to take effect : MSExchangeTransport

   Identity                                     Enabled        Priority
   --------                                     -------        --------
   Content Filter Agent                         True           5
   WARNING: Please exit Windows PowerShell to complete the installation.
   WARNING: The following service restart is required for the change(s) to take effect : MSExchangeTransport
   WARNING: The following service restart is required for the change(s) to take effect : MSExchangeTransport
   Sender Id Agent                              True           6
   WARNING: Please exit Windows PowerShell to complete the installation.
   WARNING: The following service restart is required for the change(s) to take effect : MSExchangeTransport
   WARNING: The following service restart is required for the change(s) to take effect : MSExchangeTransport
   Sender Filter Agent                          True           7
   WARNING: Please exit Windows PowerShell to complete the installation.
   WARNING: The following service restart is required for the change(s) to take effect : MSExchangeTransport
   WARNING: The following service restart is required for the change(s) to take effect : MSExchangeTransport
   Recipient Filter Agent                       True           8
   WARNING: Please exit Windows PowerShell to complete the installation.
   WARNING: The following service restart is required for the change(s) to take effect : MSExchangeTransport
   WARNING: The following service restart is required for the change(s) to take effect : MSExchangeTransport
   Protocol Analysis Agent                      True           9

   WARNING: The agents listed above have been installed. Please restart the Microsoft Exchange Transport service for
   changes to take effect.

   [PS] C:\Program Files\Microsoft\Exchange Server\V15\Scripts>_
   ```

   This will install and configure the different agent components.

3. As mentioned at the end of the script routine, to activate the agents, we need to restart the Microsoft Exchange Transport service:

   ```
   Restart-Service MSExchangeTransport
   ```

4. As a last step, we have to configure a bypass rule for our internal SMTP servers, as we don't want those to be scanned by the sender ID agent. This list should also include your Exchange 2013 Mailbox Servers:

```
Set-TransportConfig -InternalSMTPServers @
{Add="10.0.1.10","10.0.1.11"}
```

> Note that the configuration should always be done using IP addresses, not hostnames.

Enabling or disabling anti-malware scanning

Besides anti-spam, another security mechanism which is of great importance in an Exchange 2013 organization is anti-malware. Malware is the term used to refer to all sorts of malicious code including viruses and spyware.

By default, the anti-malware engine is activated in Exchange 2013, unless you explicitly chose not to activate it during the initial Exchange Server 2013 setup. There is no latency in accessing e-mails through the e-mail client, as scanning of the message is not triggered on opening the message; it is already scanned when the message travels through Exchange's Transport Pipeline.

If, for whatever reason, you need to turn off the anti-malware engine, use the following PowerShell script:

1. From within the Exchange shell, browse to the Exchange 2013 `Scripts` folder.
2. From this folder, run the following script:

   ```
   Disable-AntiMalwareScanning.ps1
   ```

3. Restart the Exchange Transport service by running the following command:

   ```
   Restart-Service MSExchangeTransport
   ```

If the feature has been disabled (or it wasn't enabled during setup), here's how you can enable it again:

1. From within the Exchange shell, browse to the Exchange 2013 `Scripts` folder.
2. From this folder, run the following script:

   ```
   Enable-AntiMalwareScanning.ps1
   ```

   The output will be as follows:

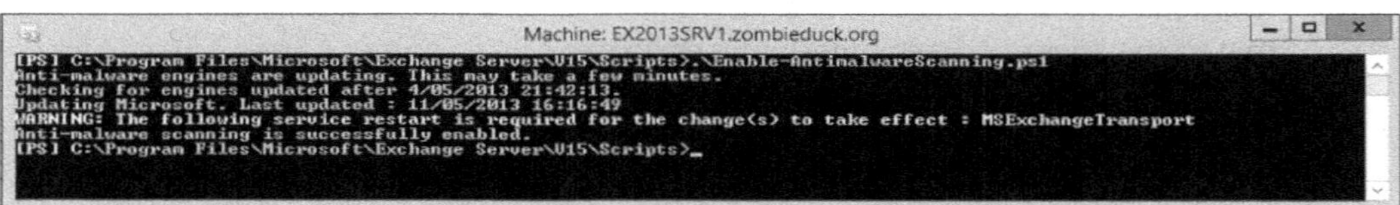

3. As mentioned at the end of the script routine, to activate the agents, we need to restart the Microsoft Exchange Transport service. Run the following cmdlet:

   ```
   Restart-Service MSExchangeTransport
   ```

Updating the anti-malware engine

Just as with any other third-party anti-malware solution, the success of anti-malware protection is determined by its definitions. These definitions contain the code that is required to detect and recognize malicious software or code. Given that malware makers continuously update their code to circumvent malware detection, the definitions that are installed will probably already be out-of-date by the time you deploy them. Even so, once they're deployed they need regular updates to be able to detect the latest threats. In normal situations, Microsoft releases an update file on a daily basis at a minimum. Sometimes, however, it multiple updates are published per day. The anti-malware engine itself will scan for updated definition files every hour.

For the updates to complete successfully, make sure the following have been checked:

- Make sure the Exchange server has access to the Internet, connecting on port 80
- Run the **Enable-AntiMalwareScanning.ps1** script again to find the latest timestamp of the installed updates

If you want to run intermediate manual updates of the engines, you can do the following:

1. From within the Exchange shell, browse to the Exchange 2013 `Scripts` folder.
2. From this folder, run the following script:

   ```
   Update-AntiMalwareScanning.ps1
   ```

The output will be as follows:

Although it is not mentioned at the end of the script routine, to activate the update of the agents, we suggest you to restart the Microsoft Exchange Transport service. (It could take up to 15 minutes before the updated engine files will be applied; in case of an outbreak this might be too late):

```
Restart-Service MSExchangeTransport
```

Verifying the installed updates

Although the update of the engines should run fine, it is always a good idea to regularly verify that the latest updates are being used.

As already mentioned, by running the `Enable-MalwareScanning.ps1` script again, the latest timestamp of the engine will be checked and shown in the shell window.

A second approach is by inspecting the Event Viewer:

1. Open the Event Viewer and navigate to **Windows Logs** | **Application**.
2. Create a filter by selecting **Filter Current Log**.
3. In this dialog box, select **FIPFS** as the Event Source and click on **OK**.

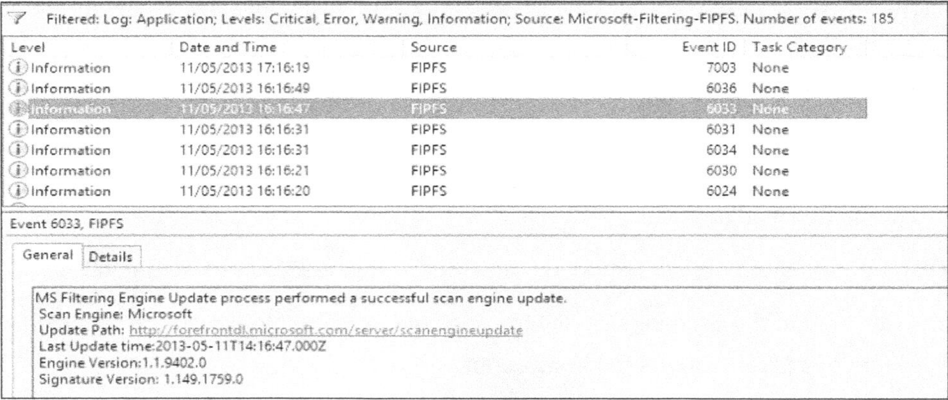

Look for event with ID `6033` which lists the last update time and engine version.

How it works...

Ever since Exchange 2003's **IMF** (**Intelligent Message Filter**), Microsoft provided some built-in configuration tools to fight against spam and malicious senders in general. With Exchange 2007 and 2010, those anti-spam agents evolved into more sophisticated agents.

Besides the internally running agents on the Exchange 2007 or 2010 Hub Transport servers, organizations could create a layered defense by leveraging adding a cloud-based or third-party filtering solution in front of Exchange such as Exchange Online Protection or using an Exchange 2010 Edge Transport Server.

Like any other transport agent in Exchange, each anti-spam agent is assigned a priority value (you can verify the priority of each anti-spam agent by running the `Get-TransportAgent` cmdlet). The lower the value, the higher the priority. So basically, an anti-spam agent with a priority 5 will run before an anti-spam agent with priority 8 on the same message.

By default, the anti-spam agents are configured in the following order and priority:

Agent	Description
Sender Filter agent	This agent inspects the From address of a sender, based on sender ID or sender domain.
Recipient Filter agent	This agent inspects the To address of a message against a recipient block list. If the recipient is on the list, the message is not allowed into the Exchange system. This mechanism also checks for existence of valid recipients. If the e-mail is destined to a non-existing address, it is rejected by default.
Sender ID agent	Almost like the Sender Filter agent, this agent inspects the From address of a sender, based on its IP address.
Content Filter agent	This agent inspects the e-mail for certain content in the message. This can be keyword or attachment based. Inspection runs against the subject and body fields. Default action here is to quarantine the captured messages, to avoid losing false-positive e-mails. Its intelligence also comes from the anti-spam configuration done by users in their Outlook or Outlook Web App.
Protocol Analysis agent	The last agent in the series is checking against the Sender Reputation Level. This is based on verifying a list of senders.

Next to the anti-spam agents, another important aspect of the anti-spam mechanism within Exchange 2013 is the anti-spam stamp.

The anti-spam stamp refers to a diagnostic code within a message as it passes through the anti-spam agents. This tells the Exchange system all information about a message, if it is classified as spam or not, and why.

The anti-spam stamp can be read from within Outlook 2010 or 2013 as follows:

1. From within your Outlook client, open a message to view it in a separate window.
2. From the ribbon, go to **Tags** | **Options**, which will display the properties of the message.
3. In the **properties** window, go to the **Internet Headers** section, and read through the anti-spam stamps:

```
X-MS-Exchange-Organization-PCL:7
X-MS-Exchange-Organization-SCL:6
X-MS-Exchange-Organization-Antispam-Report: DV:3.1.3924.1409;SID:S
enderIDStatus Fail;PCL:PhishingLevel SUSPICIOUS;CW:CustomList;PP:P
resolved;TIME:TimeBasedFeatures
```

There's more...

For more detailed information on different anti-spam agents and the actions that can be configured for them, go through the following Microsoft TechNet article:

`http://technet.microsoft.com/en-us/library/jj218660(v=exchg.150).aspx`

It is important to stress the fact that none of these features offer a 100 percent detection guarantee (not one security product that I know of does, actually). There will still be situations where certain malware is not detected by the engine because the engine has not been updated yet. If you should find such a malware in your e-mail messages, which for example could happen if an client-side anti-virus detects a virus before the malware engine has been updated, you can upload it to the Microsoft Malware Protection Center on the following web page:

`https://www.microsoft.com/security/portal/submission/submit.aspx`

Connection filtering and RBL

In Exchange 2003, connection filtering was present as one of the anti-spam mechanisms. This was updated in Exchange 2007 and 2010 to the connection filter agent. This agent allowed for creating filtering lists that contain IP addresses or hostnames which are used to explicitly block or allow connections coming from those addresses. This mechanism is also referred to as block or allow lists.

You don't necessarily have to maintain these lists manually. There are some (free of charge) services on the Internet, like Spamhaus, that offer a so-called **Real-Time Block List**. Essentially, you subscribe to their lists which are kept up-to-date by the provider. In order to create these lists, the provider uses its vast network of connections and clients to gather statistics and result, ultimately leading to an addition to the block list if a certain host is found to be sending spam. As such Real-Time Block Lists (RBLs) usually have a more extensive, up-to-date list which makes them considerably more efficient to work from.

Unfortunately, connection filtering did not make the cut in Exchange 2013. It's unclear as to whether this solution will come back at a later point. For now, you will have to revert to using third-party solutions or a cloud-based filtering service which can offer this feature.

Getting to Know Exchange Server 2013

In this appendix, we will cover:

- Exchange, then and now
- Some of the new features in Exchange Server 2013
- An explanation of the new architecture in Exchange Server 2013
- What features have been removed from Exchange Server 2013

Exchange, then and now

Did you know that with this latest release, Exchange is already in its 16th year?

In its early days Exchange 4.0 was nothing more than a simple e-mail solution. E-mail at that time was not even a business critical application and certainly not every user had an individual mailbox. During the past 15 years, the number of features, functions, and integrations with numerous other applications has expanded heavily. Ever since Exchange 2007, one could describe the product as a true unified messaging and communication solution. That description is still true today.

Out of the box, it not only includes e-mail messaging, calendaring, and contacts, just like in the early days; but it also adds archiving, shared folders, strong integration with Microsoft Lync, and Microsoft SharePoint to name just a few of the key functionalities.

From an architecture point of view, a lot of investments have been made to make it even more solid product by building further on and enhancing its features with regards to high availability. Where organizations needed to invest in expensive and complex clustering solutions to make Exchange 2000 and 2003 somewhat highly available, continued replication was Microsoft's first attempt to incorporate high availability into the product in Exchange 2007 and is basically the ancestor to the Database Availability Groups we know today. Although clustering is still used under the hood, Microsoft did a good job hiding the complexities as much as possible.

Exchange 2010 was the first version that really allowed storing data on cheap JBOD SATA storage. The replication mechanisms used in Exchange 2007 were updated and improved in Exchange 2010, which introduced **Database Availability Groups** (**DAG**); a feature that has been carried forward in Exchange 2013. A lot of effort was also put into optimizing load balancing. Inexpensive layer 4 load balancing, without requiring affinity, is now a supported scenario, potentially driving down the overall cost for load balancing.

This brings me to the latest trends in the IT industry, being "the cloud" and "mobility". Microsoft took its first steps towards a cloud-based Exchange Server environment back in 2008 with its **BPOS** (**Business Productivity Online Suite**) portfolio, which is nothing compared to what we have in Office 365 today. By making use of the so-called hybrid deployment scenario, which is basically creating a virtual Exchange organization across your on-premises Exchange and Exchange Online, companies now have a flexible way of using cloud services while still keeping some of the workloads on premises.

From a mobility point of view, **Outlook Web App** (**OWA**) is almost as feature rich as a full Outlook client. There are still some features missing, but gradually OWA is becoming a great alternative! The user experience can now be identical on all types of devices, no matter what device you are connecting from (regular desktop, laptop, ultrabook, tablet, or mobile phone), regardless of the operating system it is running (Windows, iOS, Android)

With that said, I think we have outlined a good overview of where Exchange is coming from in its early days, and what an enterprise communication oriented application it is today.

Exploring some new features in Exchange Server 2013

In this section, I'll walk you through some of the new features in Exchange Server 2013. It is not my intention to say the mentioned features are the only changes in the product, but they certainly make good part of my favorite changes:

- The Exchange Admin Center (EAC)
- The updated architecture
- The new public folders
- Outlook Web App redesign

- New security-related features
- Site mailboxes

One of the first things Exchange administrators or Exchange consultants will notice that is completely different from previous versions, is the **Exchange Management Console** (**EMC**). It's no longer there! Well, it's still there, but not as we used to know it. Exchange 2007 and 2010 (and all previous editions as well if you will) required the installation of a full-blown management console. Next to the Exchange Management Shell and the Exchange toolbox that still exist, Exchange 2013 introduces the all new Exchange Admin Center (EAC). The EAC is a web-based management tool, entirely replacing the old console. As sometimes is the case with recent Microsoft web consoles, this one is not based on Silverlight, which allows it also be used from non-IE browsers and from different types of clients.

For a complete overview of supported browsers, have a look at the following Microsoft TechNet article:

`http://technet.microsoft.com/en-us/library/jj150562(v=exchg.150).aspx`

You might be wondering how you can connect to the EAC? It's actually quite easy, but somewhat confusing. You need to surf to:

```
https://<ExchangeServerName>/ECP
```

People who are familiar with Exchange Server 2010 will know this URL already, as it refers to the **Exchange Control Panel** (**ECP**) in that version. Where the ECP was mainly used for managing users, groups, distribution lists, and so on in 2010, it is now a full administration console for managing server roles, databases, public folders, and much more. It even allows you connecting to Office365 in a hybrid scenario. All from one single console. It beats me why Microsoft didn't update the virtual directory to reflect the new name instead of still referring to the ECP. My best guess is that they didn't have enough time to make the change before the product was released.

The new public folders

Despite the rumors about public folders being removed in future versions of the product, they're still very much alive! In fact, Microsoft made quite significant changes to the public folder architecture, updating them for the future. I personally applaud this decision as public folders offer a very easy to use way of collaborating with other people in your organization, all from within Outlook.

Public folders are no longer stored in a separate public folder database, instead they are now stored as "Public Folder Mailboxes" within regular mailbox databases. As a result, public folders now use and benefit from the same high availability features as mailboxes have been doing since Exchange 2010. This includes the Database Availability Group and load balanced Client Access Servers. But there is a trade-off though: there can only be a single active instance of a public folder mailbox at any given time, before, public folders were stored in a multi-master topology. This meant that the same public folder could be replicated to different servers and be accessed simultaneously. This was especially interesting in companies that are geographically spread all over the world as every location could access a local copy of the replica. However, this approach also had its downsides. Public folder replication (which happened through SMTP) wasn't always reliable and it was a real pain to troubleshoot.

Leaving the migration of public folders aside for a moment, this can and probably will be quite challenging; its management has greatly been simplified. There is no more public folder replication and you can now manage decently through the GUI.

Outlook Web App

Outlook Web App (Outlook Web Access in previous editions) is nothing new to Exchange, but a lot has changed since Exchange 5.5. Even if you compare the new Outlook Web App with the one in Exchange 2010, there are still some noticeable differences.

One of the biggest changes in this version of OWA is the look and feel which reflects the modern UI style that Microsoft has been implementing across multiple products. It also makes it look much more like Outlook 2013 as seen in the following screenshot:

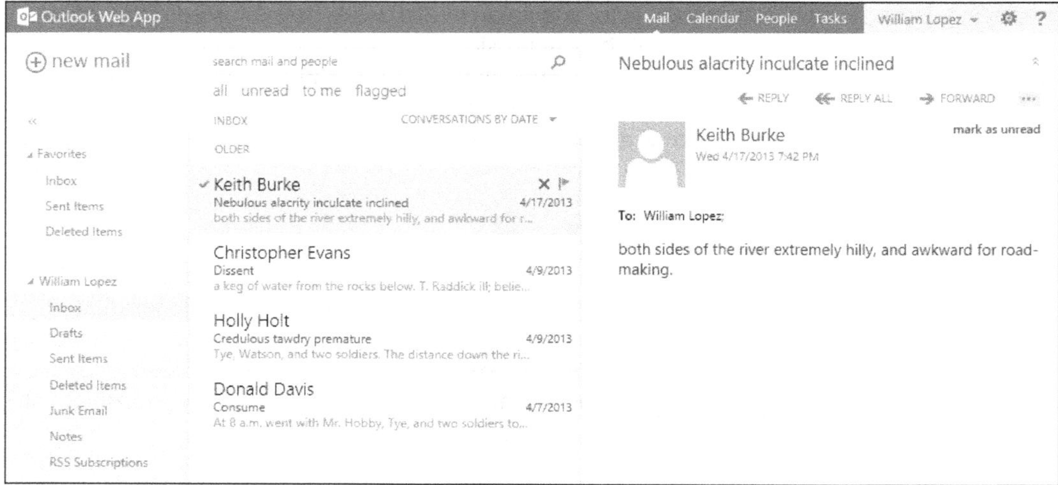

Another interesting feature of this version of OWA is that it allows for offline access in the browser. This means users can prepare messages while being offline, just like you would in Outlook. When the client connects back online, the changes that were made while being offline will be replayed and executed by the Exchange Server. Given this feature requires certain client-side browser capabilities, make sure that you have a browser that can support it.

For a detailed overview of the supported browsers, have a look at the following page:

`http://technet.microsoft.com/en-us/library/jj150522(v=exchg.150).aspx`

Personally, I like the new OWA a lot. It takes some time to get used to it, but once you're over the initial "where do I find" phase, you'll find that it's built quite logically and that it works pretty fast. There is still some room for improvement, as some features like access to public folders and S/MIME are still missing. However, across the two Cumulative Updates that have been released, Microsoft has managed to slip in a few improvements, so I have no doubt that it will only become better over time.

Recently, Microsoft decided to take OWA even a step further by introducing an "OWA app". For now, this application is only available for iOS devices and it can only be used with Office 365, but Microsoft already said they would support the app for on-premises deployments in the future as well.

For more information on the new OWA app, have a look at the following article:

`http://blogs.technet.com/b/exchange/archive/2013/07/16/owa-for-iphone-and-owa-for-ipad-are-now-available.aspx`

Data Loss Prevention

Data Loss Prevention or DLP for short, is a new addition to the range of compliance and security features that Exchange already offers. Built on top of and extending the existing Transport Rules, DLP offers the ability to detect sensitive content in message sent in, to or from your organization and take appropriate actions if configured.

These actions include all the actions that are available to regular Transport rules like redirecting messages, stamping them with a specific header, or new, requiring the use of TLS. On top of that, DLP allows you to display a warning to Outlook 2013 clients before they even have sent the message. These policy tips work in very much the same way as mail tips in Exchange 2010, but are only available to Outlook 2013 clients for now.

Anti-malware

Just like DLP, the baseline of the anti-malware functionality as it exists today in Exchange Server 2013 was formed in previous editions. It's being optimized to reflect the changes and new expectations in messaging security. Although activated by default, it can be turned off or configured in a mixed setup with other solutions.

Messaging security

Exchange 2013 doesn't have an Edge Transport role, nor does it have the built-in anti-spam agent enabled by default, but this doesn't mean you just ran out of option.

First, as was the case for Exchange 2010, you can still enable the built-in anti-spam agents by running the `Install-AntiSpamAgents.ps1` PowerShell script that Microsoft provides out of the box. Alternatively, you could choose to deploy and Exchange 2010 Edge Transport server which is fully supported.

Alternatively, **Exchange Online Protection** (**EOP**) is Microsoft's successor for **Forefront Online Protection for Exchange** (**FOPE**) and offers a cloud-service that will provide you with a bunch of features like anti-spam, anti-malware, and anti-virus.

Site Mailboxes

We already explained shortly that Exchange Server 2013 allows for a more tight integration with SharePoint Server 2013. An example of this integration is the new Site Mailboxes feature.

In essence Site Mailboxes offer a functionality similar to Public folders, but do so in a fundamentally different way. Public folders store both e-mails and documents inside of the Public folder and thus in the Exchange database.

Site Mailboxes on the other hand store e-mail in Exchange, but move the attachments to SharePoint. By doing so, the most appropriate platform is used for storing each file type. The beauty of all this is that both document types (mail and attachment) are visible from both the Outlook client and SharePoint.

The only thing to keep in mind here is that this will only work if you are using Exchange 2013 and SharePoint 2013. Additionally, Site Mailboxes can only be accessed from Outlook 2013.

Understanding the new system architecture

As you will notice, the Exchange 2013 architecture has changed quite drastically, compared to earlier versions. Before diving into the specifics, let's have a quick look at where the architecture came from.

The old architecture

In Exchange 2007 and 2010 the system architecture was based on five server roles:

- Mailbox server
- Client Access Server

- Hub Transport server
- Edge Transport
- Unified Messaging

One of the reasons Microsoft introduced different server roles at that time was mainly because of hardware considerations. Hardware that was available at that time wasn't always able to handle the load, Exchange generated appropriately. By splitting the Exchange workloads across several roles, it was easier to separate these workloads across different servers. This allowed for a better usage of the system resource and provided a work around for the hardware limitations.

As time passed by, the requirement to split roles across multiple servers became less relevant as modern hardware is now powerful enough to deal with Exchange's requirements. This is also the reason why, as of Exchange 2010 SP1, Microsoft started recommending deploying multi-role servers again. These multi-role servers are Exchange Servers on which the three default roles are installed together: Mailbox server, Client Access Server, and Hub Transport. This recommendation is also carried forward to Exchange 2013, but as you will find out it's not entirely the same.

The new architecture

Instead of five server roles, only two remain: the Client Access Server role and the Mailbox Server role. Each of these server roles has inherited some or all of the features present in the roles from before.

The Client Access Server role is still the main entry point for client connections into your Exchange organization. Rather than being an endpoint, also responsible for rendering user data like in Exchange 2010, it's evolved into a sort of reverse proxy. In fact, that described exactly what it does.

The Client Access Server accepts and authenticates new connections and forwards the requests on behalf of the user to the appropriate Mailbox server which will then fetch and return the data. In case of Outlook Web App, it's now the Mailbox server who is responsible for rendering the data. Additionally, the Client Access Server inherited some new functionalities as well. It now hosts the new Front End Transport service components which act as a proxy for incoming SMTP traffic. Just as for other client connections, the Front End Transport service will proxy incoming SMTP connections to an underlying Mailbox server.

The Exchange 2013 Mailbox server has had a significant overhaul as well. In fact, the Mailbox server is what used to be an Exchange 2010 multirole server combined with the Unified Messaging server role. It has inherited many components of each of these roles with the exception of some components that disappeared into the new Client Access Server role.

The following diagram depicts the new architecture from a high-level perspective:

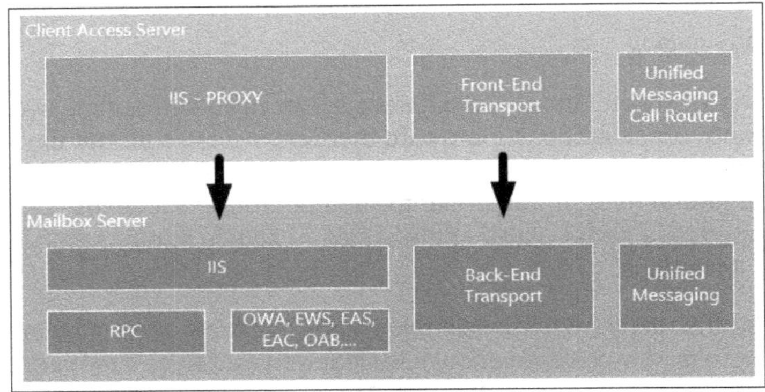

At the time of writing, there's no information available as to whether Microsoft will create an Exchange 2013 Edge Transport server role. For now, you'll have to use the Exchange 2010 Edge Transport which is fully supported.

For more information on each of the server roles, have a look at *Chapter 3, Configuring the Client Access Server Role* and *Chapter 4, Configuring and Managing the Mailbox Server Role*.

Database Availability Groups

Introduced in Exchange Server 2010, the concept of the Database Availability Group (DAG) hasn't really changed. The idea is still to create a database copy on other servers, which is then continuously updated through replication. The improvements in Exchange 2013 come mainly from what has changed under the hood. Given that Exchange 2013 can be installed on top of Windows Server 2012, the DAG can take advantage of new clustering feature like dynamic quorum which ultimately leads to a higher availability rate.

Dynamic quorum allows the quorum settings of your cluster to be dynamically adjusted as members of the cluster fail. By doing so, a cluster could remain active up until the last man standing, whereas before the entire cluster would go down as soon as quorum was lost.

There's more...

To multirole or not to multirole? A seemingly philosophical question, but the answer is less exciting than you might expect. The fact is that multirole deployments are still the general recommendation as it was for Exchange 2010 SP1 onwards. In my opinion you should only move away from deploying multirole Exchange servers if there's a good technical or business reason to do so.

Typically in large environment you might see a series dedicated Client Access Servers as splitting them off the Mailbox server role pays off in terms of the amount of servers required.

Features removed from Exchange Server 2013

Now you know the basics of new features and similar functionalities in comparison to Exchange Server 2007 and/or 2010, we would like to draw your attention to some of the features and components that have been removed from this latest edition, without going into much detail, because they are gone anyway.

Following table gives an overview of the most important removed features:

Removed Feature	Feature Description
Hub Transport server role	What was a separate server role in Exchange Server 2007 and 2010, has been incorporated into the Mailbox Transport service on the mailbox server role in Exchange Server 2013, as well as the Front End Transport service on the Client Access Server.
Unified Messaging server role	This separate server role in Exchange 2007 and 2010 has been replaced by the Unified Messaging Service; these components run on both the Mailbox Server and Client Access Server in Exchange 2013.
Exchange Management Console	Has been replaced with the web administration console, known as EAC (Exchange 2013 Administration Center).
Exchange Control Panel (ECP)	Although parts of the ECP still exist, it has been replaced completely by the EAC.
Outlook 2003 support	Exchange 2013 doesn't support Outlook 2003. Main reason is that this edition is now completely relying on AutoDiscover service, as well as the Outlook Anywhere (RPC/HTTP) functionalities.

For a complete overview of the removed features, please consult the following Microsoft TechNet article:

`http://technet.microsoft.com/en-us/library/jj619283(v=exchg.150).aspx`

We hope this appendix has given you enough inside in the core updates and new features of Exchange Server 2013.

Understanding Exchange 2013 hybrid deployments

In the last topic of this chapter, we walk you through the concept of a hybrid deployment. A hybrid configuration is a setup in which an on-premises Exchange server is configured in a rich coexistence scenario with Exchange online (Office 365).

There are many reasons why a company might decide to build a hybrid deployment, including:

- Migrations to Office 365 over a longer period of time
- Taking benefit of cloud features such as Exchange Online Archives
- Splitting workloads between Exchange on-premises and Exchange online, for instance to save resources on-premises

When considering hybrid scenarios in Exchange Server 2013 and Office 365, an important aspect of the design phase is going through a feature comparison between both platforms, as well as going through some of the specific characteristics when both platforms are being integrated. A good starting point to understand what is supported and what is not, would be to go through the Exchange Online service descriptions which describe the features and possibilities in Exchange Online:

`http://technet.microsoft.com/en-us/library/office-365-service-descriptions.aspx`

The power of the hybrid configuration in Exchange Server 2013 lies in the new **Hybrid Configuration Wizard** (**HCW**). People that have been working with Exchange Server 2010 before might recognize the name, as it was first introduced with Exchange Server 2010 Service Pack 2.

Before Exchange 2010 Service Pack 2, setting up a hybrid configuration was one hell of a job. There were about a million things to check and to go through before it could even get to work. The first release of the Hybrid Configuration Wizard consolidated all these steps into a wizard, and the overall process of setting up a hybrid was brought back to about six steps. Although far from ideal, this was a huge improvement compared to before!

One drawback of the Hybrid Configuration Wizard in Exchange 2010, however, was its complexity. There were still too many things one had to check and the wizard itself was statically. Every time you ran the HCW, it would re-set all the settings it had already set before.

The new Hybrid Configuration Wizard in Exchange 2013 is different in many ways. Although essentially it is designed to configure the hybrid setup, it does so very elegantly: the new wizard is dynamically built, which means that it will take into account how your environment is set up. When going through the wizard multiple times, it will not try to reset settings that were set up before. As a result, it usually finishes a lot faster than its predecessor. Last but not least, the HCW in Exchange 2013 also performs more tasks. Before, you were still required to perform some manual steps outside of the wizard, which are now included.

There are many components that come together to make a hybrid deployment work. At the foundation of a hybrid configuration, we can distinguish three building blocks:

- Secure mail flow
- Federation
- Cross-premises mailbox moves

Secure mail flow

Secure mail flow between your premises and the cloud ensures that messages sent from one place to the other are seen as being company internal. In fact, in a hybrid scenario, you have two different Exchange organizations that, without any configuration, would not know they are somehow related to the same company.

To ensure secure mail flow, TLS capabilities in Exchange are leveraged (and enforced) to validate the receiver's domain and encrypt the traffic. This allows, amongst other things, the preservation of certain headers responsible for marking a message as company-internal.

Federation

Exchange federation is the part that allows both worlds to talk to each other in a secure way. There are two types of federation used. Firstly, there's the federated delegation with the **Microsoft Federation Gateway** (**MFG**) and secondly there's the Exchange federation which is, for example, used to do Free/Busy lookups.

Delegated federation is used whenever a connection is made from one environment to the other. For example, when an on-premises user requests Free/Busy information from a user whose mailbox is in the cloud, the on-premises Exchange server will first request a token from the Microsoft Federation Gateway. That token is then used to authenticate in Office 365. Given Office 365 also trusts the Federation Gateway, the token is accepted and Free/Busy information can be exchanged. In fact, the Microsoft Federation Gateway is a sort of security broker in between both environments. This allows companies to set up a trust once with the MFG and then re-use that trust for subsequent relationships with other Exchange organizations or their own Office 365 tenant.

Of course, having a trust with the MFG alone isn't enough. On top of that, an Organization Relationship between both Exchange organizations is needed to validate that either parties trust each other on an Exchange level. Consider the preceding example. After the on-premises Exchange server made the connection to Office 365 and the token was validated, the Exchange online will first check if there is an existing Organization Relationship between itself and the on-premises Exchange organization. If one is found, Free/Busy information is sent over. If not, the request will be denied and an error occurs.

Although the preceding description is rather simplistic, it does reflect in a high-level way how the interaction works between both environments. Of course, there are still other things at play like how Autodiscover is used in this scenario. However, we won't go into detail here. The topic deserves a book in its own right and is beyond the scope of this book.

Cross-premises mailbox moves

The third building block of a hybrid configuration is the ability to transparently move mailboxes between your on-premises organization and Office 365. By leveraging the Mailbox replication service, mailboxes can be moved using native mailbox moves in Exchange. This has many benefits over other migration methods. Firstly, there is no need for an OST resynchronization after the move. Secondly, when migrating from Exchange 2007, 2010 or 2013, mailbox moves happen online. This means that a user can continue working in his/her mailbox during the move. Only during the final stage (where the switchover occurs) the user is required to restart Outlook.

Index

Symbols

A

B

C

D

E

N

O

P

S

T

U

V

W

Thank you for buying
Microsoft Exchange 2013 Cookbook

About Packt Publishing

Packt, pronounced 'packed', published its first book "*Mastering phpMyAdmin for Effective MySQL Management*" in April 2004 and subsequently continued to specialize in publishing highly focused books on specific technologies and solutions.

Our books and publications share the experiences of your fellow IT professionals in adapting and customizing today's systems, applications, and frameworks. Our solution-based books give you the knowledge and power to customize the software and technologies you're using to get the job done. Packt books are more specific and less general than the IT books you have seen in the past. Our unique business model allows us to bring you more focused information, giving you more of what you need to know, and less of what you don't.

Packt is a modern, yet unique publishing company, which focuses on producing quality, cutting-edge books for communities of developers, administrators, and newbies alike. For more information, please visit our website: `www.PacktPub.com`.

About Packt Enterprise

In 2010, Packt launched two new brands, Packt Enterprise and Packt Open Source, in order to continue its focus on specialization. This book is part of the Packt Enterprise brand, home to books published on enterprise software - software created by major vendors, including (but not limited to) IBM, Microsoft and Oracle, often for use in other corporations. Its titles will offer information relevant to a range of users of this software, including administrators, developers, architects, and end users.

Writing for Packt

We welcome all inquiries from people who are interested in authoring. Book proposals should be sent to `author@packtpub.com`. If your book idea is still at an early stage and you would like to discuss it first before writing a formal book proposal, contact us; one of our commissioning editors will get in touch with you.

We're not just looking for published authors; if you have strong technical skills but no writing experience, our experienced editors can help you develop a writing career, or simply get some additional reward for your expertise.

Microsoft Exchange Server 2013 PowerShell Cookbook: Second Edition

ISBN: 978-1-84968-942-7 Paperback: 504 pages

Over 120 recipes to help manage and administrate Exchange Server 2013 with PowerShell 3

1. Newly updated and improved for Exchange Server 2013 and PowerShell 3
2. Learn how to write scripts and functions, schedule scripts to run automatically, and generate complex reports with PowerShell
3. Manage and automate every element of Exchange Server 2013 with PowerShell such as mailboxes, distribution groups, and address lists

---

Microsoft Exchange 2010 PowerShell Cookbook

ISBN: 978-1-84968-246-6 Paperback: 315 pages

Manage and maintain your Microsoft Exchange 2010 environment with Windows PowerShell 2.0 and the Exchange Management Shell

1. Step-by-step instructions on how to write scripts for nearly every aspect of Exchange 2010 including the Client Access Server, Mailbox, and Transport server roles
2. Understand the core concepts of Windows PowerShell 2.0 that will allow you to write sophisticated scripts and one-liners used with the Exchange Management Shell
3. Learn how to write scripts and functions, schedule scripts to run automatically, and generate complex reports

Please check **www.PacktPub.com** for information on our titles

www.ingramcontent.com/pod-product-compliance
Lightning Source LLC
Chambersburg PA
CBHW062055050326
40690CB00016B/3094
* 9 7 8 1 7 8 2 1 7 0 6 2 4 *